# English Literature

## A Student Guide

Third edition

Martin Stephen

An imprint of Pearson Education
Harlow, England · London · New York · Reading, Massachusetts · San Francisco · Toronto · Don Mills, Ontario · Sydney
Tokyo · Singapore · Hong Kong · Seoul · Taipei · Cape Town · Madrid · Mexico City · Amsterdam · Munich · Paris · Milan

**Pearson Education Limited**
Edinburgh Gate
Harlow
Essex CM20 2JE
England
and Associated Companies throughout the

*Visit us on the World Wide Web at:*
http://www.pearsoneduc.com



First published 1986
**Third edition 2000**



ISBN 0-582-41451-2 PPR

**British Library Cataloguing-in-Publication Data**
A catalogue record for this book is available from the British Library

**Library of Congress Cataloging-in-Publication Data**
Stephen, Martin, 1949–
English literature : a student guide / Martin Stephen. – 3rd ed.
p. cm.
Includes bibliographical references and index.
ISBN 0–582–41451–2
1. English literature–Examinations Study guides. I. Title.
PR87.S814 1999
820′.76–dc21 99–36743
CIP

10 9 8 7 6 5 4 3
05 04 03 02

Set by 35 in 9½/12pt Concorde BE
Produced by
Printed in Malaysia,LSP

English Literature

We work with leading authors to develop the strongest educational materials in literature, bringing cutting-edge thinking and best learning practice to a global market.

Under a range of well-known imprints, including Longman, we craft high quality print and electronic publications which help readers to understand and apply their content, whether studying or at work.

To find out about the complete range of our publishing please *visit us on the World Wide Web at*: http://www.pearsoneduc.com

# Contents

# Preface

This is the third edition of *English Literature*. In Christopher Marlowe's play *Dr Faustus*, the hero sells his soul to the devil in exchange for an earthly lifetime of whatever he desires. Like you, the reader, Dr Faustus thirsts after knowledge. He asks Mephistophilis, the devil sent to gain his soul, a series of searching questions about the world and the Universe. In answer to each one, Mephistophilis points to the book he has already given Faustus, and tells him all the answers are in that one, single book.

*English Literature* is rather like that book, except that to buy it one has to part only with money, and not with one's immortal soul. Its aim, quite simply, is to pack in to one cover most of the background information that an A-level or degree-level student might need, thereby removing the need to purchase a whole library before one starts the course.

Since its first publication in 1986 it has become an accepted classic of its type, and one of very few 'textbooks' for A-level and degree-level students of English literature. It has now been completely re-written in the light of new AS-level and A2 examinations, both of which are for the sake of simplicity and brevity still referred to jointly as 'A-level'. It contains:

- **A Course Companion and a Basic Primer**
  *English Literature* is an introduction for advanced level and degree students to literary studies. The advanced study of English literature has basic rules and conventions, as does any other academic discipline. These range from technical ways of describing the metre of poetry to specialist definitions of words such as 'conceit' and 'image'. What follows is in part what used to be called a 'primer', and which now might be called a 'course companion'. It gives basic guidance on all the specialist techniques, rules and conventions of studying English literature, with guidance where

applicable for further reading. Part of the genesis of the book was the realisation that many schools and colleges no longer taught these basics, whilst many universities assumed a knowledge of them on the part of their students. *English Literature* is intended to fill this gap, and also to spare the student the need to purchase separate guides to the practical criticism of poetry, prose and drama.

- **A Dictionary of Literary Terms**
  Knowledge of literary terms is an essential tool of the English literature student's trade. Clear and simple definitions are given for all the major literary terms an A-level or degree-level student is likely to need.
- **A Guide to Study, Examination and Revision Technique**
  The book gives crucial advice on how to study a work of literature, on work, examination and revision techniques and on essay-writing.
- **A Key-Note Guide to Major Authors and Texts**
  The hardest thing for a student to do who comes new to a text is to find a foothold in it, a starting point. *English Literature* gives a basic overview of the major examined texts and authors in English literature. The notes here do not even begin to tell the whole story of a text or an author. What they do is prime the pump, and give the student at least an outline map of where he or she is on the daunting new territory of a hitherto unread text, or an unknown author.
- **A History of English Literature**
  The chapters which follow place authors and text in their historical and social context, without fuss and without overwhelming the student with detail. The result is that the student can find out easily and quickly what other related texts they might read by the same author, or what other texts and authors from the same period need to be or should be read. *English Literature* cannot do the reading for you; it can tell you what you might care to read. It therefore removes the need for the student to purchase a separate History of English Literature.
- **A Guide for Choosing Projects**
  *English Literature*'s pen-sketches of writers and periods allow a student to forage through them to isolate possible topics for self-chosen projects or long essays. To this extent the book can be seen as a 'sampler', giving a brief taste of a period or genre to a student without excessive investment of time or effort in these early stages of choice.
- **A Critical Reading List**
  The book contains modern, revised reading lists, suggesting some of the best and most accessible 'classic' and modern critical works on the various authors and texts.
- **A Guide to Developments in Modern Literature**
  The issue of a third edition allows for up-to-date guidance on recent developments in modern drama, poetry and prose.
- **Examples of Good Practice**
  Specimen answers illustrate all the points made in the book.

- **A Guide to Critical Theory**
  Recent years have seen an upsurge in new critical theories, ranging from structuralism to feminism. *English Literature* charts a simple and above all comprehensible path through this potential minefield for students.
- **New Chapters on War Literature and Gothic**
  The new edition advises on two new growth areas in English literature, the study of War Literature and Gothic writing.

English remains one of the most popular subjects at A-level and at University because it is about reading and interpreting works of art from an individual starting point. If any one book contains all the answers it is the text which the student is studying, and it would be a brave critic who would ever state that every last nuance of interpretation had been squeezed out of any work of art. Critical works are simply a rung on the ladder towards the student's own understanding. Unlike many study guides, *English Literature* does not aim to provide all the answers. Hopefully, it has over the years allowed a number of students to know the right questions.

The new edition contains expanded reading lists for all the major areas covered. Please remember that any such list represents only a fraction of what is available, and that no such list can claim to be either exact or binding. Wherever possible I have listed the most recent edition of a book, as far as possible in its cheapest, paperback form. Thus the date given for publication of classic critical texts such as A. C. Bradley's *Shakespearean Tragedy* is not when the book was first published, but rather the date of its most recent edition. Details of the British edition have been given where there is one. Some of the works listed are available only in libraries.

Dr Martin Stephen

# Publisher's Acknowledgements

The examination questions provided in this book are representative compilations rather than actual questions taken from any specific syllabus. The author accepts sole responsibility for the sample answers.

We are grateful to the following for permission to reproduce copyright material:

Faber & Faber Ltd/Grove Press Inc for extracts from *WAITING FOR GODOT* (1977) by Samuel Beckett; Faber & Faber Ltd for 'Preludes' from *COLLECTED POEMS 1909–1962* by T. S. Eliot; Faber & Faber Ltd/Farrar Straus & Giroux Inc for the poem 'Mr Bleaney' from *THE WHITSUN WEDDINGS* by Philip Larkin.

# Author's Acknowledgements

I would like to express personal thanks to the Librarian and staff of The Cambridge University Library, the John Rylands Library of the University of Manchester and the long-suffering staff of Waterstone's Bookshop, Manchester.

CHAPTER ONE

# Study and examination techniques in English literature

## Introduction

English literature is, arguably, the most enjoyable, the most creative and perhaps even the most individual of all the standard academic disciplines. It might therefore seem a killer to start this book with a chapter on examination technique, rather similar to mentioning a funeral at a christening. We all know examinations have to come, just as we all know we are going to die, but to mention the stark truth at the start of a book or the start of a life might be seen as very insensitive.

The reason for doing so is simple. Everyone reading this book will have received at some time in their life a new computer or board game. The game comes with instructions on how to play. They are often quite difficult to master, but once mastered they make the game fun, and they make it playable. Every academic subject has its own rules and regulations – remember the hours spent in Science lessons learning how to present the results of a practical? English has fewer than many, but they act in the same fashion as the rules of the game. Know the rules and you can enjoy playing it; fail to learn them and you could spend hours and get nowhere. This chapter is an instruction book – and as they say with every game, a few moments spent studying it will greatly increase your enjoyment . . . !

What follows does not distinguish between the various levels of learning a student might have, be they studying for A-level, at University or a mature student. It assumes total ignorance on the part of the reader, and if that makes it appear rather similar to the dummy's guides that one can find on the market for various computer programmes it is not intended to call the reader a dummy. What it is intended to do is to recognise that the 'formal' disciplines of how to write on and about English literature are taught less and less often in schools and colleges, and never taught at University. The result is a black hole of ignorance into which a number of students tend to fall, where teaching the basic disciplines of the subject becomes a classic S.E.P., or Somebody Else's Problem.

The major method by which literature candidates are examined is the essay, with variations that are discussed below. Before discussing the various types of essay question it is essential to grasp the basic principles and conventions that govern almost all essay writing.

## What is the examiner looking for?

'It's so *vague*!' is the most common complaint from students facing up to writing a literature essay, the alleged vagueness being in what the question is actually demanding from the candidate. There will always be a degree of vagueness in the questions set on a subject such as English Literature, which requires a significant element of personal response from a student. This is compounded by the fact that the rules and regulations of essay writing itself will always be a little vaguer than for a number of other forms of written examination. Nevertheless, the degree of uncertainty that you face in interpreting and answering questions can be significantly reduced.

Most important of all, distinguish between what happens when you read a book for personal pleasure, and what happens when you read it for an examination. In the first case you can think what you like about the book, and will probably first of all decide whether or not you enjoy it. Words such as 'boring' or 'interesting' are the first ones that are likely to spring to mind. When you read a book for an examination these are the last things you should think of. It is a bonus if you enjoy a book, but what the examiner wants to know is if you have *understood* it; a very different thing. When you read a book that you will be examined on you are reading it to judge or find out what the author wanted to say or achieve in that book (the content), and to expose the techniques or methods by which he or she went about that aim (the form). Again, you can think what you like about a book when you read it as part of an examination course; the difference from personal reading is that in literary criticism you have to be able to justify or prove everything you think by reference to the text. You will be reading the work of creative or imaginative writers, but your essay will need a style more akin to that of a lawyer, presenting a viewpoint and then establishing it through firm evidence, than to that of an author. It follows that with any essay there are certain basic dos and don'ts.

### Style

Write *on* an author, not *like* him or her! Flowery language, magnificent similes and metaphors, long words, and intricate sentence structure often interfere with an examination candidate's aims more than they help. Simplicity, clarity, and economy are the most valuable stylistic features in any literary essay. One of the most common mistakes is to use a flowery or ornate style, and to go for the sound of an essay over its content. One example is:

> This question is one of the most difficult of all to answer, and I propose to look at both sides of the case before proceeding to my conclusion. What are we to think of this issue? The multi-layered phenomenon of a great tragedy with its eponymous hero and final catharsis presents such a magnitude of experience that only excessive insight can provoke a final and complete understanding . . .

Convinced? You shouldn't be. The problem with this is that *it does not say anything*. You might usefully note a number of other points on style:

1. Never say how difficult the question is, or that you cannot make up your mind on it. You are only stating the obvious or displaying to the examiner the fact that you are inadequate.
2. Never *ask* questions in an essay; your task is to *answer* them.
3. Never write gobbledygook, or language so puffed-up as to be incomprehensible.
4. Never use words because they 'sound good'; it is what they mean that matters.
5. Never use a word unless you are absolutely sure of what it means. Certain words and phrases should be avoided at all costs, such as 'brilliant', 'terrific', 'nice', 'nasty', 'naughty', 'boring', and 'super'. Try to use 'however' as little as possible, and never as a conjunction.
6. Never try to ram your argument down an examiner's throat. Saying something many times over is not the same as proving it, so writing 'No one could deny that . . .' or 'It is absolutely obvious that . . .' achieves nothing. In practice most students only say things like this when they are actually quite unsure of what they should think.
7. Never patronise or condescend to the reader, or try to show off your knowledge, as in 'When one has studied the book in great depth, and thought long and hard over it . . .'; the examiner expects you to have done all that, and does not need telling. It is the weight of your arguments that wins marks, not the loudness of your voice.

## Answering the question

The single most common cause of failure to write an effective answer is failure to answer the question. This usually takes two forms. The first is where the student writes an answer to the question he wants to be asked, instead of writing an answer to the question he has been asked. The second is where the student gives a plot summary, or piles up details of the story, instead of answering the specific question as set. A long, rambling account of the plot gets you nowhere; the examiner can find the plot when he reads the book, and does not need you to tell it to him. It is what you make of the plot that matters, not your knowledge of it. Your essay should contain quotations from the text and references to incidents in it, but only as back-up or evidence for a point you are making.

*Ask yourself at all times if what you are writing down is wholly and totally relevant to the question you have been set.* If the examiner ever has cause to want to write down 'So what?' in the margin of your answer, you will almost certainly lose marks. The examiner wants to see that you can *choose* the few relevant facts from a mass of information, and then apply them to a specific area of the text and its content. Nor is it enough merely to provide relevant information: you have to show the examiner *why* it is relevant. Very often candidates will put down a quotation and just leave it, wrongly assuming that it is obvious why it is there in the essay. It never is obvious: you should always explain why you have chosen to include a quotation, or a reference to an incident or character.

A major help in making sure that you are answering the question is the use of the *topic* or *theme* sentence. This is always the first sentence in any paragraph, and in it you make sure that you have summed up exactly and precisely what that paragraph is going to be about. Thus each paragraph falls into three sections:

1. The topic sentence which sums up the statement made in that paragraph;
2. Some more lines to elaborate on that topic or theme;
3. Quotation and evidence to prove it.

Many candidates find this a difficult technique, because we are conditioned to think of a conclusion as something that comes at the end, and a topic sentence is in a way a summary of an argument or viewpoint – yet it comes at the start of a paragraph. There is a good reason for this. If you start your paragraph with a great long list of evidence for a certain point you wish to make, the examiner cannot judge whether or not this evidence is relevant to the point you are trying to make and the question you have been asked to answer. He or she needs to know what you are trying to say before he can judge your evidence, and so by far the best technique is to provide him with this before you get into detail. If you look at the plan for your essay and cannot think of a sentence to sum up what the paragraph is trying to say, it is probably that the paragraph is saying nothing at all, and needs to be re-thought. Equally, a glance at your topic sentence and a glance at the essay title tells you immediately if the content of that paragraph is relevant to the question.

## Punctuating the title

*The title of a book or poem is always given special punctuation in an essay to mark it out from the rest of the text.* First of all, find out the correct title of the book you are studying, and how to punctuate it; this is on the fly leaf or title page of the book, and may not be what is printed on the spine. The title of a *book* or *play* should be underlined throughout, if you are writing by hand, or put in italics if you are using a word-processor. The title of an individual *poem* should be placed in inverted commas, whichever method you are using. Some other useful points on punctuation and presentation are:

1. Never underline *and* put inverted commas round a title if you are handwriting, or underline and put in italics if you are using a word processor; you can have too much of a good thing.
2. Never write a title out in a different coloured ink – examiners do not mark you on artistic skills, and you do not have the time to change pens in an examination. Never use more than one font if you are word-processing, and make it a standard one such as Times New Roman or Arial, for the same reasons.
3. Use single-spacing, or 1.5 line spacing if the piece you are writing will be written on by whoever reads it and returned to you.
4. Always write the title out in full. Shakespeare wrote *Much Ado About Nothing*, not *Much Ado*; Tom Stoppard wrote *Rosencrantz and Guildenstern Are Dead*, not *Rosencrantz and Guildenstern*.
5. Start each word of the title with a capital letter, unless the title page of the book does it differently, as in *The History of Mr Polly*, where the 'of' does not require a capital. As with all rules, it helps to understand why it is necessary. The answer is that it can cause terrible confusion if the examiner thinks you mean Hamlet the character when actually you mean *Hamlet* the play; similarly, words in a poem sometimes appear as the title, and the examiner needs to know if you are talking about the whole poem, or individual lines from it. Thus you would refer to Thomas Hardy's *Selected Poems* (underlined, because it is the name of a whole book), but write 'The Darkling Thrush' when you referred to a poem in that book.

## Quotations

Any good essay will contain quotations. Provide none, and you are depriving yourself of your main evidence for proving any point that you might make. Equally, if you provide too many the examiner might think he or she could just as well have read the book in its original form! There are three basic mistakes which commonly occur in essays with regard to the use of quotations:

1. *Misquoting* or presenting the quotation wrongly;
2. *Quoting too much*;
3. *Turning poetry into prose.*

It is essential that you quote accurately, down to the last comma and full stop, even if you think the original writer has made a mistake. If the original is wrong in some way, either grammatically or because it does not make sense, you can always write *sic* – Latin for 'thus' – to show the mistake is not your own. Do be careful. Errors in original texts are very rare – even in a book such as this two or three people will have gone over the text with a fine-tooth comb, and with the help of sophisticated error-checking computer programmes. Nothing makes you look more foolish than writing *sic* against something that is your misunderstanding.

Remember that if your quotations are not accurate your whole knowledge of the text is thrown into doubt, together with the accuracy of anything you might say. It is also grossly insulting to an author to change what he or she originally wrote.

Long quotations are a menace; after all, the examiner is marking you, not the original author. Always remember that at Advanced level the examiner *expects* you to know the text in detail, and wants to read your comment on it. The best quotations are usually not more than four or five lines long at most, and are often shorter than that. In any event, very few candidates can learn more than forty or fifty lines for every text they are examined on.

The rules for presenting a quotation are quite simple. If a quotation is *two lines or less* in the original, it can be *run on* in your essay without starting a new line. All that is needed is a comma before the quotation, and the quotation to be marked off with inverted commas, as follows:

> Hamlet's bitterness and anger towards women come to the surface with increasing frequency as the play progresses, as when he orders Ophelia, 'Get thee to a nunnery!'

If it is poetry that you are quoting you can still *run on* a quotation of *two lines or less*, but the end of one line in the text and the start of another must be marked by a diagonal line:

> Othello's anger is clearly heard in the lines, 'Now, by heaven,/My blood begins my safer guides to rule.'

Where a quotation occupies *more than two lines* in the original text, it should be preceded by a comma, started on a new line, and indented (given an extra left-hand margin). Inverted commas are not strictly necessary, but can be useful for complete clarity:

> Othello's anger is clearly heard in the lines,
> 'Now, by heaven,
> My blood begins my safer guides to rule,
> And passion, having my best judgement collied,
> Assays to lead the way.'
> This speech marks the start of Othello's breakdown.

If something is written as poetry it is written on a line-by-line basis, and *it is essential that you should quote it as poetry, keeping to the original line arrangements*. Poetry (or *verse*) is written in lines, and if you ignore the division into lines you convert poetry into prose, and in so doing tell the examiner that you cannot tell the difference between poetry and prose.

## Planning

As a very rough guide the time spent on an essay written in your own time (that is, not under examination conditions), should be divided into three.

- *Part one* consists of going through the text and notes assembling information that is relevant to the essay title you are answering.
- *Part two* consists of taking this raw material and working up an essay plan for it.
- *Part three* consists of actually sitting down and writing the essay.

Each part should take roughly the same amount of time.

In an examination, there is less time for planning. A question requiring an hour to answer can allow for up to ten minutes' planning time, but you will not be able to produce an effective plan in this time unless you have learnt the techniques we have mentioned when working under more relaxed conditions.

The first stage of planning is to make yourself want to do it, because it can be very tedious and unexciting. When you walk into an examination you will know quite literally thousands of pieces of information about your set texts. Your examination will test you on perhaps twenty per cent of what you know. You are tested on your ability to *select* the right information from a very long list. If you do not select you do not pass, but this selection is impossible if you write spontaneously and off-the-cuff.

Try an experiment. Take an essay question on a book you know and write down *everything*, in the briefest note form, that comes into your head as a possible answer to that question. This is actually the first stage in planning. Then look at what you have jotted down. There should be a large quantity of relevant and useful information, but it will all be jumbled up, in no logical order. Your notes will also contain repetitions, and ideas that looked good at first sight but are quickly shown up with a little thought as being irrelevant. Yet this is what goes down on paper if you *do not plan* an essay. Someone has compared an unplanned essay to a chef trying to cook a five-course meal with all the ingredients for every course in the same saucepan at the same time. It is not only that the unplanned essay is chaotic, repetitive, irrelevant, and anarchic; it is also often inconclusive. Time after time literature students take a quick look at an essay title (it is sometimes known as the 'smash and grab' technique of essay writing) which seems horribly complex, reach an instant conclusion, and start writing with the first thing that comes into their head. What then follows is like a Shakespearean tragedy – inevitable, and very sad.

Imagine a candidate answering the question 'Is Hamlet mad?', with his immediate response being to think that he is mad. The candidate starts to write. He or she thinks up one, two, possibly three ideas that seem relevant, and tries to hold ideas number two and three in his head while he is writing down the first one. He will probably forget idea number three somewhere in between changing from his first to his second idea, and remember it three hours after the end of the examination. Idea number one happens to be a point that suggests Hamlet is not mad; no problem here, the candidate thinks – it is right and proper to put down both sides of an argument. Then idea number two goes the same way. Idea number four (number three got lost some while back) suggests Hamlet *is* mad, but number five suggests he is not . . . by this time the examiner is moving so rapidly from Hamlet not being mad to his being mad and back again that he feels rather like someone on a roller-coaster. By the end of the essay and the time allotted the candidate has actually written an essay in which two-thirds of the information he has presented suggests the opposite of what he originally thought, namely that Hamlet is mad. He might realise this half-way through the essay. He can then either carry on and change his mind half-way through, thus providing half an essay that suggests Hamlet was mad, and another half that suggests the opposite (not a very convincing technique), or he can cross out what he has written and start again. If he does he has almost certainly failed the question, because he will not be able to write an effective essay in the time he has left. He can, of course, continue to put down his information, the balance of which suggests Hamlet is not mad, but end the essay with something utterly feeble such as 'Although there is a great deal of evidence to suggest Hamlet is not mad . . . I think he is.' The examiner's blue pen will move so fast that it will put scorch marks on the script. The point is that:

(a) You must always argue on the side for which you have the most evidence.
(b) You must know what your viewpoint is *before* you start to write the essay.

It is terrifyingly easy to jump to the wrong conclusion when you first see a title, and a *preliminary plan* lets you see what your available evidence does actually prove.

1. The first stage is to jot down everything you can think of that might be useful for that essay.
2. The second stage is to go through your rough jottings, taking out any repetitions, looking again at all the information and checking if it is as good and relevant as you first thought. Try to knock the remaining information into four or five paragraphs. Of course some essays will need more paragraphs than this, others less, but it is surprising how often four or five paragraphs turn out to be the ideal number.
3. The third stage is to put the four or five paragraphs you have isolated into a logical order.
4. The fourth stage is to think of an introduction and a conclusion (see below).

After you have been through all these stages, you can then write the essay with a clear conscience.

### The Introduction

An introduction is a preliminary paragraph that comes before the main discussion of an essay title. It should rarely, if ever, be longer than half a side of standard line A4 examination paper. It could sketch in background information for an author or book, but be careful not to be irrelevant. If the essay asks for discussion of a specific topic, the introduction could sketch out the main other areas of critical interest in a book, to show the examiner that the candidate is aware of issues other than that specified in the essay title. An introduction can show where the book being examined fits in with the rest of an author's work ('*Our Mutual Friend* is an example of "late Dickens", more sombre and pessimistic in its mood than his earlier novels'), or can relate the book to other books being written at the time. The introduction can also state what the candidate sees as being the main point of the essay title, tying it down, if it is a rather vague and open-ended question, to certain issues and topics. The purpose of the introduction is to give a gentle lead-in to an essay. It may either give any relevant background information to the book being studied or to the essay title, or it may clarify the essay title and the line of approach that the candidate proposes to take. Six or seven lines of normal handwriting is usually enough.

**The Conclusion**

A conclusion is simply a very brief summary of the main conclusions raised in each paragraph, and a more or less bald statement of the conclusion the essay has reached. It is sometimes suggested that the candidate leave a new point to be raised in the conclusion. This is usually a very bad idea. If the new point in question is that effective or interesting, it is worth more than a few lines at the end, and if it is not, it is not worth stating anyway.

**General errors**

There is a catalogue of errors that are very simple to avoid, but which occur time after time in the scripts of advanced-level candidates and obscure whatever literary insight and judgement they may have.

1. Never try flattery on an examiner, with comments such as:

    > Dickens' masterly grasp of style, his superb command of the English language, and his tremendous insight make him wholly admirable, and a genius in every sense of the word . . .

    Presumably at some stage the candidate who wrote the above is going to start answering the question he was asked. In the meantime, it is a long wait, and the examiner knows Dickens is good; he would not be on the syllabus otherwise.
2. Avoid slang or casual phrases in your essay. Some have been mentioned already, and a full list would occupy a whole chapter. Examples from a recent batch of scripts include 'nice', 'naughty', 'terrific', 'fabulous', 'mind-blowing', 'nasty', 'earth-shattering', 'quantum-leap', 'clever', and 'slap-bang'. No one minds inventive use of language, but everyone who marks examinations minds *casual* use of it.
3. Never describe a book as 'boring' – it only shows what type of mind you have.
4. Try not to be flippant in an essay. My favourite example (favourite in the sense of summing up beautifully how-not-to-refer-to-a-text) is,

    > The moment when Macbeth peers into the witches' cauldron is of great dramatic significance and tension – unless, of course, his beard falls off into the steam and goes in with the witches' brew!

Ho, ho ho laughs the examiner, on the way to the waste-paper bin. If you feel like putting an exclamation mark on the end of a sentence, think again; you are not in the examination to exclaim, but to explain and understand.

5. Never start an essay with 'I propose to look at both sides of the question and then come to a conclusion' (known sometimes as a *CGO*, or Crashing Glimpse of the Obvious), or end an essay with 'This is a very difficult question, and I find it impossible to reach a conclusion.' Of course the essay is difficult; it is advanced level after all, and it is your job to come to a conclusion.
6. Always write in the present tense when referring to a book. The events in a book, play, or poem happen anew every time the book is read. They have happened (past tense) when the book was looked at in the past, they are happening, and they will happen. As it would clearly not be a good idea to state 'Hamlet was, is, and will be killed by Laertes', the best compromise is to write 'Hamlet is killed by Laertes'. Always remember that you are writing *on* an author, not *like* him or her.

## The various types of essay and other questions

### Practical criticism

'Practical criticism' essays are sometimes referred to as 'comment and appreciation', or even 'unseens'. They can consist of a passage from a book which the candidate has not been required to read before, and require her or him to comment on it, sometimes in a very general way, sometimes on specific points or areas of interest. They can also come from a book that the candidate has not seen or read before. Practical criticism essays are of such importance in English Literature examinations that they are dealt with in three separate chapters below, as regards poetry, prose, and drama respectively.

### Context questions

A context question in its simplest form is an examination question which presents the candidate with a short passage from a set text, and asks for it to be placed in context. This can simply mean stating where the passage occurs in the book (done not by act and scene, or chapter references, but by referring to the incident immediately before and after the period covered by the passage), or identifying which character is speaking. Advanced-level questions are usually rather more complex than this, and ask the candidate to comment on one or two specific areas highlighted in a passage.

In days gone by questions on authors such as Shakespeare and Chaucer used to ask the candidate to translate selected passages in to 'clear, modern English'. This is now a virtually extinct mode of questioning.

Questions asked on a passage vary a great deal. Some of the most common are:

(a) Comment on what is revealed about a character by the chosen passage.
(b) Comment on the descriptive or narrative technique of the author in the passage – how he or she tells the story and creates atmosphere.
(c) Comment on any themes covered in or advanced by the passage in question.
(d) Say what contribution is made to the book, play, or poem by the passage.

Certain basic rules govern all answers to context questions. Some of them are covered in the chapters on practical criticism below. The main point to bear in mind is that a context question is on a specific passage. It is *not* a general essay, and though of course you may refer to general issues in the book, and indeed need to say how the passage you are studying links into the rest of the book, the majority of your answer is based on that passage and that passage alone. Do not write lengthy quotations from the passage; the occasional line or two is perfectly reasonable to back up what you are saying, but resist the temptation to write out the whole passage. Resist also the temptation to write on only one idea. There should be more than one point of interest in the passage, or more than one example of what the examiner is interested in, and you need to make sure that there is a *quantity* of ideas in your answer, as well as *quality*. A context question is a short essay, and short essays need to be more distilled and concentrated than longer essays.

## Character sketch

A straightforward character sketch – 'Give a full account of the character of King Lear' – is rarely set at advanced level, but questions of a more complex nature on characters are frequently set. The major mistake here is to give an account of a character's *actions* when what is wanted is something on his *personality* or *motivation* – in other words, what those actions lead us to assume about a character. In general terms then major points of information about any character in a novel or play are:

1. What the character says;
2. What the character does;
3. What other characters say about him or her;
4. What other characters do to him or her;
5. What the particular tricks of language or expression used by that character are;
6. What the character looks like;
7. What association the character has with any given place, setting, or even incident. A character such as Krook in Charles Dickens' novel *Bleak House* is characterised as much by the place in which we usually see him as by any other method.

## Discuss

One of the most common styles of examination question is a quotation (one wonders sometimes how many of these are invented by the examiners), followed by the word 'Discuss', as in, ' "The central concern of *Hamlet* is revenge." Discuss.' *Discuss* does not mean *illustrate*; the candidate does not have to agree with the statement, but merely to discuss it. The word discuss means 'explore' or 'analyse the truth of'. Discussion means working round an essay title or topic, analysing its wider implications and the truth or otherwise of the assertion in the title. *You do not have to agree with the title*. You do have to reach a conclusion in your discussion, but it need not be the one implied in the title.

## Dramatic significance and contribution

If your set text is a play you may be asked to comment on the dramatic significance of a scene, episode, or character. If it is a novel, you may be asked what contribution is made to the book by a character or episode. This type of essay is asking you to illustrate the manner in which an episode or character fits in and contributes to the wider effect of the novel. Examples are 'What is the dramatic significance of music in *Twelfth Night*?', or 'Discuss the contribution made to Charles Dickens' *Our Mutual Friend* by symbolism and imagery.' A useful start is to list all the possible contributions made by the item you are being questioned on. In the first question ask yourself if *music* in the play contributes to the plot or story, to our knowledge of any of the characters, to any of the themes of the play, to its general atmosphere, and to its value as an entertainment (in this case the answer is yes to all except the area of contributing to the plot); in the second question the answer should suggest that *symbolism* and *imagery* have almost come to dominate the technique of the novel.

## Style

A majority of students arrive at Advanced level convinced that there is 'hidden meaning' in every work they read. As the function of every author is, more or less, to communicate something to a reader or audience, it might be asked why they bother to hide their meanings. What the phrase 'hidden meaning' usually means in practice is 'themes in the book which I cannot perceive when I read it'. Just as a young child will always choose to write a story if given a choice of essays, so an older student will always tend to write about themes, or 'meanings'. Themes are only one part of a book, its 'content'. Examiners are equally interested in the *techniques* used to convey these themes, in other words, in the book's *form*. Therefore questions about style, narrative techniques, use of imagery and symbolism, and other technical matters abound, though they are very often unpopular with students. These are the mechanics of writing, how an author actually conveys what he or she wants to say by the use of language.

The only general point here is a reminder that an essay on form must not be turned into an essay on content. Thus if you are asked 'Discuss Chaucer's use of irony' that is what you must do; no matter if Chaucer's 'The Franklin's Tale' has a thousand and one fascinating themes in it, with this essay you can only write about irony and where that leads to. You can say that one particular theme is conveyed largely through irony, but any theme is largely irrelevant to your essay if it does not rely heavily on irony.

## Opposed viewpoints

One of the most common types of essay is that which presents the candidate with two opposed viewpoints, as in 'Is Hamlet best described as a "sweet prince" or an "arrant knave"?' Here you need to know what your answer is *before* you start to write the essay, because if you do not, you will either ramble and reach no conclusion, or end up arguing both sides with equal fervour, and never reach a conclusion.

A convincing treatment of any one viewpoint always has to consider the other side of the question. If you happen to think that Hamlet is a 'sweet prince' you must look at the reasons why he might be considered an 'arrant knave' *as well as* at the reasons why he is a 'sweet prince'; you cannot persuade someone into taking one point of view unless he also knows why he should not take the other side as the truth.

It is no good ignoring contrary evidence; you simply have to show why your view is more powerful or convincing. You can do this in a number of ways. List all the reasons why you think Hamlet is a 'sweet prince'. Then list all the reasons why he might not be thought of thus. Some of these you might be able to prove wrong. For example, Hamlet tells Ophelia to get into a nunnery and is very violent and offensive towards her. You could argue that this is simply to drive her away from him, because he knows he is in danger and that anyone who supports or loves him might suffer as a result. In this case you could say that what seems to be rudeness is actually Hamlet trying to protect Ophelia. You do not always have to prove the opposition viewpoint wrong. You could argue that Hamlet is offensive *and* an 'arrant knave' towards Ophelia, but that there are more instances of his behaving like a 'sweet prince' in the play, and that these outweigh the negative side of his character.

In any event, never just say that an argument or viewpoint is wrong; saying is not proving, and you have to provide evidence and a justification for everything you say. As ever, it is your personal viewpoint, backed up by evidence, that really matters. The answer is not as important as the methods by which you reach that answer. The examiner does not want you to come down on any particular side; he or she just wants a convincing argument in favour of any reasonable viewpoint. You could even argue that Hamlet is neither a 'sweet prince' nor an 'arrant knave', but something completely different, and not covered by these descriptions. If you feel it to be true and you can argue it, go ahead.

## Problems of maturity

The further up the academic ladder that the student climbs, the vaguer the guidelines become, and the more initiative is required. An Advanced-level question often defines its own structure and plan for an answer; the next level of question may well require the student to define his or her own parameters.

One of the most common errors for the student who has been exposed to differing critical viewpoints for the first time is to write an essay that merely balances out a list of opposing critical viewpoints, moving like a see-saw between them, and at the end making a feeble stab at supporting one view or the other. The 'list of critics' essay satisfies no one; the student *must* define a viewpoint of his or her own, using criticism to inform and focus this viewpoint but not control it. This failure is little more than an extension of the Advanced-level essay that does not know where it is going; there is no substitute for the writer of an essay knowing what he or she wants to say. *Never* rest content with listing other people's viewpoints. In doing so the student must look more critically than is sometimes demanded at Advanced-level at how a particular critic *arrived* at their particular view, and not just at what that particular point of view might be. The only sure rule is to have a firm grounding in the primary texts themselves and to use that familiarity critically in approaching the secondary literature.

## Word processing

A significant amount of work done at home by students will be written on a computer with a standard word-processing package. In two respects this has made life harder for the student, albeit easier for the examiner.

Firstly, a word-processed essay reveals simple errors far more clearly than a hand-written piece of work. Mis-spellings and faulty punctuation are highlighted by the clarity of a word-processed page. Furthermore, any modern word-processing package has a spell and grammar check program. If simple spelling and other mistakes are allowed through in to the final version it argues for a very casual attitude on the part of the writer.

Secondly, technical factors can mean that hours of work are thrown away when a hard disc or a floppy becomes corrupted, or there is a power failure. A surprising number of students do not take precautions against the technical failure of their machine, and suffer accordingly.

There are some basic dos and don'ts if you are using a computer for your work. A simple 'do' when using a spell-check device is always to check that it is in UK English mode, not US English. Many programs come with the US setting as standard, and will therefore want you to spell 'favourite' as 'favorite' or 'colour' as 'color'.

Always name your file as the first thing that you do, before you write down a single word. Make the name reflect what it is you are actually writing, so that you can identify it and pick it off a menu immediately without having to wade through hundreds of similarly-named files, or files named after some form of short hand which felt really good when you invented it but have now forgotten.

Always copy your work on to the hard disc, if there is space, and also on to a floppy disc. You must have two separate sources for any important piece of work. If you come in to your room in the morning, turn on the machine and find that the hard disc has crashed and taken your last essay along with it, you can at least take the floppy and carry on the work on a college or school computer, or even a friend's. You may not even be able to rescue the file from the hard drive after it has been repaired, and so have lost it for good if you did not make a back-up copy on a floppy disc. Consider adding a ZIP drive to your computer if it does not have one. It is a relatively cheap way of storing huge amounts of information as a back-up.

Save your work every five or ten minutes, and do not rely on AUTO-SAVE. It is not widely know that the 'AUTO-SAVE' facility on many computers does not actually save what is on the screen. Instead it saves a special version of that for use if the machine should crash. Large numbers of people have been surprised after a problem to re-load the file and find that they have only saved the material that was there after their last manual save, not after the last AUTO-SAVE.

If you are writing a project or long essay consider breaking the material up in several files. Apart from being safer if your computer develops a problem, it makes it far easier for you to work on the material if the text-distance you have to cover for corrections and additions is shorter.

Do you put pictures or illustrations in to your work, now that technology makes it so easy to do so? Probably not. It is content you are being measured on, not design, though it is always worth checking with some projects whether attractive design is something that is given a mark and a value.

Finally, beware the availability of entries on famous authors and works of literature in the numerous encyclopaedias that flood the market. Many examiners, teachers and lecturers get these extracts quoted back at them by students so often that they know them off by heart. It is your words the examiner and the reader is interested in.

## Conclusion

*Clarity*, *economy*, *relevance*, and a *detailed knowledge* of the text are what the best examination candidates carry into the examination, together with a capacity for *independence*. Independence is the ability to come to a conclusion about the work being studied, and to argue that conclusion convincingly. Never undervalue the importance of 'background knowledge', be it other texts, or an awareness of the social, literary, and historical background to a set text. Most examination boards expect the candidates to know about Elizabethan society and literature in at least some areas if they are studying a play by Shakespeare, or to have a basic grasp of some of the factors that operated in medieval society where Chaucer is being studied.

Most of all, never be frightened of holding your own view on a book, poem or play. That personal feeling and insight is the most valuable thing you bring to being a student of literature. The only difference is that you have to explain why you hold that view, and make it valid for someone else. You might find yourself surprised at how much fun it is. You will not be surprised as how totally boring it is to undertake a course in English literature and for anything up to three years become simply a mouthpiece for other people's views.

## Further reading


- Francis Casey, *How To Study: A Practical Guide* (Macmillan, 1993)
- John Clanchy and Brigid Ballard, *How To Write Essays: A Practical Guide for Students* (Longman, 1992)
- Nigel Fabb and Alan Durant, *How To Write Essays, Dissertations and Theses in Literary Studies* (Longman, 1993): this is a text for the student who is working at degree level.
- Richard Gill, *Mastering English Literature* (Macmillan, 1995)
- Steven Lynn, *Texts and Contexts. Writing About Literature with Critical Theory* (Longman, 1998): also a book for the degree-level student.

CHAPTER TWO

# Revision, project work and research techniques

## Revision

There is an obvious oddity in putting a section on revision at the start of a book, when revision clearly comes at the end of a course. There is some method in the madness. Revision can only be based on work done much earlier. If you know what will be required of you in revision at the end of the course, it is far easier to get things right as you undertake the early stages of it. In effect the guidelines for revision double up as guidelines for good work practice throughout your course.

A student will have to revise a text at whatever level he or she is operating. The object of revision is to bring a candidate's knowledge of a text up to examination standard just in time for the examination; *time* is therefore as important an element in revision as *content*, or what is actually revised.

### Preparation

The first essential is to make sure that you have an accurately noted text and an organised set of notes. As regards the latter, this means checking through your files, putting all the information (lesson notes, duplicated sheets, notes on critics and essays) into separated headings, and checking that you have all you need. This is best done in the holiday before the term of the examination. It is at this time that you should copy the notes you missed when you were ill, find that book you always meant to read but never quite got round to and generally tidy up your file, so that when hard revision starts you can turn over the pages of your file as you would a book. The aim of your preparation is to ensure that the material you will need to learn is all present and correct in your files or your bookshelf. The term of the actual examination is too late to start plugging gaps in your knowledge. No one will want to lend you their notes, the local bookshops will have sold out of the standard texts and the book you need will be in permanent and heavy demand from the library.

## Revision

The following hints can sometimes smooth a path to effective revision.

### General

1. **Time** Always try to work in blocks of time equal to that of your examination. If you are sitting a three-hour examination then work in three-hour sessions in your revision. This way your mind will become accustomed to concentrating for this length of time.
2. **Texts** Try to obtain a cheap and unmarked copy of your set texts, and when revising from your own text transfer to the unmarked copy at regular intervals to check your learning and see how much you have remembered.
3. **Quotations** If you are not allowed to take a text into the examination room you will need to learn lines from the text. Start off by writing down all the lines you think you might learn, then edit this list down to about 40 or so lines, chosen to reflect the widest possible number of issues and topics in that text. *Keep the quotations short* and never have more than one extract to learn on each separate topic.
4. **Location** Vary where you work occasionally so that you do not become stale and over-tired simply through being in the same place for your revision all the time. The Icelandic section of your local library is often a very quiet place to go . . .
5. **Summary** It can sometimes help to give a point to revision if you work towards boiling down all your notes onto one side of close-written A4 paper, effectively providing a summary for yourself. The advantages of this are that it makes you think about what is truly important in your notes and requires you to discriminate, and the piece of paper that results is very useful as something to glance through just before the examination.

### Drama

(a) Try summarising the content of each scene in a play as briefly as possible.
(b) Identify and write out the six most important speeches in a play.
(c) Identify the six most crucial episodes or scenes in a play and write a short critical commentary on each.
(d) Read through the play concentrating on one major character.
(e) Do the same as for (d), but with a minor character.

### Poetry

(a) Write out and learn by heart 50–100 lines, either whole poems or extracts from poems.

(b) Read aloud into a tape recorder any number of poems.
(c) Choose three topics from a poet's work and read through his work listing every poem where that topic occurs.
(d) Do a new contents table for a book of poems, grouping each poem by theme.
(e) Take five poems at random and list their particular elements of style.

**Prose**
(a) Examine in detail the first and last chapters of a novel, and see the extent to which the last chapter finishes off the issues and themes started in the first chapter.
(b) Write the briefest possible summary of each chapter in a novel.
(c) Identify the five most crucial episodes in a novel and write brief critical notes on them.
(d) Take an unmarked copy of the novel and read through it simply as a novel, rather than a set text. Note what your response has been at the end.
(e) Attempt to reconstruct an incident in the novel from memory, and then check your recall by reference to the text.

All the above suggestions should help to stop you from becoming stale, and allow you to inject something new into your revision.

## Conclusion

Always keep a note of how long you have worked during a given period, and what you have worked at. It is surprisingly easy to spend far too much time on one book to the exclusion of others, and to think you are spending far more time revising than is actually the case. *Consistency* is what makes for good revision, not sudden huge bursts of work punctuated by equal bursts of indolence! Remember that if you know your texts and have read each one thoroughly at least three times there is little you need to fear from an examiner.

## Project work

Project work is increasingly being looked on with favour by Advanced level examination boards, and in tertiary education the same techniques are expanded to provide the dissertation or long essay.

Some projects allow the student almost a free choice of topic. Just as the success of an essay depends in large measure on the amount of time spent in advance preparation, so the choice of subject for a project (or dissertation) is *the* crucial decision. Books such as this can help the student get a taste or flavour of given subjects; use them to the full. You should know what your own tastes or preferences are – poetry, novel or drama, classic works or modern ones – and base your choice, if you have one, on what you *enjoy*.

There are two common failings at the outset with project work. One is to choose too large a subject. It is a very common mistake to choose a field of enquiry that is simply too big. A project or a dissertation entitled 'Feminist Criticism' is simply too open-ended and big; far better to tie it in to the study of one or two authors – George Eliot, Charlotte Bronte – the perception of whom has been greatly affected by feminist criticism. Similarly, 'Early Science Fiction' is far too broad a canvas. Concentrate instead on one or two authors (H. G. Wells, Jules Verne), or on a specific topic, such as the way science and scientists have been viewed in a select number of science fiction works.

The second most frequent error is to choose a topic on which assistance is not available. The average student will need a good supply of primary texts and criticism to assist in the writing of his or her own project. A fascinating African author, a fashionable and outrageous modern poet or the headline-hitting author of one successful play may be exciting prospects, but the student who chooses to write on them will be on his or her own. That can be no bad thing, but it needs thinking about in advance.

There is a principle in engineering that the larger a structure, the more thought needs to be given to its supports. So it is with a project; the longer essay needs very careful thought over its plan or structure.

If choice of subject is crucial, so is choice of viewpoint. Projects fall into two very basic types – an *account* of a given field or area of study, or an *exploration* of certain issues within a topic. At Advanced level more often than not what is needed is a competent summary of a given field or author, giving no surprises but providing a broad, general account. Tertiary education – and occasionally some Advanced-level boards – demand rather more. A project on the poetry of the First World War might provide an account of the major poets and the prominent features of their work, with some detail about why the war provoked so much poetry. A dissertation is going to need to examine the basic debate about that poetry. The poet and critic W. B. Yeats described the poetry of Wilfred Owen as 'all blood, dirt and sucked sugar stick', implying that the poetry of the First World War was one-dimensional and sentimental at the same time. This has spawned a debate that continues to the present day. Was it, as Yeats said, limited and not proper material to be considered as 'true' poetry, or is it classic poetry that will continue to have relevance and power long into the future? This will need to be the dynamic behind the dissertation and the student needs to consider how motivated and knowledgeable he or she will be in finding something interesting to say.

If the student wishes to rise above the simple account, it is essential to choose an area with some meat to be plucked from its bones. It is beyond the scope of this work to suggest what these meaty areas might be, but as a passing thought some areas that adapt well to a challenging examination are the reputation and standing of authors and schools; the less well-known work of major authors (Chaucer's *Troilus and Criseyde* is one such); relatively neglected genres, such as Restoration tragedy; new media-based approaches to old topics, such as changing production ideas in Shakespeare from Olivier to Polanski. If you are going to look at wider themes, such as the influence of irony on twentieth-century literature, make sure you know the basics of the existing debate before you add to it.

It may well be made clear before you start that you should prepare a plan of the whole dissertation, detailing individual chapters and as much as you can of the general direction of your arguments. If it has not been made clear, it stands as an essential before making a start. Firstly, you may find you do not have enough material when you actually get down to a detailed plan. Secondly, the detailed plan can be presented to your tutor or supervisor for him or her to pick holes in! Writing a lengthy dissertation or essay reveals very clearly how much work has gone into it in advance, and depends on it.

## Research techniques

The project or dissertation relies heavily on techniques of research that branch out far wider than was ever needed for the conventional, examination-based Advanced level. The first port of call for any student is the library; that at least has not changed in many years.

Libraries offer a wealth of assistance, some of it not realised by students until too late in the day to be of any assistance. For basic information about what subject to choose for a project, and for basic information on that subject, there are a number of standard works that give details about all and anything in English and other literature. Margaret Drabble's *The Oxford Companion to English Literature* (Oxford University Press, various editions), *The Concise Oxford Dictionary of English Literature* (Oxford University Press, various editions) and the three-volume Penguin *Companion to Literature* (Penguin, various editions) are invaluable research aids. There are numerous histories of English literature. Some of the most effective are David Daiches, *A Critical History of English Literature*, Volumes 1–3 (Secker & Warburg, 1969); A. Fowler, *A History of English Literature* (Basil Blackwell, 1989); the *New Pelican Guide to English Literature*, Volumes 1–9, edited by Boris Ford (various editions); the *Sphere History of English Literature*, edited by Christopher Ricks (various editions); *A Literary History of England*, Volumes 1–4, edited by A. Baugh (Routledge & Kegan Paul, 1967) and *The Short Oxford History of English Literature*, edited by Andrew Sanders (Oxford University Press, 1996).

These are fairly obvious research aids. Good libraries contain a number of other surprises, and if they do not hold them in stock they can usually be obtained through inter-library loan schemes. For example, the *Dictionary of National Biography* and *Who Was Who* are very useful indeed for basic biographical details of an author. There are regular productions which allow the student to find details of every postgraduate thesis written in the United Kingdom and in English-speaking universities overseas; of every book published in Britain and America; of every published review of every book in English. These reference works usually operate two or even three years in abeyance, but that does not usually matter to the student writing a project or dissertation. Copies of contemporaneous newspapers and journals are also available, and projects and dissertations can be livened up significantly by reference to contemporary reviews or obituaries of an author. Remember to use the books and articles you find as means to further research, scanning their apparatus of references and further reading to find out what may be relevant and important.

Video and audio tape loom ever larger as research aids. There is as yet no central cataloguing agency for these resources, but tapes of 'classic' and other productions are widely available. Sometimes this material can provide the basis for a project in itself: a comparison between the Roman Polanski film of *Macbeth* and the BBC Television Shakespeare version of the same play reveals wholly opposed attitudes to and versions of Shakespeare.

Increasingly students will tend to turn to the computer and word-processor for the preparation of projects and dissertations. The presentation of a work should not differ from that given in the first chapter of this book – and resist at all costs the temptation offered by some computers of different typefaces! The only word of warning to be offered to students is to separate a long project or dissertation into separate small 'files' or 'documents'. Alterations, printing and reference are made much easier if the text is divided up into digestible chunks.

CHAPTER THREE

# A guide to basic literary terms

All academic disciplines have their own specialised language. Literature's is more simple than most, with the possible exception of the terms applied to technical aspects of poetry. The following brief guide to some of the literary terms in most common usage is intended to stop the student feeling the need to purchase an expensive specialist guide to literary terms. The definitions assume no specialist knowledge on the part of the reader. They also contain elements of literary history (see the first entry on the *Theatre of the Absurd*). One reason for reading through the whole chapter is to acquire background knowledge. A second reason for reading the chapter, even if one does not require a specific definition, is to check on the literary meaning of certain words and phrases, which can be different from their meaning in normal usage. 'Image' and 'conceit' are only two examples.

Where a word appears in capital letters in the text of the definition it means that it is the subject of a separate entry in this chapter.

ABSURD, THEATRE OF THE ABSURD: in 1961 the critic Martin Esslin published a book called *The Theatre of the Absurd*, and the term has now become common as a description of the work of such authors as Edward Albee (b. 1928), Samuel Beckett (b. 1906), Eugene Ionesco (b. 1912), Arthur Adamov (1908–1970), Jean Genet (b. 1910), and N. F. Simpson (b. 1919). The early work of Harold Pinter (b. 1930) and Tom Stoppard (b. 1937) is also often linked with this group. These dramatists shared a belief that human life was essentially irrational, purposeless, and out of harmony with its surroundings, the result of this being a chronic state of uncertainty, anguish (*angst*), and depression. Other authors had reached this conclusion before; none had allowed it to dictate the *form* of their work as well as its *content*. Absurdist plays can drop all logic and rationality, and allow absurd, illogical, or irrational things to happen on stage in order to illustrate the central thesis that this is the nature of life. The opening shot in this revolution was fired by Samuel Beckett's *Waiting for Godot* (1953), which shocked theatre audiences at first by its absence of plot or structure, its bare set, and its central concept that 'nothing happens'. Absurd drama could be seen as a blend of surrealism and farce. An excellent example is Ionesco's *Rhinoceros* (1960), in which people keep turning into rhinoceroses, whilst others frantically try to ignore the fact. In the novel, works such as *The Trial* (1925) and *Metamorphosis* (1912) by Franz Kafka (1883–1924) have absurdist elements in them.

AESTHETICISM and DECADENCE: the **Aesthetic Movement** originated in France in the latter part of the nineteenth century, and in English literature its best-known adherents are Oscar Wilde (1854–1900), Algernon Swinburne (1837–1909) and the artist Aubrey Beardsley. The Aesthetes believed in 'art for art's sake', and the pursuit of beauty to the exclusion of all else, particularly materialistic or worldly values. The Aesthetic Movement was closely linked with the **Decadent Movement**, with its search for exquisite sensations, its hatred of all that was 'natural' and its obsession with high artifice. Aesthetes and Decadents were associated with the flouting of conventional morality.

AFFECTIVE FALLACY: the attempt to evaluate a poem by its emotional effect upon the reader. It is therefore part of a plea for objective criticism that seeks to ascertain how a work achieves its effects, rather than describing the effect on the critic personally.

ALIENATION EFFECT: in a conventional play the members of the audience tend to get swept up in the action, suspend their disbelief, and believe in what they are witnessing as reality. Certain authors, notably the playwright Bertolt Brecht (1898–1956), considered that this illusion of reality stopped the audience from judging what they were seeing with sufficient objectivity and detachment. He therefore inserted specific devices into his plays to remind his audience that what they were watching was an illusion, thereby forcing a more critical judgement on them. The so-called alienation effect is sometimes given rather more attention than it deserves; soliloquies, 'asides', and other techniques such as the use of a Chorus in Greek drama have long been doing much of what is done by Brecht's alienation effect.

ALLEGORY: allegory is a story or narrative, usually of some length, which carries a second meaning, as well as that of its surface story or content. It is a method of telling one story whilst seeming to tell another. *The Pilgrim's Progress* (1684) by John Bunyan (1628–88) is one of the most famous prose allegories. As with many of its kind, it personifies abstract ideas and human virtues and vices in characters such as Mr Worldly-Wise, Giant Despair, Hopeful, Lechery, Pride, and Christian, the pilgrim. Famous allegories include the poem *The Faerie Queene* (1596) by Edmund Spenser (?1552–99),

*Absalom and Achitophel* (1681) by John Dryden (1631–1700), and Chaucer's *Roman de le Rose*, which describes at great length a lover's attempt to win his lady in terms of a man trying to enter a garden and pluck a flower. Allegory and satire sometimes go hand in hand, a neat way of ridiculing people being to characterise them as other than themselves; one example of this is George Orwell's (1903–50) novel *Animal Farm* (1945), where the setting of a farm, the story of the animals overthrowing their human owners and the eventual imposition of tyranny by one set of animals on to another is an allegory of the story of the Communist revolution in Russia and the rise of Stalin.

ALLITERATION: the repetition of the same consonant sound (as in the repetition of the 's' sound in 'Whispering silently in the shaded streets'), and very common in Old English and medieval poetry. Two famous examples of its use are Hopkins' 'The Windhover' and Keats' 'Ode to Autumn' (1820).

AMBIGUITY: describes language with a doubtful meaning, or with several meanings. It can be used where meaning is unclear because of a fault or weakness on the part of the author. Its more modern usage, sometimes described as *multiple meanings*, *fruitful*, or *wilful* ambiguity, is in describing a situation where an author deliberately suggests several layers of meaning, all of which can be kept in the reader's mind at the same time.

ANACHRONISM: a historically inaccurate episode or event, as when Shakespeare has a clock chime in *Julius Caesar*; mechanical clocks had not been invented in Roman times, in which the play is supposedly set.

ANAPAEST: a metrical FOOT consisting of two unstressed syllables followed by one stressed syllable (see Ch. 4).

APRON STAGE: a part of a stage which projects into the audience, allowing the audience to view the action from three sides.

ARCHETYPAL CRITICISM: a critical theory which emphasises the importance of archetypal myths in the creation of and response to literature. See Chapter 25.

ASSONANCE: the repetition of vowel sounds, where ALLITERATION is the repetition of consonantal sounds.

AUGUSTAN: a term used to describe the early years of the eighteenth century, dominated in literature by the poetry of Alexander Pope. The term derives from the Roman Emperor Augustus, and implies a return or adherence to 'classical' values in literature.

BALLAD: a narrative poem, telling its story (often at some length) in a simple, unadorned way, and with a minimum of characterisation and description. Original ballads were often anonymous folk tales, but the style has been copied copiously by many authors. An ancient ballad is the Scottish poem *Sir Patrick Spens*; a modern variation of the technique is Oscar Wilde's harrowing *The Ballad of Reading Gaol* (1898).

BATHOS: a sudden descent from the serious to the ludicrous. Bathos is usually unintentional, whereas *anti-climax* is used deliberately by an author, often for comic effect.

BLANK VERSE: poetry which does not rhyme, but which is metrical, in that it uses a regular and repeated pattern of rhythm rather than relying on rhyme to bind the poem together.

BURLESQUE: a work of literature that sets out to ridicule a style or type of writing, by exaggerating the features of the original and making them appear ridiculous. Shakespeare's play put on by the 'rude mechanicals' in *A Midsummer Night's Dream* is burlesque, ridiculing the 'theatrical interlude' of the day. PARODY is a form of burlesque, ridiculing a specific book or work by imitating it badly. Henry Fielding's *Shamela* (1741) mocks Samuel Richardson's *Pamela* by imitating its style and applying the style to ludicrous situations. The MOCK HEROIC style of writing is also a member of the burlesque family, as in Alexander Pope's (1688–1744) poem *The Rape of the Lock* (1712) where the full-blown heroic style of writing is applied to the theft of a lock of hair from a young girl, thus creating a total mis-match of style against content that makes the incident look ludicrous. This, of course, was Pope's intention. The actual incident on which the poem was based was threatening to do harm out of all proportion to its importance, and by writing of it in such an important style Pope ironically makes it clear how trivial the incident is. TRAVESTY is also a form of burlesque: Tom Stoppard's play *Travesties* (1974) has great fun with the form. One of the funniest of all modern parodies in Stella Gibbons' *Cold Comfort Farm* (1932), which manages to be hilarious even if one does not know the school of 'rural primitivism' whose style it sets out to parody. Try reading it alongside Emily Bronte's *Wuthering Heights*.

CARICATURE: a character whose personality is described in terms of a very small number of features, often grossly exaggerated.

CATHARSIS: sometimes spelt Katharsis (originating from Greek tragedy), the word describes the purging of emotions (usually defined as pity or fear) that takes place at the end of TRAGEDY.

CHORUS: originally a body of performers in Greek drama who recited or chanted lines commenting on the action of the play before them. Nowadays the term is used of any character who acts as commentator in a play. A famous example is Chorus in Shakespeare's *Henry V*.

CHRONICLE PLAYS: chronicle plays were primitive plays dealing with English history, popular in the latter half of the sixteenth century, and a significant influence on Elizabethan dramatists.

CLASSICAL: originally this term described Greek or Roman literature, or works written in the Roman or Greek style. It is increasingly used nowadays to describe writers who value tradition in their work, or who are very concerned with form in their work. *Romantic* and *classical* are sometimes used as opposites in describing an author's work. A rule-of-thumb method for deciding if an author is writing in a Romantic or classical mode is to look at his or her treatment of children. The Romantic will tend to see them as pure and unspoilt humanity, valuable in their own right as symbols of the essential goodness of humanity. The classical writer will tend to value them only for their adult features, and may indeed view childhood as a nuisance, and a phase to be passed through as quickly as possible.

CLICHÉ: a phrase or idea that has been used so often, and is so well-worn, that it has lost its original inventiveness, freshness, and appeal.

COMEDY: in modern usage the term now means something that makes an audience or reader laugh; in its original form, it simply meant a play or other work with a happy ending. It is tempting and very wrong, to see comedy as very lightweight. A comic work, with either or both of the above meanings, can make extremely serious points.

CONCEIT: an elaborate, extended, and startling comparison between apparently dissimilar objects, associated in particular with METAPHYSICAL POETRY. When in his poem 'The Flea' John Donne (?1571–1631) compares his lover and himself to a flea (the flea has sucked the blood of both, and by carrying their mixed blood in his body becomes a symbol of unity) he is composing a textbook conceit: unexpected, lengthy, and ultimately both convincing and intriguing.

COUPLET: a two-line section of a poem which rhymes, and which has a meaning complete within itself. Alexander Pope is probably the most famous user of 'heroic couplets'; Elizabethan dramatists frequently rounded off a scene with a pair of rhymed verse lines.

COURTLY LOVE: a philosophy of love, and an attitude towards it, that influenced medieval literature. It flourished and was formalised in the royal courts of the South of France in the twelfth century. It dealt with aristocratic, extra-marital love conducted in secret. The male lover was totally subservient to his mistress, worshipped her as a goddess, and was completely at her mercy. Though the love affairs are often sexual and sensual, the physical side of the affair is treated with great dignity and decorum, and the love is a rarified spiritual experience as much as a physical one. Geoffrey Chaucer

(?1340–1400) makes significant use of the courtly love mode of writing, but can also satirise it, as in the *The Merchant's Tale*. By Chaucer's time middle-class morality was beginning to creep into courtly love tales, with an attempt to combine the idealism of courtly love with the morality of marriage, a very difficult balancing act as the two ways of looking at relationships view the relative dominance of man and woman quite differently. Chaucer's *The Franklin's Tale* is the best-known example of such an attempt to combine the different outlooks of marriage and courtly love.

DACTYL: a metrical FOOT consisting of one stressed syllable followed by two unstressed syllables.

DECONSTRUCTION: a critical theory that attempts to dismantle the views of STRUCTURALISM, arguing that all works of literature deconstruct themselves and collapse into a multitude of meanings. See Chapter 25.

DÉNOUEMENT: the ending of a work of literature where all the necessary information is revealed and the plot concluded.

DICTION: a poet's choice and arrangement of words; in normal usage the word is equivalent to 'vocabulary'.

DIDACTIC: something with a lesson, moral, or teaching in it. Aesop's *Fables* are clearly didactic.

DRAMATIC IRONY: see IRONY.

DRAMATIC MONOLOGUE: a speech written as if spoken by an imagined character, in his or her voice and tone. It is 'dramatic' because it comes from a character created by the author in the manner of that character speaking or thinking out loud. It is a 'monologue' because it comes from one character only. It should not be confused with SOLILOQUY, which takes place within a play. Dramatic monologues are usually complete within themselves and written as prose or poetry, not within the confines of a play or dramatic event.

ELEGY: a mourning or lamentation poem, usually of a reflective nature, though not always about a specific dead person. Good examples are John Milton's (1608–74) *Lycidas* and Alfred Lord Tennyson's *In Memoriam* (1850). A very famous, though rather different, example is Thomas Gray's (1716–71) 'Elegy Written in a Country Church-Yard'.

ELEMENTS: Up until about the seventeenth century it was thought that all matter on earth was made up of the four elements, *earth*, *air*, *fire*, and *water*, and that these were the basic building blocks of the Universe. See HUMOURS.

END STOPPING: a verse line with a pause or stop at the end.

ENJAMBEMENT: running on the sense of one verse line to the next, without a pause.

EPIC: a long narrative poem, written in an elevated style and with heroic subject matter. Classical epics include the *Iliad* by Homer (*c.* ninth century BC), and the *Aeneid* by Virgil (70–19 BC). More modern attempts at epics include *The Divine Comedy* by Dante (1269–1321), and *Paradise Lost* by John Milton (1608–74). The true epic starts in the middle of the action, after a grand announcement of theme and an appeal to the MUSE. The noble hero performs many deeds of courage, there are great battles, and the central characters have long speeches in which they tell of themselves. As with all literary styles, individual works all have their own individual features.

EPIC SIMILE: sometimes known as a Homeric simile, an epic simile is an extended and elaborate simile, not to be confused with a CONCEIT. The epic simile is lengthy and elaborate, but rarely shocking or apparently outrageous in the manner of the conceit.

EPIGRAM: a brief, pointed, and often witty statement, found in all forms of literature.

EPISTLE: verse or poetry in the form of a letter.

EPITAPH: a short composition in memory of a dead person.

EUPHEMISM: expressing something unpleasant in milder, more inoffensive language. In the novel *The Loved One* (1948) by Evelyn Waugh (1903–66) the title itself is a euphemism for a corpse or dead person.

EUPHONY: pleasantly smooth and melodious language.

EXEMPLUM: a story told to illustrate a moral point, or an 'example' of morality in action and practice.

EXISTENTIALISM: in existentialist philosophy, existence is the only thing we are certain of; man's life begins and ends in nothingness, and life is inexplicable, meaningless, and dangerous. The nature of our existence is decided by the choices we make to determine its nature. There are many variations of this philosophy, including even a Christian one, but its main appearance in literature is in the THEATRE OF THE ABSURD.

EYE RHYME: rhyme based on words which look similar but which are pronounced differently, as in 'how/bow' where 'bow' is pronounced as in 'bow and arrow'.

FABLE: a short tale or story conveying a clear moral lesson, as in the sixth-century *Aesop's Fables*.

FABLIAU: a short satirical or comic tale with a strong bawdy element; Chaucer's *The Miller's Tale* is one of the best-known examples.

FARCE: a play intended to provoke non-censorious laughter by presenting absurd and ridiculous characters and actions. Complicated plots, mistaken ideas, and marital infidelity are the stuff of farce.

FEMININE ENDING: a line of verse ending on a weak or unstressed syllable.

FEMINIST CRITICISM: the literary and critical theory that explores the bias in favour of the male gender in literature, and which re-examines all literature from a feminist viewpoint. See Chapter 25.

FLAT AND ROUNDED CHARACTERS: a FLAT character is one who is one-dimensional, often characterised through one feature or mannerism. He or she is a type, a CARICATURE, or someone who behaves with little depth and complexity. A ROUNDED character is more complex, can surprise the reader with his or her actions, and can change or grow over the course of a book or play. In general, flat characters are simple, and rounded characters are complex. Thus in *Great Expectations* (1861) by Charles Dickens (1812–70) Pip, the hero, is a round character, whilst Trabb's Boy (who has only the one feature of being cheeky) is a flat character.

FOOT: a group of syllables forming a unit of verse.

FREE VERSE: poetry which does not have a regular metrical structure.

GENRE: a kind or style of writing.

GEORGIAN POETRY: a school of poets whose main expression was through the five *Georgian Poetry* anthologies edited by Edward Marsh between 1911 and 1922. It included such poets as Rupert Brooke (1887–1915), Walter de la Mare (1873–1956), W. H. Davies (1871–1940), D. H. Lawrence (1889–1930), and Edmund Blunden (1896–1974). Georgian poetry was SUBJECTIVE, concentrated on rural subjects, and appeared simple. As such it has tended to be dismissed by post-T. S. Eliot and modernist poetry as a decayed and decaying last fling of the Romantic poetry movement. It is now increasingly recognised that, though the Georgian poets did not experiment with the form of poetry, they were both skilful and the pioneers of new subject matter in poetry.

GOTHIC NOVEL: a type of novel popular in the eighteenth and nineteenth centuries which dealt with supernatural events, high passion, and violence, frequently set back in the Middle Ages. Interest in the Gothic novel has now spread out and encompasses interest in a wide range of literature seen as being Gothic: see Chapter 16.

HALF RHYME: imperfect rhyme; see RHYME.

HEPTAMETER: a verse line containing seven feet.

HEROIC COUPLET: see COUPLET.

HEXAMETER: a verse line containing six feet.

HORATIAN ODE: an ODE written in a restrained manner, and to a regular metre.

HUBRIS: the pride that allows a tragic hero to ignore the warnings from the gods, and so bring about his NEMESIS (downfall).

HUMOURS: the four humours were originally thought of as four liquids existing in the human body, and the balance of the humours dictated a person's personality and his health. Much medieval and Jacobean writing refers to this theory. Earlier references tend to refer to the basic fluids and the features they were meant to give people. A person with an excess of the humour *blood* in him was called *sanguine*, and was pleasure-loving, amorous, kind, and jovially good-natured; the Franklin in Chaucer's *The Canterbury Tales* is such a figure. Someone with an excess of *phlegm* in them was described as *phlegmatic* and was dull, cowardly, unresponsive, dour, and unexciting. An excess of *yellow bile* gave rise to a *choleric* person: vengeful, obstinate, impatient, intolerant, angry, and quick to lose his temper. An excess of *black bile* produced a person who was *melancholic*: moody, brooding, sharp-tongued, liable to sudden changes of mood, and often lost in thought and contemplation. The poet John Donne was supposed to be highly melancholic. By the start of the seventeenth century the 'comedy of humours' had developed, in which people's behaviour was linked to one humour or feature. *Every Man in His Humour* by Ben Jonson (1572–1637) is a good example of such a play. Humour here is coming to have its wider meaning of personality, rather than the specific four humours meant in medieval times. In medieval and Jacobean times the four humours were thought of as equivalents of the four ELEMENTS around which the Universe was created.

HYPERBOLE: a figure of speech which uses exaggeration.

IAMB: the most common metrical FOOT in English poetry, consisting of an unstressed syllable followed by a stressed syllable.

IMAGERY: a word used by a great many critics to mean a great many different things. In its most basic form imagery is descriptive language, most commonly SIMILE or METAPHOR. Anything which creates a picture in the mind can be said to be an image.

INTENTIONAL FALLACY: the supposed error of looking to explain a point or feature of a literary work by reference to the intentions of its author. In this view such 'external' evidence is inadmissible, with the work having to stand or fall merely on what is locked within it.

INTERNAL RHYME: rhyming words within a line, rather than at the end.

IRONY: saying or writing one thing whilst meaning another. Irony occurs when a word or phrase has one surface meaning, but another contradictory meaning beneath the surface. This should not be confused with *sarcasm*, which is very blunt and unsubtle spoken irony. *Verbal* or *rhetorical irony* occurs when a character says something which is the exact opposite of what they mean. When Hamlet says he is 'but mad north-northwest' he means he is not mad at all. *Socratic irony* occurs when a character appears to adopt a view he does not share in order to make it appear ludicrous. *Dramatic irony* occurs when a character speaks lines which have a totally different meaning – for the other characters on stage, or for the audience – to the one he or she means. Thus when in Shakespeare's *Macbeth* Duncan says, 'This castle hath a fine and pleasant seat', the audience know from what they have heard before that this castle is actually where Duncan will be cruelly murdered. Irony can also be used in a general sense to apply to any complex work of literature that suggests the many 'ironies of life'. The novelist Jane Austen (1775–1817) is a master of irony, as are Chaucer and the novelist Henry Fielding (1707–54).

KITCHEN SINK DRAMA: a type of play associated with the play *Look Back in Anger* (1956) by John Osborne (b. 1929). The term usually refers to plays with a true-to-life, rather seedy setting and action. This type of play also gave rise to the term 'angry young man', implying youth in rebellion against older people and the restrictive ways of the society they have created. For some years it was felt that Osborne's work had aged badly, but recently there has been an increased interest in his work with a number of successful revivals of *Look Back in Anger* in particular.

LAMENT: a poem expressing immense grief.

LYRIC: originally a song accompanied on the lyre, an early form of stringed instrument. It can now mean a song-like poem, or a short poem dealing with the thoughts and feelings of a single speaker, usually but not always the poet.

MALAPROPISM: the muddled use of long or complex words in the wrong place or context. The term is derived from the name of Mrs Malaprop, a character in *The Rivals* (1775) by Richard Brinsley Sheridan (1751–1816). However, the concept is considerably older than this. Malapropisms are the main comic feature of Dogberry in Shakespeare's *Much Ado About Nothing*.

MARXIST CRITICISM: examines literature from the perspective of Marxist thought, class structures and class warfare. See Chapter 25.

MASCULINE ENDING: a line of verse ending on a stressed syllable.

MASQUE: a lavish form of dramatic entertainment relying heavily on song, dance, costumes, extravagant spectacle and special effects. The genre flourished in the first part of the seventeenth century, having been imported from Italy. Ben Jonson is sometimes seen as the greatest of masque writers. *Comus* (1634) by John Milton is a particularly famous masque, and the scene of its first performance can still be visited at Ludlow Castle.

MELODRAMA: now a derogatory term, melodrama is drama that is sensational, highly emotional, full of excitement, with very little depth to it, and usually given a happy ending. It was very popular in Britain in the late nineteenth century.

METAPHOR: a comparison between two objects for the purpose of describing one of them. A metaphor states that one object is another, as when John Keats the poet (1795–1831) refers to a vase and the decoration on it as 'Thou still unravish'd bride of quietness'. The vase is clearly not a bride, but the comparison is made more forceful by being written in this manner. For the above to be a SIMILE, Keats would have had to say that the vase was *like* a bride.

METAPHYSICAL POETRY: the Metaphysical poets were a diverse group of poets writing between, roughly, 1610 and 1680. Metaphysical poetry (a term invented quite a while after the poets wrote and lived) is both intellectual and emotional, and operates at a high pitch of intensity. It uses ordinary speech as well as scientific concepts and terms drawn from the science of the day. Technical devices associated with the school are PARADOX and CONCEIT. Love and religion were probably its commonest themes. Authors generally held to belong to the school are John Donne (?1571–1631), Andrew Marvell (1621–78), George Herbert (1593–1633), Henry Vaughan (1621–95), John Cleveland (1613–58), Abraham Cowley (1618–67) and Richard Crashaw (?1612–49). The Metaphysical poets have become highly fashionable in the twentieth century, but before this were often considered eccentric and difficult: see Chapter 10.

METRE: the regular and repetitive use of stressed and unstressed syllables in poetry. Metre is the formalised use of rhythm in poetry, formalised in the sense of its using regular and repeated rhythmic patterns. See Chapter 5.

MILTONIC SONNET: a form of SONNET introduced by the poet John Milton which has the rhyme scheme *abbaabba cdcdcd*, but which has no turn or change of meaning in the second half.

MIRACLE/MYSTERY PLAYS: these plays marked the high point of medieval drama, reaching a peak in the fourteenth and fifteenth centuries. The plays were essentially dramatisations of episodes and scenes from the Old and New Testaments of the Christian Bible. They were presented from a series of wagons, complete with complex stage effects, so that a whole 'cycle' of plays could be seen performed in one spot before each individual wagon moved on. The most famous English cycles were York, Coventry, Wakefield, and Chester. They became so complex and demanding of time and resources that they were taken over by the immensely powerful medieval trade guilds (a cross between a modern trade union and a professional association). As these guilds tended to refer to their trades as 'mysteries' the plays came to be called mystery plays. Miracle plays could deal with miraculous events and legends, whereas the mystery plays dealt solely with biblical episodes.

MOCK HEROIC: treating a trivial subject with the grandeur and style of the EPIC mode of writing, so as to make the subject appear ridiculous and to provoke laughter. A famous example is *The Rape of the Lock* (1714) by Alexander Pope. See also BURLESQUE.

MONODY: a poem of mourning presented by one person.

MONOMETER: a verse line with only one foot or unit of stressed and unstressed syllables.

MORALITY PLAYS: the successor to MIRACLE and MYSTERY plays. Morality plays were simpler, and mounted on a primitive stage. A famous example is *Everyman* (c. 1500), which in common with many morality plays is in the form of an ALLEGORY.

MUSE: originally, one of the nine Greek goddesses who presided over the arts. Poets used to invoke the aid of the Muses to inspire them, as in Shakespeare's appeal 'for a Muse of fire' in *Henry V*.

MYTH: an anonymous story which tells of mysterious and strange events far back in history. *Mythology* is a collection of such stories. Myths often deal with elemental situations such as the creation of the world or the actions of the gods, and are associated with primitive societies. These stories are often basic to the nature of human existence, and as such exert lasting appeal. Many authors have either used myths in their work, or attempted to create myths of their own. *The Waste Land* (1922) by T. S. Eliot (1888–1965) uses the myths of the Holy Grail and the Fisher King, whilst J. R. Tolkien's

(1892–1973) *The Lord of the Rings* (1955) uses a personal mythology that borrows heavily from a wide range of other mythologies.

NATURALISM: a view of mankind which sees man as no more than an animal, and life as a squalid and meaningless tragedy.

NEGATIVE CAPABILITY: a phrase derived from the poet John Keats. It can mean two things: either the capacity on the part of an author to remain in doubt and uncertainty, without wishing to give a final answer to all things; or the capacity to forget one's own personality and blend totally into the experience of other people.

NEMESIS: the fate that overtakes the tragic hero, or the punishment that he deserves and cannot escape.

NEW CRITICISM: a school which believed in close reading of a text, minimal reliance on external factors for understanding it and an objective scrutiny of what had been written. See Chapter 25.

NOBLE SAVAGE: the idea that primitive man is somehow better and more pure than his civilised counterpart, whose civilisation serves merely to corrupt him. The concept is frequently associated with ROMANTIC writing, and in more popular culture the figure of Tarzan comes very near to summing up the basics of the concept.

NOVEL: an extended and fictional work in prose.

OBJECTIVE CORRELATIVE: A set of objects, situation or chain of events that represent in tangible form an emotion – according to T. S. Eliot, the only way that such emotion can be represented. In general usage an objective correlative is seen as a method of portraying emotion in and by a concrete image or form. Its validity has been much debated.

OBJECTIVITY: an impersonal and detached style of writing in which the author treats a subject impartially. It is doubtful whether any book is truly objective; some appear to be more so than others. See also the opposite, SUBJECTIVITY.

OCTAMETER: a verse line consisting of eight feet.

OCTAVE/OCTET: the first eight lines of a SONNET.

ODE: a serious and lengthy LYRIC poem.

OMNISCIENT NARRATOR: a narrator in a novel who knows and sees all that is happening in the plot of the novel and to its characters. Charles

Dickens' (1812–1870) *Bleak House* (1853) is interesting in that it combines a personal narrative from the heroine Esther Summerson and an omniscient narrator.

ONOMATOPOEIA: a word which sounds like the noise it describes, such as 'splash' or 'thwack'.

OXYMORON: a figure of speech in which words of opposite meaning are joined together, as in 'a damned saint'.

PARADOX: an apparently self-contradictory statement that on closer examination is shown to have a basis of truth. As well as illustrating a truth, a paradox concentrates the reader's attention on what is being said, through the initial shock of an apparently nonsensical statement, as in the following example from *Holy Sonnets* by John Donne:

> One short sleepe past, we wake eternally,
> And death shall be no more, Death thou shalt die.

PARARHYME: another name for HALF RHYME; see RHYME.

PARODY: a work written in imitation of another work, usually with the object of making fun of or ridiculing the original. See BURLESQUE.

PASTORAL: in general, literature that concerns country life. It is usually used of writing which describes the idyllic life of shepherds and shepherdesses who fall in love and pass the time by singing and playing songs, and is thus somewhat distanced from the real life of actual shepherds. *As You Like It* by William Shakespeare and *Lycidas* by John Milton are two works with elements of pastoral in them that are commonly set at Advanced level.

PATHETIC FALLACY: a term used originally by John Ruskin (1819–1900) to describe the links that poets and authors saw between their own moods and the natural world about them. Ruskin thought the idea of a causative link between man and nature was a fallacy because it was clearly untrue, and pathetic because it merely showed a man's desire not to be alone in the world, and his tendency to overestimate his own importance and influence. The term nowadays can be used without the original pejorative tone.

PATHOS: moments in literature which evoke strong feelings of pity and sorrow.

PENTAMETER: a line of verse with five feet.

PERSONIFICATION: giving to inanimate objects or abstract ideas, human qualities or actions; making non-human things appear as human.

PETRARCHAN SONNET: a fourteen-line poem divided into two parts, an eight-line OCTAVE and a six-line SESTET. The octave usually rhymes *abbaabba*, the sestet *cdecde*. The octave generally states the theme, the sestet its answer or reconciliation. The rhyme schemes can be varied.

PHENOMENOLOGY: a critical theory linked with the Geneva School that sees the act of reading as leading to a powerful and unique form of empathy with the author. See Chapter 25.

PICARESQUE: in Spanish the *picaro* was a rogue or villain. The term 'picaresque' traditionally refers to a novel with a central figure or picaro who is a low-born rogue or knave, who goes on a journey which involves him in a sequence of adventures, frequently unconnected, and which are comic or satirical. The hero in certain picaresque novels, such as *Tom Jones*, is not low-born, or a rogue. Most novels by Daniel Defoe (1660–1731) are picaresque. Tobias Smollett (1721–71) also wrote many novels in this style.

PROSCENIUM ARCH: the picture frame stage, with a curtained square arch over the acting area. Plays set within a proscenium arch give the impression of watching events in a room one wall of which has been taken away.

PROSE: any language that is not VERSE; language which is not made to obey a metrical pattern of regular and repetitive stressed and unstressed syllables.

PROSODY: not to be confused with PROSE, prosody is the science and study of versification.

PYRRHIC: a metrical FOOT consisting of two unstressed syllables.

READER RESPONSE CRITICISM: analyses and is concerned with the response of the reader when coming to a work of literature. See Chapter 25.

REALISM: one of the most misused words in criticism. Realistic works attempt to show life as it really is, idealistic works to show it as it should be. The term is almost impossible to define, and as a result should be left alone as far as possible!

RENAISSANCE: the Renaissance was the rebirth of learning, art and literature deemed to have taken place from late in the fourteenth century onwards in Europe. The collapse of the Roman Empire was followed by a period of relative barbarism in Europe (the 'Dark Ages'), and then by the Middle Ages. Visions of the Dark Ages have been coloured by the fact that their history was written by later, Christian historians, most of whom have tended to see the period as the historical irritant that took place in between the Roman Empire and the establishment of Christianity in Europe. Anyone who has seen Viking silver work and jewellery might question at least the suggestion that the Dark Ages lacked artistic sensitivity. The Middle Ages managed to reimpose a degree of stability on European society, but the age saw itself as clawing back some of the advances made by the Romans, the paragons of civilisation, and certainly not improving upon them. The Renaissance marked the time when European art, thought and religion began to believe it could improve on Roman knowledge on the one hand, and on the other hand move out from a specifically Christian interpretation of classical material. This produced a feeling of heady excitement, but, as a movement which also challenged all existing knowledge, it could also produce the black depression and loss of all certainty seen in some Elizabethan and particularly Jacobean work. The Renaissance is at best a very loose concept, deemed to have lasted until early in the seventeenth century. Perhaps the greatest symbol of the Renaissance is Shakespeare's *Hamlet*, containing as he does within himself in almost equal measure the potential for perfection and the potential for self-destruction.

RESTORATION: the period of Charles II's restoration to the English throne produced both comedy and tragedy in the newly built theatres, but Restoration comedy is now far better known than Restoration tragedy. In the Restoration period the nature of the plays being performed changed radically from Shakespearian and Jacobean times. Restoration comedy deals almost exclusively with the affairs of the London upper classes. It is graceful and sometimes bawdy, heavily concerned with sexual behaviour and money, and places a huge premium on WIT as a major social virtue. It tends to contain several stock figures, such as the beau, the dandy or fop, the young rake, and the country or rustic bumpkin. Best-known authors are William Congreve (1670–1729), William Wycherley (1640–1716), Sir George Etherege (?1634–91), George Farquhar (1678–1707), and Sir John Vanbrugh (1664–1726). Congreve's *The Way of the World* (1700) is often viewed as the masterpiece of the GENRE. Wycherley's *The Country Wife* (?1675) is one of the most cynical and unpleasant of restoration comedies, whilst Vanbrugh's *The Relapse* (1696) illustrates the free and easy ways of the time. It was written in a matter of weeks to bail a friend out of debt, allows the sub-plot to take over the main plot in riotous disregard of proper plotting and has some marvellous characterisation.

REVENGE TRAGEDY: the name given to a style of dramatic writing associated with the Shakespearian and Jacobean period. See Chapter 8 below.

RHETORIC: the art of speaking and writing so as to win an audience round, and the subject of several books by Greek and Roman scholars. Nowadays the term is just as likely to be used to imply something empty and false, or ornate but meaningless statements.

RHYME: the use of similar sounding words in poetry. See Chapter 4 below.

ROMANTIC POETRY: Romanticism is one of the most complex terms in literature, so much so that no exact definition exists. Romantic poetry in English literature is easier to define, but even here the term covers some very dissimilar poets. The beginning of Romantic poetry is usually identified with the publication of *Lyrical Ballads* (1798, 1800, 1803) by William Wordsworth (1770–1850) and Samuel Taylor Coleridge (1772–1834). The Romantic poet believes in the emotions and the imagination, rather than reason or the intellect. He believes in man as an individual, rather than as a member of society, and in the cultivation and revelation of the individual soul. Man is seen as essentially or instinctively good, but corrupted by civilisation. The Romantic poet can be a political revolutionary, but more often has a high regard for nature and the natural environment, seeing in it unspoilt beauty, basic truths, and even the hand of the Creator or guiding spirit of the Universe. He is often searching for a transcendental moment of insight, the sublime and wonderful experience that makes life worthwhile, and frequently writes in a highly SUBJECTIVE manner. Romantic poets include Percy Bysshe Shelley (1792–1822), Robert Browning (1812–89), Alfred Lord Tennyson (1809–92), Lord Byron (1788–1824), as well as Keats, Wordsworth, and Coleridge. See also CLASSICAL.

ROUNDED CHARACTER: see FLAT AND ROUNDED CHARACTERS.

SATIRE: exposing human vice and folly to laughter and ridicule. Satire can be light or amusing, or savage in the bitterness of tone with which it exposes human frailty. Examples of both can be found in *Gulliver's Travels* (1726) by Jonathan Swift (1667–1745). Some satirists believe that by exposing folly to laughter they render it ineffective; its danger and weakness is that it can be wholly negative and destructive, and fail to suggest positive alternatives to what is being criticised. In modern usage satire is often used to denote humour created by making fun of someone, but true satire always has a moral aim.

SCANSION: the analysis of metrical patterns in poetry.

SCHOOL: a term used of a group of authors who are seen to share certain features in their work. The term needs to be treated with caution; members of the same school can be very different, and authors are usually grouped into a school by critics, rather than by the authors themselves.

SEMIOTICS: a critical theory which examines the signs that humanity adopts in order to communicate, though in literary terms the movement has concentrated on linguistic signs and the mechanics of language. See Chapter 25.

SENTIMENTALITY: writing which calls forth an excessive emotional response from a reader usually by means of an oversimplification of reality. It has been described as 'emotion without thought', or 'an outpouring of emotion unimpeded by thought'. It is usually scorned by critics, and quite often adored by the reading or viewing public.

SEPTET: a seven-line STANZA.

SESTET: the last six lines of the PETRARCHAN SONNET.

SIMILE: a comparison between two objects where one object is said to be like or as another. See METAPHOR.

SLAPSTICK: broad, coarse, physical comedy.

SOLILOQUY: a long speech in which a character expresses his thoughts out loud on stage, usually when he or she is alone.

SONNET: a fourteen-line poem with a complex rhyme scheme and structure. See PETRARCHAN and MILTONIC SONNET, OCTAVE, and SESTET. A *Shakespearian sonnet* has fourteen lines of iambic pentameters, a variable rhyme scheme, and is divided up into three quatrains with a concluding *couplet* that usually expresses the theme of the sonnet. A *Spenserian sonnet* has the rhyme scheme *ababbcbsodcdee* and no break between the OCTAVE and the SESTET. It is named after the Elizabethan poet Edmund Spenser (?1552–99).

SPEECH ACT THEORY: a linguistic theory of criticism that concentrates on explaining the underlying assumptions of authorial and character language. See Chapter 24.

SPONDEE: a metrical FOOT consisting of two stressed syllables.

SPOONERISMS: transposing the initial consonants of two words, as in 'half-warmed fish' for 'half-formed wish'. Named after Rev. W. A. Spooner (1844–1930). A common line in University debates is for the speaker to describe his opponent as a 'shining wit, as the Rev. Spooner might have said'.

STANZA: a group of lines in a poem divided off from the others. A stanza is the correct term for what is often referred to as a 'verse' of poetry.

STREAM OF CONSCIOUSNESS: the attempt in novel writing to recreate the actual flow, pattern and sense of thoughts as they pass through a person's head in real life, or to describe experience as it is actually felt by a person as it is taking place. James Joyce (1882–1941) and Virginia Woolf (1882–1941) are two well-known exponents of this style.

STRUCTURALISM: a linguistic-based theory of criticism suggesting complex structures governing the meaning and interpretation of language. See Chapter 25.

STYLE: in its simplest form the collective impression left by the way an author writes. An author's style is usually individual, his literary fingerprint.

SUBJECTIVE: a personal, individual outlook as distinct from an OBJECTIVE outlook.

SUB-PLOT: a secondary plot or story line in a book or play, often provides either comic relief from the main plot, or a different way of looking at the themes and interests of the main plot.

SYMBOL: a symbol is similar to an image in that it stands for something else, but unlike an IMAGE it is not merely descriptive. Literary symbols, such as the great white whale in *Moby Dick* (1851) by Herman Melville (1819–1891), or the lighthouse in *To The Lighthouse* (1927) by Virginia Woolf, are multi-layered in their meanings. They mean different things to readers of the book and to characters within it. A symbol frequently sums up abstract virtues or features. It has been said that a symbol works like a stone thrown into a pond, sending ripples in all directions, it being very difficult to see where the ripples end.

TETRAMETER: a verse line of four feet.

THEME: the central idea or ideas examined by a writer in the course of a book. Conclusions can be presented on a theme, or the theme simply explored and final conclusions left to the reader. When a student refers to the 'meaning' of a book he or she usually means its theme.

TRAGEDY: the derivation of this word from a Greek word meaning 'goat-song' is not very helpful. Tragedy developed from ancient rituals, worked through to Greek drama, and has been a lasting presence in literature ever since, though as with so many of the terms used in literature its precise meaning is very difficult to arrive at. In its simplest terms, a tragedy is usually a play with an unhappy ending, though both poetry and novels can contain strong elements of tragedy. The Greek scientist and philosopher Aristotle (384–322 BC) wrote that tragedy had to be serious, wide in its scope, and complete in itself. The tragic hero was high-born, and neither particularly good nor particularly bad, merely normal in his balance of the two. Due to some tragic flaw (a weakness or mistake on his part) the tragic hero goes from happiness to misery and death. There is often a supernatural element in tragedy, and the feeling that the tragic hero has somehow aroused the anger of the gods or controlling powers of the universe. There is also frequently a sense of waste at the death of the tragic hero, a feeling also of relief that he or she is spared more pain and suffering, and a moment of tragic recognition where the tragic hero recognises both his fate and his weaknesses. CATHARSIS occurs at the end of a tragedy, often with a sense of final peace and regeneration. All authors, including those from Greek times, have rung the changes on these features, which should not be viewed as in any way binding.

TRAGICOMEDY: a mixture of tragedy and comedy.

TRIMETER: a verse line consisting of three feet.

TROCHEE: a trochee is a FOOT consisting of a stressed syllable followed by an unstressed syllable.

VERSE: the correct term for poetry.

WIT: a term which has gone through several meanings. It can mean intelligence or wisdom, or the application of those features to experience. It can mean 'quick-witted', implying excellent imagination, originality, and the capacity to think quickly. It can mean excellence of judgement and a reasoned, balanced outlook. Its most modern meaning is something intellectually amusing, often with a mildly shocking or surprising element in it. Alexander Pope defined it as 'What oft was thought, but ne'er so well exprest.' It can also mean verbal brilliance.

## Further reading


- M. H. Abrams, *A Glossary of Literary Terms* (5th edn, Holt, Rinehart & Winston, 1988)
- Martin Gray, *A Dictionary of Literary Terms* (Longman, 1992)
- John Peck and Martin Coyle, *Literary Terms and Criticism* (Macmillan, 1993)

CHAPTER FOUR

# Practical criticism: poetry

Practical criticism is sometimes known as Comment and Appreciation. It consists of a short passage from a poem, or a complete short poem, or fairly brief extracts from a novel or play. Usually the extracts are 'unseen', meaning that the candidate will not have previously seen that extract or read it before.

Two sets of skills are required for answering a practical criticism exercise effectively and efficiently. The first is general: the candidate must know what the most likely areas of interest in a poem are likely to be. Second, the candidate has to be able to respond to the specific and distinguishing features of the poem or poems set, which give it its uniqueness. In the chapters which follow the distinguishing features associated with all the major schools of poetry through history are briefly described. These chapters need to be read alongside the material below.

Poetry is often thought of as the most 'difficult' of the three literary modes or *genres*. This may be true of certain types of modern poetry, but it is not true of poetry as a whole. Early ballads are very simple and vivid stories originally written for mass entertainment of a sometimes unsophisticated audience. The poetry in Shakespeare's plays appealed to all levels of society. Many poets have been relatively simple and hugely popular; John Betjeman, a former Poet Laureate who died in 1984, is one example, and there have been many others. Poetry can be obscure and difficult; so can novels and plays.

If poetry is generally seen as being complex, it is partly because certain modern authors such as T. S. Eliot deliberately accepted that their poetry would be more obscure to allow it to carry a greater weight and profundity of meaning. Eliot thought that poetry in his own time had become so simple as to be banal and trivial. It is also because poetry uses several specialised techniques, some of which have rather terrifying names. Poetry tends to compress and condense a lot of experience into a limited length, making it tightly packed, so that it usually requires more than one reading for it to be understood. Again, this is nothing to be alarmed about. One expects to eat a sweet in almost one gulp, but a four-course meal takes longer; the end result is more satisfying, so the extra effort is worthwhile, as it is for spending time with a good poem. Be warned about one feature of poetry. It is sometimes possible, though not advisable, to read a novel or a play with one eye on something else, such as glancing at a television set. It is not possible to do this with poetry. Poetry demands full concentration from the reader.

The term 'poetic' can sometimes mean the same thing as 'artificial', suggesting that poetry is removed from real life, and experience forced out of its natural shape into something false and pretentious. In some senses poetry is artificial. It uses features which exist naturally in language – rhythm, imagery, diction, rhyme – and boosts them unnaturally to a much larger presence than that which they occupy in normal, everyday language. It is essential to realise that artificial *techniques* do not necessarily give an artificial or unreal *result*. A play is wholly artificial, in the sense that it is an act or performance in front of an audience who know, if they think about it, that the actors are only actors. A film uses all the paraphernalia of modern technology to produce its result. In both cases, play and film, the result can be grippingly 'real', and actually a stronger experience than real life. Some poets are exceptionally skilful at hiding the advanced techniques of poetry, and making what they write appear totally fluent and normal, or 'colloquial' (similar to everyday speech).

## Poetic stance and tone

Before moving on to the technical aspects of poetry it is essential to emphasise that writing about poetry does not mean simply being able to list technical terms. Technique may underpin a poem, as foundations underpin a building. Your job as a student is to come to an idea of the overall impact of a poem, just as someone commenting on a building needs to describe its overall impact. Both people need to be aware of the foundations; both need to see them as a means to an end.

In this sense there are issues that need to be decided before the technique of a poem is examined. For example, from what direction does the poet himself come? Does he or she appear as an active figure in the poem, one of its 'characters' even, or is the poet invisible within the framework of the poem? Is the tone of the poem subjective (highly personal and linked to the outlook of one specific individual), or is it objective (impersonal, seeking to speak for all people and not just one individual)?

Certain techniques will have a major effect on the overall tone and effect of a poem. Tone is a difficult word to define, as is style. It is a poet's way of speaking, something almost akin to her or his manner. It is a composite feature, built up from many individual inputs. Irony is a crucial feature in it, perhaps one of the most complex of literary forms and a hallmark of much modern poetry. Irony means that there is always at least one 'alternative' meaning beneath that which appears on the surface. It can be satirical, or reveal complexities of which the reader was previously unaware. It can be savage in its effect, or gently self-mocking. A sensitivity to irony, and a realisation that it is one of the most complex and subtle of all literary techniques, is essential to any effective student of literature. A sensitivity to humour is also a very useful starting attribute. A feeling for what is meant by 'wit' is also very useful in poetry criticism, remembering that wit does not mean simply being funny but is more often in poetry the display of intelligence.

If poetic tone is crucial, remember also the importance of style in a poet's work. A poet's style is the way he or she writes, and is arrived at as a result of a combination of all the things discussed above – the poet's stance, use of irony, subjectivity or objectivity – and the things discussed below – the poet's imagery, diction, use of rhyme, use of rhythm and metre. A poet's style is likely to be hugely personal, but remember that it can change dramatically over the course of a poet's life: you might care to plot the changing style of a poet such as W. H. Auden as one example. The only way to develop a feel for the vastly different styles of the poets whose work you will be reading is to read as many as possible of them yourself, and if you need to be convinced how very, very different individual styles are read a translation into good modern English of Chaucer's 'The Miller's Tale', and follow it with Tennyson's 'The Lady of Shallott' and Seamus Heaney's 'Death of a Naturalist'.

Try always to use detail, not to get bogged down in it. Sometimes it can help to do this if you remember some of the grand themes or issues in poetry. For example, the twentieth century poet T. S. Eliot said that poetry did not have to be understood in order to communicate. Can you believe this to be true? Can poetry communicate to you as a reader even though you cannot outwardly understand large areas of what is being written? Another famous poet, the Irishman W. B. Yeats, said that out of the conflict with others comes mere rhetoric, but out of the conflict from within ourselves comes great art. Is it true that internal conflict produces great poetry? The Romantic poet William Wordsworth believed that poetry should be emotion reflected in tranquillity, implying that in the heat of emotion communication is almost impossible, the very strength of feeling overwhelming the person who feels and denying them the ability to say effectively to another person what it is they feel and why. By 'taming' such emotion the poet allows it to be expressed. Is the poet you are reading seeking to express emotion by controlling it with poetic technique, or are they instead whipping up that emotion? Is poetry actually to do with emotion, or should it have more to do with intellect? There are no simple answers to any of these questions, but there is a tremendous excitement in pursuing them to an answer you the student can at least agree with.

# Metrical structure and rhythm

If gaining an overall understanding of a poem is the equivalent of driving a fast car along a beautiful road, then gaining an understanding of poetic techniques is the equivalent of learning how to strip the engine down to see how it works.

Metre is outwardly the most daunting of all poetic techniques. All language has its own natural rhythm. Words are composed of syllables ('so' has one syllable, 'So/phie' two, 'in/so/far' three, and 'so/phist/ic/a/ted' no fewer than five syllables). In normal speech we do not give each syllable the same stress or emphasis. We put a heavier stress on certain syllables than we do on others. Thus when we say 'Sophie' we would put a slightly heavier stress on the first syllable than on the second, and say it as Sō–phĭe, without having to think about it. An Englishman will always pronounce 'novel' stressing the first syllable, as 'nōv–ĕl'; the ¯ is the sign for a *stressed* syllable, the ˘ for an *unstressed* syllable. We use rhythm without thinking. If we want to lull a child to sleep we will use a sing-song rhythm, that is a regular unstressed/stressed mode of speaking to induce drowsiness. If we want to sound firm and full of authority we will use very heavy stresses, as in 'Gō–ā–wāy', with each syllable heavily stressed.

All a poet does is to take these natural rhythms that exist in all language and to use them in an artificial pattern that will augment and amplify the sense, mood, and meaning of what he is trying to say. The poet who does this is using *metre*. Metre is simply a rhythm that has been chosen by the poet and which he repeats and uses consistently over the length of a stanza or complete poem. For a poem to be described as being written in metre it has to have a specific rhythm that is repeated and used continually. The metre chosen will vary with the subject of the poem and with the effect that the poet wishes to create. A poet who wishes to create a solemn mood might use a ¯ ˘ pattern, called *trochaic*, or a ¯ ˘ ˘ pattern, called *dactylic*, because starting with a heavy, stressed syllable can give an air of solemnity to a poem. If he wanted to suggest movement and excitement he might use a ˘ ˘ ¯ pattern, called an *anapaest*.

There are various units of metre, or patterns, that a poet is likely to use. Each individual unit or collection of stressed and unstressed syllables is called a *foot*. When you read through a poem to see if it is written in metre, and if so what the metre is, this is called *scanning* a poem. You must first decide which type of foot the author is using. You are helped in this by the fact that there are only a fairly small number of feet available to the poet, and the main ones are four in number.

- An *iambic* foot (the most commonly used in English poetry) has a pattern, as in ŭn–rēst or dĕ–fēat.
- A *trochaic* foot has a ¯ ˘ pattern as in wēl–cŏme and ēmp–tў.
- An *anapaestic* foot has a ˘ ˘ ¯ pattern, as in măsq–uĕr–āde and sĕ–rĕn–āde.
- A *dactylic* foot has a ¯ ˘ ˘ pattern, as in wīll–ĭng–lў and mē–rrĭ–lў.

It is normal to find whole poems written in one of the above feet or patterns of rhythm, though sometimes an author might combine two types of foot. Sometimes the poet will use what are known as occasional feet, one of which might occur in a line. A whole line or poem would not normally be based on these.

A *spondaic* foot has a ¯¯ pattern.
A *pyrrhic* foot has a ˘˘ pattern.
An *amphibrach* has a ˘¯¯˘ pattern.

Only assume one of these is being used when all else fails!

The next stage in scanning a poem is to decide how many feet are being used in a line. The terms are:

*monometer*: one foot or units of metre per line.
*dimeter*: two feet or units of metre per line.
*trimeter*: three feet or units of metre per line.
*tetrameter*: four feet or units of metre per line.
*pentameter*: five feet or units of metre per line.
*hexameter*: six feet or units of metre per line.
*heptameter*: seven feet or units of metre per line.
*octameter*: eight feet or units of metre per line.

When describing the metre of a poem, start with a description of the foot used, then say how many are in a line; thus you would talk about an 'iambic pentameter' or an 'anapaestic trimeter'. These are difficult words, but they are describing something relatively simple.

To scan a poem, read through it as naturally as you can and mark down which syllables you are stressing as you read it. You will make mistakes early on, and put stresses in where you would normally never dream of saying them. Even so, have your first attempts checked by an expert, and keep trying. Some examples are:

> I grant indeed that fields and flocks have charms
> For him that grazes or for him that farms.

Pencil in where you think the heavy stresses fall: then put in the unstressed syllables. Now see what type of foot the poet is using, and put a diagonal line between each separate foot. Count them up and you have the metre, which should look like this:

> Ĭ grānt/ĭndēed/thăt fiēlds/ănd flōcks/hăve chārms/
> Fŏr hīm/thăt grāz/ĕs ōr/fŏr hīm/thăt fārms./

This is an iambic (˘¯) pentameter (five feet per line). Note that metre is based not on words, but on syllables, so the foot division can quite correctly split 'grazes' down the middle. Now try,

> Though thy slumber may be deep
> Yet thy spirit shall not sleep

This should scan as:

Though thy/slumber/may be/deep,
Yet thy/spirit/shall not/sleep

Basically this is a trochaic trimeter, with an extra stressed syllable at the end of each line. Now try:

Earth, receive an honoured guest
William Yeats is laid to rest

This is the same metrical pattern as for the previous example,

Earth, re/ceive an/honoured/guest
Willi/amYeats/is laid/to rest

but the second line reverts to an iambic metre with a trochaic foot at the start.

Season of mists and mellow fruitfulness!
Close bosom-friend of the maturing sun

should appear as,

Season of/mists and/mellow/fruitfulness!
Close bosom/friend of the/matur/ing son

This has trochaic and dactylic feet, and one final iambic foot.

Just for a/handful of/silver he/left us,
Just for a/riband to/stick in/his coat

The above is primarily a dactylic tetrameter.

O, he flies/through the air/with the great/est of ease
The dar/ing young man/on the fly/ing trapeze

is an anapaestic tetrameter.

Text books frequently quote the poem by the Romantic poet Samuel Taylor Coleridge which illustrates five metrical patterns.

Trochee trips from long to short,
From long to long in solemn sort.
Slow Spondee stalks; strong foot! yet ill able
Ever to come up with Dactyl trisyllable,
Iambics march from short to long
With a leap and a bound/the swift Anapaests throng.

The pronunciation of the metrical terms follows their metre:

I–amb, Tro–chee, Ana–p–ae–st, Dac–tyl–ic, Spon–dee.

A metre that is too regular can send the reader to sleep, or simply become monotonous. As well as putting in slight variations to the metre, a poet will often put a *caesura* into a line. This is simply a pause, usually in the middle of a line, and marked by a punctuation mark, such as a full stop, comma, or semi-colon. An example occurs in Hamlet's most famous speech: 'To be, or not to be: that is the question.' The caesura or pause comes with the colon. The reader has to pause there, and this injects variety into the metre, which is predominantly an iambic pentameter.

Once you have spotted if a poem is written in metre and what that metre is you can then set about using that knowledge in practical criticism answers. Take care. Nothing is more tedious than a blow-by-blow description of a poem's metre, such as:

> The poem starts with a line containing three iambic feet and one trochaic foot. The second line has four iambic feet with a caesura, and the third line has two trochaic feet and one dactylic foot . . .

Firstly, tell the examiner what the general metre of the poem is, and how that metre contributes to the atmosphere and meaning of the poem. It is perfectly acceptable to use emotive words in describing the effect of the metre, as in, 'The iambic pentameters give a relaxed and tranquil feeling to the poem' or 'The use of anapaestic trimeters adds urgency and a sense of relentless persecution'. Never say that metre *creates* a mood: the words of a poem do that, and metre merely augments or amplifies that feeling or impression.

Secondly, scan the poem and see where the poet varies or changes the metre. When the poet does so there is a good chance that he is doing it in order to achieve some special aim or purpose, and these are the areas that the examiner wishes you to comment on. There are good examples of this in the specimen answer below on Andrew Marvell's 'To His Coy Mistress'. *Never comment on metre in general simply for the sake of it*; only comment when by so doing you add something useful to our stock of knowledge of the poem.

## Rhyme

Very often people think of poetry as something that rhymes. In fact poetry need not rhyme, nor need it have a metre. Poetry with no rhyme but with a metre is called *blank verse*, whilst poetry that rhymes (or can rhyme) but which has no metre is called *free verse*. Rhyme is an obvious feature to comment on when answering a practical criticism question, and there are various types of it.

1. *Masculine* rhyme is rhyme on one syllable as in boat/coat, fast/last, will/kill, sad/bad, sag/bag.
2. *Feminine* or *Double* rhyme is rhyme on two syllables, with the second syllable being unstressed, as in wilful/skilful, stranger/danger, master/plaster.
3. *Triple* rhyme is rhyme on a stressed syllable followed by two unstressed syllables, as in laborious/victorious, sufficiency/deficiency.

4. *Internal* or *Middle* rhyme is used to describe where rhyming occurs in the middle of a line, rather than in the usual place at the end of lines.
5. *Pararhyme* or *Half rhyme* occurs when the first and last consonants in words are the same, but the intervening vowel is different, as in flip/flop, leaves/lives, grained/groined, slip/slop.
6. *Eye* rhyme occurs when two words look alike, but do not sound the same, as in bough/rough, love/move, low/how.

Rhyme is pleasing to the ear, or can be, and adds the musical, sound quality in poetry that can be so important to it. It can emphasise certain words, as words which rhyme are obviously more prominent than those which do not. It can unify a poem and draw it together, or give a ritualistic, almost mystic element to it. The system of rhyme within a poem is called its *rhyme scheme*. This is ascertained by giving each rhyming sound at the end of a line a letter of the alphabet, and repeating this letter when the sound is repeated.

Thus one might say that a poem has the rhyme scheme aabbccdddd, as in,

The Harlot's cry from Street to Street a
Shall weave Old England's winding Sheet. a
The Winner's Shout the Loser's Curse b
Dance before dead England's Hearse. b
Every Night & every Morn c
Some to Misery are Born. c
Every Morn & every Night d
Some are Born to sweet Delight. d
Some are Born to sweet Delight. d
Some are Born to Endless Night d

(William Blake, 'Auguries of Innocence')

## Diction

A poet's diction is his choice of words, or vocabulary. Diction can be archaic (using old-fashioned words), colloquial (like everyday speech), formal, refined, elegant, technical, or any number of things. A phrase such as 'Jesus Christ! I'm hit!' uses colloquial diction, whilst the diction of 'Avenge, O Lord, thy slaughter'd saints, whose bones/Lie scattered on the Alpine Mountains cold' could be described as exalted, dignified, or formal – or all three. Again, *only comment when there is something to say*. Remarks such as 'The diction in this poem is normal' gain no marks.

## Imagery

An image is usually a simile or metaphor, but can be used to mean any picture that an author creates in the reader's mind. An author's descriptive or figurative language obviously exerts a strong influence on his writing and its effect. Comment on the individual effect of each image in a poem, and explain precisely what impression the image gives of the object described. Then look at *all* the images in a poem, and see if *collectively* they are linked so that they have a cumulative effect on the reader. For example, Thomas Hardy's poem 'The Darkling Thrush' contains several images that refer to death or ghosts, such as 'spectre-grey', 'haunted', 'Century's corpse outleant', 'crypt', and 'death-lament'. Each *individual* image has strong powers of association and suggestion; *collectively* they add up to the fact that the reader cannot reach the end of the poem without having acquired a strong feeling of imminent death and mortality.

## General features

There are a number of other features in poetry to look out for, and comment on. *Enjambement* occurs when there is no punctuation mark at the end of a line of poetry, so when reading it is should be 'run on' without a pause. *Alliteration* is the repetition of a consonant sound; *assonance* the repetition of a vowel sound. As with metre and rhyme, be very cautious about saying that either technique creates an impression or feeling; the words do that. A poem which features rain falling might well repeat the 's' sound to suggest the gentle hiss of soft rain, but repeating that sound does not *create* the sound of falling rain. You can check this by going up to someone and repeating 'sssss' at them. Provided they do not think you mad they are just as likely to think that you are imitating a snake or a gas leak as suggesting rainfall. The 's' sound *helps to suggest* the rain falling, it does not *create* it.

## Questions, notes and answers

**Question 1**
Write an appreciation of the poem below:

**To his Coy Mistress**
Had we but World enough, and Time,
This coyness Lady were no crime.
We would sit down, and think which way
To walk, and pass our long Loves Day.
Thou by the Indian Ganges side
Should'st Rubies find: I by the Tide
Of Humber would complain. I would
Love you ten years before the Flood:
And you should if you please refuse
Till the Conversion of the Jews.

My vegetable Love should grow
Vaster than Empires, and more slow.
An hundred years should go to praise
Thine Eyes, and on thy Forehead Gaze.
Two hundred to adore each Breast:
But thirty thousand to the rest.
An Age at least to every part,
And the last Age should show your Heart.
For Lady you deserve this State;
Nor would I love at lower rate.
But at my back I alwaies hear
Times winged Charriot hurrying near:
And yonder all before us lye
Desarts of vast Eternity.
Thy Beauty shall no more be found,
Nor, in thy marble Vault, shall sound
My ecchoing Song; then Worms shall try
That long preserv'd Virginity:
And your quaint Honour turn to dust;
And into ashes all my Lust.
The Grave's a fine and private place,
But none I think do there embrace.
Now therefore, while the youthful hew
Sits on thy skin like morning dew,
And while thy willing Soul transpires
At every pore with instant Fires,
Now let us sport us while we may;
And now, like am'rous birds of prey,
Rather at once our Time devour,
Than languish in his slow-chapt pow'r.
Let us roll all our Strength and all
Our sweetness, up into one Ball:
And tear our Pleasures with rough strife,
Thorough the Iron gates of Life.
Thus, though we cannot make our Sun
Stand still, yet we will make him run.

**Notes**

Any essay needs a structure or plan for the student to work to, and some essays give what is in effect a plan by the way the title is phrased; there is no such luck with this title. Rather than just writing down straight away an answer to this question it might be worthwhile working through it in rough, as one might plan it out, and then giving the answer from the plan.

Technique is usually a good starting point for a practical criticism of a poem, so the first step is to see if the poem is written in metre. The answer is a firm yes:

> Had we/but World/enough,/and Time,
> This coy/ness La/dy were/no crime.

The metre is iambic, and there are four feet in each line, allowing the poem to be written in iambic tetrameters. There are, of course, variations from this, as can be discerned in the first line above, where a trochaic foot starts off the poem. Why? Probably to give it a dramatic start . . . or is it that the first syllable is actually unstressed, and the foot merely a standard iambic one? The only way is to read it through and see which reads naturally and most easily. When the metre is established you should look through the poem and see where the poet varies the metrical pattern. The opening line might be one example. Line four ('long Loves Day') is another, the extra stress presumably being there to emphasise the heavy length of time stated in the words. A trochaic foot starts off line 5, presumably for variety, and there is another in line 6. There is a spondee in line 12 ('Vaster'), again probably to give added weight and significance to the word. A spondee and a pyrrhic foot start off line 18. Work through the rest of the poem on your own and see what other variations you can find, and then compare your answer with that given later in this section. At first jot down all variations or significant points about the metre; then see if they form a pattern, and look for the major points of significance, and transfer both items of information onto a note plan.

The poem has a clear aabbcc rhyme scheme, and so rhyme might well be the next point to look at. Occasionally the rhyme is not exact ('would' and 'Flood'), but in general there is little sign of strain in the rhyming. This, when taken in conjunction with the regular metre, gives the poem a controlled tone, rather than the feeling of an experience being lived through then and there on the page in front of the reader. One effect of the rhyme is to give the poem a pleasant musical effect, whilst at the same time making it slightly less immediate than might otherwise have been the case.

The poem is definitely shaped or structured by the poet. The imagery is superficially unremarkable. The contrast between the exotic 'Ganges' and the filthy 'Humber' suggests the author has a sense of humour – as does another passage. Can you find it? In fact there are two examples of sexual humour in the poem. At this point the student might begin to feel he has exposed something important in the poem. The imagery becomes more specific as the poem progresses, and the pattern follows the division of the poem into three separate sections. For example, Time and Death dominate the imagery of the second section, but Death does not appear at all in the first. What dominates the third section, if anything does?

The fact that the imagery alters as the poem progresses should alert you to the fact that this tripartite division of the poem is of considerable significance. Again, it is not so much the patterns and style set up at the start of the poem which matter, but rather the things that change. The reason for isolating rhyme, metre, imagery and all the other techniques is to let you see when a poem is moving on to another target, or changing meaningfully, or simply losing its grip. This ability to see beyond the immediate facts staring you in the face is a vital asset for a student of literature – in effect it is the capacity for independent thought, i.e. for adding two and two together and presenting the examiner with a deduction as well as a statement.

By this stage of the proceedings you should be starting to gain a general idea of the poem's main theme or statement – if, of course, it has one. It is essential to realise that this overall grasp of a poem's aims and achievements is not gained the instant you set sight on the poem; it is something that you work towards gradually, and a rash, instant decision that a poem or any other literary extract is trying to achieve a certain aim or effect is prone to disaster, even in an examination where time is short. Let the words work on you before jumping to a conclusion.

A reasonable answer to the question, using material given in the 'thinking-out-loud' above but adding to it, is as follows:

**Answer**

The diction and language of the poem suggest a seventeenth-century poet of the Metaphysical school. The subject of the poem is love of a sexual nature between the poet and his mistress. It is phrased in the form of an argument, employs conceits or fanciful imagery, combines reason and passion, and shows considerable wit, all of which suggest the Metaphysical school of writing.

[The above shows the advantages of wide reading, even if only of works such as the present one. The poem, by Andrew Marvell, is Metaphysical, and could be seen as such by anyone who was familiar with the two descriptions of Metaphysical poetry given in this present work. It is one thing to persuade an examiner you can understand and comment on a poem; it is a decided bonus to suggest to him you are well-read as well.]

The poem is written in iambic tetrameters for the most part, with occasional departures from this pattern in individual feet. The departures are sometimes for variety. ('Ănd thĕ/lāst Āge . . .'), but sometimes appear to be there in order to enhance the sense of the words being used, as in 'hŭrryĭng nēar' and 'ĕcchoĭng sōng'. The regularity of the metre in general gives an ordered, composed tone to the poem, as does the straightforward aabbcc rhyme scheme, suggestive of experience recollected in tranquillity, rather than experience presented in the first fire of action. The diction is simple yet elevated, without gross use of colloquial language but at the same time clear and straightforward.

The poem is divided into three sections, and is written in the form of an argument to the poet's mistress that she should allow him her favours. The first section suggests what might happen if the two lovers had all the time in the world, and to make his point the poet imagines a ludicrously extended period of courtship, including the lines,

> An hundred years should go to praise
> Thine Eyes, and on thy Forehead Gaze.
> Two hundred to adore each Breast:
> But thirty thousand to the rest.

After the sexuality implicit in 'Breast' the reader is expecting more specific description of erotic areas; instead, they are simply described as 'the rest', but the time span allotted for their adoration suggests their vast importance. There is more dry humour in the comment that couples do not embrace in the grave. The second section recognises that humanity is mortal, and that Time is always eating away at a person's life, bringing them nearer to death. The third section presents the conclusion. If we had all the time in the world we could take as long as we wished and as was proper to woo each other; we do not have much time; therefore we must act now, 'And tear our Pleasures with rough strife'.

There is a sudden injection of violence into the poem in this last section, and urgency and passion that are not present in the same mixture in the preceding two sections. The 'birds of prey' image takes the reader away from the world of languid lovers into a world of harsh reality where pleasure and time are both in short supply. Timelessness dominates the first section, and an awareness of how short man's life is dominates the second section. The third section is dominated by images of violence and action.

Superficially this is a love poem, but the final lines 'Thus, though we cannot make our Sun/Stand still, yet we will make him run' suggest that sexual love is only the excuse to present a poem which is in effect about mortality, the grip that time holds over man's life, and the shortness of his time on earth. Thus though the poem is written in the first person, the reader learns very little about the author, who remains a representative figure – as does his mistress; the 'I' of the poem can speak for all men because he is not identified with any one particular person. There is even a hint of the tragic mode in the final lines, in that though defeat is shown as inevitable for mankind, in the sense that all people will die, time can still be given a run for its money, and not be allowed to break man's spirit. There is a feeling of exultancy in the poem that, even though time will win in the end, there are some things that it can never remove completely, at least in the short term.

**Question 2**

Compare and contrast the following two poems:

**Preludes**

**I**

The winter evening settles down
With smell of steaks in passageways.
Six o'clock.
The burnt-out ends of smoky days.
And now a gusty shower wraps
The grimy scraps
Of withered leaves about your feet
And newspapers from vacant lots;
The showers beat

On broken blinds and chimney-pots,
And at the corner of the street
A lonely cab-horse steams and stamps.
And then the lighting of the lamps.

**II**

The morning comes to consciousness
Of faint stale smells of beer
From the sawdust-trampled street
With all its muddy feet that press
To early coffee-stands.
With the other masquerades
That time resumes,
One thinks of all the hands
That are raising dingy shades
In a thousand furnished rooms.

**III**

You tossed a blanket from the bed,
You lay upon your back, and waited;
You dozed, and watched the night revealing
The thousand sordid images
Of which your soul was constituted;
They flickered against the ceiling.
And when all the world came back
And the light crept up between the shutters
And you heard the sparrows in the gutters,
You had such a vision of the street
As the street hardly understands;
Sitting along the bed's edge, where
You curled the papers from your hair,
Or clasped the yellow soles of feet
In the palms of both soiled hands.

**IV**

His soul stretched tight across the skies
That fade behind a city block,
Or trampled by insistent feet
At four and five and six o'clock;
And short square fingers stuffing pipes,
And evening newspapers, and eyes
Assured of certain certainties,
The conscience of a blackened street
Impatient to assume the world.
I am moved by fancies that are curled
Around these images, and cling:
The notion of some infinitely gentle

Infinitely suffering thing.
Wipe your hand across your mouth, and laugh;
The worlds revolve like ancient women
Gathering fuel in vacant lots.

(T. S. Eliot)

**Mr Bleaney**

'This was Mr Bleaney's room. He stayed
The whole time he was at the
Bodies, till
They moved him.' Flowered curtains, thin and frayed,
Fall to within five inches of the sill,
Whose window shows a strip of building land,
Tussocky, littered. 'Mr Bleaney took
My bit of garden properly in hand.'
Bed, upright chair, sixty-watt bulb, no hook
Behind the door, no room for books or bags–
'I'll take it.' So it happens that I lie
Where Mr Bleaney lay, and stub my fags
On the same saucer-souvenir, and try
Stuffing my ears with cotton-wool, to drown
The jabbering set he egged her on to buy.
I know his habits–what time he came down,
His preference for sauce to gravy, why
He kept on plugging at the four aways–
Likewise their yearly frame: the Frinton folk
Who put him up for summer holidays,
And Christmas at his sister's house in Stoke.
But if he stood and watched the frigid wind
Tousling the clouds, lay on the fusty bed
Telling himself that this was home, and grinned,
And shivered, without shaking off the dread
That how we live measures our own nature,
And at his age having no more to show
Than one hired box should make him pretty sure
He warranted no better, I don't know.

(Philip Larkin)

**Answer**

T. S. Eliot's poem is divided up into four sections, each of which takes as its theme a different time of day. The first section concentrates on a winter evening – 'Six o'clock', the second section on the following morning. The third section then switches back to the intervening night time, and the fourth and final section goes back to morning again. This cyclical pattern suggests an endless round, something that goes on and on ever repeating itself. The first section is written predominantly in iambic tetrameters ('The winter evening settles down'), but lines three, six, and nine shorten to dimeters, again predominantly iambic ('The showers beat'). This complements the atmosphere of evening, of something (day) coming to an end, and perhaps even of exhaustion. The second section uses four, three, and two feet to a line, perhaps suggesting the rush and bustle of morning. The third section more often than not has four feet to a line, but in this section an extra weak syllable is often placed at the end of the line with a trochaic foot ('revealing', 'waited', 'constituted', 'shutters', 'gutters'). The impression this gives, in conjunction with the content, is of restlessness, uncertainty, things failing to come to a conclusion, emphasising the tedium of a sleepness night. The fourth section starts with regular iambic pentameters, as if the poet felt a new certainty, but towards the end this collapses, with the lines being lengthened and the metre lost, as in 'Infinitely suffering thing'. The cumulative impression created by the metre is of something that should run smoothly, but which perpetually falters, like an engine that will fire on all its cylinders only for a few minutes.

The poem is clearly written about city life, and it emphasises the sordid and decrepit nature of this life. 'The burnt-out ends of smoky days', 'grimy scraps', 'withered leaves', 'faint stale smells of beer' and 'dingy shades' all convey misery and seediness. Even though the poem looks at different times of day it is almost as if it were perpetual evening on a wet and cold winter's day. Everything is 'soiled', 'stale', 'muddy', or 'blackened'. Certain images recur, such as darkness, grime, dampness, stale smells, newspapers, smoke, and ineffective light. The poet's phrase 'The thousand sordid images' almost describes his poem, and 'sordid' is a key word which summarises many of the images in the poem.

The poet starts by using 'you' and 'your'. He then moves on to 'he', and finally to 'I'. However, the reader learns very little about the figure or figures at the heart of the poem, and great care is taken to make the comments refer to anyone, perhaps leading to the conclusion that this could be any one of a thousand people living 'In a thousand furnished rooms'. What does emerge is that the human or humans in the poem are soiled, grey figures, only vaguely aware of their misery, and comforting themselves that they are 'Assured of certain certainties'. Only in the final section is there a strong note of compassion and suffering, in 'The notion of some infinitely gentle/Infinitely suffering thing'. This is followed by an almost flippant line, 'Wipe your hands across your mouth and laugh', suggesting almost a fear of facing up to the truth, and a retreat away from reality into satisfaction of physical desires, and defensive or protective laughter. 'Gathering fuel in vacant lots' suggests emptiness and hence the emptiness of people's lives, and that living from day to day is all that can be expected of human beings. There is a huge sense of inertia in the poem. Like smoke that is 'curled' and which clings, realisation of the pointlessness of life can be seen and smelt, but is insubstantial for all that and can easily be pushed away. Life is a 'masquerade', an act that has to be carried out because there is nothing better to do. The rhyme scheme is strong but intermittent, helping to create a mood in which things repeat themselves, but in a rather vague and uncoordinated manner.

Everything in the poem seems disheartened. Dawn can only creep up, and the lively sparrows can only inhabit the gutters.

'Mr Bleaney' is on the surface a rather different poem. Its seven stanzas have a regular abab rhyme scheme, and though it is quite loose each stanza is based round iambic pentameters, with five stressed syllables to a line. There is considerable use of enjambement, which together with the use of dialogue gives a colloquial and almost relaxed feeling to the poem. The situation is urban, and unattractive ('building land,/Tussocky, littered'), but there is much less description of scenery than is found in 'Preludes'. The faceless figures of Eliot's poem are replaced by three people (the landlady, Mr Bleaney, and the author) all of whom are characterised to some extent. Whereas Eliot describes what is and what happens outside the room, Larkin concentrates almost exclusively on the room itself and the house in which it is situated. The tone of Larkin's poem is more forthright and direct, its descriptive range narrower, and there is even a slight trace of bitter humour ('Stuffing my ears with cotton wool, to drown/The jabbering set . . .') in the poem.

Despite these differences the two poems take a different path to a similar destination. Both poems show human beings in decayed, seedy, and sordid surroundings, and show hopeless people leading hopeless lives. In 'Mr Bleaney' Larkin looks at Mr Bleaney and how he lived, and the realisation that the sum total of Mr Bleaney's life was possession of 'one hired box' (which could be his rented room, or even his coffin) terrifies Larkin. If 'how we live measures our own nature' then the suggestion is that humans are worth and achieve very little. 'Mr Bleaney' is perhaps a sharper poem than 'Preludes'. The fear that existence is useless and life pointless is brought to a head by the word 'dread' in the penultimate stanza, and the observation of the lifestyle of a single man living in a rented room is very acute. A sense of impermanence is given in the observation that there was no hook 'behind the door', and an overwhelming impression of bleakness by the bareness of the room, with 'Bed, upright chair, sixty-watt bulb'). Eliot talks about 'the world', Larkin about 'Mr Bleaney' and, indirectly, himself, and whilst Eliot tries for a universal feeling to his poem, Larkin is content to let it rest at close observation of three people. Yet the effect is almost the same. Both poems paint a bleak picture of human life, showing it to be tedious, dull, and concerned mostly with putting off serious thought. Eliot observes this mood and records it with almost sardonic objectivity. Larkin is himself a part of it, ending his poem with 'I don't know'. In both poems people seem to be born, to live, and to die and leave hardly a ripple on the face of the world, but whilst Larkin's poem suggests this is a cause for worry and concern, Eliot's suggests it is inevitable and must be accepted. The yearning for a richer life is more marked in 'Mr Bleaney'; in 'Preludes' the whole business has gone too far to be worth worrying about overmuch. To use two poem titles of T. S. Eliot's, both poems show 'hollow men' inhabiting a 'wasteland' in which all the splendour and all the joy have gone out of human life, to the extent of making the reader wonder if they were ever there in the first place.

## Further reading


- James Caddan, *Poetry Appreciation for A-level* (Hodder & Stoughton, 1988)
- Tony Curtis, *How to Study Modern Poetry* (Macmillan, 1990)
- Barbara Everett, *Poets In Their Time. Essays on English. Poetry from Donne to Larkin* (Oxford University Press, 1992)
- John Lennard, *The Poetry Handbook. A Guide to Reading Poetry for Pleasure and Practical Criticism* (Oxford University Press, 1996)
- John Peck, *How To Study a Poet* (Macmillan, 1988)
- Clive T. Probyn, *English Poetry* (Longman/York Press, 1984)
- James Reeves, *Understanding Poetry* (Pan, 1967)
- Christopher Ricks, *Essays in Appreciation* (Oxford University Press, 1988)
- ––, *The Force of Poetry* (Oxford University Press, 1995)
- Philip Davies Roberts, *How Poetry Works* (Penguin, 1991)
- Philip Robinson, *Practical Approaches to Literary Criticism: Poems* (Longman, 1987)
- F. Scott, *Close Readings* (Heinemann, 1968)
- Barry Spurr, *Studying Poetry* (Macmillan, 1997)

CHAPTER FIVE

# Practical criticism: prose

## The novel

The novel is the youngest of the three main literary mediums, with what is usually recognised as the first novel (*Don Quixote* by Miguel de Cervantes (1547–1616) being published in two parts in 1605 and 1615. The reason for this late development is practical, rather than literary or aesthetic. Poetry can thrive very happily in an oral tradition, with verse being recited and passed on by word of mouth. Drama also relies on performance, and need rely little on the printed word. There were probably only a handful of 'scripts' for Shakespeare's actors to work with, and the plays were only published in book form long after the plays had been performed and enjoyed by live audiences. Stories, of course, can be passed on and passed down the generations through the oral tradition, as can poetry, but the novel has to be read from a printed page simply because of its length. For this to be possible there has to be the sophistication of printing techniques required to print and bind a large book. There has to be the transport system that can take the copies from the point of manufacture to the point of sale. Most of all, there have to be enough people who can read with enough disposable income to buy a relatively expensive and non-essential product. Such conditions did not apply in Europe until the seventeenth century, so one can argue that economic, technological and social development were what made the novel possible.

The traditional view of the novel is that it tells a story, though this view has been criticised in more recent times. Perhaps such criticism is only to be expected given that the twentieth century has produced plays that consist of little more than a few seconds of heavy breathing off stage, and poems written by means of the author cutting up a newspaper, throwing the cut-out words to the floor, and publishing as a poem the words simply as they appear on the floor. Although the novel as a story-telling vehicle has been criticised and challenged, the plot remains a significant element in most of the novels that an Advanced-level student will have to face. More advanced students will find themselves faced with passages that challenge traditional theories about plot and structure, and which give an opportunity for the student to show her or his knowledge of modern critical and literary theory (see Chapter 25).

However much critical fashions, and fashions in writing, may change, you are likely to find yourself criticising any extract from a novel on two main fronts – plot or 'narrative technique', and characterisation. As a very rough, rule of thumb guide, novels are usually positioned on a sliding scale: the more they are interested in characterisation the less significant is the plot, and vice versa. Many of the early novels are firmly plot-based (see the entry for PICARESQUE NOVEL in Chapter 3), many modern novels far more interested in characterisation. Ian McEwan's *Amsterdam* (1998) is an excellent example of a modern novel where the plot is simply a device to squeeze out the maximum understanding of the two central characters. A novel such as Christopher Wallace's *The Pied Piper's Poison* (1998), however, shows how easily such broad generalisations can be disproved. This is again a novel about character, but it is blended with one of the great stories of all time, The Pied Piper of Hamelin. The combination gives significant narrative suspense, as well as high detail and intimacy of characterisation.

## Plot and Story

Telling a story sounds the simplest of tasks, but it is actually one of the most difficult. A starting point for practical criticism of a novel is the narrative viewpoint adopted by an author, or the stance from which the author tells his story.

The first-person narrative, where the story is told in the 'I' or first-person mode, is an obvious viewpoint to adopt. The first-person speaker is usually a character in the novel, but can sometimes be a version of the author himself. The first-person mode or technique has a number of advantages.

1. It can be realistic. We see life through the eyes of one person, ourself, and if a novel is told through the eyes and ears of one person the reader can relate this to his or her own experience.
2. The technique also brings the reader very close to the narrator, thus helping to make it very vivid and immediate. The more the reader identifies with the narrator, the more whatever happens to the character affects the reader.
3. The technique can also be seen as more realistic with regard to other characters. In real life we can only see 'inside the head' of one person, ourself, and a first-person narrator must judge and form his or her opinion of other people in the novel on the basis of external features, as we ourselves do in real life.

The first-person technique also has a number of disadvantages.

1. It is restrictive. For the sake of realism, the first-person narrator can only be in one place at one time, and tell the reader things that would be naturally known to one person. There is therefore the risk that events vital to the novel will not be witnessed by a first-person narrator, and that rather clumsy techniques will be brought in to widen the range and scope of the novel.
2. If the first-person narrator is a strong personality he or she will impose strong views on events and other people, thus not allowing the readers to form their own conclusions as easily as might otherwise be the case. On the other hand, if the narrator is a weak personality he or she might become insipid and unattractive, thus putting off the reader.
3. Equally the first-person narrator can be a means whereby the author imposes his or her own views strongly on the novel.

A technique which gives rather more range is that of the omniscient narrator. It can be a narrator who is both omniscient and invisible – that is, a narrator who never appears as a person in the novel, never says anything, and never appears to impose his judgement on people or events. All the reader has is an apparently factual account of what took place, and what people said or did. Charles Dickens uses both a first-person and an omniscient narrator in *Bleak House*.

A variation is where the narrator actually steps forward and does appear in the novel, and comments directly on what took place. Early novels, such as Fielding's *Tom Jones*, have a narrator who not only tells the story but also takes time to lecture the reader, share opinions with him, and tell him what he should be thinking. When referring to such interference always remember to refer to the narrator and not the author. The figure who appears in *Tom Jones* is a character as much as those in the novel proper. He is not simply the author himself, but an edited version of that author, given certain features and personality traits to allow him to help the novel along. This trait is not restricted to the novel. Chaucer appears as a pilgrim in *The Canterbury Tales*, but the person who carries his name tells the worst tale of any pilgrim, and is an object of derision to the other pilgrims.

As a general rule, the later the novel the more likely it is to be told by an omniscient, invisible narrator, with the characters and events allowed to speak for themselves.

A wide variety of narrative techniques is possible within these two extremes. A plot can be related by means of letters, as is the case with one of the famous early novels, *Pamela* (1740) by Samuel Richardson (1689–1761). A number of separate narrators can be used, or the story told to one central figure by those involved in it; the latter being a technique used sometimes by Joseph Conrad (1857–1924).

## Characterisation

Characterisation is a central feature in very many novels, and in many modern works has overwhelmed plot as the main centre of interest in the typical novel. When answering a practical criticism question the student is on the way to a good answer if he or she can ascertain the main technique of plot or characterisation used by the author. Characters are often described as either 'flat' or 'rounded' (see Chapter 4). The simplest way of presenting a character to a reader is through the external means we use to form our judgements in real life, effectively by showing us what the characters say and do. In addition, a character can be vividly characterised by being associated with a particular setting which colours our image of them. The wildness and bleakness of Heathcliff's character in Emily Brontë's (1818–48) *Wuthering Heights* (1847) is continually emphasised and brought home by his being associated with rough weather on the Yorkshire moors. A character's friends can also influence the reader's judgement, and the style or manner of their speech. The halting manner, full of 'um's' and 'ah's' in which Frederick Dorrit speaks in *Little Dorrit* (1857) by Charles Dickens (1812–70) sums him up. Dialogue is clearly important in many novels; some authors write it extremely skilfully, others less so. Charlotte Brontë (1816–55) is never at her best when trying to recreate upper-class dialogue and speech.

Characters can also be portrayed by going inside their heads, and the reader being made privy to their every thought and feeling. This has a number of advantages. Early novelists tended to stick to external characterisation, with the reader having to assume what was happening inside a character's head from the external signs of it. At times of great stress or emotion this could produce almost ludicrous situations, as when Emily Brontë is forced to have Heathcliff smash his head against a tree, or Fielding have Tom Jones quite literally tear his hair out, in order to suggest the extreme of emotion the character is in. A quasi-social justification for keeping out of a character's head was offered by the writer and wit Lady Mary Wortley Montagu (1689–1782), when she stated that fig leaves are as necessary for our minds as for our bodies. This is a typically eighteenth-century comment, reflecting the classical view that external manners and decorum are essential for social integrity. Lady Mary would no doubt have been horrified by the ultimate in going inside a character's head, the 'stream of consciousness' technique (see Chapter 4), where the author tries to recreate exactly thoughts, feelings and emotions as they pass through a single character's mind. The problem here is that only a few of the things inside our mind are actually put into words, but words are all the author has to work with on the page.

## General points

There are a wide variety of other features which the examination candidate can look out for when answering a practical criticism question on a novel. The tone in which an author writes or his style are often the first features to be noticed when reading a passage, and are as crucial to criticism of the novel as they are to poetry.

A formal or informal tone is usually easy to spot, as is whether the author is writing in a comic or serious vein. In the hurry of an examination it is sometimes surprisingly easy not to recognise irony, and to take at face value a passage or phrase that has an undertone of satire, humour, or criticism. Heavy use of dialogue, lengthy descriptions of settings, extended use of imagery are all prominent and worthy of comment.

It is usually easy to spot whether an author is writing didactically, instructing the readers about what their proper response should be. A rather more vague term, beloved of examiners, is dramatic style. Sometimes this can simply mean an author who works in strong colours, and who goes for an immediate and vivid impact. More correctly the term is used of an author who uses certain theatrical techniques. Dickens, who was in love with the theatre and with acting, as well as with a number of actresses, does this in *Little Dorrit*. Episodes tend to be placed firmly against a vividly realised backdrop or 'scene setting', and follow on from each other like scenes in a play. Dialogue is extensively used, sometimes with long sequences where there is nothing but direct speech, as in a play. There are clear climaxes in the book, built up to in a sequence of episodes, and characters are given distinctive physical features and mannerisms of speech, as they often are in the theatre.

It is also worth looking to see if an author uses colloquial language (the language and style of everyday speech), and also to see if there are any hints as to whether or not the novel was first published in serial form. This latter is often hard to judge from a short extract, but an unresolved climax at the end of a passage might just be the lure left by an author who wishes the reader to purchase the next instalment of a novel. This technique of serial publication was used quite widely in Victorian times, as it allowed the cost of a novel to be spread out over months and years.

## Questions and notes

Write a critical appreciation of each of the three passages presented below.

**Passage 1**

The following extract is from *A Portrait Of The Artist as a Young Man* (1914–15) by James Joyce (1882–1941)

> Once upon a time and a very good time it was there was a moocow coming down along the road and this moocow that was coming down along the road met a nicens little boy named baby tuckoo. . . .
>
> His father told him that story: his father looked at him through a glass: he had a hairy face.
>
> He was baby tuckoo. The moocow came down the road where Betty Byrne lived: she sold lemon platt.
>
> *O, the wild rose blossoms*
> *On the little green place.*
>
> He sang that song. That was his song.

*O, the green wrothe botheth.*

When you wet the bed first it is warm then it gets cold. His mother put on the oilsheet. That had the queer smell.

His mother had a nicer smell than his father. She played on the piano the sailor's hornpipe for him to dance. He danced:

*Tralala lala,*
*Tralala tralaladdy,*
*Tralala lala,*
*Tralala lala.*

Uncle Charles and Dante clapped. They were older than his father and mother but uncle Charles was older than Dante.

Dante had two brushes in her press. The brush with the maroon velvet back was for Michael Davitt and the brush with the green velvet back was for Parnell. Dante gave him a cachou every time he brought her a piece of tissue paper.

The Vances lived in number seven. They had a different father and mother. They were Eileen's father and mother. When they were grown up he was going to marry Eileen. He hid under the table. His mother said:

– O, Stephen will apologize.

Dante said:

– O, if not, the eagles will come and pull out his eyes. –

*Pull out his eyes,*
*Apologize,*
*Apologize,*
*Pull out his eyes.*
*Apologize,*
*Pull out his eyes,*
*Pull out his eyes,*
*Apologize.*

**Notes**

The first reaction to a passage such as this is quite possibly going to be sheer horror. A teacher with a desire to ease a student's mind might well utter soothing noises; a realistic one might well admit that this is a make-or-break question. If the student recognises that the passage is written to suggest the workings of a child's mind then all is well; if this fact is not realised, then it is going to be very difficult indeed for the student to gain any marks, however long the answer. As to how one recognises this fact, there is no simple answer. It is one of those things which looks very simple when explained, but which in the pressure of an examination can be completely overlooked.

The first task in answering a question of this nature is to state the obvious, that the passage seems to be designed to imitate or suggest the thoughts of a child, possibly a five or six year old. The next task is to state the techniques and devices which the author uses to create this effect. They can be listed as follows:

- 'Once upon a time' is a phrase associated with stories for young children.
- 'moocow' is a child's name for a cow.
- 'nicens' is baby talk.
- 'baby tuckoo' suggests a nickname given to a child.
- 'He was baby tuckoo' suggests the narrator is baby.
- Inability to pronounce 'r' and 's' sounds correctly suggests a child learning to speak.
- The reference to wetting the bed suggests a young child.
- 'When they were grown up' suggests that the narrator is not yet grown up.
- The sentences in the passage are either very long, linked by a string of conjunctions, or very short. The contrast and the jerkiness that result again suggest a child's way of speaking.
- Adults, including mother and father, are described only in the most immediate sensory terms (father's beard, mother's smell), and not in terms of personality or character.
- The concern with age ('They were older than his father . . .') suggests a child coming to terms with the concept of age, and some people being older than others.
- The sudden changes in subject (a song, wetting the bed, hair brushes) and thought association (one thought leading on to another without a logical link, as when the smell of urine links in with the smell of the boy's mother) again suggest a child.
- The use of song suggests a child.

However, a comprehensive commentary on this passage will include more than the above. The first danger is that the student will not recognise the most obvious feature of the passage (one student in an actual examination wrote down in a tone of utter condemnation that the author of this passage was an idiot because he wrote no better than a child could have done); the second is that once recognised the passage is left there, and not analysed any further. For example, the link between the smell of urine and the smell of a mother is comic, as the insult to mothers is clearly unintentional. The sudden changes of subject are quite amusing in a general sense, and not merely in connection with this one passage. The author also suggests with some intensity the uncertainty and strangeness of a child's world, its inability to understand why anything happens, its clinging on to certain certainties ('He was baby tuckoo' and 'That was his song'), and its capacity to note what happens without making any judgement on it. Thus events and people are recorded in the passage, but hardly commented on; the child does not have the knowledge, maturity, or detachment to make comments, merely to experience whatever surrounds him. Something of the terror that the world can hold for a child is suggested by the final refrain 'Pull out his eyes,/Apologize', and is there possibly even to suggest how guilt is programmed into a child from a young age.

If the question seems to invite such comment, a passage such as this is a good opportunity to talk or write about narrative technique. Simple as it is, it could be argued that the language of the passage is too complex for a young child, the vocabulary ('oilsheet', 'queer') too mature. The passage could be seen as an extreme of first-person narrative, or as an approach to the 'STREAM OF CONSCIOUSNESS' (see Chapter 4) technique. Certainly the limitations of the passage are the limitations of its narrator. It is extremely vivid, demands attention, and paints an effective picture of the world seen through the eyes of a child.

**Passage 2**

One law of reading the novel (and other forms of literature) is to assume right from the start that anything odd, unusual, or out of the ordinary has a reason for its existence, and that it is your job to find that reason. If a reason cannot be found after long and exhaustive effort, then perhaps what is there in the passage is simply inexplicable; it is safer to assume that everything has an explanation. Another law is not to take a passage always at face value; IRONY can quite easily be missed, as in the following passage from an eighteenth-century novel:

> He now lived, for the most part, retired in the country, with one sister, for whom he had a very tender affection. This lady was now somewhat past the age of thirty, an aera at which, in the opinion of the malicious, the title of old maid may with no impropriety be assumed. She was of that species of women whom you commend rather for good qualities than beauty, and who are generally called, by their own sex, very good sort of women – as good a sort of woman, madam, as you would wish to know. Indeed, she was so far from regretting want of beauty that she never mentioned that perfection, if it can be called one, without contempt; and would often thank God she was not as handsome as Miss Such-a-one, whom perhaps beauty had led into errors which she might have otherwise avoided. Miss Bridget Allworthy (for that was the name of this lady) very rightly conceived the charms of person in a woman to be no better than snares for herself, as well as for others; and yet so discreet was she in her conduct, that her prudence was as much on the guard as if she had all the snares to apprehend which were ever laid for her whole sex. Indeed, I have observed, though it may seem unaccountable to the reader, that this guard of prudence, like the trained bands, is always readiest to go on duty where there is the least danger. It often basely and cowardly deserts those paragons for whom the men are all wishing, sighing, dying, and spreading every net in their power; and constantly attends at the heels of that higher order of women for whom the other sex have a more distant and awful respect, and whom (from despair, I suppose, of success) they never venture to attack.
>
> Henry Fielding, *The History of Tom Jones*

**Notes**

On the surface this passage does no more than paint a picture of a certain lady, in guarded terms of praise. Closer examination reveals a cutting irony in almost every line.

> This lady was now somewhat past the age of thirty, an aera at which, in the opinion of the malicious, the title of old maid may with no impropriety be assumed.

At first sight this says that the lady in question is a little over thirty. The key phrase is 'somewhat past the age of thirty', the word 'somewhat' being particularly influential in shaping the reader's response. The fact that care has been taken to qualify the statement that she is over thirty warns the reader and makes him suspicious, adding to the number of years awarded to the lady. The author then states two things: malicious people call such women old maids, and there is nothing wrong or improper in the term. By stating that only malicious people would call her an old maid the author is neatly avoiding calling her one himself, but at the same time planting firmly in the reader's mind the idea that she is an old maid. By telling the reader that there is nothing improper in the term, he alerts the reader to the idea that there might be something improper in the term. The outcome of all this is a firm message that the lady is considerably older than thirty, and perhaps lies about her age to conceal it, and that she is a true old maid, or a woman ignored by men. This may be what is implied by the passage, but the author has apparently taken great pains to imply nothing of the sort, a fact which adds to the humour of the passage.

The author then states that the lady was known for good qualities rather than beauty – outwardly a harmless statement, but one which could easily be taken as stating that she is ugly. The repetition of the phrase 'good woman', and its rendering in semi-colloquial speech, also makes this phrase somewhat suspicious, as though it is of doubtful truth and so has to be repeated if anyone is to believe it. When the lady goes on to condemn beauty in others, it is clear that she is envious of those who have the beauty she cannot claim. The author tells us that she condemned beauty in an apparently neutral tone, but the ironic interpretation given to earlier lines warns the reader to interpret these lines as well in an ironic manner.

The author then tells us the woman's name, which has been withheld up to this point. The author carries on his pretence of innocence by stating that Miss Bridget Allworthy takes every possible defensive action against seduction, despite the fact that she seems to be in little real danger. The comment on life which follows ('prudence . . . is always readiest to go on duty where there is the least danger') is again apparently innocent, a mere observation on one of the oddities of life, yet it condemns the woman by revealing her hypocrisy and jealousy of those who are in danger of seduction. The author completes the irony by commenting that prudence seems to desert those most in danger when they most need it, but that men do not attempt to seduce women like Miss Allworthy 'from despair, I suppose, of success'. By this time it is quite clear why men do not approach women such as she: they are far too ugly and unattractive to be worth bothering about.

The danger for the author in a passage such as this is that the reader will take what he says at face value. The author avoids this with a number of techniques. The woman herself is of a type familiar to most people: born in an age when marriage was the only realistic career possibility for a well-bred woman, neglected by men, bitter, self-righteous, sour, unattractive. All these features are suggested by the phrase 'old maid', and once the author can forge a link between the woman and the phrase 'old maid' the damage to her reputation is half-way towards being done – no matter that he hedges the phrase round with qualifications. Then he qualifies everything he says, as with her age being somewhat past thirty. The author also makes points by what he does not state. He states she is called a very good sort of woman by her own sex, implying that the opposite sex have a very different view of her. The author adopts a tone of bland innocence in his comments, seemingly unable to see the real meaning behind what he is stating, and that meaning is left to the reader to unravel. All the information necessary for the reader to form a hostile picture of Miss Allworthy is there in the passage; the skill of the irony lies in the reader's being allowed to draw the conclusions from it himself, and not have the author spell out to him what he should be thinking. This process of finding out for himself is attractive for the reader. His perception of the gap between what appears to be stated and what is actually stated is also comic, an added bonus for the author. The author can claim to have written a straightforward description of an admirable sort of woman, with a few wondering comments on certain ironies of human behaviour; the effect is of a straight condemnation of a hypocritical woman.

**Passage 3**

An equally useful weapon in a novelist's armoury is that of description. This extract from *Bleak House* by Charles Dickens shows a master of description at work.

> While Esther sleeps, and while Esther wakes, it is still wet weather down at the place in Lincolnshire. The rain is ever falling, drip, drip, drip, by day and night, upon the broad flagged terrace-pavement, The Ghost's Walk. The weather is so very bad down in Lincolnshire, that the liveliest imagination can scarcely apprehend its ever being fine again. Not that there is any superabundant life of imagination on the spot, for Sir Leicester is not here (and, truly, even if he were, would not do much for it in that particular), but is in Paris, with my Lady; and solitude, with dusky wings, sits brooding upon Chesney Wold.
>
> There may be some motions of fancy among the lower animals at Chesney Wold. The horses in the stables – the long stables in a barren, red-brick courtyard, where there is a great bell in a turret, and a clock with a large face, which the pigeons who live near it, and who love to perch upon its shoulders, seem to be always consulting – they may con-

template some mental pictures of fine weather on occasions, and may be better artists at them than the grooms. The old roan, so famous for cross-country work, turning his large eyeball to the grated window near his rack, may remember the fresh leaves that glisten there at other times, and the scents that stream in, and may have a fine run with the hounds, while the human helper, clearing out the next stall, never stirs beyond his pitchfork and birch-broom. The grey, whose place is opposite the door, and who, with an impatient rattle of his halter, pricks his ears and turns his head so wistfully when it is opened, and to whom the opener says, 'Woa grey, then, steady! Noabody wants you today!' may know it quite as well as the man. The whole seemingly monotonous and uncompanionable half-dozen stabled together, may pass the long wet hours, when the door is shut, in livelier communication than is held in the servants' hall, or at the Dedlock Arms; – or may even beguile the time by improving (perhaps corrupting) the pony in the loose-box in the corner.

So the mastiff, dozing in his kennel, in the court-yard, with his large head on his paws, may think of the hot sunshine, when the shadows of the stable-building tire his patience out by changing, and leave him, at one time of the day, no broader refuge than the shadow of his own house, where he sits on end, panting and growling short, and very much wanting something to worry, besides himself and his chain. So, now, half-waking and all-winking, he may recall the house full of company, the coach-houses full of vehicles, the stables full of horses, and the outbuildings full of attendants upon horses, until he is undecided about the present, and comes forth to see how it is. Then, with that impatient shake of himself, he may growl in the spirit, 'Rain, rain, rain! Nothing but rain – and no family here!' as he goes in again, and lies down with a gloomy yawn.

So with the dogs in the kennel-buildings across the park, who have their restless fits, and whose doleful voices, when the wind has been very obstinate, have even made it known in the house itself: upstairs, downstairs, and in my lady's chamber. They may hunt the whole countryside, while the raindrops are pattering round their inactivity. So the rabbits with their self-betraying tails, frisking in and out of holes at roots of trees, may be lively with ideas of the breezy days when their ears are blown about, or of those seasons of interest when there are sweet young plants to gnaw. The turkey in the poultry-yard, always troubled with a class-grievance (probably Christmas), may be reminiscent of that summer morning wrongfully taken from him, when he got into the lane among the felled trees, where there was a barn and barley. The discontented goose, who stoops to pass under the old gateway, twenty feet high, may gabble out, if we only knew it, a waddling preference for weather when the gateway casts its shadow on the ground.

Be this as it may, there is not much fancy otherwise stirring at Chesney Wold. If there be a little at any odd moment, it goes, like a little noise in that old echoing place, a long way, and usually leads off to ghosts and mystery.

**Notes**

The opening of the passage – 'While Esther sleeps, and while Esther wakes' – gives the impression of something taking place over a long period of time, spanning at least a night and a day. The repetition of 'drip' and the further reference to something lasting more than a day ('by day and night') concentrate the description on the twin concepts of rain and wetness, and something which has continued and is continuing for a long period of time. The absence of the presumed owners of the house gives a feeling of emptiness, aided by the words 'solitude', 'dusky' (with its hint of 'dusty'), and 'brooding'. The author takes pains to emphasise the absence of 'imagination', perhaps because it suggests liveliness – the one feature absent from the house.

The mention of 'imagination' in the first paragraph is carried through into the remainder of the passage, the difference being that the term now used is 'fancy'. Both terms imply something other than bare fact, a certain liveliness of mind and spirit, but 'fancy' perhaps has a more playful feeling to it, more gaiety and spirit. In any event, the author chooses to use the animals in or around the house to convey his description of it at this particular time. This is seemingly rather strange. The author clearly wishes to present a description of a lifeless house almost inundated with rain and dreary weather, and he might be expected therefore to describe long empty halls, the noise and feel of the rain, and keep any hint of life out of his description. As written he does almost the exact opposite. The house itself is hardly mentioned, the description concentrates on the only things (the animals) that have any life in them at all, and even then describes largely what they felt like or might feel like at more cheerful times. The author wonders if the 'old roan' remembers summer, if the mastiff remembers the 'hot summer', the goose the time when the hot sun cast a shadow from the gateway.

However, this apparently contradictory method of describing a sodden house and countryside does have an effect. There are continual reminders throughout the passage of the weather and emptiness of the house. The 'human helper' is suggested as being sunk in apathy. The statement that the 'seemingly monotonous' stable might hold more life than the local inn or the servants' hall in effect suggests that all three are dead and silent, as the reader knows already that the stable appears to be still and silent, and the author is only wondering if the animals may have these stimulating thoughts. The mastiff is imagined as saying 'Rain, rain, rain!'; the following paragraph has 'while the raindrops are pattering round their inactivity', combining wetness and inaction in one phrase. Thus the author takes care that the reader never loses sight of the prevailing conditions.

The reader knows that the glimpses of summer or a full house given in the passage are imaginary concepts in the minds of animals; as such, they lose a little of their force and power, the force and power they might have had if they had been seen working in a human mind. In effect the reader knows from the start that the idea of the animals imagining anything in this way is fanciful right from the start, and increases the fictitious element in what is said. The scenes summoned up of hot summer days and bustling activity are therefore made to seem unreal, and their presence serves to emphasise the bleakness and isolation that starts off the passage. The description is oblique: it does not describe the issue in hand, but something else very different from it, and in so doing heightens the reader's awareness of what the original issue is. The descriptions of the heat and activity are different, each animal being associated with a different one; the concept of a drenched emptiness and solitude is a constant, to which the passage returns at regular intervals, and the preceding description emphasises the dreariness that is at the heart of the passage, rather than destroying it. Even the fact that animals are imagined as being provoked into yearning for better days carries with it a feeling that the present must be truly dreadful to cause this reaction in animals.

Another technique is the situation of the animals. The horses are locked in a stable; the mastiff is confined to his kennel; the dogs are confined to their kennels; the rabbits are diving for cover into their holes in the ground; the turkey is cooped up in the poultry yard. Only the goose is moving, and he 'waddles' and 'stoops', suggesting almost an old and crippled fat man. Everywhere the animals are confined, hemmed in by the rain and the isolation, afloat in a sea of solitude, almost in hibernation. The author could have chosen to describe buildings or the countryside in the rain; instead he chooses animals with life in them, but shows this life at so low an ebb, so run-down and constrained, that it suggests something so dispirited as to drain all but the barest flicker of animation from living things. By describing images of summer and heat the author is showing the reader what things might be like, but in so doing is emphasising how differently they actually are, and how low things have sunk. There is 'fancy' in the passage, an almost playful wandering in and out of stable and kennel and field and poultry yard, as if the author delights in the freedom he has given himself to go where and when he pleases. Tiredness is suggested a number of times, with the mastiff 'dozing', and giving a 'gloomy yawn', and discontent is also suggested with the 'doleful' sound of the dogs, the turkey with a 'class grievance', and the 'discontented goose'. However much the description might seem to stray from the two concepts of rain and dreary emptiness, these two concepts underpin the whole passage, and are its most consistent element. The description is visual, but not exclusively so; sound and smell are used consistently, as are descriptions of various abstract moods. The sheer variety of the techniques used can serve to hide the extent to which the passage concentrates on the atmosphere suggested in the opening section and in the final paragraph.

## Further reading

### Classic Texts


- E. M. Forster, *Aspects of the Novel* (Penguin, 1990)
- H. Burton, *The Criticism of Prose* (Longman, 1973)
- Walter Allen, *The English Novel* (Pelican, 1958)

- Arnold Kettle, *An Introduction to the English Novel* (Volumes 1–2, Hutchinson, 1967)
- Ian Watt, *The Rise of the Novel* (Hogarth Press, 1987)

## Modern Texts

- Andre Brink, *How to Study a Novel* (Macmillan, 1995)
- Jeremy Hawthorn, *Studying the Novel. An Introduction* (Edward Arnold, 1997)
- John Peck, *The Novel. Language and Narrative from Cervantes to Calvino* (Macmillan, 1998)
- James Cadden, *Prose Appreciation for A-level* (Edward Arnold, 1986)

CHAPTER SIX

# Practical criticism: drama

Poetry and prose each have features that are peculiar to them: the main distinguishing feature of drama is that it is designed for performance in front of its audience. This is so obvious a remark as to be accepted by most students, without the realisation that this basic factor is the start and finish of most practical criticism of drama and dominates the way drama is written.

The problem is that when plays are studied for examinations they are usually read from a printed text, as are poems and novels, but right from the start this puts the student in a false position if he or she treats drama in the same way as poetry or prose. Drama was meant to be seen and heard, not read. Everything the student writes must be based on the written text, but that text needs to be enlivened by a vivid visual and auditory imagination. Every time a student reads a play he or she needs to be seeing a performance of it in his or her mind. Even if the student has seen a performance in the live theatre, the cinema or on television the dangers are still there. Each production of a play has its own individual interpretations and 'feel', and having seen one production the student can have his or her horizons hemmed in by that memory, and see the play purely in terms of the one production he or she has witnessed.

The artificial situation that students finds themselves in when appreciating drama can create a number of problems. Shakespeare's plays present perhaps more problems than many others, because we only have the words and very little insight as to how Shakespeare wanted them performed. This applies to many dramatists, the general rule being that the more modern a play, the more the author will give specific instructions on how he wants his work staged, acted, and presented. George Bernard Shaw (1856–1950) gave the clearest possible instructions as to how he wished his plays to be staged and the lines to be spoken, and the *Preface* to his plays is often nearly as long as the play itself. However, in pre-Restoration drama all we have is the text and virtually no stage directions. This means that first of all we have to guess at how the play might have looked and how the lines might have been spoken.

Secondly, reliance on pure text with no insights from the author creates other problems. In Shakespeare's *Macbeth* Lady Macbeth makes it clear that she has breast-fed an infant, but it is also clear in the play that Macbeth and Lady Macbeth have no children. Such inconsistencies can get totally out of proportion when the play is read rather than seen, and in this instance led to a famous essay attacking the very literal approach to criticism of A. C. Bradley, entitled 'How Many Children Had Lady Macbeth?' Reading *Macbeth* the student has time to note and dwell on the inconsistency. On stage the remark about breast-feeding makes a valuable point at the stage in the play, which is that Lady Macbeth is prepared to deny her basic feminine and human instincts in order to gain the crown for her husband. A great deal happens between that remark and the realisation that the Macbeths have no children, and in the theatre the audience have neither the time nor the inclination to dwell on the conflicting statements. Even if they are apparent, simple answers are available, the simplest of all being that Lady Macbeth's child died in infancy. The hurry and excitement of a dramatic performance can bulldoze its way over details such as this, so that they simply do not cross the audience's mind.

A minor problem can occur where music features largely in a play, and this has to be imagined by the student who is simply reading the text. The impact of the songs in Shakespeare's *Twelfth Night* is huge, but obviously depends to quite a large extent on tunes and voices. The impact of pomp, ceremony, and processions in an Elizabethan play is also liable to be lost. A simple stage direction such as 'Flourish. Enter Claudius, King of Denmark, Gertrude the Queen, Councillors, Polonius and his son Laertes, Hamlet cum aliis' is a bare statement of fact when written. On stage it can be translated into a blare of ceremonial music that can make the audience jump in their seats, followed by a glorious pageant of extravagantly and luxuriously dressed characters streaming onto the stage in a riot of colour and noise. The entry of the full court of Denmark is visually immensely exciting, but it is an effect that a mere reading of the play does not necessarily bring out. Nor does a bare reading bring out the contrast between this scene and the one that immediately precedes it, with a few cold and frightened soldiers perched on the wind-swept battlements of Elsinore. As regards practical criticism, the student must be aware of what is suggested or implied in a passage, and the appeals to the imagination contained in bare stage directions.

## Characterisation

The simplest method of characterising a person on stage is by what he or she does and says, from which the audience can form their own conclusions. Occasionally a Chorus or narrator figure will appear in a play to tell the audience what to think of a character, but for the vast majority of time our judgement of the characters is based solely on their actions on the stage, and their words. Insight into a character's private thoughts can be given by means of a soliloquy, or monologue, where the character speaks out loud to the audience, usually when he or she is alone on stage. There is a problem with realism here; we tend to think our thoughts, not speak them out loud, and any soliloquy or monologue needs to be examined for the subtlety and conviction with which it is blended into the main action.

It may sometimes be a strain on credibility to have a character speak out loud on an empty stage; it is much less of a strain to have another character speak about someone else. Look for points of characterisation in what other characters say about a character. Standard devices are to boost a major character before his or her entry by a preliminary speech praising or damning them, thus arousing tension and expectation in the audience. Remember that the character of the speaker can be judged from what they say, as well as the character of the person they are talking about. A grudging or generous comment about another character may tell the audience something about the other character, but it definitely tells them something about the personality of the speaker. It is a very effective and common technique to have a character who we know has no reason to praise or love another character speaking in his or her praise. Thus Enobarbus in Shakespeare's *Antony and Cleopatra* does not like Cleopatra, but when even he is forced to speak in glowing terms of her immense presence and sensuality we know how strong these features must be to have overcome his other feelings. Similarly Claudius hates Hamlet, so when he says that the people of Denmark love Hamlet we recognise that this must be so abundantly true as to be accepted even by Hamlet's enemies. Another device is to have a character the audience hate or find ludicrous speak in praise of someone else, and thus damn him by association.

Imagery can play a vital part in forming our opinion of a character. If a person's speech is laced with references to illness, disease and decay, as Hamlet's is, then it does not take the audience long to associate these features with the character in question. When answering a question look out for mannerisms of speech, as suggested by spelling, stage directions or comments from other characters. Look closely for hints as to a character's appearance and age; in older plays these are frequently buried, or wrapped round in so many jocular remarks that they go unnoticed. The author of this book read *Twelfth Night* three times in detail as a student, and totally failed to recognise until he was told that there are several references in the play that make it clear Maria is a very small person. In a novel, character is often stated; in a play, it has to be deduced.

## Plot

The majority of plays have a strong plot, and even those that do not, such as Beckett's *Waiting for Godot*, obtain some of their effect by challenging the audience's expectation that there will be a plot. In modern plays the plot is more likely to be original, and sometimes merely an excuse for the author to characterise or make thematic points. Therefore in a modern play the balance between plot, characterisation, and themes can be a good starting point in a practical criticism.

A simple plot with limited settings and characters may not just be the product of a modern writer's desire to focus on characterisation and themes. Numerous expensive sets and a large number of actors make for a very expensive production in the modern theatre, and one of the great unsung influences on modern drama is cost-consciousness. A new young writer stands the best chance of seeing a play performed in a studio theatre, which has limited staging facilities and only a few actors on call. A play such as Tom Stoppard's *Jumpers* (1972) is an exception. Stoppard knew this play was destined for the prestigious and relatively rich National Theatre in London, and so could afford to write a play which required, among other things, a troupe of gymnasts and a huge television screen. A modern writer who wished to tell the story of Antony and Cleopatra would probably go to the film studios, not the live theatre. However, look for hints that a modern writer may be telling an old story in allegorical form. A simple dramatisation of a novel such as *Of Mice and Men* (1937) by John Steinbeck (1902–68) may appear to be a story about two American vagrants; it can quite easily on stage be made into an allegory of the fall of man. Where a play is using an old and well-known story, such as Shakespeare's *Antony and Cleopatra*, look to see if the author is assuming any knowledge on the part of the reader, or deliberately varying the story or characterisation for effect.

A sub-plot is a feature of many plays. It is not unknown for examination boards to set parallel extracts, one from the main plot of a play and one from its sub-plot, and ask the student to compare and contrast them. A sub-plot provides variety and a change of scene from the main plot, whilst at the same time keeping the audience in touch with the concerns and themes of the main plot. An excellent example of what a sub-plot can be is to be found in Shakespeare's *King Lear*, where the main and sub-plots are carefully interleaved, in roughly alternating sequence. The sub-plot examines the themes of the main plot, but from a different viewpoint and with different characters. Certain characters and scenes overlap, ensuring that the play as a whole is not split down the middle. At the climax of the play, sub-plot and main plot are brought together, with the sub-plot concluding just before the main plot so that the latter is not reduced in effectiveness at its climax.

Sub-plots can also go gloriously wrong, though that fact alone need not ruin a play. In *The Relapse* by Sir John Vanbrugh the main plot starts off in fine style, but the sub-plot with its coarse and bawdy concentration and complete lack of morality soon takes over. The sub-plot dominates more and more of the play, until the main issues in the main plot are left unresolved, and the sub-plot finishes the play in complete control, with only the merest token gesture towards the main plot. Other plays have parallel plots, such as Shakespeare's *Much Ado About Nothing*, in which one story line provides much of the narrative and a comment on romantic love, whilst the other provides much of the comedy and a comment on real love.

## Dialogue

Plays centre on dialogue, or the verbal exchanges between characters on stage. Very often individual characters will have their own specific and individual style of speaking, but remember that in appreciating drama it is not only what each individual character says that matters, but the skill of the author in linking characters to each other by means of what they say. Thus the effect of a word, sentence or speech on another character can be as important as the word, sentence or speech itself. One example is Jimmy Porter, the 'angry young man' who is the central figure in John Osborne's play *Look Back in Anger*. Jimmy is superb at launching darts at those to and with whom he speaks, darts that he knows will both have an explosive effect and demand that attention be paid to him. Or look at the punning and word play in many Restoration Comedies, where the pace of the exchange between characters seems to get faster and faster as each one tries to cap the other's wit.

*Irony* in all forms plays a crucial part in theatrical dialogue, and in many post-war plays it is the dominant feature – see the entry for DRAMATIC IRONY in Chapter 3. Remember that irony can be very subtle, and look for it in particular between characters at the extreme end of relationships – those who are very close to each other, and those who are very far apart. In this, as in so many areas, it is the student's sensitivity that is tested. Irony is a delicate flower. The student who sees his or her task as bashing through a text for an examination is likely to trample on irony before they have even realised it is there.

## General points

As with all practical criticism questions, look out for the prevailing tone of an extract, be it comic, serious, reflective, or whatever. Where comedy is the dominant effect, be careful to specify what the comic effect is, and how it is achieved, be it slapstick, bawdy or coarse humour, word-play, or emphasis on wit. Learn to follow a dialogue through: good dialogue shows characters changing, flexing, and developing their attitudes, so that the audience and the characters are at a different point towards the end of an extract from that which began it. Comment on the presence of stock types if characters appear to be cast in this mould. Examples might be the malcontent or bastard in Jacobean drama; the stupid, unsophisticated rustic or country bumpkin; the fop or dandy in Restoration comedy; the old man or woman desperately trying to pretend they are young; the star-struck lovers.

## The context question

When answering on a passage from a play you have studied for Advanced level it is perfectly allowable and desirable to make use of the wider knowledge that you have, and to relate the passage to the play as a whole – but be careful! Such wider references should only form a small part of your answer, and never let your answer turn into another general essay on the play. Look carefully for the direction the examiner wants you to go in. The questions are often specific, and ask you to comment on an author's technique in a given passage. 'Discuss Shakespeare's comic technique in the following passage' and 'How does the author reveal the tensions between the characters in the scene below?' are examples of questions where the examiner does not want a general analysis of a passage; more candidates fail through failure to read the question than fail it through inadequate knowledge of the text. You may quote lines from a context passage in your answer, but exercise moderation: there are no marks merely for being able to read the question and write out the text.

## Questions, notes and answers

### Context, Comment and Appreciation questions

**Question 1**

(a) What does this passage tell us about Hamlet's state of mind at this point in the play?
(b) What is the significance of this extract, coming as it does in this point in the play?

*Enter Hamlet.*

*Hamlet.*
To be, or not to be: that is the question:
Whether 'tis nobler in the mind to suffer
The slings and arrows of outrageous fortune,
Or to take arms against a sea of troubles,
And by opposing end them. To die, to sleep
No more and by a sleep to say we end
The heartache, and the thousand natural shocks
That flesh is heir to! 'Tis a consummation
Devoutly to be wished. To die, to sleep.
To sleep, perchance to dream: ay, there's the rub,
For in that sleep of death what dreams may come
When we have shuffled off this mortal coil,
Must give us pause. There's the respect
That makes calamity of so long life:

For who would bear the whips and scorns of time,
Th'oppressor's wrong, the proud man's contumely,
The pangs of despised love, the law's delay,
The insolence of office, and the spurns
That patient merit of th'unworthy takes,
When he himself might his quietus make
With a bare bodkin? Who would fardels bear,
To grunt and sweat under a weary life,
But that the dread of something after death
The undiscovered country, from whose bourn
No traveller returns, puzzles the will,
And makes us rather bear those ills we have,
Than fly to others that we know not of?
Thus conscience does make cowards of us all
And thus the native hue of resolution
Is sicklied o'er with the pale cast of thought,
And enterprises of great pitch and moment,
With this regard their currents turn awry,
And lose the name of action.

**Question (a)**

This question specifically asks about what is learnt of Hamlet's state of mind from this soliloquy. The student who has studied *Hamlet* has to be careful not to bring in irrelevant information when answering a question of this nature and to stick to what is asked. An answer might read as follows:

**Answer**

The speech opens with a question, and there are two other extended questions in the passage, all of which suggests that Hamlet is undecided, and either unable or unwilling to make up his mind. Hamlet appears to be contemplating suicide. His comments on human life suggest that he sees it in terms of suffering, anguish, and pain. Hamlet's explanation for people's failure to commit suicide is a cynical one, being simply that people are frightened that worse things await them after death. When the speech opens its metre is broken and jagged, again suggesting uncertainty and confusion, but it becomes more ordered as the speech proceeds. Hamlet appears to take solace and comfort in explaining away the situation he finds himself in, perhaps suggesting that he calms his fears by apparently rational thought. In some respects Hamlet is describing himself when he states that 'conscience does make cowards of us all'. Hamlet's imagery centres on pain and suffering, suggesting man in continual pain. His final reference to Ophelia might also suggest a man tortured by a sense of guilt, an awareness of his own sins.

Therefore this soliloquy suggests that Hamlet is unable to make up his mind, contemplating suicide, and disenchanted with the suffering of human life. He is cynical, but comforts himself with reflection, even though he is clearly suffering greatly and aware of his own sins and weakness.

**Notes**

The answer given is brief and strictly relevant, working through the passage line by line, and tying it all up at the end with a two-line conclusion. Questions of this nature are rarely aiming for a lengthy answer, and the one that is short and to the point usually scores the highest marks.

**Question (b)**

This speech marks a turning-point in the play. In Hamlet's first soliloquy he gives vent to an intense, suicidal depression, following this by equally intense anger when he hears the truth of his father's murder from the figure purporting to be his father's ghost. He then moves with equal intensity to self-hatred, berating himself for not avenging his father when a mere player can summon up more apparent feeling than he can. In this soliloquy, the high-emotion, anger and self-recrimination have gone, to be replaced by an almost thoughtful, contemplative and reflective reflection not only on suicide as it might affect Hamlet, but suicide as it affects all human beings. This speech is therefore the calm before the storm. It is a turning point because increasingly after it events move beyond Hamlet's power to control them. Prior to this speech he has used a cloak of madness to hide his true motives and retain some control of events. This control is soon about to leave him. His ability to trust anyone except Horatio is about to be shattered by the apparent betrayal of him by Ophelia and his University friends, and he will inadvertently kill Polonius, thus placing himself at Claudius's mercy. This is perhaps the last time in the play before the very end that we see the Renaissance Prince, the man whose gifts and intelligence make him the sum of all men.

## Comment and appreciation questions

**Question 2**

Comment in any way that seems suitable on the passage given below:

> The light suddenly fails. In a moment it is night. The moon rises at back, mounts in the sky, stands still, shedding a pale light on the scene.
>
> *Vladimir*: At last! (Estragon gets up and goes towards Vladimir, a boot in each hand. He puts them down at the edge of stage, straightens and contemplates the moon.) What are you doing?
>
> *Estragon*: Pale for weariness.
>
> *Vladimir*: Eh?
>
> *Estragon*: Of climbing heaven and gazing on the likes of us.
>
> *Vladimir*: Your boots. What are you doing with your boots?
>
> *Estragon*: (turning to look at the boots). I'm leaving them there. (Pause.) Another will come, just as . . . as . . . as me, but with smaller feet, and they'll make him happy.
>
> *Vladimir*: But you can't go barefoot!
>
> *Estragon*: Christ did.

*Vladimir*: Christ! What's Christ got to do with it? You're not going to compare yourself to Christ!
*Estragon*: All my life I've compared myself to him.
*Vladimir*: But where he lived it was warm, it was dry!
*Estragon*: Yes. And they crucified quick.
*Silence.*
*Vladimir*: We've nothing more to do here.
*Estragon*: Nor anywhere else.
*Vladimir*: Ah Gogo, don't go on like that. Tomorrow everything will be better.
*Estragon*: How do you make that out?
*Vladimir*: Did you not hear what the child said?
*Estragon*: No.
*Vladimir*: He said that Godot was sure to come tomorrow. (Pause.) What do you say to that?
*Estragon*: Then all we have to do is to wait on here.
*Vladimir*: Are you mad? We must take cover. (He takes Estragon by the arm.) Come on.
*He draws Estragon after him. Estragon yields, then resists. They halt.*
*Estragon*: (looking at the tree). Pity we haven't got a bit of rope.
*Vladimir*: Come on. It's cold.
*He draws Estragon after him. As before.*
*Estragon*: Remind me to bring a bit of rope tomorrow.
*Vladimir*: Yes. Come on.
*He draws him after him. As before.*
*Estragon*: How long have we been together all the time now?
*Vladimir*: I don't know. Fifty years perhaps.
*Estragon*: Do you remember the day I threw myself into the Rhone?
*Vladimir*: We were grape-harvesting.
*Estragon*: You fished me out.
*Vladimir*: That's all dead and buried.
*Estragon*: My clothes dried in the sun.
*Vladimir*: There's no good harking back on that. Come on.
*He draws him after him. As before.*
*Estragon*: Wait.
*Vladimir*: I'm cold!
*Estragon*: Wait! (He moves away from Vladimir.) I wonder if we wouldn't have been better off alone, each one for himself. (He crosses the stage and sits down on the mound.) We weren't made for the same road.
*Vladimir*: (without anger): It's not certain.
*Estragon*: No, nothing is certain.
*Vladimir slowly crosses the stage and sits down beside Estragon.*
*Vladimir*: We can still part, if you think it would be better.

*Estragon*: It's not worth while now.
*Silence.*
*Vladimir*: No, it's not worth while.
*Silence.*
*Estragon*: Well, shall we go?
*Vladimir*: Yes, let's go.
*They do not move.*

CURTAIN

**Answer**

The passage appears to be taken from a modern play, possibly of the Drama of the Absurd school of writers.

The style of the passage is that of a dialogue between two characters, Vladimir and Estragon. Stage effects are minimal, but the sudden failure of the light and equally sudden rising of the moon has a comic element to it which may have been intentional on the part of the author. The two characters speak to each other in alternate lines, usually quite brief. The conversation itself is very varied. It can be commonplace ('What are you doing?'), poetic ('Pale for weariness'), religious ('Christ did'), philosophical ('We've nothing more to do here'), and personal ('Are you mad? We must take cover'). The language is simple and unadorned, for the most part.

The two characters seem to have known each other for a long time. Vladimir suggests (although without a great deal of conviction or certainty), that they might have known each other for fifty years, and the way they speak to each other is familiar (Vladimir uses a nickname, Gogo, to refer to Estragon). They reminisce about times past, and show concern for each other, but nothing they say appears to have very much effect, and they never remain on one topic for any length of time, almost as if their conversation had been used up many years ago, and they were still going through the motions of talking without really ever communicating. Both characters appear ineffectual, something emphasised by the last lines of the extract and the stage direction which follows ('Well, shall we go?/Yes, let's go. *They do not move.*').

There appears to be a religious theme in the passage. Estragon compares himself to Christ who went barefoot, but the real significance of Christ for the two characters seems to be firstly that where he lived it was warm (the fact that Vladimir and Estragon are both cold is referred to several times in the passage), and secondly that in Christ's day 'they crucified quick', suggesting that Vladimir and Estragon are being slowly tortured to death, in a harder way than Christ's. The second reference that might be religious is to Godot, who is coming tomorrow, and whose arrival will, according to Vladimir, make everything better. It is possible that the author is referring here to people's religious beliefs which allow them to suffer misery and misfortune in the hope that religion will produce something that will suddenly make things satisfactory, or better. If so, the suggestion would appear to be that people are wrong to wait in this manner, and act instead on the basis of what they know to be true. On the other hand the fact that someone has said Godot will come could be seen as a valid reason for awaiting his arrival.

An atmosphere of chronic indecision is created by the passage. Its theme might be stated as 'nothing is certain'; it certainly seems that the two characters on stage are certain of nothing except their coldness, and the existence of each other. Anything else, from what they should do to whether or not they should remain friends, or were mistaken in becoming friends, is shrouded in uncertainty and indecision.

The passage seems to present a picture of two people alone against the world, uncertain about what they should do, and even about what they are. Their relationship is the only sure thing they have, yet even that seems to be automatic and unthinking, more a question of habit and apathy than a conscious choice on their part to be friends. Both characters are frozen by inertia, lack of motivation, and lack of confidence. Their relationship is partly comic and partly tragic. Religion appears to be a theme in the passage, although the exact nature of what is being stated about religion is unclear and ambiguous.

**Notes**

As with any essay of this type, the above answer is only one of many that might be written, all of which could have validity. The writer is prepared to make educated guesses about the 'meaning' of the passage, but is not afraid to admit to uncertainty, and as much time is spent on style and technique and characterisation as on themes, recognising that all four elements balance each other out. The essay is based firmly on the set passage, not on a view of the play as a whole – an essential part of all answers of this type.

## Further reading

- John Cadden, *Drama Appreciation for A-level* (Hodder & Stoughton, 1988)
- Linda Cookson, *Practical Approaches to Literary Criticism: Plays* (Longman, 1987)
- Kenneth Pickering, *How To Study Modern Drama* (Macmillan 1988)
- Mick Wallis and Simon Shepherd, *Studying Plays* (Arnold, 1998): for the more advanced student.

CHAPTER SEVEN

# Chaucer

Geoffrey Chaucer (?1340–1400) and John Milton (1608–74) (see Ch. 12) are, with Shakespeare and Dickens, the most commonly set 'classical' authors by examining boards, and are also often found at the core of many traditional and modern degree courses. However, there is a movement away from the traditional 'big four' of Chaucer, Shakespeare, Milton and Dickens in certain universities, though a general trend is difficult to isolate with the fragmentation of so many degree courses into hitherto unexplored areas.

In Chaucer's case the reasons for his popularity are two-fold. Firstly he is a truly magnificent poet who, like Shakespeare, has something in his work for everyone, from the soaring dignity of *The Knight's Tale* to the scurrilous and extremely coarse humour of *The Miller's Tale*. Secondly, he was effectively the first English poet, or at least the first one to write in what is recognisably English. Actually what Chaucer writes in is largely a London and East Anglian dialect, but the point is that he is the first truly great English author to write in his own language, rather than French or Latin.

## Chaucer and Modern Critical Theory

For many years Chaucer was deemed more or less immune to the onslaught of new critical theories that began to dominate English literature from the 1970s onwards. (These theories are described in Chapter 25, which you might wish to read alongside this chapter). Medievalists erected barriers round Chaucer and other early medieval authors, insisting that the new waves of Freudian, Marxist, Feminist, Postcolonial, Structuralist, Poststructuralist and other criticism had little to offer. Chaucer's world was one of stable, orthodox Christian values and a hierarchy that was as far from 'postmodernism' as could be. What relevance had feminism to a society where it was accepted that the married woman became the property of her husband? What relevance had Marxism to a ruthlessly authoritarian society where power was held by a hereditary monarchy and privilege accepted as being ordained by God?

In fact new criticism has much to offer Chaucerian studies. Critical theories based on linguistics and theories of language are bound to find fertile fields with an author writing to complex laws of 'rhetoric', and who seemed at times obsessed with the mechanics of the story and the multi-faceted ironies 'the teller within the tale' could be used to produce. The supposed social orthodoxy of Chaucer can be challenged from the outset when his major work involves people from all strata of society riding together on a joint enterprise, thereby providing a form of social mixing that medieval society was supposed to discourage. In one interpretation, the supposed symbol of chivalric virtue, The Knight, is little more than a time-serving mercenary. Perhaps feminist criticism has found most of all in Chaucer. In *The Canterbury Tales*, is Griselda in *The Clerk's Tale* the perfect wife, or is she a symbol of incomprehensible femininity that terrifies men through their inability to understand it? Is the Nun a silly girl using religion as a cover-up for a flirtatious nature, or is she a woman taking one of the few routes to freedom, the Church, offered to medieval women? Is the Wife of Bath a dreadful symbol of medieval anti-feminism, or a freed creature in touch with her sensuality? A specimen answer below attempts to disentangle some of the issues modern critical theory has brought to *The Canterbury Tales*.

## Chaucer's Work

*Troilus and Criseyde* by Chaucer is sometimes set as an Advanced-level text, but for the vast majority of students Chaucer means one or more of *The Canterbury Tales*, one of Chaucer's later works. The plan for *The Canterbury Tales* was grandiose. Twenty-nine pilgrims meet in London to embark on a pilgrimage to the shrine of St Thomas Becket in Canterbury. Organised by the Host or landlord of the inn where they meet, each pilgrim is to tell four tales on the pilgrimage to help pass the time, with a dinner paid for by the others at the Host's inn (the Host is no fool!) for the best storyteller and story. Chaucer never completed the whole scheme, and only twenty-four tales have come down to us, with four of these incomplete in one respect or another. The most popular material set at Advanced level is *The General Prologue*; *The Knight's Tale; The Pardoner's Tale*; *The Wife of Bath's Tale*; *The Nun's Priest's Tale*; and *The Franklin's Tale*. Next come *The Man of Law's Tale* and *The Clerk's Tale*, and *The Merchant's Tale*. *The Miller's Tale*, *The Reeve's Tale*, and *The Summoner's Tale* are excellent stories, but are sometimes given the cold shoulder by examining boards because they are highly scurrilous and coarse. The remaining Tales hardly feature in any examination syllabus, but each Tale which is set normally includes the Prologue to the Tale, which in the case of the Wife of Bath is as long and as interesting as the Tale itself. Sometimes the section in *The General Prologue* which describes the teller of the set Tale is also included for study. Most examining boards use context questions, as well as essays, for Chaucer, and quite detailed textual knowledge is usually required, though the Tales themselves are quite short. Beyond Advanced level, interest branches out from *The Canterbury Tales*, and Chaucer's other main works (*The Book of the Duchess*, *The House of Fame* and *Troilus and Criseyde*) are likely to feature in the syllabus. The discussion below is restricted largely to *The Canterbury Tales.*

## Approaching the text

Chaucer is difficult in the initial stages of study because his Middle English is very different from modern English: vocabulary, syntax, construction, and pronunciation have all changed since the fourteenth century. Despite this apparent problem, Chaucer often proves to be one of the most popular authors set at Advanced level; hold on to this reassurance if the early stages of tackling a Tale prove difficult.

Firstly remember that although the language and vocabulary can be difficult they are consistently so. It is a very strange experience to meet the word 'eek' for the first time, but the strangeness soon wears off when it is realised that it simply means 'also', and that it always means this whenever you meet it. The same is true of other words, syntax, and construction; enough of the language is recognisable to give the student a head start, and the differences from modern English are consistent and fairly simple. Take your text and work through it line by line, pencilling in translation (which should be given in the notes carried by any respectable academic edition) over the relevant words or passages. In doing this you will gain an instinctive and almost subconscious grasp of the basics of Chaucer's language, and be able to understand much more without reference to notes.

Secondly remember that pronunciation is different, the tendency being to pronounce rather more syllables than in modern English. Get hold of a record of someone reading Chaucer: the language has a gorgeous, rich sound to it, and hearing it well read is an experience not to be missed. For background reading buy or borrow a copy of the Nevill Coghill translation of *The Canterbury Tales*. This is often scorned by critics, as distorting what Chaucer originally wrote, and losing much of the original richness of the language. Of course your set text must be read in the original Chaucerian form, but Coghill was an excellent academic, and his translation, though not to be relied on for academic purposes, does retain much of Chaucer's freshness and originality, and is a stimulating and easy way of reading a great many of *The Canterbury Tales*.

## The biographical, literary and historical background

A comparison of the graffiti left on the walls of Pompeii with that found on, say, the London Underground, suggests that basic human nature has changed surprisingly little over the years. Chaucer's characters are very recognisable in their personality traits, even if the society in which they portray these features and in which they live is vastly different from our own. There is no substitute for going and reading a book on the form and nature of medieval society. The basic facts about Chaucer's England are that it had a far smaller population in the Middle Ages (under five million as distinct from over fifty million), and was dominated by the King, the Court, the great noble families, and the Roman Catholic Church.

Chaucer was the son of a prosperous businessman who became a member of the King's Court. Thus he was not a professional author. What he actually was is much more difficult to define in modern terms. The lowest classes in medieval society, and by far the most numerous, were non-landowning agricultural workers. In modern terms they lived static lives of appalling poverty and degradation. As if to compensate, the ruling elite, of which Chaucer was a member and which formed a tiny percentage of the population, was immensely sophisticated and had a wide range of skills and abilities. This elite was dominated by those born into the noble classes, but wealth and the ownership of land could provide a place in it for the sons of wealthy upper-middle-class parents such as Chaucer's.

Chaucer's life was typical of his class. He was a courtier, well-versed in the tremendously complex etiquette and manners of court life. He was a soldier, being captured at one time by the French and ransomed by the King for £16.00, and a diplomat. He was a Civil Servant, holding a post such as Controller of Customs in London. He was familiar with European languages, literature, and culture, and had an excellent knowledge of literature, the law, the 'science' of the day, and medicine. His poetry was written for his own personal pleasure and for that of a group of friends and courtiers, with no thoughts of publication, which in any event was hardly technically possible. Writing and literature were merely an accepted hobby and accomplishment for someone operating at Chaucer's level in society.

## Basic examination questions on Chaucer

### Teller and tale

Each one of *The Canterbury Tales* is not just a story, but a story told by a very specific individual. More often than not each Tale tells us as much about the person relating it as it does about itself. There are effectively three layers in each Tale. There is the story itself. Then there is the teller. The teller chooses the story and the way it is told, and in so doing can tell us a great deal about him or herself, sometimes willingly, but sometimes without realising what they are revealing. There is even a possible third layer, with Chaucer himself manipulating the relationship between teller and Tale to make a point about the character. Both the characterisation and the story can be enhanced by this interplay of relationships, which gives Chaucer endless opportunities for irony, dealt with in detail below, where the surface or superficial meaning of what is said is very different from the real meaning.

Sometimes the Tale appears merely to reflect the character of the Teller as it has been established in *The General Prologue*. The Knight is 'a verray parfit, gentil Knyghte', and tells a noble, chivalric tale which reflects and exemplifies the values he stands for and believes in. The Squire is young, hugely enthusiastic, and in a rather attractive way is in love with both chivalry and himself. He tells a rather silly and overdone Tale of chivalry that is so bad that it has to be stopped before it is finished. On another level, the Franklin is a very rich landowner, but not technically a noble or member of the ruling class. By the time his Tale comes round, the pilgrims have had enough of stories about nobility, chivalry, and gentlemanly behaviour, so the Franklin lulls them into a false sense of security by appearing to start a Tale about love and marriage. What he actually wants to talk about is nobility, and his Tale subtly changes emphasis as it progresses to become a Tale about how common people (indirectly, the Franklin and his son) can be as noble and 'gentil' as true-born nobility.

The Franklin at least knows what he is doing. Other characters tell stories that reveal rather more about themselves than they might imagine or wish. The Miller tells a Tale that is verging on the obscene (Chaucer, who invented the whole lot of them, has great fun telling the audience that he is very sorry if the Miller offends people, but it is not his fault, because he can only write down honestly and accurately what is said), but his Tale is very funny and strangely harmless and inoffensive. The Miller is a shrewd buffoon, and his Tale mirrors that exactly. The Merchant, on the other hand, tells a Tale that is utterly foul, and which leaves a very bad taste in the mouth. Its foulness is a comment on his own foulness as a human being, though he does not realise it or see it as such. The Pardoner tells a Tale that is a rip-roaring condemnation of greed and the lust for money; what he apparently fails to realise is that he is as much a sinner in this respect as are the characters in his Tale. The fact may be lost on him, but it is not lost on the audience.

Examiners expect candidates to be aware of the complex interrelationships between Teller, Tale, and Chaucer, to show how they work, and to realise that the end result is not just a good story, but a marvellously detailed and vigorous character sketch as well, full of irony, insight, and humour.

## Irony and satire

The apparent simplicity of *The Canterbury Tales* is misleading. There is a rich and varied use of irony in his work. Irony is very economical, as one line or phrase can contain several meanings, and it is usually funny. Irony is often linked with innuendo and satire in Chaucer, satire being the exposure to laughter of vice or stupidity, thereby reducing it to size and diminishing its effect and importance. Chaucer's irony is very varied. There is the slapstick and highly obvious irony of his pretending to have no responsibility for the content of *The Miller's Tale*, or the cruel and tragic irony of *The Knight's Tale* that allows Arcite to triumph in the battle but die an accidental death just before he can claim Emily, his prize. There is the gentle irony that accompanies the description of the Nun, who has taken holy vows of poverty, chastity, and obedience, but who sports a brooch saying 'Love conquers all', and who is far more vain and worldly than she should be. Chaucer's irony here is gentle, because though the Nun is weak and fallible, she is harmless and her behaviour hardly damages anyone other than herself. With other characters Chaucer's irony can be savage, as is the case in *The General Prologue* with the Friar. This man, a wandering monk charged with the care of men's immortal souls, not only is personally corrupt, but also threatens the souls of other people. 'And pleasaunt was his absolucioun,/He was an esy man to yeve penaunce' writes Chaucer, apparently praising the Friar. What is actually meant is that the Friar forgives people their sins without demanding true repentance from them, possibly in exchange for money or favours. The person confessing thinks his sins have been forgiven, but unless he has truly repented this is not so, and so that person is still carrying sin that could condemn him to an eternity in Hell. There is damning irony in the final line of the Merchant's description – 'But, sooth to seyn, I noot how men hym calle' (But to tell you the truth I don't know what his name was); in other words, the Merchant is so despicable that Chaucer will not even acknowledge he has a name.

It is usually a feature of Chaucer's style that the more pure and virtuous a character, the less irony there is in his description. The Knight and the Parson are described in straightforward, glowing terms. (It is worth noting that some modern critics challenge this traditional moral judgement.) As a footnote, the more admirable the character, the less physical description Chaucer tends to give him or her. Details of face, body, and clothing abound when the character is vicious, evil, or morally deficient, but good characters such as the Knight, the Parson, and the Ploughman are described almost exclusively in terms of their deeds and their thoughts.

## The 'marriage' group of tales

Some years ago a theory was produced that certain of *The Canterbury Tales* were written to be read in sequence as a deliberate treatment of the theme of marriage. This idea is dealt with fully in the specimen answer later in this chapter, as an example of the traditional type of question that has dominated examinations for many years.

## Chivalry and courtly love

Courtly love is a phrase invented in the nineteenth century to describe a style and mode of writing that originated in eleventh-century France, and which was still going strong when Chaucer wrote *Troilus and Criseyde* and *The Knight's Tale*. Courtly-love stories are about high-born men and women falling in love. In medieval times marriage was often a business or financial arrangement, rather than a matter of love. A courtly-love affair is almost always adulterous, outside of marriage. Love is seen as something noble and almost divine. The male lover adores his mistress even though she is the wife of another man. He places himself completely at her mercy, thus reversing the social convention of the Middle Ages whereby the male was dominant. He venerates and idealises her, suffers, pines, and falls ill for her, devotes himself to the high ideals of chivalry for her sake, and will sacrifice everything, including his life, to preserve her honour.

It is debatable how much of this was true-to-life, and how much a romanticised, 'literary' view of life. In its pure form courtly love provides an experience rather similar to that of a precious stained-glass window – artificial, idealised, fragile, yet strangely moving and beautiful. Courtly love comes into *The Canterbury Tales* in a number of ways. *The Knight's Tale* is a fine example of conventional courtly love, with the one exception that Emily, loved by both the knights Palamon and Arcite, is not married when they fall in love with her. One rung down the ladder comes *The Franklin's Tale*. This story has many of the conventions of courtly love, but pure courtly love is exclusively an upper-class or noble preserve, and the Franklin keeps injecting middle-class attitudes into the story. Thus the lovers, Arveragus and Dorigen, are in love as courtly lovers, but are also married. This is almost an impossible compromise, because in medieval marriage the man is in complete charge, whilst in courtly love the situation is reversed. This leads to the rather ludicrous, but amusing, situation whereby the man and woman agree that she will have power inside the house, but he will have it outside. This is not a matter of honour, rather a middle-class concern with appearances and with the husband's not being shamed. When Dorigen gets into real trouble all pretence of her being in charge vanishes, and she gives her husband complete control over her destiny. *The Franklin's Tale* could thus be said to be written in a diluted form of the courtly-love mode. Another rung down, if not several, is *The Merchant's Tale*. This tale has all the ingredients of the courtly-love story – a husband, a wife, and a young courtier who loves the wife to distraction – and some of the action; but in the hands of the Merchant this pure and idealised form of love story is made filthy, and the conventions of courtly love are seen as merely a way of dressing up brutal lust and physical desire. There is nothing noble or edifying in either the husband's love for his wife, or the courtier's love for her; in both cases it is simply lust and straightforward carnal desire that prompts them and the wife, made all the worse by the husband being a wizened old man who marries a young girl purely to ensure a continuation of his sexual satisfaction. Here Chaucer is using the courtly-love convention to illustrate the seediness of human nature, and of the Merchant himself. A man without nobility cannot hope to see anything in love that is noble.

Chivalry and courtly love go hand in hand. Chivalry was the code of conduct that was meant to govern the life and behaviour of knights and noble people. It emphasised total devotion to God and one's temporal lord, purity of the soul, and the use of strength only in support of the weak and helpless. A knight's 'trouthe' and honour were vastly more important than his life. A knight was, of course, also an excellent fighter and militarily skilful, but never ostentatious or a braggart. Chaucer's Knight is usually seen as the symbol of all that was best in chivalry and knighthood. As with courtly love, Chaucer can present chivalry at its face value, as in *The Knight's Tale*, or poke fun at it, as in *The Wife of Bath's Tale.*

## The Church

No fewer than nine of *The Canterbury Tales* are told by people who have a significant connection with the Church. The Parson, The Second Nun, The Nun's Priest, The Monk, The Prioress, The Pardoner, The Clerk (who would be in training for holy orders), The Summoner, and The Friar. Examiners rarely ask questions specifically about the Church, but it is essential to know what the role of each character is within the Church if that character is to be judged and seen accurately. Essentially the Parson, a simply country curate or vicar, is the most saintly of the clerics on the pilgrimage, and the most admirable. We are told little about the Second Nun and the Nun's Priest. The Monk is venal and corrupt, but not disastrously so. The Prioress is the highest-ranking cleric on the pilgrimage, and is rather too much the young courtly woman and rather too little the nun. The Clerk is sincere and harmless, and the Summoner, the Pardoner, and the Friar are all evil and rotten personalities, using religion for purely selfish and corrupt ends. Chaucer is careful never to deny the basic doctrine of the Church, or belief in God, but he is ready to criticise people who do not live up to its high ideals or who bring it into disrepute.

## General points

Examiners sometimes favour questions about Chaucer's skill at describing places and settings, his ability to draw vivid character portraits by means of external detail and irony, and the way in which figures who are conventional types are given individuality and freshness in their portraits. His narrative skills are also significant, and *The Canterbury Tales* are after all first and foremost a magnificent collection of stories, with another story to link them all together. In the area of narrative technique it is worth noting the variety of styles that Chaucer can muster, and the manner in which many of the stories are designed with reading aloud in mind. Plot and character details are introduced carefully and in sequence, dialogue (which can be 'acted out') is a major technique, and a listener who cannot flip back through the pages to see who is who, and what happened when, is always given necessary information in a simple and digestible form. The links between the Tales are also worth studying, and display all the same skills that are found in the stories themselves. The breadth of Chaucer's knowledge in astronomy and astrology, medicine, the law, chivalry, the art of rhetoric, and all the other skills of the medieval courtier are rarely the subject of a full essay, but are relevant to some other questions, and crop up continually in context questions. The question of how much we sympathise with the characters may also be set on occasions, most notably in connection with *The Wife of Bath's Prologue and Tale*.

## Questions, notes and answers

Outline answers to many of the standard Advanced-level questions on Chaucer are in fact contained in the section above. Here I present a full answer to a specific question.

**Question 1**

To what extent is it true to say that there is a specific group of marriage tales in *The Canterbury Tales*?

**Notes**

The question as written above would only be rarely asked, because it covers more than one Tale. However, the answer to the above contains the information needed to answer the more likely question, which is the extent to which marriage can be seen as the theme of any one of the Tales covered below.

**Answer**

*The Canterbury Tales* are incomplete, and have come down to us only in fragmented form. This makes it difficult to decide with any complete certainty if Chaucer intended some of the Tales to be read in sequence. However, there are definite narrative links that join together some of the Tales, and there is no reason why Chaucer should not have intended some of the parts of such a long work to throw light on each other.

The idea of a marriage group centres on four Tales, separated by other Tales, but as far as modern scholarship can judge, following on after each other in sequence. The first of these is *The Wife of Bath's Tale*, and its *Prologue*. The Wife of Bath quickly establishes herself as a merry widow, and announces proudly 'Housbondes at chirche dore I have had fyve'. In her comments on marriage she makes it clear that she considers herself the dominant partner. She is the master, they the slaves,

But sithe I hadde hem holly in myn hond,
And sith they hadde me yeven al hir lond,
What sholde I taken keep hem for to plese,
But it were for my profit and myn ese?

When she makes a mistake and marries for love she becomes locked in almost mortal combat with her fifth husband, Jankyn, until he too submits to her completely. The Wife's Tale has as its theme the fact that what women most desire is 'sovereyntee', or complete domination over their husbands.

The Clerk makes no reference to the Wife of Bath when he starts his Tale, but it is so directly opposed to everything in *The Wife of Bath's Prologue and Tale* that it is tempting to see it as an indirect reply to that Tale, and an attempt to refute it. His Tale tells of 'patient Griselda', a woman whose noble husband decides to test her loyalty and obedience by subjecting her to a wide range of tests and humiliations. Griselda remains loyal and faithful, and the story ends on a triumphant note, with Griselda rewarded and back in her place of honour. She is the opposite of the Wife of Bath, and is a model of wifely servility and obedience who accepts totally her husband's control over herself and her family.

After these totally different viewpoints on marriage *The Merchant's Tale* appears to suggest that there is little to choose between male and female in marriage. Each partner does exactly what they want. January, the husband, may command his wife outwardly, but in private she does precisely what she wants and is willingly seduced by the first young man who attempts to gain her favours. January is disgusting, an old, gloating lecher who has married a young woman purely for sexual gratification, but convinces himself that 'A man may do not synne with his wyf'. May, his wife, is no better, and her nature is summed up when she commits adultery, and gets rid of her lover's letter down the lavatory. Damian, the squire, is no better, and he achieves his ambition when in a pear tree, in front of his master, who is now blind, he 'pullen up the smok, and in he throng'. The Merchant's comment on marriage seems to be that sovereignty, 'dominaunce', and 'maistrie' are irrelevant; the real holder of sovereignty in marriage is selfishness and personal gratification, coupled with lust.

Finally the Franklin smoothes over the debate with his Tale in which a man and a woman strike a happy medium, have genuine love for each other, and do not allow their marriage to overwhelm or conquer basic good manners or the code of honour. Arveragus offers Dorigen complete mastery over him, whilst she in turn promises to be his 'humble trewe wyf'.

It might therefore seem that these four Tales are carefully designed to reveal differing attitudes towards marriage and the status of the partners within it, finishing with a true and balanced compromise. Yet this can also be seen as a gross misreading of the text. *The Wife of Bath's Prologue and Tale* certainly talks about marriage, which is the Wife's hobby, pastime and business, but the fact that her *Prologue* is both about herself and much longer than the actual Tale suggests that her section in the book is much more about herself than about marriage. The Wife of Bath is a remarkable woman, a towering individual, and a fascinating study of sentimentality coupled with brute strength.

Similarly, *The Clerk's Tale* can be seen as a story about suffering, endurance, and humility. The Clerk himself says:

> This storie is seyd, nat for that wyves sholde
> Folwen Grisilde as in humylitee,
> For it were inportable, though they wolde;
> But for that every wight, in his degree,
> Sholde be constant in adversitee

This translates as 'The point of this story is not to impress upon wives that they should be as humble and forgiving as Griselda. That is impossible, even if they wished to be so. Rather it is told so that everyone, regardless of their place and station in society, should learn to endure suffering and bad fortune.' In other words, this story is not about marriage, but how to cope with bad fortune and suffering, the answer being to endure and suffer with patience and without complaint. The Tale is therefore about fortitude, courage, and stoic endurance, not about marriage.

In a sense *The Merchant's Tale* is not about marriage either, but about a sour and corrupt man's vision of the world. The Merchant has no love in him, so he can see none in others. He lives and works without morality and purely for his own gratification, and so he tells a story in which others do the same. *The Merchant's Tale* is a comment on his own sickness of mind and diseased outlook, a warning that those who are sordid and corrupt lose the eyes with which to see the world in any other light.

Equally, *The Franklin's Tale* is based on a marriage and a triangle of lovers, but partly this is a ruse to fool the pilgrims who have had enough talk about nobility. The real point of the Tale is the question at the end – 'Which was the moste fre . . . ?'. It is a tale about nobility of mind and action, and sets out to prove that nobility is not the sole preserve of those born into the upper or chivalric classes. The magician who frees Aurelius of his bond is a mere scholar, but as he says:

> But if a clerk koude doon a gentil dede
> As well as any of yow, it is no drede!

Marriage is hardly the point in *The Franklin's Tale*; nobility is its main theme. Undoubtedly many of *The Canterbury Tales* comment on marriage but at best the four Tales in question have this as a subsidiary and minor theme. Each has its own concern, more linked to the character of the Teller than to any grandiose scheme of summing up marriage and the issue of sovereignty in it.

**Question 2**

What are the main techniques by which Chaucer describes and evokes atmosphere in the following passage?

Why sholde I noght as wel eek telle yow al
The portreiture that was upon the wal
Withinne the temple of myghty Mars the rede?
Al peynted was the wal, in lengthe and brede,
Lyk to the estres of the grisly place
That highte the grete temple of Mars in Trace,
In thilke colde, frosty regioun
Ther as Mars hath his sovereyn mansioun.
First on the wal was peynted a forest,
In which ther dwelleth neither man ne best,
With knotty, knarry, bareyne trees olde
Of stubbes sharpe and hidouse to biholde.
In which ther ran a rumbel in a swough,
As though a storm sholde bresten every bough.
And dounward from an hille, under a bente,
Ther stood the temple of Mars armypotente,
Wroght al of burned steel, of which the entree
Was long and streit, and gastly for to see.
And therout came a rage and swich a veze
That is made al the gate for to rese.
The northren lyght in at the dores shoon,
For wyndowe on the wal ne was ther noon,
Thurgh which men myghten any light discerne.
The dore was al of adamant eterne,
Yclenched overthwart and endelong
With iren tough; and for to make it strong
Every pyler, the temple to sustene,

Why should I not as well also tell you all
Of the paintings that were upon the walls
Inside the temple of mighty Mars the Red?
The walls were covered in paintings, in length and breadth
Similar in style to the interior of the terrible place
That is known as the great temple of Mars, in Thrace.
It is in that cold and frosty area
That the home of Mars is to be found.
First on the wall was painted a forest
In which neither man nor beast lived.
It had knotted, gnarled, and bare ancient trees
With sharp stumps that were hideous to look at,
Through which there ran a rumbling and a sighing
As if a storm were about to smash every bough.
At the foot of a grassy slope
Stood the Temple of Mars, mighty in arms,
Built out of burnished steel, of which the entrance
Was long and narrow, horrible to behold.
Out of this came such a raging blast
That it made all the gate shake.
The northern light shone in at the doors,
Because there were no windows on the walls
Through which anyone might see some light.
The door was made of eternal adamant,
Riveted across and along
With hard iron; to make it strong,
Every pillar which held the temple up

| | |
|---|---|
| Was tonne-greet, of iren bright and shene. | Was as big as a barrel, and made of shining bright iron. |
| Ther saugh I first the derke ymaginyng | There I saw first the dark mind and imagination |
| Of Felonye, and al the compassyng; | Of criminality, and every detail of its execution; |
| The crueel Ire, reed as any gleede; | Cruel Wrath, red as any ember from the fire; |
| The pykepurs, and eek the pale Drede; | The pickpocket, and also pale Fear; |
| The smylere with the knyf under the cloke; | The smiling man with the knife hidden beneath his cloak; |
| The shepne brennynge with the blake smoke; | Ships burning with black smoke; |
| The tresoun of the mordrynge in the bedde; | Treason, with someone murdered in their bed; |
| The open werre, with woundes al bibledde; | Open warfare, with wounds all covered in blood; |
| Contek, with blody knyf and sharp manace. | Strife, with bloodstained knife and sharp threat. |
| Al ful of chirkyng was that sory place. | All full of grating noises was that dismal place. |
| The sleere of hymself yet saugh I there,– | I saw the suicide victim there,– |
| His herte-blood hath bathed al his heer; | Blood from his heart smearing his hair; |
| The nayl ydryven in the shode a-nyght; | The nail driven into a person's temple at night; |
| The colde deeth, with mouth gapyng upright. | Cold death, lying on his back with gaping mouth. |

**Answer**

Chaucer makes strong use of sight, sound, and touch imagery. The images used of the temple of Mars are often metallic – 'burned steel', 'iren tough', 'iren bright and shene'. On their own these suggest the spirit of war, cold, hard, unyielding, strong, and inhuman. Images of cold, frost, raging winds, grating noises, and a lifeless forest all augment and confirm this impression of a lifeless, freezing desert. However, the strongest and most effective invention in the passage is the device of having paintings on the wall. These allow Chaucer to extend his description into every sphere of life and nature. There is a risk that Chaucer's emphasis on the absence of light in the temple could make the reader question the vivid and detailed way in which the paintings are perceived. The risk is lessened by Chaucer deliberately not stating whether the lightless and windowless temple is the one in which the paintings are situated, or the one depicted in the paintings. Even without this the sheer power of the description is sufficient to overwhelm any doubts, and the absence of light (often a symbol of hope) suggests with full force the terror and evil of the place.

The paintings themselves are a catalogue of human violence and horror, made all the more horrific by the door 'Yclenched overthwart and endelong' which suggests that the viewer is locked in, prison-like, with this terror, with no chance of escape, just as humans are imprisoned by war. Colour is brought into the descriptions, all the more startling because of the absence of light and the darkness mentioned earlier. The colour is the angry red of fire, or the scarlet of blood. 'Pale Drede', 'blake smoke', and 'colde deeth' repeat and emphasise the imagery of the earlier lines, but this time associate them with real human beings and life on Earth. The first section ignores life and humanity, suggesting the sterility and destruction that Mars brings. The second section uses specific and vivid imagery to emphasise the effect of war on man – bloody wounds, the cold, gaping corpse, and the man with the nail driven through his forehead. In one sense Chaucer cheats. This is the temple of Mars, God of War, and pickpockets, thieves, traitors, and suicides are not solely aspects of war. In another sense this extension of the imagery is a triumph. It allows Chaucer to present an expanded impression of Mars as not just god of war, but also god of all that is destructive, terrifying and violent in man. Chaucer's Mars becomes the god of all violence and sterility in human nature.

Chaucer's basic technique is to choose a small number of key motifs – cold, darkness, sterility, tearing noise, blood, violence, and the colour red, and then to pile image after image of these onto the reader with relentless force. The result is an impression of something inevitable, unstoppable, and immensely violent and destructive. A simple technique is to show every human being in the passage as malevolent, agonised, or dead. Taken in conjunction with the lightless gloom of the temple this produces a stifling sense of asphyxiation and terror. Chaucer also personifies 'Felonye', 'Ire', 'Drede' and 'Contek'. His skill is shown in the way that he appears to be describing the paintings (a notoriously difficult thing to do in words) but is actually describing their effect. The reader provides much of the detail of the pictures from his own imagination, with Chaucer merely fuelling these.

Rhythm is also significant in the passage, with a relentless five stresses to a line driving the extract on like a stark drum-beat. The images are remarkable for their clarity, and for the fact that they are accessible to anyone even if they have no experience of war; hardly anyone can be unfamiliar with the type of person described as 'The smylere with the knyf under the cloke'. The images are driven home remorselessly, but each one is given almost always a line to itself, so that the reader has time to take each one in before passing on to the next. There is absolutely nothing in the passage which tells of life, hope, or softness, and the clarity, economy, and acute observation of the imagery has nothing to lessen its impact. It is descriptive language that combines simplicity with total effectiveness.

**Question 3**

What advantages have new theories of criticism brought to our understanding of *The Canterbury Tales*?

**Answer**

For many years it seemed that new theories had little to contribute to our understanding of the man who is often the oldest writer represented on any syllabus. Geoffrey Chaucer, viewed backwards from the twenty-first century, might seem to have lived in an age of utter certainty. Absolute power was vested in the twin pillars of monarchy and Church. Christian belief was universal, and orthodoxy was enshrined not just in the law, but in the whole fabric of social belief. A student seeking to understand and write about Chaucer's work needed detailed knowledge of his language, and detailed knowledge of the very specific society in which he lived, worked and wrote.

This belief has been challenged by the growth of new theories of criticism, such as feminist theory, Marxist theory, structuralism and deconstruction. Outwardly these might seem not to apply to Chaucer's work. Feminism, it could be argued, has little relevance in a society where the woman had no rights as an individual, and her secondary status to man was deemed a matter of religion and law, not just a matter of opinion. Marxism, the political theory born out of concern for the masses, seems also to have little relevance to a society where there was no industry, no seething mass of the proletariat and hardly any concept of equality or egalitarianism. Structuralism is immersed in language and seeks to understand how works come to have the meaning and effects that they do. Chaucer's work is based in effect on an earlier version of English, and can appear to have meanings and effect that are so relatively simple as to deny the complexities of structuralism. Poststructuralism and Deconstruction emphasise disenchantment, hardly relevant to an age where every person had the right to salvation and a place in Heaven, and Deconstruction's questioning of any lasting certainties seems at odds with an age which such outward certainty in so many areas of human experience.

Yet modern critical theory could be said to have put new energy and life into Chaucerian studies, and produced numerous new insights. Structuralist and Poststructuralist theory see everything as human, and thereby flawed. From this vantage point it can be argued that the disenchantment of much of *The Canterbury Tales* can be seen far more clearly than otherwise might be the case, and Chaucer be seen as someone in opposition to many of the outward standards of his day. For example, the clear corruption of so many of the pilgrims who work in and for the Church can be seen as a symbol of an institution that is permanently deconstructing itself. Chaucer frequently denies responsibility for what is written in *The Canterbury Tales*, as is the case with the content and style of the scurrilous *The Miller's Tale*, or with the ranking of the pilgrims,

Also I prey yow to foryeve me,
Al have I nat set folk in hir degree,
Here in this tale, as that they sholde stonde.

Modern critical theory has pointed out that such denials of responsibility can be seen as a subversive criticism of what is being written about, undermining the apparent adherence to conventional values. It is as if Chaucer is saying, 'This is what I have to write – but I don't have to like it'. Structuralist emphasis on linguistics and how effects are created is also ideally suited for examination of the immense complexity and multi-layered irony that Chaucer brings to the mechanism by which a story is told. This is particularly true in analysis of the relationship between teller and Tale in *The Canterbury Tales*.

There may have been no industrial proletariat in Chaucer's time, but the exploitation for economic advantage of the majority by a tiny minority was around long before the Industrial Revolution. The Knight appears as the symbol of chivalry in *The Canterbury Tales*, 'a verray parfit, gentil Knyghte', yet the Marxist critic might just as easily see him as the exploiter of those over whom he rules. Does Chaucer see him as such? He allows the Knight to be given pride of place in the pilgrimage, and awarded the first story – and then allows his authority to be challenged by the hugely proletarian Miller, whose bawdy tale is directly at odds with every value the Knight has espoused. Perhaps in this clash of wills Chaucer is making a far wider point about the conflict in medieval society. Marxist criticism also makes it easier to examine the campaigns the Knight is listed as having been on, to see if they are indeed 'crusades' or mere mercenary expeditions.

Feminist criticism can give a radical new perspective on many of *The Canterbury Tales*. From such a perspective Alison in *The Miller's Tale* can appear not so much as a young adulterous female, but rather as a young person finally able to claim their right to enjoyment and fulfilment because Nicholas uses male, patriarchal authority systems such as the Bible against themselves to fool the husband. Griselda in *The Clerk's Tale*, far from being the perfect wife, can appear as someone whose ability to suffer and remain loyal in fact challenges the men who seek to control her more than it comforts or reassures them. The Wife of Bath can similarly be seen as a challenge to male domination and a challenge to male concepts of femininity, and particularly those contained in *The Knight's Tale*. In this tale the heroine, Emily, is divorced from sexuality, and a battle fought, won and lost for the lust of two young men for one woman. Its protagonists are described as if they did not exist from the waist down. Feminist criticism can throw startling new light on to jaded concepts of sexuality and gender in many of *The Canterbury Tales*.

Yet new critical theories are not the whole answer to our understanding of Chaucer's work, even though they are certainly a part answer. The danger with all theories of criticism is that they impose a meaning on a text, rather than reveal it. The disenchantment of a Deconstructionalist vision is in part itself a reaction of an age that has seen Hiroshima and Dachau, and to perceive too much disenchantment in Chaucer is also to deny the huge energy and simple optimism of the description of Emily in *The Knight's Tale* – 'Up roos the sonne, and up roos Emelye', in modern English, 'Up rose the sun, and up rose Emily'. Alison in *The Miller's Tale* may claim her rights after a male-dominated society has forced her into an obscene marriage with an aged lecher. Yet her cry of triumph after she has fooled Absolon – 'Teehee!, quod she, and clapte the window to', is as much about one human being in comic triumph over another as it is about a woman in triumph over a man. The complexities of teller and tale relationships can be explained without reference to 'signifier' and 'signified', even if these latter can help understanding. Perhaps the story of Griselda is so awful to modern taste that we have to impose an alternative, feminist meaning on to it if the alternative is to consider that Chaucer supported its apparent moral.

Perhaps it is The Wife of Bath who shows us most clearly the usefulness of modern critical theory to an understanding of *The Canterbury Tales*. Thirty years ago there might have been little challenge to the vision of the Wife as a blood-sucking variation of the music hall mother-in-law, albeit one possessed of considerable humour, a terrifying energy and almost elemental strength. Thirty years on we can still see her as this, and also as someone in touch with her sensuality, or as someone who is 'an unstable projection of male fear and desire'. New critical theory cannot tell us what to think. It can, and has, opened our eyes to many more things that we might consider in our judgement of Chaucer. Its advantage has been to bring a great widening of vision to Chaucerian studies.

## Further reading


- David Aers, *Chaucer* (Harvester, 1986)
- Valerie Alicen and Ares Axiotis, ed., *Chaucer* (New Casebooks Series, Macmillan, 1997)
- Valerie Allen, ed., *Chaucer* (New Casebook Series, Macmillan, 1997): excellent collection of critical essays.
- Gail Ashton, *Chaucer. The Canterbury Tales* (Macmillan, 1998)

- Peter G. Beidler, ed., *The Wife of Bath's Prologue and Tale* (Case Studies in Contemporary Criticism, Macmillan, 1996): a series designed to show how new critical theories have changed or challenged existing perceptions of authors.
- Lillian M. Bisson, *A Chaucer Resource Book. The Poet and the Late Medieval World* (Macmillan, 1997): a historical companion to *The Canterbury Tales*.
- Piero Boitani and Jill Mann, ed., *The Cambridge Chaucer Companion* (Cambridge University Press, 1986)
- Derek Brewer, *A New Introduction to Chaucer* (Longman, 1998)
- Helen Cooper, *The Canterbury Tales* (Oxford Guides to Chaucer Series, Oxford University Press, 1996)
- W. A. Davenport, *Chaucer and his English Contemporaries* (Macmillan, 1998)
- Steve Ellis, ed., *Chaucer, The Canterbury Tales* (Longman, 1998)
- S. Hussey, *Chaucer: An Introduction* (Methuen, 1981)
- Terry Jones, *Chaucer's Knight. A Portrait of a Medieval Mercenary* (Methuen, 1994): a highly controversial but extremely interesting work, suggesting that the Knight is simply a mercenary, and not the symbol of chivalry he is usually shown as.
- Derek Pearsall, *The Canterbury Tales* (Routledge, 1994)
- S. H. Rigby, *Chaucer in Context* (Manchester University Press, 1996)
- Beryl Rowland, ed., *Companion to Chaucer Studies* (Oxford University Press, 1979)
- Brian Stone, *Chaucer* (Penguin, 1987)

For comparative purposes the student might also like to read *Sir Gawain and the Green Knight* in 'translation' into modern English, and *Piers Plowman*; both are available in various modern editions. Good critical background is James Simpson, *Piers Plowman* (Longman, 1990).

CHAPTER EIGHT

# Elizabethan and Jacobean drama

## The literary and historical background

No one has ever really explained why the thirty years from 1580 to 1610 saw one of the greatest flowerings that has ever taken place in English literary history, and probably in the history of world literature. Shakespeare, dealt with in the following chapter, was only part of this literary and dramatic boom, and perhaps not even the most highly thought-of by the age in which he lived. As with any intense flowering of literature, the reasons are historical, political, social, and economic, as well as literary. It is tempting to see a link between great outbursts of creativity in literature and social upheaval. English society in the Jacobean period had to come to terms with the Renaissance (the end of medieval thinking in Europe), the end of Queen Elizabeth I's reign and the accession of a Scottish King (James VI of Scotland) to the throne of England, as James I, as well as the aftermath of its own battle with the Roman Catholic Church.

As far as the Elizabethan and Jacobean period goes the flowering in the theatre was brought to an abrupt end by the English Civil War in 1642, when theatres were closed. They remained closed until 1660 and the restoration of the monarchy under Charles II. However, signs of decadence in the theatre had been visible much earlier than 1642, possibly even as early as 1615; certainly from the mid-1620s drama seemed to have little new to offer.

### The Theatre

The Elizabethan and Jacobean theatre was the first fully professional theatre in England, in the sense of professional actors performing in purpose-built theatres. There certainly had been acting before, with a religious and a secular input from the medieval mystery, morality, and miracle plays, and wandering troupes of performers putting on acts with no religious content. A favourite place for performing any travelling theatre or entertainment was the yard of an inn. These were often built on three sides of a square, the fourth being open for access by horses and wagons. The inn was a natural meeting point for the locality, could offer accommodation for the players, entertainment for guests, and presumably an increased profit for the innkeeper. By mounting a portable stage at the far end of the inn yard, more expensive seats could be sold for the galleries and rooms that overlooked the yard, whilst cheaper viewing positions could be offered on the floor of the yard itself, at ground level.

The first public theatre, called logically enough The Theatre, was opened near the site of Liverpool Street Station in London in 1576. It seems that the designers based their plan to quite a large extent on the lay-out of the medieval inn. As far as we know the acting area jutted out into an uncovered 'pit' or flat floor area, where cheap seating, probably on stools or perhaps standing only, was offered. There were galleries and rooms, roofed over, on three sides, where more expensive covered seating was available. The acting area probably had a trap door, a curtained recess at the back of the stage, and a back wall with galleries or balconies on it. This allowed for devils to rise up from hell (the trapdoor), witches' dens or private rooms in the curtained alcove, and the balcony or gallery to stand for the battlements of a castle, or an upstairs room. A canopy jutting out over the acting area gave some protection to the actors. The discovery of the site of various Elizabethan theatres has provided new insight into the design of Elizabethan theatres, and the reconstruction of The Globe Theatre in London is a best-guess as to how the theatre in Shakespeare's times looked and worked.

Productions took place in the afternoon, in daylight, and there was little or no artificial light for performances. Fairly complex sound effects were available, luxurious costumes and music, but little in the way of sets or painted backcloths seems to have been used. There were also an increasing number of private theatres built in the period, which were indoors and allowed for rather more complex staging effects, and of necessity had to use crude artificial lighting. One result of the lack of scenic effects in the public theatre is that a sense of location is conveyed by words and costume. In Shakespeare's case, the move to the indoor theatre at Blackfriars relatively late in his writing career creates significant changes in the plays he writes for this theatre, including clear division into five acts for the first time. The breaks were needed to change the candles that were then the only lighting for an indoor theatre.

The actors were formed in companies, under the nominal patronage of a great lord, with probably fifteen or more 'sharers', or people with a right to share in the profits of the company. Those profits came directly from the sale of seats or tickets. There was fierce rivalry between the companies, and with a fairly small audience available in London there was also a huge demand for new plays to perform; one company, the Admiral's Men, performed eleven different plays in twenty-three days. With new material in such demand a script would never be published until such time as 'pirate' or unofficial copies were in wide circulation. The original scripts would be zealously guarded, but the words of a play could be taken down in shorthand from a performance, or an actor or actors bribed to dictate their lines to a rival. Publication of plays, when it came at all, seems to have been an afterthought, and there were no copyright laws to protect authors. Publishers did not return manuscripts to the authors, so we have hardly any surviving manuscripts of Elizabethan or Jacobean plays. There is evidence that a large number of plays were collaborative, that is written by two or more authors. One of the few surviving manuscripts from the time is that of *Sir Thomas More*, a multi-authored history play one page of which is probably in Shakespeare's handwriting. He was called in to 'make over' an unsatisfactory scene that in its original form had caused trouble with the censors, and the idea of bussing in another author to make good bits and pieces of an existing play seems to have been commonplace. All female parts were played by boys, though these boys appear to have been highly trained and thoroughly convincing. The effect of this restriction can be seen in Shakespeare's plays, where physical contact between male and 'female' is limited, and huge ironies can be created by a boy acting a woman dressing up in 'disguise' as a man. There was no director in the modern sense of the person responsible for the artistic content and the interpretation of a play, but plays were frequently written round the capabilities of individual actors. The clown or fool parts written by Shakespeare change dramatically when a more melancholic and intelligent character, Robert Armin, came into his company, as distinct from the coarse and bawdy clown parts that had been written for the previous actor. Certain plays appear to have been written for performance to specific audiences, but in general Elizabethan and Jacobean plays might be performed in front of poor apprentices and nobility, a fact which required them to have a wide range of emotion and humour to copy with audiences of all types.

## Plot

A large number of Elizabethan and Jacobean plays were based on famous stories from the past; very few had entirely original plots, partly because the age considered that anything that had not been said before over two thousand years of human civilisation might well not be central enough to be worth saying. It is always worth remembering that originality was perceived more as a weakness than a virtue in these times.

## Seneca

The classical author Seneca (c. 4 BC–AD 65) exerted a significant influence on Elizabethan and Jacobean drama. His tragedies were widely known and read. They were full of bloody and horrific events, often with a theme of revenge and with ghosts and other strange events peppering the action. The gore, the ghosts, the violence, and the gloom caught the Elizabethan imagination, but whilst his plays were more pessimistic than at least some works by earlier Greek authors, they did have positive points. In Seneca's world of cruelty, suffering, and misery the capacity to endure suffering becomes an essential element in the survival of humanity. Indeed endurance was seen as perhaps the only way that humans can retain their dignity and triumph over Fate, Destiny, or gods who seem certain to be cruel, unfair and random in the suffering they inflict. Thus humans can achieve heroic status through this capacity to endure, and retain their mental spirit even as they lose their physical lives.

## Revenge

Seneca undoubtedly helped the popularity of revenge as a theme and subject in Elizabethan and Jacobean drama, but the subject itself had many attractions for the dramatist. It was exciting and violent, but also posed a stimulating moral dilemma. The Christian ethic specifically condemns revenge and makes it a right that only God has – 'Vengeance is mine saith the Lord'. Yet it is very natural for someone who has been wronged to wish to take the law into his own hands, and exact his own vengeance. If he does so he clears his honour and his burning desire for vengeance, but also loses his immortal soul, both through having taken vengeance upon himself and having killed in so doing. The inherent drama and tension of this conflict between moralities made for exciting and stimulating drama. The fact that the subject of revenge is so popular nowadays with thriller writers and film-makers suggests that the earlier dramatists were not far wrong in their assessment of at least one situation that seems to be everlastingly fascinating to ordinary people.

## The Renaissance

The Renaissance is the name given to the 'rebirth of learning' that is visible in Europe from the sixteenth century onwards. Civilisation slipped back dramatically in Europe with the collapse of the Roman Empire, and for many hundreds of years the most that could be hoped for was that one day society would return to the level of civilisation and understanding shown in Greek and Roman days. In the medieval period people saw themselves as clawing slowly back up to the old levels of civilisation, not improving on them. In the sixteenth century a feeling began to develop, after centuries of relative stability in Europe, that new horizons did exist. This meant more than the acquisition of new knowledge; it meant that all issues and institutions were open to question, if only because the spirit of enquiry cannot be restricted to any one specific or 'safe' area. The Reformation and challenge to the Roman Catholic Church was only one manifestation of this desire and willingness to break new ground. It is tempting to see the Renaissance as Europe throwing off the chains of the Dark Ages and reaching out for the sunlight and freedom, a very exciting and stimulating activity. It also needs to be remembered that the slave who gains his freedom also loses his security, and is well and truly on his own, whereas previously he never had to take a decision for himself. Medieval society may have been primitive and cruel, but it was also secure, predictable and known. The Renaissance brought stimulation, excitement and discovery, but also fear, insecurity and uncertainty. Two plays discussed below, Marlowe's *Doctor Faustus* and Shakespeare's *Hamlet*, reveal more than any others the fear and loneliness that come when man tries to stand on his own two feet, defy the old order, or face up to life with nothing but his own resources to lean on. Like most blessings, the Renaissance was mixed. It let man find out much more, and at the same time showed him how much he did not know.

## Machiavelli

Niccolo Machiavelli (1469–1527) was another major influence on Elizabethan and Jacobean drama. He was a civil servant and politician in what was then the independent state of Florence. In 1512 Florence was defeated and Machiavelli was imprisoned, tortured, and eventually exiled. In his exile he wrote *The Prince* (1513) in which he stated that strong government was the only method of securing a happy and stable society, but that people were fundamentally greedy, envious, and ambitious. The effective ruler thus had to be prepared to match people at their own game, and might have to lie, deceive, cheat, and even murder in order to maintain a stable government that would provide the greatest happiness for the greatest number. The good ruler at the same time had to keep up an appearance of being above all evil.

This summary of Machiavelli's views makes them sound a great deal more horrific than they actually were. His philosophy that the end justifies the means has been a major element in a great many governments for very many years, and in some respects is merely practical politics. However, Machiavelli made the mistake of being honest about it, and his views, inevitably enlarged and taken out of context, caused vast shock and horror when they appeared. Elizabethan and Jacobean dramatists seemed gripped by this doctrine of power politics, although their version of it frequently bore little or no resemblance to what Machiavelli said. The cynical, totally unscrupulous villain in so many plays of the period probably owes his inspiration as much to Machiavelli as to any other agency, though the popularity of such figures is also due in large measure to the fact that regardless of Machiavelli they make very gripping characters in their own right.

## Modern Criticism and Renaissance Drama

A considerable amount of attention has been focused on all Renaissance writing by advocates of the various new schools of criticism. A world of drama set so often in courts and dealing with the exercise of raw power, frequently by a traditional and authoritarian hierarchy that is both decadent and wholly out of sympathy with the needs of common people, has a clear attraction for Marxist criticism, whilst Feminist criticism is also bound to be attracted to plays where women are so often either the apparent cause of corruption (Webster's *The White Devil*) or its clearest victim (Webster's *The Duchess of Malfi*). Psychoanalytic criticism has a field day with figures such as The Duke in *The Duchess of Malfi*, whilst any school of critics interested in language and the linguistic elements of drama can find plenty to interest them in the word-play of Renaissance drama. In Renaissance drama reality (or what is initially perceived as reality) often deconstructs itself to the extent where the only moral or social certainty is uncertainty. No 'centre' of meaning, no moral or social structure that can be guaranteed either validity or existence: such talk is the life-blood of deconstruction. Postcolonial theory might also find a character such as the Jew in Marlowe's *The Jew of Malta* an interesting figure – the outcast or alien in a trading and colonising society. The critic Michel Foucault, probably best defined as a poststructuralist for the technically-minded, writes more interestingly than some on the Renaissance period, pointing out in particular the immense importance of resemblance in the writing of the period – the belief that everything in creation resembled something else, and that nothing stood alone. This is an instinctive conclusion for writers of the time, in Foucault's opinion, so instinctive that it is unconscious and therefore requiring us in our time to approach and dissect these resemblances so that they can be seen objectively for what they are. A cynic might point out that E. M. W. Tillyard had said much the same thing in one sense at least many years earlier in *The Elizabethan World Picture*, but such cynicism should not hide the fact that Foucault is both a valid and interesting writer on the Renaissance period.

## The authors and their plays

### Christopher Marlowe

Marlowe lived from 1564 to 1593. He came from a rumbustious family, was almost certainly a spy in the service of Queen Elizabeth's secret service agency, and may have been involved in black magic. He was killed under highly suspicious circumstances in a room in an inn when on his way to answer a court case. As his murderer was later pardoned, guesses have been made that he was killed on the orders of the government for fear that he would attempt to bribe his way out of trouble by telling all he knew about espionage activities. It has even been suggested that he was not killed at all, and that the whole business of his death was staged to allow him to escape to Europe, from where he then wrote plays using Shakespeare's name. It should be stated that this theory is normally sufficient to bring about severe illness on the part of an examiner.

Marlowe's first plays were *Tamburlaine the Great Part 1* and *2* (1587, 1588). These pioneered the use of blank verse in the theatre of the time, but rarely appear on an Advanced-level syllabus. *Doctor Faustus* is a very different story. It examines the life of the infamous Faustus who was reputed to have sold his soul to the Devil in exchange for some years of having his every desire satisfied. The play symbolises Renaissance man, given an aspiring, ambitious and hugely talented mind by God, but then denied by God the freedom to do with it as he wishes; it shows the conflict between the new faith in man which saw him as limitless in his potential, and the older faith which saw him always subservient to God. The opening sequences when Faustus decides to take up magic, his conversations with Mephistopheles (the spirit given to him by the Devil to assist him in achieving his desires), and the final sequence in which Faustus waits out the night that must end with him being taken into Hell for eternity, are superb. Some of the intervening sections are appalling slapstick comedy of the lowest kind, producing the inevitable response that questions whether all the play was written by Marlowe. The battle between good and evil in Faustus's mind is the central theme of the play, and provides its most gripping moments. Standard issues are the dominance of Faustus as a character in the play, and the relative absence of any other developed characterisation; the techniques by which the battle between good and evil in Faustus's mind are suggested; the extent of the audience's sympathy with Faustus; the contrast between high tragedy and low clowning in the play; the character of Mephistopheles and his dramatic significance; and the power of Marlowe's verse, particularly in the final scene.

*The Jew of Malta* (1590) is in the tradition of Senecan revenge tragedy, and Barabas, the Jew of the play's title, is thoroughly and straightforwardly evil, as are the rest of the play's characters. Issues include the role of humour in the play, and even whether or not it is a farce. The violence and barbarity in many Jacobean plays is so extreme as to be grotesque and even funny, and the question arises of whether it was intended to be so. Perhaps the term 'black comedy' is the most useful one to apply, recognising as it does that laughter can disturb and unsettle an audience, and indeed is perhaps the only sensible response to a world without morality or sanity. Other questions centre on the central character, his dominance in the play, and the extent to which the audience can feel sympathy for him, and on whether or not any moral structure or lesson can be perceived in the play.

*Edward II* (?1592) tells the story of the ill-fated monarch of England, imprisoned by his own barons and eventually murdered. As with all Marlowe's plays the central figure dominates the play, although given the weakness of Edward II it is perhaps hardly surprising that this play lacks the heroic feeling and language of Marlowe's previous plays. Despite this, examining boards usually stick to the same general line of questioning as applies to the other plays, with the occasional extra questions on whether or not the play develops any strong line of political thought.

## Cyril Tourneur

Tourneur (?1575–1626) probably wrote *The Atheist's Tragedy* (1611) and *The Revenger's Tragedy* (1606), and it is the latter upon which his fame rests. The central character of the play is Vindice who, as his name suggests, is the spirit of revenge, and the play itself is almost the archetypal revenge tragedy. The society it depicts is almost wholly corrupt, and where goodness does appear it is either ineffective or unattractive. The revenger becomes as evil as those upon whom he seeks revenge, and the characters are largely one-dimensional, and summed up by names such as Lussurioso, Ambitioso, and Supervacuo. The violence is horrific and frequently farcical, as when the aged and lecherous Duke is tricked into kissing the poison-smeared skull of a woman he once raped, and then has his tongue nailed to the ground while he is forced to witness the love-making of his wife with his bastard son. Despite this, Vindice, the revenger, achieves some magnificent moments of dark and intense lyric poetry, musing bitterly and viciously on corruption and a hopeless world. Again the central character and the comic or farcical elements in the play dominate examination questions. Questions may also involve the morality the play evinces, if any; the nature of the portrayal of good in the play; and the question of whether the play is a pure spectacle of blood-letting and violence, or an attempt at a more serious comment on life.

## John Webster

Webster (?1580–?1634) wrote two of the plays most commonly set for examination purposes, *The White Devil* (?1608) and *The Duchess of Malfi* (?1614).

Many of the themes and issues already mentioned in this chapter recur in *The White Devil.* It has a horrifically corrupt court, and a 'heroine' (Vittoria Corombona) who is 'the white devil' of the title – a character as evil as those she destroys. The themes of revenge and justice dominate the play, and it has a dark, brooding, and claustrophobic atmosphere, with incidents of appalling violence and cruelty. Goodness is rather more of a weakness than a virtue in the play, and natural human relationships outside and inside the family are shown as twisted, perverted and corrupt. A courageous attitude to death is seen as almost the only virtue open to a human being.

The whole morality of the play is a major issue. It is as if Webster were saying that in a world of almost total evil, conventional distinctions between good and evil cease to have any meaning or validity: a new moral code has to be evolved to cope with the reality and all-pervasiveness of evil, and in that morality we should place the virtue of survival at a premium. Thus, though Vittoria Corombona is evil, we can almost come to admire her, because her evil is a courageous and realistic response to the world in which she finds herself.

A favourite with examiners is the idea that Webster wrote individual scenes of brilliant intensity, but was unable to link these effectively into a whole, coherent unit of a play, the alleged result being that the overall effect and impact of a play by Webster is rarely as telling as the impact of the individual scenes and episodes. In one of the strange oddities that sometimes crop up in criticism and in the thinking of examination boards, justice is often implied as the major concern of Webster's plays, and you should be ready to address this issue. *The Duchess of Malfi* differs from *The White Devil* and many other Jacobean plays in that its central couple, the Duchess and her husband, are not evil, but become the victims of evil by marrying against the wishes of the insane Duke, the Duchess's brother. Cruelty, corruption, grotesque violence, madness, and all the hallmarks of Jacobean tragedy are there, but the characterisation in the play is remarkably subtle, the boundaries between good and evil more clearly marked, and many of the characters genuinely fascinating psychological studies. Bosola, the malcontent figure in the play, and the Duke are particularly worthy of note, both for what they are and for the fact that they are frequently involved in questions set by the examiners. Bosola is a far more complex portrayal than many of his kind in Jacobean drama, whilst the Duke is a terrifying study in obsessional madness combined with bizarre sexual overtones, and convincing in spite of his grotesqueness. Thus variety and depth of characterisation are standard examination questions for this play. The Duchess' death scene and the famous echo scene where, by simply repeating a character's words, a menacing and ominous prophecy and commentary on what has happened is made, are highly examinable. As a sidelight on the play, the subtlety of its characterisation and the fact that most of its scenes are set in dimly lit rooms has given rise to suggestions that the play was specifically written for private performance in an indoor theatre.

## Ben Jonson

After the brooding violence and horror of so many Elizabethan and Jacobean plays, the works of Ben Jonson (1572–1637) can come as a refreshing change. Jonson was an extremely skilful writer of masques (see Ch. 3), a man of huge energy and varied talents. At varying times he was a bricklayer, a soldier and an actor, and also managed to walk from London to Edinburgh, and spent various spells in prison. He and Marlowe are the authors closest in stature to Shakespeare from this period. His tragedies did not succeed nearly as well as his comedies, and of these latter *The Alchemist* (1610) and *Volpone* (1606) are the most commonly set, with *Bartholomew Fair* (1614) and *Every Man in His Humour* (1598) also examined with some frequency. Although his plays are all obviously different, examination questions on Jonson do have a certain uniformity to them, and most can be applied to almost all the plays.

### Satire

Satire is a major element in all Jonson's plays. As someone who took classical models very seriously, his satire has the plain purpose of exposing human vice and folly to ridicule, and thus correcting it. It is actually said (though not always reliably) that *The Alchemist* did focus public attention on the number of villains preying on the gullible in London (alchemy was a mock science devoted to refining the 'philosopher's stone' that could turn all it touched into gold), and thereby helped reduce them. Jonson's satire can be vicious and biting, but it is also driven home by a tremendous zest, energy for life, and sense of humour. Jonson never makes the mistake of some satirists whereby the vices under scrutiny are treated so seriously as to make them appear more important than they are, as distinct from merely ludicrous. Techniques of satire are therefore an important area for the examination candidate to understand. Label names are used frequently by Jonson as a satiric technique; characters such as Justice Overdo and Zeal-of-the-Land-Busy hardly need any further characterisation. Vice-ridden characters are used to expose the imbecility and gullibility of their victims, and then these characters are themselves exposed to ridicule. One of Jonson's techniques is to let the audience enjoy with the main characters the duping of stupid folk, and at the same time enjoy the manner in which these supposedly superior tricksters are finally exposed by the greed and ambition that they prey on in others. Jonson is very much a dramatist of city life, and London in particular. Examination candidates are sometimes asked to discuss how much of Jonson's satire is merely topical and related only to his own particular society.

**Characterisation**

Characterisation is a major issue in Jonson's work. Jonson is famous for his humour characters (see Ch. 3), or characters given one ruling trait or passion. One interesting feature of his work is the manner in which his comedies can appear very realistic, despite so many of the characters being effectively rather one-dimensional 'humour' caricatures. A sharp examination candidate might dare to take issue with the whole concept of 'humour' characters, which is possibly overdue for a critical re-evaluation, and has become something of a cliché. Many of Jonson's characters are dominated by one humour but, when it comes down to it, greed, ambition and sheer naiveté appear very frequently on the list. It could be argued that Jonson's famed and undeniably effective humour characters are in fact based on a very small range of personality features.

**Dramatic unities**

Jonson was something of a scholar, and probably knew classical writing better than any of his contemporaries. As such the concept of the dramatic unities appears in his plays. This is a belief derived from Aristotle, and based on tragedy, that states that plays should show one complete action, with events which take place within a single day and night, and in a single place. These are sometimes referred to as the three dramatic unities of action, time, and space. Jonson did try to adhere to these principles wherever possible, and this whole area leads on to the excellence with which Jonson constructed the plots of his plays.

### The Spanish Tragedy

*The Spanish Tragedy* (1592) by Thomas Kyd (?1558–?1594) sometimes surfaces on the occasional syllabus, and was the first major revenge tragedy. It is interesting by virtue of being one of the first of its kind, but also rather clumsy. Other plays which are sometimes set, and which make excellent comparative reading for those studying the more frequently set plays, are *The Maid's Tragedy* (1601) and *The Knight of the Burning Pestle* (1613) by Francis Beaumont (?1584–1616) and John Fletcher (1579–1625); *The Shoemaker's Holiday* (1599) by Thomas Dekker (?1572–?1632); *The Changeling* (1622) by Thomas Middleton (1580–1627); *A New Way to Pay Old Debts* (1625) by Philip Massinger (1583–1640); and *'Tis Pity She's a Whore* (1627) and *The Broken Heart* (?1630) by John Ford (1586–?1640).

## Question and answer

**Question**

Would it be accurate to describe Marlowe's *Doctor Faustus* as a justification of conventional Christian morality, or is the play an attack on that morality?

**Answer**

Christopher Marlowe had the reputation of being a violent man, to have damned religion, and to have been involved in black magic. As such it seems extremely unlikely that such a man could have written in *Doctor Faustus* a play which wholeheartedly supports conventional Christianity. However, an author's work need not reflect his life, and what later ages have heard about Marlowe may not be accurate.

Certain features of *Doctor Faustus* might suggest that it is at least partially an attack on Christianity and its beliefs. It is possible to feel considerable sympathy for Faustus. He is a great man with a vast array of talents at his disposal. He can speak in magnificent and stirring poetry, suffers greatly, and his complaint about the limitations of being a human – 'Yet art thou still but Faustus, and a man' – must strike a sympathetic chord in anyone who has ever wished for more than life appears willing or able to offer. Faustus may be foolish and frivolous at times in the play, but he is rarely if ever criminal. His actions for the most part hurt himself far more than they do any other character in the play, and he attempts to protect his friends at the end of the play, refusing them permission to be with him in his final torment. For his sins he is condemned to everlasting torture, and it might appear that this punishment far outweighs his crime. It could also be said that Faustus represents the fight for intellectual freedom against an oppressive and tyrannical God. The line 'heavens conspired his overthrow' can suggest almost a conspiracy on the part of God to damn Faustus, not for his sins but for his desire to break free. It is this line of thought that has given rise to the vision of Faustus as a symbol of the Renaissance, and of mankind trying vainly to break free from the chains of the past. His final scene, as he is dragged down into Hell, is intensely moving, nor does he lose his essential honesty even in the last moments of his trial, as he shows when he says:

Curs'd be the parents that engender'd me!
No, Faustus, curse thyself, curse Lucifer
That hath depriv'd thee of the joys of heaven.

Throughout the play it can be argued that God appears as totally severe and without mercy or compassion, and that the symbol of goodness, the Good Angel, is a weak, bleating figure who has no powerful lines and is usually reduced to threatening punishment. Pleasure is made vivid in the play, Heaven less so, and the Christian virtues appear as rather flat and meaningless. It is notoriously difficult to make pure good appear convincing on stage, and Marlowe's play gives a high proportion of the most powerful and moving lines to the powers of evil.

There are a number of dissenting voices to this view of the play as an anti-Christian parable. The audience may sympathise with Faustus, but this does not invalidate the morality in the play which makes him a figure who deserves his fate. The audience sympathise with Shakespeare's Macbeth, but their sympathy does not stop Macbeth from being evil, nor does it stop the audience from recognising that he must die for his sins. Faustus may have great talents, but he is also a fool. He fools himself into thinking that he has control over Mephistopheles, as when he says, 'How pliant is this Mephistopheles,/Full of obedience and humility!', when it is clear that it is the devils who are in control. He ignores direct warnings, such as 'O Faustus, leave these frivolous demands,/Which strike a terror to my fainting soul'. He also has a number of features which are certainly not attractive. He is avaricious, conceited, arrogant, dominated by physical desire, and in his displays of magic can appear as a cheap entertainer who has given away his soul in order to be able to perform a few cheap conjuring tricks. Furthermore, it is made clear to him that the powers of evil cannot in the final conclusion triumph over those of good. When Faustus asks for the Old Man to be punished, Mephistopheles reveals the limits of his own power:

His faith is great; I cannot touch his soul;
But what I may afflict his body with
I will attempt, which is but little worth.

He shows fear when threatened by the Devil, and the point that is made repeatedly in the play is that Faustus' search in the play is not for heroic knowledge or freedom, but for simple pleasure – 'For the vain pleasure of four-and-twenty years hath Faustus lost eternal joy and felicity' and 'He that loves pleasure must for pleasure fall' both illustrate this repeated message. Faustus is honest enough to recognise that he has struck a bad bargain, which increases sympathy for him, but the pursuit of pleasure is not particularly noble, and is remarkably selfish and therefore unattractive. The play makes it clear that Faustus is 'swollen with cunning of a self-conceit'. He worships himself in place of God, and that makes him merely selfish, rather than heroic or a spokesman for atheism.

Doctor Faustus points out the difficulties of religious belief. It shows faith and goodness as being hard, unrewarding on Earth, unyielding in their demands, and difficult to apply. It also shows how attractive vice and self-indulgence are, but none of these areas make the play an attack on religion. Rather they make it an honest description of a man's life and what happens when the attractive but false gods of pride and appetite are worshipped. Marlowe's play does not state that following Christian ethics is easy; it does state very vividly what happens if the dictates of religion are not followed, and is thus best seen as a harsh reminder of the realities of faith.

## Further reading

### Anthologies

There are two excellent anthologies on the market at present which allows the reader to gain access to several plays at a very reasonable cost. These are Katharine Eisaman Maus, ed., *Four Revenge Tragedies: The Spanish Tragedy*; *The Revenger's Tragedy*; *Bussy D'Ambois*; *The Atheist's Tragedy* (Oxford University Press, 1995), and Colin Gibson, ed., *Six Renaissance Tragedies: The Spanish Tragedy*; *Doctor Faustus*; *The Revenger's Tragedy*; *The Duchess of Malfi*; *The Changeling*; *'Tis a Pity She's a Whore* (Macmillan, 1997).

### General

- M. C. Bradbrook, *Themes and Conventions of Jacobean Drama* (Cambridge University Press, 1980): a classic text on the period.
- A. R. Braunmuller and Michael Hattaway, ed., *The Cambridge Companion to English Renaissance Drama* (Cambridge University Press, 1997)
- Una Ellis Fermor, *The Jacobean Drama* (Methuen, 1965): another classic and highly readable text.
- Alison Findlay, *A Feminist Perspective on Renaissance Drama* (Blackwell, 1999)
- John Kerrigan, *Revenge Tragedy. Aeschylus to Armageddon* (Oxford University Press, 1996)
- Alexander Leggatt, *English Drama: Shakespeare to the Restoration 1590–1660* (Longman, 1988)
- Richard Wilson and Richard Dutton, *New Historicism and Renaissance Drama* (Longman, 1992): an excellent example of critical analysis based round one particular school of criticism.

Though published in 1934 and 1950 respectively, Basil Willey, *The Seventeenth Century Background*, and C. V. Wedgwood, *Seventeenth Century English Literature*, have much to offer.

## Ben Jonson

- Martin Butler, ed., *Re-Presenting Ben Jonson. Text, Performance, History* (Macmillan, 1998)
- David Riggs, *Ben Jonson: A Life* (Harvard University Press, 1989)
- Julie Sanders, Kate Chedgzoy and Susan Wiseman, ed., *Refashioning Ben Jonson. Gender, Politics and the Jonsonian Canon* (Macmillan, 1998)

## Christopher Marlowe

- Judith O'Neill, ed., *Critics on Marlowe* (Allen & Unwin, 1969)
- Roger Sales, *Christopher Marlowe* (Macmillan, 1991)
- William Tydeman and Vivien Thomas, *State of the Art: Christopher Marlowe* (Bristol Press, 1989): details much modern Marlowe criticism.
- A. D. Wraight and Virginia F. Stern, *In Search of Christopher Marlowe* (Adam Hart, 1993)

## John Webster

- Richard Cave, *The White Devil and the Duchess of Malfi* (Casebook Series, Macmillan, 1988)
- Rowland Wymer, *Webster and Ford* (Macmillan, 1995)

CHAPTER NINE

# Shakespeare

## The author and his work

Shakespeare has a strong claim to be regarded as the greatest dramatist of all time. This creates a double set of problems. It can lead to him being seen not as an artist, but as a pillar of the Establishment and as a symbol of all traditional virtues. This view of him is a travesty of the meaning of his art, which conforms to no single line and observes no external authority. His reputation can also create problems for the student, who sometimes cannot see what all the fuss is about, and who can sometimes be overwhelmed by the reputation. In fact, Shakespeare is often one of the most popular authors with students, albeit sometimes to their surprise. There are always new things to be said about his work, and he is in some respects a very accessible author. For the degree-course student Shakespeare offers even more exciting possibilities. Whatever the changing fashions are in criticism and literary theory, there is always something in Shakespeare to provide meat for them, always a perspective or idea that can be turned to modern and current usage.

### Shakespeare and Modern Criticism

Just as every mountaineer wants to climb Everest, and every athlete to win a gold medal at the Olympics, so every critic sometimes seems to want to prove their worth on Shakespeare. He has not disappointed them. One of the greatest aspects of Shakespeare's genius is his capacity for apparently infinite reinterpretation, with each age being able to see in his work aspects of its own needs and its own beliefs. It is perhaps no surprise therefore that Shakespearean criticism has not suffered from new schools and theories, but been enhanced by it. Marxist theory, and the writing of the French critic Michel Foucault (one of whose main tasks has been to seek to revise our concept of sexuality), are particularly well represented in new approaches to Shakespearean criticism.

## Shakespeare's Plays

Any modern edition of a Shakespeare play will contain a list of all Shakespeare's plays, and an educated guess at when they were written. It is sometimes only a guess, because there is little documentary evidence that has survived to give an exact date. The table below lists Shakespeare's plays in rough chronological order. It also gives each play a number (invented purely for use in this book), and a string of such numbers after each individual play title. The numbers after the title refer to other plays which are linked in some way to that particular play. Thus the numbers after *Hamlet* refer the reader to *Othello*, *King Lear*, and *Macbeth*, the other three great Shakespearean tragedies. All are excellent background reading to *Hamlet*, will throw more light on it and should be read if at all possible.

There then follows a brief description of the category to which that play is generally assigned by modern critics. These are only very rough guides. For example, a play such as *Antony and Cleopatra* is generally seen as a tragedy, but there is a strong historical and political element in it. Other plays simply do not fit neatly into any of the accepted categories, and if this is the case it is suggested by a question mark after that categorisation. Plays marked * are those most commonly set for examination purposes, though any of the plays can be, and sometimes are, set.

| Date | Play | No. | Background reading | Category |
|---|---|---|---|---|
| Pre-1592 | *Henry VI, Part 1* | 1 | | |
| | *Henry VI, Part 2* | 2 | 5, 15, 16 | History/ |
| | *Henry VI, Part 3* | 3 | | Early plays |
| ?1592–93 | *The Comedy of Errors* | 4 | 7, 8 | Comedy |
| | *Richard III** | 5 | 6, 10 | Tragedy/ History? |
| 1593–95 | *Titus Andronicus* | 6 | 5, 10 | Tragedy |
| | *The Taming of the Shrew* | 7 | 4, 8 | Comedy |
| | *The Two Gentlemen of Verona* | 8 | 4, 20 | Comedy |
| | *Love's Labour's Lost* | 9 | 8, 21 | Comedy |
| 1595–96 | *Romeo and Juliet** | 10 | 5, 30 | Tragedy |
| | *Richard II** | 11 | 15, 16, 18 | History |
| | *A Midsummer Night's Dream** | 12 | 17, 20, 21 | Comedy |

| Date | Play | No. | Background reading | Category |
|---|---|---|---|---|
| 1596–98 | *King John* | 13 | 5 | History? |
| | *The Merchant of Venice** | 14 | 17 | Comedy? |
| | *Henry IV, Part 1** | 15 | 11, 16, 18 | History |
| | *Henry IV, Part 2** | 16 | 11, 15, 18 | History |
| 1598–1600 | *Much Ado About Nothing** | 17 | 12, 20, 21 | Comedy |
| | *Henry V** | 18 | 11, 15, 16 | History |
| | *Julius Caesar** | 19 | 30 | Tragedy |
| | *As You Like It** | 20 | 12, 17, 21 | Comedy |
| | *Twelfth Night** | 21 | 12, 17, 20 | Comedy |
| 1600–02 | *Troilus and Cressida* | 22 | 25, 27, 35 | Problem play |
| | *Hamlet** | 23 | 26, 28, 29 | Tragedy |
| | *The Merry Wives of Windsor* | 24 | 15, 21 | Comedy |
| 1602–06 | *All's Well That Ends Well* | 25 | 22, 27, 35 | Problem play |
| | *Othello** | 26 | 23, 28, 29 | Tragedy |
| | *Measure for Measure** | 27 | 22, 25, 35 | Problem play |
| | *King Lear** | 28 | 23, 26, 29 | Tragedy |
| | *Macbeth** | 29 | 23, 26, 28 | Tragedy |
| 1606–09 | *Antony and Cleopatra** | 30 | 19, 10, 23 | Tragedy |
| | *Timon of Athens* | 31 | 32, 33 | Tragedy |
| | *Pericles* | 32 | 31, 33 | Tragedy |
| | *Coriolanus* | 33 | 31, 32 | Tragedy |
| 1609–10 | *Cymbeline** | 34 | 27, 35, 36 | Romance |
| 1610–13 | *The Winter's Tale** | 35 | 27, 36 | Romance |
| | *The Tempest** | 36 | 34, 35 | Romance |
| | *Henry VIII* | 37 | 1, 36 | History |

It is dangerous to spend too much time putting labels onto Shakespeare's plays, such as 'comedy' or 'tragedy'; the categories frequently overlap, and categorising a play is much less important than your understanding it. The first and main aim of any student must be to try to see a live performance of his set text, and failing that, any play by Shakespeare. There are now a large number of high quality film productions of Shakespeare's plays available on video. The health warning here is never to see one production only of a play if at all possible. Let your own imagination visualise the play, not the imagination of a film director. One way to achieve this is to see as many different productions as possible, or to compare the effect of a video with the effect of an audio tape of the play.

All three types of performance – live theatre, video, and audio – raise the play out of the text and make it what it was originally meant to be, a performance. The plays were never designed to be read, but to be acted. Some of the impact of a play depends on purely physical elements, such as Falstaff's huge size in *Henry IV, Part 1* and *Henry IV, Part 2*, Sir Andrew Aguecheek's thinness and lank yellow hair in *Twelfth Night*, or King Lear's age and frailty in *King Lear*, and these can be missed from the hints in the text when the play is read. Tone of voice can give a completely new meaning to a line, violence be much more frightening, and deliberate contrasts much more obvious, when a play is seen or heard.

Perhaps comedy needs live acting more than any other type of play. Very often in Shakespeare it is the people who make lines funny, more than the lines they say. One example is Beatrice and Benedick in *Much Ado About Nothing*. These two characters have been sparring partners for years, but actually love each other. They are involved in much sharp, witty word-play which needs the pace and timing of a good actor to give it life and breath, and it is not the words which are funny as much as the character insight given by these words. One of the funniest scenes in drama is the orchard scene in *Twelfth Night*, where the Puritan steward Malvolio reads a false love letter from Olivia, his employer and someone far above him. He is overheard by three roisterers who eavesdrop on him, but the real humour only comes through when these three rogues are seen peering out and ducking behind the bushes with Malvolio failing to spot them. If you have no opportunity to see or hear a performance it will be helpful to read a plot summary of a play before reading the actual text. Get hold of a good edition of the play in question. Read through the play in as near to one sitting as you can manage, and try to see and hear the characters as you read. Make very brief notes in the margin in pencil, either when you come across something you simply cannot understand, or when you meet a line or passage that seems to you particularly significant. Use the notes in your text for translation. Do not pay much attention at first reading to the critical hints contained in most notes; that can come later.

If you have seen a production of a Shakespeare play, or even if you are reading it without having seen it, remember that the production you have seen, or the image you hold in your head, is only one possible viewpoint or interpretation. Shakespeare is endlessly adaptable and flexible, which is one reason why he has survived as he has. Whilst the basic text remains the same, each new age can interpret the plays in the light of their own concerns, worries, and beliefs. Thus Hamlet can be portrayed as a mighty hero. He has also been played by a woman several times, as a gawky university student, complete with long scarf, as a 'snivelling adolescent', as a ruthless politician, and as a madman. When the Berlin Wall fell and a new era was ushered in to European politics, *Hamlet* was chosen as the play to reflect a society poised between an old and a new path, and uncertain of its direction. All these interpretations are possible within the text, and each different interpretation says something about the director and actors, as well as the age which produced the production.

On first reading, fix the main points of the play firmly in your mind, such as characters, plot, and themes, together with any obvious techniques, such as the use of blank verse, or the introduction of a Chorus – and take brief notes. Always try to remember what your first impression of a play was; it will come in useful later on.

## General themes and issues in Shakespeare's work

Perhaps the most significant thing to realise about Shakespeare is that he did not write his plays in order to gain a doctorate in advanced philosophy. The 'meaning' of a Shakespeare play is only a part of the whole. There are such matters as entertainment, stagecraft, observation of human nature, emotion, language, tragedy, and comedy to discuss as well. There are no 'hidden meanings' in Shakespeare. There are meanings, but they lie on the surface, merely waiting to be picked up.

A theme is an issue or group of issues examined by an author. Sometimes the work may reach a conclusion about this issue. There is no rule saying that is has to. Never look at a play by Shakespeare as if it were an Aesop's fable, a little story with a neat moral at the end, such as 'The Tortoise and the Hare'. Shakespeare did not write his plays like that. The most significant thing to realise is that Shakespeare tended to observe life as much as comment on it. Sometimes the conclusions are left to the audience, or the experience on offer simply cannot be summed up that easily. *Antony and Cleopatra* shows us a love affair that can be seen in two completely different lights. Antony is a member of the ruling elite of the Roman empire, Cleopatra the Queen of Egypt. These two have a tempestuous love affair which leads directly to their deaths at the end of the play. One view has it that the love affair between Antony and Cleopatra was thinly disguised lust, an animal instinct that led both to destruction and the senseless loss of power and life. This view has it that Antony throws away his life and ambition for a useless and sordid affair. Another view has it that their love was magnificent, transcendental, and something so rich and powerful as to justify any sacrifice in order to enjoy it for a few moments. In other words, this viewpoint has Antony and Cleopatra possessed of something in their love that makes even power over the whole world appear trivial by comparison. Shakespeare shows both views. He simply observes that human beings are immensely complex, and can fall in love in a manner that is both heroic and seedy, worthwhile and a waste. A computer could not understand this. It is illogical, but utterly convincing. Shakespeare observes and records, but does not force a conclusion on us. This is why Feminist criticism can come along and show us that in having the symbol of masculinity – Antony – lose all his power because of his relationship with a woman, and in having as the eventual victor Octavius Caesar who is shown as having no 'softening' relationship with a woman, the play confirms men's traditional fear of women as a threat to their power. Such fear and possibly even loathing can be seen in the biblical story of the destruction of Samson. Full credit to Shakespeare that the play can also take the weight of an opposed view, that Antony can only be brought to proper emotional fulfilment by the perceived femininity of Cleopatra, so she becomes not a destroyer but the creator of the true Antony.

Some individual issues in specific plays are looked at below. Certain general themes do recur in most of Shakespeare's work, and these can be discussed as follows.

## Appearance and reality

Very often in a Shakespeare play there are two worlds: what we see on the surface (appearance), and the truth that lies underneath (reality). The world of appearance shows what seems to be true, whereas the world of reality shows what actually is true. Learning to distinguish between these two, and not being fooled by outer show, is often what makes the difference between a happy or an unhappy life for characters in a Shakespeare play. Thus Lear in *King Lear* cannot distinguish between the apparent love afforded him by his daughters Goneril and Regan, and the real love offered by his daughter Cordelia. The former is flattery and hypocrisy, the latter is genuine, but Lear sees the real love from Cordelia as being more opposition to his will. He is a proud, angry man used to exercising power without challenge. His pride colours his view of the real world so that he cannot see any longer what is real and what is unreal. Vanity and pride make people look at the world through a distorting lens, seeing it falsely.

Shakespeare emphasises that self-knowledge, a clear and honest vision of one's own personality with all its strengths and weaknesses, is essential if one is to be able to distinguish appearance from reality. If you do not know who you are you will not be able to see who and what others are, and such misjudgements can be horrifically dangerous. In tragedies, the penalty for failing to distinguish good from bad is immense suffering and death; in the comedies the characters get off more lightly, but still have to go through suffering to learn their lesson. The difference is that in comedies, more people live on to use what they have learnt. Shakespeare is also honest enough to know that certain people can never learn about themselves, or face up to facts. At the end of a comedy there is often a figure left out, unable to reconcile himself with other people and the society in which he lives: Malvolio in *Twelfth Night* and Jaques in *As You Like It* are two examples.

## Love

Love between the sexes has little part to play in the History plays, in which it tends to be either bawdy and coarse (see the relationship between Falstaff and the prostitute Doll Tearsheet in *Henry IV, Part 2*), or rather clumsily comic and pure, as with Henry V's wooing of Katharine of France in *Henry V*. The love mentioned in these plays is of one's country or one's King.

In the comedies, love is at the heart of the plays. The plots usually feature one, two, or even three lovers. Good, healthy, and happy relationships end in marriage, used as a symbol of harmony and happiness. The capacity to give and receive love is what makes a hero or heroine in the comedies, as witnessed by such characters as Viola in *Twelfth Night* and Rosalind in *As You Like It*. In the tragedies, love is often defenceless against evil. Lady Macduff cannot stop either herself or her children being murdered on the orders of *Macbeth*, despite her goodness and innocence. Cordelia is the only one of Lear's daughters in *King Lear* who really loves him, but her capacity for love does not save her life, and indeed she dies almost as a result of it. However, love is the basis of all decency and goodness in the tragedies, the yardstick by which we measure everything else.

Love can be a tremendous source of strength, but it can also become a force for evil. Lady Macbeth loves her husband, and it is possible that this love becomes perverted into a desire to see him become King at any price. Othello's love for his wife Desdemona is so powerful that when it is turned into jealousy by Iago it destroys both man and wife. Hamlet's love for his mother and father mean he can be devastated by what he sees as a betrayal.

In Shakespeare love is the ability to commit oneself utterly to the care and service of another person. It is shown as a prime human need, and even the most evil characters, such as Goneril and Regan, sometimes fall in love. It is immensely strong, has vast powers of healing and reconciliation (best seen perhaps in *The Winter's Tale*), and if thwarted or mishandled has an equal capacity for doing harm. *Romeo and Juliet* and *Antony and Cleopatra* are the flagships of Shakespeare's achievement in commenting on and revealing love, but it is a fleet with a great many ships in it. Feminist criticism has given sharp new insight into many of the apparently traditional love stories and relationships in Shakespeare.

## Kingship and politics

Kingship can appear an outdated and outmoded theme when so few modern countries are run by monarchs, but the theme Shakespeare conveys through the agency of his Kings and Queens is as old as time itself, and concerns the wielding of power, the morality of government, and the reality of politics. The basic attitude towards kingship is that the King is appointed by God through the hereditary principle, a concept sometimes referred to as the 'Divine Right of Kings'. It is thus almost the ultimate sin to kill or remove a King, because to do so is to challenge not only men's laws, but the rule of God. A usurper (someone who takes the throne illegally) is usually condemned in a Shakespeare play to a reign of huge turmoil and revolt.

Shakespeare was not only a theoretician and moralist, but also a practical observer. He knew that once it was shown as possible to remove a King many others would try to repeat the exercise, through ambition and lust for power. The King is the source for the whole strength and stability of the state. Removing him is to threaten the whole state with dissolution, and a bad King infects the state from the top downwards, in the manner of a mortal illness. The History plays deal with Kingship most fully, though the theme appears in tragedies and in other plays.

Marxist criticism sees the plays not so much in terms of kingship but more in terms of the wielding of power. A writer who offended the authorities in Shakespeare's time might end up as did Ben Jonson, threatened with having his nose and ears slit, and so Shakespeare's capacity to deny the political correctness of his time was severely limited. Marxist interpretations of the plays, and especially the History plays, are very stimulating, tending to suggest that Shakespeare was far less orthodox in his political views than might be imagined. One example must stand for many. In *Troilus and Cressida*, Ulysses gives a famous speech extolling the absolute virtue of rank, precedence and order. The speech is unequivocal in its support for a traditional, authoritarian view of society. Yet Ulysses is the most Machiavellian character in the play, and a few minutes after giving this fine speech rigs an election. Does this mean that the sentiments expressed in his speech stand proud, regardless of his actions, or does it mean that Shakespeare is seeking to deny those stated 'truths' in the only devious, indirect way that the politics of the time allowed him?

## Good and evil

The eternal battle between good and evil features strongly in Shakespeare's plays. Evil is sometimes manifested directly, as in the Witches in *Macbeth*, but more often it is found within humans. Evil people in Shakespeare are selfish, self-centred, and incapable of love. They are frequently hypocrites. Good triumphs in the end when a battle takes place, but only after much suffering and anguish on the part of those who are good.

Shakespeare frequently blurs the distinction between good and evil, showing that opposites can and do exist within the same person. Claudius in *Hamlet* has murdered Old Hamlet, who was both King and Claudius' brother, a terrible act of evil, yet the play shows clearly that Claudius is a firm, efficient, and effective monarch. Falstaff in the two *Henry IV* plays, is a knave but also attractive, as is Edmund in *King Lear*. Both these latter characters are surprisingly honest and open, to the audience at least, about their misdeeds, and in them and other characters Shakespeare makes two points, firstly that evil has to be attractive at times or else it would not be so popular, and secondly that the most frightening evil is that which cloaks its true nature, a link with the appearance and reality theme. Distinguish between evil characters and those who are misguided, dull, or stupid. Iago in *Othello* is evil whilst Malvolio in *Twelfth Night* is simply a flawed human being. Probably the most specific and comprehensive treatment of the battle between good and evil in Shakespeare is *Macbeth*.

One aspect of Shakespeare's writing that is infuriating and stimulating in equal measure is his unwillingness to explain his characters' behaviour. We never really know why Iago does what he does. Shakespeare's source for *Twelfth Night* gives a perfectly clear reason why Viola chooses to dress as a man: she has suffered an attempted rape on her earlier sea voyage which has taught her how vulnerable a young woman is. In Shakespeare's play this reason is omitted, and very little of a clear one put in its place. Similarly, perfectly good reasons for Leontes' insane jealousy in *The Winter's Tale* are given in the Shakespeare's source, but left out when he comes to write the play. There are risks in leaving an open canvas. There is great profit in the way this allows us, the reader, to paint our own picture on top of what Shakespeare provides, or perhaps even to finish it off.

## Energy and time

Energy and enthusiasm for life are major virtues in Shakespeare's plays. He cannot abide people who want to hide away from life, praises those who meet it head-on, and is attracted by energy and enthusiasm. Olivia in *Twelfth Night* is an example of someone who tries to block life out, whilst Viola in the same play shows all the virtues of energy and enthusiasm. Even Falstaff, who has joyfully partaken of every sin the world has to offer, is excused some of the blame because he is so full-blooded and alive. These energetic and active heroes and heroines also know about time, a major theme in Shakespeare. The wise person knows when to act, and when to wait and acknowledge that instant action is not always the right thing. Time is shown as a great healer in the plays (a character called Time actually appears in *The Winter's Tale*, a play very much concerned, as are many of Shakespeare's later plays, with time).

## Destiny, fate, stoicism, and courage

Destiny and Fate are the controlling and often unseen powers of the Universe. Convention and morality in Shakespeare's day did not allow God to be mentioned on stage, so the convention of referring instead to pagan gods adds to the impression of an unseen controlling power at work in everyone's lives. The tragedies look most closely at this power (see below). In *Macbeth* there is a straight fight between good and evil, and an evil Destiny in the shape of the Witches at work in the world. *Othello* looks much less closely at Destiny, but Hamlet acknowledges the existence of a shadowy force which cannot be understood by humans, but which controls their lives fully. *King Lear* looks at Destiny and Fate most closely, and contains a host of contradictory remarks, suggesting among other things that God does exist and is benign, that he exists and is cruel and that he does not exist at all. The basic issue is what it is that controls our lives; *King Lear* comes near to saying at times that nothing does. Love takes the place of Fate and Destiny in the comedies, as the major influence on our lives.

In the tragedies the Universe is often a hostile, threatening, and in the final count, incomprehensible place. Courage, stoicism (the capacity to endure), love and the determination to take whatever comes with dignity are the prime virtues. Death may be inevitable in the tragedies, but one can still die on one's own terms, and with the mind unbroken, whatever may happen to the body.

### Stagecraft and technique

There are certain aspects of Shakespeare's style and technique that fascinate examiners.

1. *Blank verse* is unrhymed metrical poetry, usually in Shakespeare a loose iambic pentameter. Shakespeare tends to use blank verse for nobler characters, and never for the low-born or common, except to mock them or when they imitate their betters. The more important the character, and the more lofty or intense the subject, the more likely Shakespeare is to use blank verse. Conversely, most comic scenes and those featuring low-born characters are in prose, as are straightforward conversations or exchanges of information.
2. *Contrast* is a major technique. With little or no set, scene changes in Shakespeare's plays were swift, giving ample opportunity to emphasise a point by contrast. The loneliness and coldness of the castle guards in *Hamlet* is conveyed even more strongly when one of their scenes is followed instantly by the warmth, wealth and luxuriousness of the whole Danish court. Contrast also comes in the shape of characters. Again in *Hamlet*, Hamlet the young prince is placed side by side with Laertes, comparable in age and ability; the audience learn more about each character from the comparison they inevitably make.
3. A number of other techniques might usefully be noted. *The technique used to portray battle scenes* fascinates some examiners, as does the means by which characters are portrayed and brought to life. *The use of boys to act female parts* and the opportunity for ironies that this gives, together with the use of disguise, are fruitful areas of study, as is *music* in the plays, and *imagery*.

## Specimen topics on individual plays

### The early plays

Some authorities finish Shakespeare's early phase of writing as late as *Romeo and Juliet*; others end this period earlier, with *Love's Labour's Lost*, as does this author. As a group the early plays are still performed, but can appear quite clumsy in comparison with Shakespeare's later work. Their language tends to be artificial and forced in comparison, the plots more cumbersome and less well controlled by the author, and the conclusions and characters more stereotyped. The three *Henry VI* plays, *The Comedy of Errors* (a comedy with a plot based on two identical twins), *Titus Andronicus* (a blood bath), and *The Two Gentlemen of Verona* are rarely set for examination purposes.

***Richard III*** is part history, part tragedy, part comedy. Richard III is an evil, hunchbacked King who delights and revels in his evil. The fact that he is a King injects a history element into the play, the fact that he dies makes it partially tragic and his enjoyment of his outrageous actions produces a comic element, which we would think of nowadays as black comedy. Some common examination topics are:

(i) The character of Richard, the nature of his evil, and whether or not the audience can feel any sympathy for him. It is worth noting that one of the changes Shakespeare brought to Elizabethan drama from Marlowe's pioneering example was a willingness to have essentially weak men as the central figure or hero.
(ii) The blending of comic, tragic, and historical elements in the play.

***The Taming of the Shrew*** can be difficult for a modern audience because its story of a 'shrewish' woman 'tamed' by a man can seem to go against modern ideas of the equality of men and women. A reading of feminist critiques of this play is essential.

ISSUES
(i) The attitude to women expressed in the play.
(ii) The attitude to love and human nature expressed in the play.
(iii) Comic techniques used by Shakespeare.

## The Comedies

The term 'comedy' originally meant merely a play with a happy ending, which is why a number of rather disturbing plays without much humour in them are called comedies. *Love's Labour's Lost* is only very occasionally a set text, and could be described as an early play. It may have been written for a court audience, and is about courtiers in love, and the fallibility of human nature.

***A Midsummer Night's Dream*** is an early comedy, but also a masterpiece. It is peopled partly by fairies, and partly by humans, with the two crossing each others' paths, usually in pursuit of love affairs that range from the solemn to the ludicrous.

ISSUES
(i) Does love represent the highest or the lowest emotion to which mankind can aspire, in *A Midsummer Night's Dream*?
(ii) What is the importance of the dream world in the play, and how does Shakespeare reconcile the real and the unreal world in it?

(iii) Is it fair to say that the characterisation in the play is weak, superficial, and insubstantial?
(iv) How closely are comedy and tragedy linked in the play?
(v) What is the attraction of Bottom in the play, and why is he such a successful comic creation?
(vi) What are the advantages in having a fairy-tale world in *A Midsummer Night's Dream*?

***The Merchant of Venice*** is a forceful illustration of the fact that Shakespearean comedy need not make the audience laugh. Indeed, it is sometimes referred to as a problem or 'dark' comedy. One of its central figures is a young woman who is empowered in the course of the play, and Portia in *The Merchant of Venice* can be interestingly compared with Viola in *Twelfth Night* and Rosalind in *As You Like It.*

ISSUES
(i) Are the audience meant to sympathise with or despise Shylock?
(ii) How well does the happy ending of the play fit in with what has gone before?
(iii) How convincing is the portrait of Portia, and the episode of the caskets? Is the play best thought of as a fairy story?
(iv) How easily can the postmodern generation, with its knowledge of the Holocaust, watch a production of the play?

***Much Ado About Nothing*** is often seen as a rather light comedy, it has become more popular recently, and is quite frequently set. The play lacks a truly evil presence, but this does not make it the frothy, light mix that might be supposed. Feminist writing has much that is stimulating to say about the relationship between Beatrice and Benedick.

ISSUES
(i) Would a more accurate title for the play be 'Beatrice and Benedick'?
(ii) Discuss the assertion that this is one of Shakespeare's most 'intimate' plays; does the description fit?
(iii) What does a comparison of the two sets of lovers in the play tell us above love?
(iv) Discuss the relationship between the two plots in the play.
(v) Are Hero and Claudio ineffective presentations?
(vi) How is the comic atmosphere preserved in a play so full of potentially damaging action and events?
(vii) What is the importance of eavesdropping in the play?

***As You Like It*** is set in the forest of Arden, and hence often seen as a 'pastoral' play (see Ch. 3). It and *Twelfth Night* contain the two most famous examples of cross-dressing in Shakespeare, and are endlessly fascinating in their questioning and portrayal of conventional sexual roles.

ISSUES

(i) Discuss the allegation that *As You Like It* is a failure, 'full of casual workmanship, lacking in unity, with a feeble opening and a feeble ending'.
(ii) What is the attraction of Rosalind? Why is she a dramatic success?
(iii) What is the importance of pastoral in the play?
(iv) What is the dramatic function of Jaques and Touchstone?

## The history plays

***King John*** is a difficult and obscure play, rarely performed or set.

***Henry VIII*** may well have been written in conjunction with other authors, and is rarely if ever a set text. This leaves the so-called 'second tetralogy' of History plays, discussed below.

***Richard II*** can be seen and understood perfectly as a play in its own right, as can all four plays discussed here, but it is also the start of the sequence which has its conclusion in *Henry V*. *Richard II* poses the question of what to do when a rightful King is also a very bad ruler, though in some ways an attractive man. Even though Richard is a bad King, no man has the right to remove him, and Bolingbroke (Henry IV) will suffer terribly for so doing. It is also clearly stated that being a good man does not necessarily mean one will be a good King.

ISSUES

(i) How is it that a man with 'the soul of a poet' can fail to be a good King in *Richard II*?
(ii) Is the character of Richard interesting because of or despite his weaknesses and failings?

***Henry IV, Part 1*** and ***Part 2*** are two separate plays, but continue on from each other chronologically, and share the same central characters.

ISSUES

(i) What evidence is there for believing that Shakespeare originally intended to make only one play out of the story of *Henry IV*?
(ii) Discuss the blending of comic and serious scenes in *Henry IV Part 1* or *Henry IV Part 2*.
(iii) Discuss the treatment of honour in *Henry IV, Part 1*.
(iv) Do we sympathise with Falstaff or Hal when Hal rejects Falstaff?
(v) How is it that such a rogue as Falstaff can be attractive to an audience, and to Prince Hal?
(vi) What conclusions, if any, are drawn about kingship in *Henry IV, Part 1* and *Henry IV, Part 2*?
(vii) Is the real hero of *Henry IV, Part 1* and *Henry IV, Part 2* England?
(viii) Can we sympathise with the rebels in these plays?

(ix) How does Shakespeare prepare the audience for Hal's reformation?
(x) What is the price of Kingship in these plays, and is it too high?

***Henry V*** is the culmination of the History plays, to show Henry V as the 'ideal King'.

ISSUES
(i) What is the role and function of Chorus in *Henry V*?
(ii) Is it true that the final Act of *Henry V* is an anti-climax after Agincourt?
(iii) 'If *Henry V* is the ideal King, then the price paid in human terms is too high.' Discuss.
(iv) How does Shakespeare overcome the limitations of the Elizabethan stage in *Henry V*?
(v) 'Patriotism at the expense of sensitivity and feeling.' Discuss this judgement of *Henry V*.

## The Tragedies

For a definition of tragedy, see Chapter 3. Shakespeare's tragedies are not 'pure' tragedies according to classical definitions.

***Hamlet*** is possibly the most famous tragic hero of all time, and many of the lines from the play have passed into common usage.

ISSUES
(i) Is Hamlet a 'sweet prince' or an 'arrant knave'?
(ii) Why does Hamlet delay in killing Claudius?
(iii) Is Hamlet mad?
(iv) To what extent is it accurate to call *Hamlet* a revenge play?
(v) How important are politics and comedy in *Hamlet*?
(vi) Is it true, as stated by Laurence Olivier in his film of *Hamlet*, that the play is about as man who cannot make up his mind?

***King Lear*** is the most terrifying of all Shakespeare's tragedies, and the deepest in terms of its moral probing. The authoritarian father-figure opposed by two daughters and supported by a wronged and subservient daughter makes this play in particular a fascinating one for feminist and Foucauldian critics, as well as for Marxist thought.

ISSUES
(i) To what extent should *King Lear* be seen as a Christian and redemptive play, or as a play which offers no hope for humanity?
(ii) What is the importance of madness in *King Lear*?
(iii) What is the dramatic significance of the Fool? (Once, famously, written as, ' "And my poor Fool is hang'd." Discuss.')
(iv) Discuss the relationship between plot and sub-plot in the play.

(v) Is Lear 'more sinned against than sinning?'
(vi) How effective is the portrayal of Cordelia?
(vii) Does King Lear die happy?

***Macbeth*** is meant to be a play that brings bad luck along with it, and may have come down to us with certain of the original scenes missing. It may have been written with more than half an eye on the new King James I, a Scottish king and heir of Banquo (who appears and is murdered in play). James was a published authority on witchcraft, which features strongly in the play.

ISSUES
(i) 'This dead butcher and his fiend-like Queen.' Is this an accurate judgement of Macbeth and Lady Macbeth?
(ii) Is it Macbeth's fault that he murders Duncan, or that of his wife, or the Witches?
(iii) How does Shakespeare produce sympathy for so evil a man as Macbeth?
(iv) Discuss the theme of evil in Macbeth.
(v) Account for the intensity of mood and atmosphere in Macbeth.

***Othello*** is sometimes seen as a 'domestic' tragedy, in that it has little to do with the supernatural or the gods. The fact that Othello is 'black' (actually, he is a Moor), and isolated within a white society, has made this play of particular interest to critics allied with the Postcolonial school of critical theory.

ISSUES
(i) 'Motiveless malignancy.' Is this an accurate description of Iago?
(ii) Is jealousy Othello's tragic flaw?
(iii) Is Othello a noble Moor or a hollow egotist?
(iv) 'A tragedy of misunderstanding'; 'a domestic tragedy'. Comment on these two views of the play.
(v) How significant in the play is the difference in race and culture between Othello and the society which employs him?

***Julius Caesar*** is one of the best-known of Shakespeare's 'Roman' plays. The term 'Roman' is misleading; *Julius Caesar* is a play about power and ambition, effectively a history play set in Roman times.

ISSUES
(i) Discuss the assertion that *Julius Caesar* lacks both variety and a true tragic hero.
(ii) To what extent is there an anti-climax in the second half of *Julius Caesar*?
(iii) Is Brutus justified in killing Caesar?
(iv) Compare and contrast Caesar, Brutus, and Mark Antony.

***Antony and Cleopatra*** has many of the same characters as *Julius Caesar*, but is a totally separate play. The relationship between the two lovers has in history been seen in two different lights. The 'classical' view, expressed by Alexander Pope in his version of the story, *All for Love*, is that Cleopatra ruins Antony, who throws away an empire for mere sensual pleasure. The 'romantic' view is that the loss of an Empire is more than justified by the overwhelming, transcendental nature of the love between Antony and Cleopatra. Shakespeare manages to portray both views, side by side.

ISSUES
(i) 'The world well lost'; 'the world ill lost'. Which of these two views seems to you to best sum up the action of *Antony and Cleopatra*?
(ii) 'Age cannot wither her,/Nor custom stale her infinite variety.' Is this an accurate description of Cleopatra?
(iii) What different values are represented by Rome and Egypt?
(iv) *Antony and Cleopatra* is set on a vast scale, spanning the world. How does Shakespeare cope with a play on such a vast scale?
(v) Does Antony achieve true tragic stature?
(vi) What is the role and function of Enobarbus?
(vii) Is *Antony and Cleopatra* about love or about power?

***Romeo and Juliet*** is probably Shakespeare's most famous love story. Despite being a relatively early play it has adapted very well to modern times, being used both as the basis for the American musical *West Side Story* and a gripping production set in Northern Ireland with Romeo and Juliet's families representing Catholic and Protestant. It is also at the centre of the film *Shakespeare in Love*.

ISSUES
(i) Discuss the assertion that *Romeo and Juliet* is 'clumsy' and 'long-winded'.
(ii) How much does *Romeo and Juliet* rely on its plot?
(iii) Why have the lovers in *Romeo and Juliet* been so successful as representatives of all young lovers?
(iv) What are the features that have allowed the play to be successfully adapted to modern times and circumstances?

## Problem plays

There are three plays which are generally seen as problem plays, sometimes referred to as problem comedies, and certain other plays (and even *Hamlet*) have sometimes been included in the group. These plays usually have a happy ending, but enough tragic or unhappy incident in the run-up to that ending to throw the credibility of the ending into question. Of the three plays, *Troilus and Cressida* and *All's Well That Ends Well* are rarely set. All the characters in *Troilus and Cressida* seem dark grey in tone, with neither good nor evil allowed to reach any heights, and much philosophical debate which seems to lead nowhere. *All's Well That Ends Well* contains folk-tale elements of riddles and mystery cures, and centres on the relationship between the lowly

Helena and the noble Bertram. Their marriage at the end of the play, after Helena has done a series of unlikely things in order to satisfy the conditions for marriage set by Bertram, can appear unsatisfactory and disturbing.

***Measure for Measure*** starts off in what seems to be full tragic vein, and then slips into folk-tale and a happy ending. It may be a confusing play, but it is also potentially very powerful on stage. Antonio's conversion from severe judge to corrupt philanderer raises issues of sexuality, morality and power that have proved as interesting to new critical theories as they have over the years to traditional criticism.

ISSUES

(i) How convincing is the ending of *Measure for Measure*?
(ii) Should Angelo be forgiven?
(iii) Can the contradictions in the Duke's character be satisfactorily explained?
(iv) Discuss the theme of justice in *Measure for Measure*, considering particularly whether justice is done at the end.
(v) Should *Measure for Measure* best be seen as a folk or fairy tale?
(vi) Does *Measure for Measure* make a statement about human sexuality?

## Romance plays

These are sometimes referred to as the late plays. The two which most concern examination candidates are *The Winter's Tale* and *The Tempest*.

***The Winter's Tale*** has a plot that is split into two by a fifteen-year gap. It is a play that is particularly challenged by feminist theories, focusing as it does on a man's irrational jealousy that seems to destroy his wife, and issues of forgiveness.

ISSUES

(i) Discuss the theme of Time and reconciliation in the play.
(ii) To what extent should the play be seen as a religious allegory?
(iii) How does Shakespeare attempt to portray perfect goodness in Hermione?
(iv) To what extent is the politics of power the dominant theme in the play?

***The Tempest*** is Shakespeare's penultimate play, and in one sense combines the moral outlook of the comedies, the histories, and the tragedies. Critical interpretations of it have been turned on their head by postcolonial critics, who have pointed out that the arrival of Prospero on his island and his subjugation of the 'native' Caliban prefigures exactly the process of colonisation and Empire that started in seventeenth century Europe. As with so many of Shakespeare's plays, the text has been able to take on board new interpretations without loss of grandeur or authority.

ISSUES

(i) What power does love have in *The Tempest*?
(ii) What significance do Caliban and Prospero have in the play?
(iii) 'Power; knowledge; love; mercy.' Is this an accurate list of the themes of *The Tempest*?
(iv) Is our vision of the play helped or hindered if we view Prospero as a coloniser and an agent of Empire?

## Questions, notes and answers

**Question 1**
Is Hamlet a 'sweet prince' or an 'arrant knave'?

**Answer**
Hamlet is referred to as both a 'sweet prince' and an 'arrant knave' in the text of *Hamlet*. The tragic hero usually has a tragic flaw or weakness of character which helps to bring about his downfall, and as such one might expect Hamlet to have something in him that merits the 'arrant knave' accusation, if this implies someone not worthy of respect. However, if Hamlet were to be too much the 'arrant knave' it would be difficult for the audience to feel any sympathy for him in his suffering, and much of the play would be wasted. In both his actions and his words Hamlet can sometimes justify the description 'arrant knave'. He subjects Ophelia to mental torture, insults her obscenely on occasion (as when he remarks 'That's a fair thought to lie between maids' legs' at the play scene), and is largely responsible for her suicide. He murders Polonius, and seems to show a complete lack of feeling about the murder of an innocent man when he says of him merely 'I'll lug the guts into the neighbouring room'. He arranges for his old friends Rosencrantz and Guildenstern to be murdered, and places the players in extreme danger. He is violent towards his mother, and gives a repulsive reason for not killing Claudius at prayer, which is that if he does so Claudius will not burn in Hell. He shames Ophelia and himself by leaping into her grave, and spends the majority of the play acting like a madman.

On the other hand, there are possible excuses for most of the above weaknesses. He may be trying to frighten off Ophelia in order to protect her from the dangerous game which he is playing with his father's murderer. Furthermore, Ophelia has obeyed her father in acting as a spy and a lure for Hamlet, and he may be quite right to feel resentment at this betrayal. Similarly, he is betrayed by Rosencrantz and Guildenstern, who side with Claudius in spying on Hamlet, and in having them killed he is only doing to them what they would do to him. Polonius is as Hamlet describes him, a 'rash, intruding fool'. Hamlet clearly thinks it is Claudius behind the arras when he stabs through, and thus kills Polonius by mistake. This may not technically lessen the crime. But it makes it much more easily understandable.

Hamlet also has many features that merit the description of him as a 'sweet prince'. In Ophelia's words he is, or was,

> The Courtier's, soldier's, scholar's, eye, tongue,
> sword;
> Th'expectancy and rose of the fair state,
> The glass of fashion and the mould of form,
> Th'observ'd of all observers . . .

He is popular with the people of Denmark, a fact which Claudius comments on when he says Hamlet is 'much beloved of the distracted multitude'. He is clearly well-educated and cultured, as well as being an excellent swordsman. He proves his courage when he faces the Ghost, the pirates, and Laertes, and he meets his death with calmness and tragic dignity. He is a loving and a loyal son, placed in an impossible and horrific situation, to which he responds with courage and great strength.

Hamlet convinces himself that he is an 'arrant knave' because he fails to kill Claudius immediately. This is more likely to make the audience respect him than condemn him, as a man who killed too easily would indeed be despicable. Hamlet's self-condemnation reveals the features that help to make him a 'sweet prince' – compassion, sensitivity, and awareness.

Hamlet is both a 'sweet prince' and an 'arrant knave', but the balance is weighted heavily towards the former. The evil in him is largely a result of his own suffering and anguish, and the terrifying situation he finds himself in. It is always explicable, often excusable, and cannot blot out his essential nobility and tragic stature. If anything, the weaknesses revealed in him serve to make his goodness all the more credible. As Fortinbras says at the end of the play, had he come to Kingship he would have proved 'most royal'.

**Question 2**

When Henry V rejects and banishes Falstaff at the end of *Henry IV, Part 2*, does the audience sympathise with Henry, or with Falstaff?

**Suggested points**

(a) Although Falstaff is a glutton, a thief, a liar, and a totally unscrupulous rascal, he is liked by the audience because he makes them laugh, and is a great entertainer. Falstaff may be a villain, but he can be an amiable one; his villainy is so obvious that it does not threaten the audience; he has a huge and attractive energy and zest for life. There is much to like in Falstaff, and his banishment might seem unduly harsh.

(b) Falstaff is rarely seen as doing any major act of evil in the play, and Henry's action might therefore be seen as too severe and out of proportion.

(c) Falstaff represents a happy, carefree way of life. In banishing and rejecting him Henry could be seen as also banishing this way of life, rejecting a friend and putting cold duty before personal relationships and people. Henry can appear as ruthless, cold and uncaring when he banishes Falstaff.

(d) On the other hand, Falstaff represents riot, anarchy and misrule, and is based on the Vice character in medieval plays. Vice is always attractive, otherwise it would not be so popular, but the King cannot consort with Vice if his country is to be well-governed and its people cared for.
(e) Falstaff is made deliberately less attractive in *Henry IV, Part 2* to prepare for his rejection. His antics are shown as being more dangerous, less amusing and more seedy than in *Henry IV, Part 1*, and include his ruthless and unattractive manipulation of Mistress Quickly, his recruits and Justice Shallow.
(f) Henry banishes Falstaff from his presence, but gives him a pension. He has told Falstaff in *Henry IV, Part 1* that he will be rejected, and it is Falstaff's fault if he does not heed the warning.

The audience therefore feel sorry for Falstaff, but accept that his rejection is necessary and inevitable. A good King must banish Vice, however painful that might be.

**Question 3**
What is the dramatic significance and contribution of Feste to *Twelfth Night*?

**Suggested points**

(a) Feste provides a great deal of entertainment to the audience, by virtue of his wit and humour, and his songs. As the licensed fool of the play his job is to provide humour, often at the expense of others, and this he does admirably.
(b) His obvious depression at the loss of his master, his worry over losing his post in Olivia's household, and his 'Wind and Rain' song at the end of the play provide a glimpse of a harsher world than is sometimes seen in the rest of the play, and make the point that life is not always comic, thus increasing the reality of the play and making the happiness it portrays more worthwhile.
(c) Feste is highly intelligent and shrewd, and sees through other characters' pretence and hypocrisy. His comments on other characters help the audience to see their true nature, and their weaknesses. He judges characters for us, and is vital to our judgement of them.
(d) He acts as a vital link between the main plot (Viola, Orsino, and Olivia) and the sub-plot (Sir Toby, Sir Andrew, Maria, Fabian, and Malvolio), appearing in both.
(e) He prompts and inspires much of the comic action of the play, most notably the duping of Malvolio.
(f) By remaining as an outsider at the end of the play he emphasises that happiness is not something everyone achieves.
(g) He is a stimulating and fascinating character in his own right. By being one of the most intelligent characters in the play, but also one of the characters who is lowest in society and scorned by it, he emphasises one of the play's main themes, that how someone appears to be in society at large is not always a guide to their real nature.

Feste is therefore one of the most significant characters in the play, contributing widely to it on a number of levels.

**Question 4**

(b) What does this extract tell us about the character of Isabella, and what technique does the author use to convey this information?

(*Measure for Measure*, Act 2, Scene IV).
*Isabella*:
To whom should I complain? Did I tell this, 1
Who would believe me? O perilous mouths
That bear in them one and the self-same tongue
Either of condemnation or approof,
Bidding the law make curtsy to their will;
Hooking both right and wrong to th'appetite
To follow as it draws! I'll to my brother.
Though he hath fall'n by prompture of the blood,
Yet hath he in him such a mind of honour
That, had he twenty heads to tender down
On twenty bloody blocks, he'd yield them up
Before his sister should her body stoop
To such abhorr'd pollution.
Then, Isabel, live chaste, and, brother, die:
More than our brother is our chastity.
I'll tell him yet of Angelo's request,
And fit his mind to death, for his soul's rest.

*Modern English Version:*
Who can I complain to? If I were to say what had happened on one would believe me. [Author's note: Isabella, about to become a nun, has found that her brother is under sentence of death for making his fiancée pregnant. Angelo, the temporary ruler of the state, has offered to save Isabella's brother's life if she will submit to having intercourse with him.] How very dangerous people are who can both condemn and pardon people, and make the law obey their will, letting their decisions not be influenced by right or wrong, but simply by their own physical desires and appetites. I will go and see my brother. Although he has given in to his instincts and physical desires, he is still such an honourable person that he would rather be executed twenty times over than let his sister be seduced and polluted sexually. So, Isabella, remain a virgin and pure, and die brother. My chastity is more dear to me than my brother. Still, I will tell my brother of Angelo's request; knowing that he is about to die will help him prepare his soul to meet death more peacefully.

**Answer**
Two questions open the extract, suggesting uncertainty, fear, and worry. This is then followed by moralising, suggesting that Isabella is genuinely outraged

by what has happened, and has a firm belief in conventional morality. Her mention of 'appetite' might imply scorn and loathing for physical drives. She seems to make her mind up very quickly, and by line 7 she has overcome her initial uncertainty, decided what to do and what the outcome will be. This might well suggest someone who makes up their mind too quickly. She shows no sympathy for her brother, and the repetition of 'I' and her instant conclusion that her own chastity is more important than her brother's life, coupled with her total certainty that her brother will willingly give up his life, suggests selfishness and a certain coldness. The line that ends 'and, brother, die' makes this point forcefully and harshly; she cares more for herself and her honour than she does for her brother. She then talks about 'our' brother and 'our' chastity, a rather pompous and formal mode that increases the impression of coldness and heartlessness. Yet there is also a suggestion in the last two lines that she is not as certain or happy in her decision as she would have the audience and herself believe. She decides to tell her brother of her decision and the offer made to her, almost as if she is hoping he will agree as she has predicted, rather than being actually certain of it. She is clearly religious, as is shown by her outward concern for her brother's soul, but she does not show very much in the way of worry or concern for her brother.

Shakespeare makes Isabella appear a rather cold and hard person with little heart and a great degree of selfishness, though there are hints that some of this is self-deception. The questions at the start of the passage break up the rhythm, suggesting uncertainty, but once Isabella's mind is made up the rhythm becomes more regular and smoother. A more sensitive person might have been expected to speak in a progressively more disorderly way as the full horror of the choice before her was realised.

**Notes**

Note that the above answer restricts itself to the passage, and is not used as an excuse for a general essay on the play. The passage does contain some comment on what is one of the most significant themes in the play, Law and Justice, but because this area is not asked on it has been left out in the answer provided. At best a candidate could afford to write only one sentence on it, as it is not what the question is about.

## Further reading

As might be expected, there is a whole library of classic Shakespearean criticism, much of it still very much worth reading. One of the first great critical works about Shakespeare was A. C. Bradley's *Shakespearean Tragedy* (with an Introduction by J. Russell Brown, Macmillan, 1985). Bradley is still hugely informative, though he has been taken to task for treating the characters in the plays as if they were real. W. H. Charlton, *Shakespearean Comedy* (Methuen, 1966), is a good general survey, and C. L. Barber's *Shakespeare's*

*Festive Comedy* (Princeton University Press, 1972) is essential reading on the social and cultural background to Shakespeare's comedy. John Dover Wilson, *Shakespeare's Happy Comedies* (Faber, 1962), is recommended, as is the same author's *What Happens in Hamlet* (Cambridge University Press, various editions). John F. Danby, *Shakespeare's Doctrine of Nature* (Faber, 1958), is a valuable study of *King Lear*. Rivalling A. C. Bradley as one of the greatest figures in Shakespearean criticism is Harley Granville-Barker, whose *Prefaces to Shakespeare, volumes 1–5* (Batsford, various dates), have lost little of their value over the years. E. M. W. Tillyard's works, notably *The Elizabethan World Picture* (Penguin, 1972) and *Shakespeare's Problem Plays* (Pelican, 1985), are essential reading. J. Dover-Wilson, *The Fortunes of Falstaff* (Cambridge University Press, 1964), exerted a major influence over criticism of Shakespeare's history plays, and in particular the vexed question of how much sympathy should be felt for Falstaff. Two books which greatly influenced thinking on Shakespeare's imagery are Caroline Spurgeon, *Shakespeare's Imagery* (Cambridge University Press, 1935), and J. Clemen, *The Development of Shakespeare's Imagery* (Methuen, 1977).

There is simply too great a volume of work on Shakespeare in recent times to give a list that is in any sense exhaustive. The following is therefore merely a sampling of some modern work.

- Jonathan Bate, *The Genius of Shakespeare* (Picador/Macmillan, 1997): a highly regarded and well-written examination of all aspects of Shakespeare's life and work.
- John Russell Brown, *William Shakespeare: Writing for Performance* (Macmillan, 1996): an interesting work reflecting growing interest in the performance of Shakespeare's plays.
- John Drakakis, ed., *Shakespearean Tragedy* (Longman, 1996)
- Michael Mangan, *A Preface to Shakespeare's Tragedies* (Longman, 1991)
- Juliet Dusinberre, *Shakespeare and the Nature of Women* (Macmillan, 1996)
- Hugh Grady, *The Modernist Shakespeare. Critical Texts in a Material World* (Oxford University Press, 1994)
- Michael Mangan, *A Preface to Shakespeare's Comedies* (Longman, 1997)
- Russ McDonald, *The Bedford Companion to Shakespeare. An Introduction with Documents* (Macmillan, 1996): an excellent source book and background text.
- Kiernan Ryan, ed., *Shakespeare's Last Plays* (Longman, 1998)
- Stanley Wells, ed., *The Cambridge Companion to Shakespeare Studies* (Cambridge University Press, 1986)

CHAPTER TEN

# The Metaphysical poets

John Donne was born in 1571, or thereabouts; Henry Vaughan, another Metaphysical poet, died in 1695, and it is hardly surprising that poets whose lives stretched out over a hundred years should be so individual. It is perhaps more surprising that there are sufficient similarities between all the poets generally held to be in the Metaphysical school to justify their all being branded with the same name.

## General issues and questions

The four Metaphysical poets who appear with the greatest frequency on examination syllabuses are John Donne (1571–1631), Andrew Marvell (1621–78), George Herbert (1593–1633) and Henry Vaughan (1622–95). All these authors are highly individual, but certain general areas in their work can be distinguished. It is very common to find a definition of Metaphysical poetry, in quotation form, as an essay title, with the candidate required to sift through this definition with reference to the author he or she is studying. Read the definition given in Chapter 3 of this work, and any other definitions you can find. Make sure you understand also the entries on conceit and paradox, two techniques central to Metaphysical poetry.

Originally the term 'metaphysical' was coined by John Dryden (1631–1700) and later popularised by Dr Samuel Johnson (1709–84), and the features of the school which unite the various authors are quite numerous. As well as making widespread use of conceit, paradox, and punning or wordplay, the Metaphysicals drew their imagery from all sources of knowledge, and in particular from science, theology, geography, and philosophy. The images are often startling in themselves, very tightly packed, and in startling contrast to each other, something which has led to the accusation that their imagery is too shocking, and their poems mere displays of wit. There is often considerable violence in the poems, not so much in what is described as in the style and the occasionally forceful and colloquial approach.

Metaphysical poets tend to take a moment of intense experience, but rarely are content just to present or recreate it. Linked to whatever is being written about there is an intense and almost overwhelming urge to argue, persuade or define what is happening; there is plenty of emotion in Metaphysical poetry, but also a fierce desire to come to terms with experience in an intellectual, rational sense. Love, religion, and nature are common subjects, perhaps because all three offer an intense spiritual moment and the opportunity to analyse, dissect and push a point of view about the experience.

These poets talk both about the world they live in, and about themselves. Historians have pointed out that these poets lived in a time of major social and political upheaval (a few years after Donne's death England was to execute its king, and do away with the monarchy for over twenty years), and this feeling of uncertainty is very obvious in Metaphysical poetry, as is the desire to impose certainty on an uncertain world. The Metaphysical poets were unfashionable during the eighteenth century, and were thought too wild and rough for contemporary poetic tastes. They did not really come into their own until the twentieth century, which may well have been drawn to them by its own uncertainty. A number of very quotable lines damning the poets for their violence are therefore available to examiners, and as there are a number of occasions when Metaphysical poets do appear to go 'over the top', or expend vast effort for little visible result, it must not be thought that a question such as this is merely an excuse for the candidate to pour praise on the poets.

## John Donne

Donne was educated as a Roman Catholic, by prosperous parents, but then became a Protestant. He married a niece of his patron's wife, Anne Moore, and so angered Sir Thomas Egerton, his patron, that he had Donne imprisoned, and removed from his job. Their dispute was later patched up, but not before Donne had to spend years living off the generosity of his friends.

Bowing to pressure from the King, James I, Donne became an Anglican priest in 1615, and became an immensely successful and popular preacher of sermons. Most of his poetry was not published until after his death. It ranges from fervent and impassioned love poetry that can also be very cynical and bitter, to remarkably powerful religious poetry. The tone of all his poems is passionate, sensual and intellectual, and much of it is highly dramatic, with a rough energy and drive that at times seems only just under control. In almost every poem he wrote Donne seemed to be looking for an all-embracing mental and physical experience, a moment of total involvement and power. In earlier poems he seeks this experience in love, but then even more remarkably he transfers it almost effortlessly (and sometimes in much the same style) into religious poetry. God in Donne's poems is sometimes talked to as if the poetry were a dialogue between two lovers.

There can be an attractive impertinence and cheekiness in his poetry, as when he opens a poem with 'Busie old fool, unruly sunne!' Yet his ironical impudence frequently conveys a very full realisation of how small and insignificant man is, and how much he overestimates his own importance. 'The Sunne Rising', from which the first line quoted above comes, is a good example. By treating the sun as an 'old fool' and saying that the lovers in their bed are superior to him, he shows a vaunting ego. At the same time the reason given for man's superiority includes the idea that the poet can blot out the sun simply by closing his eyes, an image that reminds the reader of the ostrich with his head in the sand. The pathos and even the stupidity of man's capacity for deluding himself into thinking he has control of his life is there in the poem, but so is a huge admiration of man's stature and the power of his mind. Donne frequently uses colloquial language, and a brusque, argumentative tone that stuns the reader into agreement by the speed of its mental processes, its lucidity and its clearly felt passion.

Examination questions on Donne often ask about his attitude to, and treatment of, the theme of love, and the extent to which the passion and commitment of his religious verse is expressed in the style of love poetry. The importance of argument and colloquial language in his poetry, and the tightly planned way that many of his poems move from a preliminary statement to a reasoned and resounding final line or conclusion, may also be examined. So too may the dramatic or 'rough' quality of his poetry, together with its variety. The tone and mood of his poetry ranges from the ecstatic ('The Exstasie') to the desperate melancholy of 'A Nocturnall Upon Saint Lucies Day'. His subjects and sources for his imagery are equally varied, leading to questions such as 'Discuss the assertion that Donne's poetry is typified by variety and energy'. Some modern criticism appears to be switching away from interest in his love poetry to greater interest in his religious writing.

## Andrew Marvell

It has been said of Andrew Marvell that he manages to combine 'passion with formality, lightness of touch with seriousness, and lyric beauty with intelligence of argument'. 'To His Coy Mistress' by Marvell is the subject of a full answer in Chapter 4 of this work. In his own time Marvell was best known as a writer and politician in favour of freedom of worship, a champion of liberty, and a powerful writer of prose pamphlets. He was neutral during the English Civil War, then became a supporter of Oliver Cromwell, but was allowed to retain his position under the Restoration rule of Charles. It is sometimes surprising for a modern reader to realise that many of the Metaphysical poets were simply not known as poets in their own time. Much of the poetry they wrote was very private, perhaps shown and read only to a small group of friends. Their honesty, informality of address and willingness to shock might well owe much to the personal and private nature of their poetry.

Marvell is quieter than Donne, and less dramatic, but there is an authority, dignity and elegance in his poetry that is often lacking in Donne's work, and which produces poetry that is more reflective and sometimes firmer in its arguments than Donne's work. Marvell is also less reliant on sweeping paradoxes and conceits than is Donne. His love poetry is magnificent, though examination questions do sometimes ask candidates to say whether it is 'more art than nature', suggesting by this that Marvell's love poetry is less personal than, say, Donne's. There might also be a suggestion here that Marvell's love poetry is rarely innovatory in theme or content, and can sometimes give the impression of an author writing as an exercise in technique rather than with real commitment.

Marvell made extensive use of the pastoral tradition (see Ch. 4), but his vision of Nature is far from being an idealised rural idyll. He creates a magnificent literary symbol in his use of the mower or reaper figure, who has associations with death, time, and rebirth. Examination questions on Nature in Marvell's work require the student to understand the complexity of Marvell's vision, including the enigmatic and menacing figure of the mower. Marvell does not love Nature in the raw; he is no Romantic poet. Rather it is Nature that has been controlled and civilised by the hand of man that appeals to him, as in a well-kept garden. In one sense this symbolises the classical view of Nature which sees it as incomplete and anarchic, unless it has the guiding and controlling hand of rationality and intellect to let it yield up its riches.

In 'The Garden' Marvell pours scorn on human ambition and striving after worldly success, preferring instead the 'fair quiet', 'innocence' and 'delicious solitude' of the garden, which is compared to the Garden of Eden. However, there is a clear clash between Marvell the recluse and Marvell the man of action, and an understanding of this conflict is essential for any student sitting an examination with a question on Marvell in it. Whilst in 'The Garden' Marvell seems to suggest that involvement in the world at large is fruitless and unsatisfying, in 'An Horatian Ode Upon Cromwell's Return From Ireland' and 'A Nymph Complaining of the Death of her Faun' he seems to take the opposite view. In 'An Horatian Ode . . .', Cromwell, the archetypal man of action, is seen as heaven's avenger, a man whose capacity to take the world and shake it by its shoulders is admirable. He is a natural force, like lightning, unstoppable, destructive and hence unavoidable. Marvell's complexity is seen at its best in this poem. He praises Cromwell whilst at the same time being fully aware of his weaknesses and deficiencies, and does the same for the ill-fated Charles I. In 'A Nymph Complaining of the Death of her Faun', the nymph's faun has been slaughtered by 'wanton troopers, riding by', suggesting that any pastoral seclusion is liable to be shattered by the force of worldly events.

In a dignified, yet passionate way Marvell is torn between involvement and seclusion, action and passivity, something seen as well in 'Upon Appleton

House'. Marvell was two people, the private man and the man of affairs thrust onto a public stage. He was also a political satirist, though this element in his work is rarely examined. The major areas for examination in Marvell are therefore his love poems, his use of standard Metaphysical devices and techniques, his pastoral poetry, and the whole conflict between the recluse and the man of action.

## George Herbert

George Herbert was born into an aristocratic family, and was destined for a highly successful secular career. He suddenly changed tack, and became a parish priest renowned for his piety and godliness. As with Donne and Marvell, his poems were published after his death. They are highly original and individual attempts to deal with conventional issues of Christianity. A description such as this does little to convey the drama, passion and excitement that Herbert injects into his verse. He faces up to the issues of doubt, loss of faith and anger, as well as managing to express an utterly convincing faith and belief in God. Dramatic openings to poems, colloquial language, conceits and use of paradox, intense questioning, intense personal feeling married to rigorous intellectual examination and a fierce spirituality – all these Metaphysical features are present in Herbert's verse. There is an intensity of enquiry in Herbert's writing which sums up the best of Metaphysical school, and which can also lead him in to technical experimentation, as when he makes actual shape of a poem on the page represent its subject.

## Henry Vaughan

Vaughan's poetry is sometimes set with Herbert's, with selections from both combining to form one 'set text'. In general Herbert and Vaughan are thought of rather less highly than either Donne or Marvell, perhaps because their subject matter is restricted largely to religion.

Vaughan is rather less extravagant and elaborate than Donne, though conceits and intellectual wordplay do feature in his poetry. There is an intense yearning in Vaughan's poetry, of a spiritual and religious nature, but it is often a yearning for past or future glories (the spiritual closeness of the child in 'The Retreate', friends who have gone to Paradise in 'Friends Departed'), and contains a melancholic distaste for the world the poet finds himself in. Vaughan does not doubt the existence of God or Heaven, but he despairs of finding them on Earth, and his poetry, strong as it is, can lack the exuberance and joyousness of Herbert's and Donne's verse. Vaughan was capable of producing marvellously memorable lines, one of the most famous being 'I saw Eternity the other night/Like a great Ring of pure and endless light,' from 'The World', but sometimes his poems fail to live up to the promise of the individual lines. In this area he bears comparison with John Webster, if in no other. His virtues are the Metaphysical ones of intensity, clarity and spirituality, and he has perhaps rather more simplicity than many writers from the same period. He lacks Donne's, Marvell's and Herbert's capacity to build poems up to a magnificent climax, or to pack quite the range and breadth of experience into his poems that the others seem to manage effortlessly.

## Background reading

Any student needs to read round his or her set authors. It is particularly necessary with the Metaphysical poets, because definitions of the school feature quite largely in examination questions, and because the individual poets do throw each other into relief and help a candidate's awareness of their individual strengths and weaknesses. As a basic reading list candidates should look at the following poems:

**Donne:** 'Holy Sonnets'; 'The Sunne Rising'; 'A Nocturnall upon S. Lucies Day'; 'Song: Goe, and catch a falling starre'; 'The Flea'; 'Twicknam Garden'.
**Marvell:** 'To His Coy Mistress'; 'An Horatian Ode Upon Cromwell's Return From Ireland'; 'The Mower to the Glow-Worms'; 'Upon Appleton House'; 'The Garden'.
**Herbert:** 'Easter Wings'; 'Jordan'; 'The Pearl'; 'The Collar'; 'Love'.
**Vaughan:** 'The World'; 'The Retreate'; 'Corruption'.

Other poets generally held to be members of the Metaphysical school are Richard Crashaw (1612/13–49), linked with Vaughan and Herbert because his poems are mainly religious; John Cleveland (1613–58), sometimes linked to Marvell because of the political element in his work; and Abraham Cowley (1618–67).

## Question and answer

Each individual poem written by an author is usually complete within itself. As a result there can be a problem drawing the threads together for an essay on a poet's work in general, and the tendency is to write on a one-poem-to-one-paragraph basis. This rarely works effectively. Answering a question on a poem-by-poem basis often leads to the student writing down quite a large amount of irrelevant material, and failing to develop a consistent thread of argument. Wherever possible, answer on a topic-by-topic basis, illustrating your point from a number of poems. After all, if your point is not provable by reference to a number of individual poems, as distinct from only one, the point may not actually be valid for the whole spread of an author's work.

This being said, it is a common feature in examinations to mention a general theme, and then ask the candidate to illustrate this from a designated number of poems. An answer to such a question is given below.

**Question**
Illustrate and discuss Donne's treatment of the theme of love by reference to any three poems.

**Answer**
It could be argued that Donne's religious poetry is as much love poetry as his poems which have as their subject love between the sexes. His religious poetry can at times simply seem to transfer the passion and emotion of sexual love to love of God, and do so without implying any disrespect to God. The range of emotions expressed in those poems of his which deal with love between man and woman reflect the character and virtues of Donne as a whole – intensity, variety and a forceful and even violent desire to analyse every last shred of experience for all that it can reveal.

'The Canonisation' opens in an abrupt, colloquial and abusive manner. To 'canonise' someone is to make them a saint in the Christian church, and there is an immediate irony in the blasphemous use of 'God' in the opening line: 'For Godsake hold your tongue, and let me love.' Here Donne is suggesting that love is private, always subject to prying and perhaps jealous eyes, but essentially no concern of anyone else's. This startling opening line is followed by a stanza that appears to have little to do with love. The poet laughs at himself, inviting his critic to 'chide my palsie, or my gout,/My five gray hairs . . .', all of which are features of old men, and then in inviting his critic to go elsewhere and occupy his time he satirises courtiers and flatterers: 'Take you a course, get you a place,/Observe his honour, or his grace'. The first stanza is therefore energetic, abusive, amusing and varied in its content. Donne's variety, and the sheer speed with which logical idea after logical idea flows from his pen, is suggested by the second stanza, which sets up an almost legalistic case to prove that the poet's love harms no one. Love has not 'Adde[d] one more to the plaguie Bill', and wars take place whether or not the poet follows love. It is an emotion that is being talked about in the poem, but hard and sharp intellect is used to justify and typify that emotion, albeit with the author's tongue in his cheek. A more personal element creeps in with the succeeding stanzas. Love is a beautiful, joyous experience; its sonnets are hymns, and because the lovers are the constructors of hymns they deserve to be 'Canonis'd for Love'. The reader knows full well this is carnal love that is being discussed, and that it is ludicrous to expect people to be elevated to the rank of saints for indulging in what the Church sees as sin, but somehow Donne makes his conclusion seem the more convincing. The final stanza is perhaps the most serious of all. It uses the image that is very common in Donne's love poetry, where the power of love 'did the whole worlds soul contract, and drove/Into the glasses of your eyes'. The poem is insolent, even cheeky, in its attitude to conventional morality. It celebrates the joys of carnal love, yet at the same time there is a seriousness underlying the whole poem that gives it strength and weight, making it more than just a young man's justification of casual pleasure.

If 'The Canonisation' is a celebration then 'Twicknam Garden' is more of a lament. The poet retreats to the garden 'Blasted with sighs, and surrounded by teares' as a result of the vicissitudes of love, hoping to 'Receive such balmes, as else cure every thing'. But the garden is like Paradise, and the poet by bringing the serpent of love into it renders it corrupt and ineffective. In one sense this poem strikes a conventional pose about love; tears, sighs and groans have been the other side of love's coin for hundreds of years, and it could be said that the poet in 'Twicknam Garden' is merely echoing what one of Chaucer's courtly lovers might have said and been, after a slight from his love. However, the poem is not a mere repetition of a conventional and perhaps rather hackneyed theme. The poem is skilfully structured, with each stanza having a different theme and atmosphere. The first stanza concentrates on the poet's feelings of sadness and bitterness. The second stanza takes these same feelings but gives bite and edge to them by expressing them through images of the garden. The garden is made to reflect the poet's mood, but is also personified:

> 'Twere wholsomer for mee, that winter did
> Benight the glory of this place,
> And that a grave frost did forbid
> These trees to laugh, and mock mee to me face;

The very fact that it is summer in the garden is used to emphasise the black winter of the poet's mood. So great is the poet's misery that he wishes to be turned into 'Some senseless peece of this place' so that he may 'groane here'. The selfishness of the lover and his bitterness are brought home to the reader by the suggestion that the poet's tears be put in a bottle and used to test women's tears at home, 'For all are false, that tast not just like mine'. The reader is allowed to savour in full the depths of the lover's depression, while never losing sight of the fact that this depression is also petulant, and almost grossly self-centred. The lover expresses his own feelings and characterises himself, but because the personality of the love is kept deliberately open-ended the poem can be read as typical of all lovers. The third stanza ends on a paradox. 'O perverse sex, where none is true but shee,/Who's therefore true, because her truth kills mee.' The 'truth' of woman (implying fidelity and loyalty) is that they are all untrue. The sweeping generalisation about women summarises and typifies the poet's abject misery. In this poem, as in many others by Donne, love is a savage illness, women naturally unfaithful and never to be trusted, and the man realises the stupidity of allowing himself to be ensnared by love as well as recognising that the bait is irresistible.

'Sweetest love, I do not goe' illustrates the range and variety of Donne's love poetry. Where the poems previously studied have an almost frantic energy and drive, this 'Song' is gentle, reflective, caring, and deeply moving.

It is a reassurance to a loved one, perhaps Donne's wife, on the occasion of his leaving her:

Sweetest love, I do not goe,
  For weariness of thee,
Nor in the hope the world can show
  A fitter love for mee;
    But since that I
Must dye at last, 'tis best,
To use myself in jest
  Thus by fain'd deaths to dye;

The poet reassures his listener of his fidelity, and there is more than a hint of the 'Holy Sonnets' in the conclusion to the poem. If the poet does die, he says,

  But thinke that wee
Are but turn'd aside to sleepe;
They who one another keepe
  Alive, ne'r parted bee.

In this poem, as in the others, love provokes an emotion that is eternal, and unbreakable. Here it is faithful love, in 'The Canonisation' it was the joy of carnal love, and in 'Twicknam Garden' it is the melancholy of love, but in each case what is produced by love, though abstract, is stronger than anything physical or concrete.

The sweep and variety of Donne's love poetry is very evident from the examples studied above, as is the capacity he has within the confines of tightly structured verse to create wholly different moods. In all three poems the moment or the mood must be argued and analysed, never merely recorded. In all three the intensity of expression by the poet does not blind the reader or stop him from forming an objective judgement of the experience being presented.

## Further reading

### General

- Joan Bennett, *Five Metaphysical Poets* (Cambridge University Press, 1964)
- Thomas N. Corns, *The Cambridge Companion to English Poetry: Donne to Marvell* (Cambridge University Press, 1993)
- George Parfitt, *English Poetry of the Seventeenth Century* (Longman, 1992)

### John Donne

- John Carey, *John Donne: Life, Mind and Art* (Faber, 1990)
- Andrew Mousley, *John Donne* (New Casebook Series, Macmillan, 1998)

- P. M. Oliver, *Donne's Religious Writing. A Discourse of Feigned Devotion* (Longman, 1997)

## George Herbert

- James Boyd White, *This Book of Stars: Learning to Read George Herbert* (University of Michigan Press, 1994)

## Andrew Marvell

- Tom Healy, ed., *Andrew Marvell* (Longman, 1998): an interesting collection of modern essays.

CHAPTER ELEVEN

# Milton

Shakespeare, Chaucer, and Milton were the grand triumvirate of the British examining boards and traditional degree courses. Changing times and in particular the emphasis of new critical directions emanating from the United States of America seemed to threaten this, and the situation at universities is still very fluid. In particular, authors such as Shakespeare, Milton and Chaucer have been seen as typical of the 'Dead White European Males' who were perceived as having dominated academia (and much more) for far too long. In 1992 *The Daily Telegraph* ran a story stating that the black American woman novelist Alice Walker had become a compulsory author in more higher education institutions than Shakespeare. However, new UK Government policies and the creation of a 'core' for A-level English meant that Shakespeare became a compulsory author, and traditional authors such as Chaucer and Milton received positive discrimination. There are therefore difficult and sometimes contradictory cross-currents at work at the present time. The fact that the listeners to a leading national radio programme voted Shakespeare the most influential individual of the millennium shows that both he and other traditionally revered authors have strong populist support.

In any event, Milton is a crucial figure in English literature, and a major author by any standards. The examination candidate who wrote, 'Like kippers, Milton has a strong taste, and therefore arouses strong feelings' was probably being too flippant for most examiners' tastes, but he had a point. Milton is a towering genius of English letters, but his grand, epic style is not to everyone's taste, and a totally subjective appraisal of Milton would suggest that he can be the least popular of the great writers with examination candidates, as well as being one of the most popular with examiners and teachers.

The majority of critical works cheat slightly with Milton. They mention in general terms the adverse criticisms that have been made of him, and then provide in detail the refutations of these viewpoints. It is worth reading criticism of Milton's works more widely than perhaps that of any other author, to find out precisely what the objections to Milton are. The student who finds himself ill-at-ease with Milton's works has a number of essential tasks to perform.

1. Recognise that Milton has certain huge talents. Not liking these in a personal sense has never mattered much in criticism. The student has to learn to respect and acknowledge the achievement of an author, and understand him, even if there is little or no personal sympathy towards him.
2. Remember the comment of an academic to a young student who had written an essay dismissing *Paradise Lost*, to the effect that it was perfectly fair to write that the book should be dismissed – but only after one had written something so lasting and famous oneself.
3. Find out what are the sensible objections to Milton, and make these the basis of a hostile view, not vague and wholly unscholarly attitudes such as 'I'm bored by him', or 'It needs too much work to understand him'. Never, with any author, pour praise on his works which you do not yourself feel; equally, when you do dislike an author, find scholarly reasons for your distaste, remembering that your job as a critic is to understand and appreciate, not to like an author's works.

## Milton's life

Milton lived from 1608 to 1674. As has already been noted with reference to the Metaphysical poets this was one of the most tumultuous times in the whole of English history. Milton spent the first years of his life as a student and academic, attending the University of Cambridge for seven years, and finishing off this period with a tour round Europe. His years of private study were financed by his father, and from this period dates the wealth of learning that he acquired, particularly in the classics, a wealth which sometimes makes it difficult for the student to approach his work.

The second period in his life dates from 1642 or 1643. In his first period he had completed his education, and written some poetry, including *L'Allegro* (1632), *Il Penseroso* (1632), *Comus* (1634), and *Lycidas* (1637). At first Milton appeared to ignore the Civil War that broke out in 1642, but by 1649 he had come to support Oliver Cromwell and the Puritan cause against the Royalists. In that year he became 'Secretary for the Foreign Tongues', effectively the author of the political pamphlets that sought to justify Cromwell's reign and his execution of the old King, Charles I. In this second period of his life he virtually ceased to write poetry, political writing taking up most of his time. He married for the first time in 1642 or 1643, most unhappily: he and his wife separated for most of the time, and by 1652 he had gone completely blind, having had weak eyesight from youth. The third period of his life, 1660–74, coincides with the Restoration period, in which the monarchy under Charles II was restored to England. As a Cromwellian sympathiser, Milton was in some danger, but he was rescued by other poets and authors, some of them Royalists, and allowed to live out his days in peace. He married twice more, his first two wives dying in childbirth. Deprived of political work and influence it was this last period of his life that saw the production of the long poems that have made his reputation, in particular *Paradise Lost* (1674), though parts of this epic were probably written as early as 1642. In this last period he also wrote *Samson Agonistes* (1671).

## Literary and historical background

### Puritanism

Milton is associated above all with the Puritan ethic, the ethic which drove Oliver Cromwell and has become associated above all other influencing factors with the English Civil War. It is essential to note that Puritanism was not a religion, but rather an attitude of mind which saw the Roman Catholic Church, and the Anglican Church founded by Henry VIII when he broke away from Catholicism, as corrupt and decadent. The Puritans took their name from their desire to return to a purer, more austere form of worship, and to cleanse religion of the excesses and corruption which they saw in it and in the Established Church. Literature has not been kind to Puritans. Ben Jonson (see Ch. 8) and Shakespeare in *Twelfth Night* portrayed them as ludicrously sombre and serious men, puffed up with a sense of their own righteousness, lacking a sense of humour, and concerned only to stop all manifestations of human fun and enjoyment.

Milton was a serious and austere figure, cast in a very different mould from Jonson or Shakespeare. He could inspire vast affection in those that knew him, and his particular brand of Puritanism was more that of the rebel, bravely defying the establishment for a spiritual cause, yearning for true spirituality in religion and willing to risk his life in the defence of liberty. This was the Puritanism that founded America, and did so in the face of tremendous persecution and suffering. If it also produced a particularly vicious and even scurrilous streak in Milton's political writing, which does not stop short of personal abuse, the reason is that the times in which he wrote were not suited to compromise in any sphere. Any such traits do not reduce the essential courage in the stand he took.

If there is one thing that emerges from Milton's life and his beliefs, it is the folly of seeing too great a link between a man's life and what he wrote. Milton's Puritanism comes through in his work in the tremendous spiritual clarity he expresses, in his desire to go back to the most basic of all religious stories, and in his sympathy for the individual man. At the same time here is a man with an overwhelming belief in free will and freedom of expression who at one time allied himself with the Presbyterian sect. This was the one sect which, with its all-embracing belief in predestination, denied free will and freedom of expression to man. Here is a man with the highest political ideals who engaged in vicious political tract writing. Here also is a man who seemed unable to make any success of his relationships with women, but yet can show true marital bliss existing between Adam and Eve in *Paradise Lost*. Great literature is rarely simple though one of the skills of authorship is to make it seem so. Great works of art can be and are often are immensely complex and contradictory, though often not as contradictory as the apparent clashes between an author's own life and his writings. Such contradictions should be enjoyed rather than ignored or viewed as an illogical irritant.

## Cosmology

Throughout *Paradise Lost*, Milton uses the Ptolemaic system and theory of cosmology, which had been believed throughout the Middle Ages. He did so despite the fact that Copernicus and Galileo had, by the time Milton was alive, proved the basics of the modern knowledge that the Earth revolves around the sun, and not the other way round. Milton certainly knew of the modern theories. The answer to why he still used the older system in preference is simply that the Ptolemaic system suited his literary aims much better than the newer ideas.

The Ptolemaic system (still evident in Elizabethan and Jacobean works) suggests that the world is made up of a number of concentric, crystalline spheres (opinions vary about the number, nine being a reasonable guess), each revolving inside the other, with Earth at the centre. The motive power for these spheres is provided by God's love, itself transformed into energy by the action of the outermost sphere, or *primum mobile*. As the spheres move against each other, they produce a marvellous music or sound, known as the music of the spheres. The whole created universe is suspended from Heaven by a golden chain. Various insulating layers are provided between the spheres. Among these are the Chaos and the Old Night, through which Satan has to fly to reach Paradise. It was believed that the four elements which made up all earthly matter (earth, air, fire, and water) were naturally repugnant to each other, and that only the imposition of God's will made them bend to natural laws, such as that whereby the waters of the Earth do not rise up and swamp all land. Chaos is the land where these laws do not apply, so in flying through Chaos Satan is battling with a vision of total and utter anarchy. A modern equivalent might be Satan flying through the heart of a nuclear reaction, in which all the natural force and violence of the universe's building blocks has been released from the control that normally holds them in check.

This system appears quaint and ludicrous to us nowadays, but because this system was invented as a logical response to how man saw his place in the cosmos, it makes a perfect setting for *Paradise Lost*. It may be factually inaccurate, but so was Shakespeare in the majority of his History plays. If Milton's cosmos can be viewed as a complete poetic symbol, then it comes into its own; Chaos, Hell, the golden chain, Paradise, all help and assist Milton in expressing his basic poetic desires and designs.

## The Epic

Anyone studying *Paradise Lost* quickly learns that it is an epic. Definitions of the epic abound, and can be found in this work (Ch. 3) and in a host of others. Milton's application of the epic mould is not as simple as it sometimes appears. No fewer than three epic elements contribute to *Paradise Lost.*

1. *Primary epics* are typified by the *Iliad* and the *Odyssey*, by the blind poet Homer who probably lived in the eighth century BC. These epics were designed as long narratives to be read out to an audience, and celebrate the deeds of the military aristocracy. Their hero was part human and part divine, usually having at least one parent who was a god. His deeds and military prowess were immensely heroic.
2. *Secondary epics* are associated with Virgil (70–19 BC), whose great work was the *Aeneid*, designed more for private reading, and with a more consciously solemn and dignified style. Aeneas, the hero of the *Aeneid*, is still a military hero, and still has a divine parent, but he can think and philosophise, as well as fight, and is one who needs to learn self-control before he is fit to govern. The 'grand style' and more sophisticated hero are both very present in *Paradise Lost.*
3. However, the third element which adds significantly to confusion about the role and influence of epic style in *Paradise Lost* is that Milton is deliberately applying a *pagan style* to a specifically *Christian story*. There is a conflict, though often a fruitful one, between the influence of the pagan epic and scriptural literature in *Paradise Lost.* Milton uses the style and some of the conventions of secondary epic in his work, but blends in with these many elements which are directly derived from Christian literature. An awareness of each, and an awareness of where the two blend and clash, is essential in understanding the work.

# Topic areas in *Paradise Lost*

Examiners usually set two books from *Paradise Lost*, often drawn from Books 1, 2, 4, 9, and 10, though sometimes they surprise themselves and students by choosing others. Incidentally, it is worth reading the complete books of *Paradise Lost*, daunting prospect though it might sound. Familiarity with Milton's language, and therefore understanding of it, increases with usage. There are hidden gems in the unfashionable books. Most of all, a few hours extra work gives a sense of perspective and extra detail that is a hugely marketable commodity when it comes to essays and examinations.

Degree courses may ask for knowledge of *Paradise Regained*, *Lycidas*, *Comus* and *Samson Agonistes*, though the last three are quite popular for Advanced level as well.

A quite vitriolic debate has raged over whether or not Milton was 'of the Devil's party without knowing it' (William Blake). Milton undoubtedly sets out to 'justify the ways of God to man'. Some would argue that what he succeeds in doing is showing Satan as an altogether more attractive figure than God or the forces of good. This is a fascinating area. On its widest level it relates to one of the eternal issues and problems in literature, which is that it is a great deal easier to present a realistic and convincing picture of vice than it is of godliness. After all, vice must be attractive, or it would not be so popular. Shakespeare faces this problem in his *Henry IV* where Falstaff, the 'Vice' figure, can appear more attractive than the supposed hero of the plays, Prince Hal.

Did Milton intend Satan to be the hero of *Paradise Lost*? Outwardly it is a ludicrous suggestion, but modern theories of criticism such as Deconstruction tend to show the dissolution and decay of all forms and structures, among which might be included Milton's beliefs and intentions as traditionally perceived. Milton does acknowledge Satan's grandeur, and gives him features that are undeniably heroic. He has huge courage, a willingness to fight against all odds, intelligence, and physical prowess. Satan is the archetypal rebel, and as guerrilla movements all over the world prove, rebellion itself is an attractive feature.

It is arguable that Milton deliberately set out to show in Satan a representative of the old, primary epic heroic values, and then set out to show how this type of hero should be superseded by the newer model, partly drawn from the secondary epic, and partly from scriptural authority. Temperance and self-control echo, like a clarion-call, throughout *Paradise Lost* as the virtues most praised, admired and needed by Milton. Satan may have the old heroic virtues, but what he signally lacks is this control and temperance. Milton's view is a thoughtful, serious, and well-considered one. His mistakes, if that is what they are, are to show Satan at his most heroic in Books 1 and 2, the very start of the epic, and to assume that his new mould of heroism will be strong enough to swamp the appeal of the old one. Temperance implies control of the passions, but there is a gut appeal in the old type of hero that can sweep moralising and philosophy aside. No one doubts that the reader should dismiss Satan as a hero, at least in the sense of the figure we most admire in the book. The problem with human nature is that we do not always do what we should, or what we are told.

One problem with *Paradise Lost* is that very few students read beyond the one or two Books they are set. If Books 1 and 2 are the set texts this can be lethal for a candidate faced with a question on the status of Satan, because it is in the later books that Milton deliberately blackens Satan's character. He deliberately chooses evil, and deliberately corrupts Adam and Eve. He knowingly blocks out all his finer feelings, and is shown to corrupt Adam and Eve for purely selfish reasons, using them as pawns in his personal vendetta against God. From being a heroic war leader, he turns into a 'vile politician', an arch hypocrite, and a seamy manipulator of those weaker than himself. In Book 9, Satan is a vicious actor, not a heroic leader, and it must also be remembered that by Book 9 Milton has succeeded in building up a charming picture of innocence in Adam and Eve. The victims of his corruption and flattery are not ciphers to us, but real people.

## Freedom of manoeuvre

All writers who use a story that is very well known to their readership lose an element of freedom in so doing. The story Milton chose to use presents more problems than many others, and on a variety of levels.

1. First, there is the problem of how God, who is all-knowing, permitted a third of his angels in Heaven to rebel and revolt against him. Milton answers this one very neatly, as throughout *Paradise Lost* his fervent belief in free choice is conveyed. The devotion to God shown by the remainder of the angels is meaningless unless they have the potential and the capacity to rebel, and Milton shows with the angels and with Adam and Eve that free will must involve the opportunity to make the choice in the wrong direction.
2. Although a lesser problem, the epic tradition demanded military deeds and battles, but there can be something mildly ludicrous in the sight of angels and archangels battling it out in Heaven with swords, particularly as both Milton and his audience know that angels, be they good or bad, cannot be killed in the conventional way. Milton thus has to stage a battle where biblical evidence makes it clear that the rebel angels were outnumbered two to one, where none of the contestants can actually die, and where severed limbs merely rejoin themselves back onto the main body. Something can be made out of these oddities by a critic hostile to Milton, but the honest student will recognise that they are not major blemishes on the work, simply because Milton's style makes the battle convincing. There are times, however, when Milton blunders into error, as when he gives the reader a blow-by-blow account of an angel's digestive system. Milton is determined to explain everything, and there are some things which perhaps are better left to the imagination. Explanation can sometimes merely emphasise a difficulty instead of explaining it, and create a problem where none need exist.
3. There is always a problem in sustaining dramatic and narrative tension when the outcome of a story is well known. Vividness of characterisation helps here a great deal, in that it makes the centre of our interest not what happens but to whom it happens. Satan, Adam, and Eve are vividly portrayed in a manner that makes the reader care genuinely what happens to them. There is also a genuine interest in seeing what an author makes out of characters who are widely known and portrayed, and Milton succeeds by creating this interest and feeling for his characters, in much the same way as Shakespeare makes a new play out of an old story in *Antony and Cleopatra*.

4. Milton faces a more serious problem in his portrayal of God. By his very nature God is the ultimate Divinity, and as such is unportrayable. By showing him at all, Milton runs the risk of making an all-powerful and unreachable figure mundane and approachable, thus reducing his mystique and power. It has been said that Milton's God is a pedantic schoolmaster, and Milton almost acknowledges one of his main problems when he says his task is to justify the ways of God to man; the use of 'justify' implies that it is not all plain sailing in agreeing with God's decision to oust Adam and Eve from the Garden of Eden, and to deprive all humanity thereafter of the joys of Paradise.

   There are times when Milton treads a fine line in this area, and one of the more stimulating and rare Advanced-level questions on the book is whether Milton does actually succeed in his proposed justification. The key to an answer is a reading of the whole epic, rather than isolated fragments, and a firm realisation that the whole issue hinges on free will. In Milton's terms this is a priceless gift, but to be meaningful it has to be double edged. Furthermore mankind in *Paradise Lost* is not forever banished from Paradise, but rather sent out into exile so that it can learn what it needs to learn (notably the virtues of temperance and control) in order to be a worthy inhabitant of it.

## Milton's style

Milton's style is a favourite topic for examiners. Words such as 'sublimity' and 'grand style' occur frequently in critical works on Milton, but as with so many terms in literature they can mean so much and apply to such a wide front as to be more confusing than they are helpful. For an effective answer on Milton's style the student must be aware of the 'epic' elements in it. Many of these have already been referred to in this chapter; the most obvious one for the student to grasp is the epic simile. Lines 196–209 of Book 1, where Satan is described in terms of the mighty monsters of mythology and the natural world, are a good starting point for study.

One of the great problems in Milton for any modern reader of Milton is his use of Latinate forms. Many words are used with their Latin rather than their English meaning. Thus the word 'secure' means 'safe' in English, but is used by Milton in the sense of the Latin *securus*, meaning over-confident. There are many examples of such usages in *Paradise Lost*, and the only way to avoid major misinterpretation is by an avid reading of the notes carried in all good texts.

Milton also inverts word order by putting the adjective after the noun, as in 'horror chill' or 'serpent wise', whereas conventional English usage would read 'chill horror' and 'wise serpent'. He can also sandwich a noun between two adjectives, as in 'grateful evening mild' and 'mortal sin original'. He can write immensely long sentences, and uses the technique of *epanalepsis* (repeating a word or phrase) to tie these long sentences together. He can also describe simple objects in a roundabout or diffuse way; sometimes this does present a new image of them to the reader, but occasionally it verges on the ludicrous, as when an elephant's trunk is described as a 'lithe proboscis'.

Despite these circumlocutions he is a poet who is very aware of sound, and to hear Milton's verse read out by a fine actor or reader is to have another dimension added to it. When a word appears odd or unusual in the text, it is always worth reading through to see if Milton has chosen that word for its sound value as much as for its meaning. He can occasionally come a cropper, but more usually his instinct for the most impressive or suitable sound is exactly right. It has been argued that a blind man is more attuned to and aware of sound than a sighted person. He often produces a cadence or falling-off at the end of a line, and puts names or other central words at the end of a line where they receive emphasis. He also tends to use adjectives as nouns; one of the most-quoted examples is the 'palpable obscure'. It is worth looking at the section in Book 2 where the rebel angels speak and argue, as proof of how skilfully Milton can give separate and identifiable tonal values and rhythms to his characters, thus distinguishing them and adding to the power and distinctiveness of their characterisation.

## Adam and Eve

Adam and Eve are favoured areas for examiners to set questions on, for candidates who are studying the later books. Satan occupies the same position in Books 1 and 2, although as a, if not the, central figure in the epic, he is also often the subject of questions where the later books are concerned.

Adam and Eve are human characters in a work concerned largely with the superhuman; they are duped by Satan; and they are responsible for mankind's losing Paradise and immortality. Despite these apparent inherent disadvantages they are generally regarded as successes. Their nobility, simplicity, and beauty is stressed, and they have the promise of all that is best in humanity within them. Satan is an immensely skilful corrupter, and so Eve is not as damnable as she might appear. Adam's motive in sinning is pure love; whatever will happen to him he would rather face it than face life alone without Eve, and as such his sin is both touching and tragic.

Where there is a problem is with Eve, particularly for the modern sensibility, increasingly convinced that man and woman are equals. Milton was not as arbitrary or as medieval in his attitude to woman as is sometimes stated, but he did believe that man was superior to woman, and makes this clear. Her motives for sharing the fruit with Adam are selfish, and Milton hints at the long-standing theme in literature of woman's desire to dominate man. There is a slightly tricky moment when Adam can appear as the school sneak when he instantly appears to blame Eve for his own consumption of the forbidden fruit, but this is smoothed over by his other responses to Eve. For a truly committed feminist, the story of Adam and Eve is where all the problems started, and as might be expected the treatment of the subject by feminist critics is interesting.

The examination candidate should ponder the skill with which Milton characterises Adam and Eve; the manner in which he creates them as entirely credible portraits, yet at the same time superior to ordinary men and women; the extent to which prejudice interferes with art in the portrait of Eve; and the compellingly tragic element in their fate. One question that is sometimes touched on is sexuality, but Milton is very straightforward in this area. He sees nothing wrong in a healthy sexual relationship between humans who are genuinely in love, and whose relationship is blessed by God. Sexuality can be a valid part of love; when it is lust, or mere physical desire, then he condemns it, as this is in conflict with the doctrine of temperance that pervades the whole works.

### The Garden of Eden

Book 4 contains lengthy description of the Garden of Eden, and much of the epic rests on this as the symbol and visual representation of Paradise. Those who wish to belabour Milton can sometimes do so with relative safety in terms of his description of the Garden of Eden. It is based firstly on famous gardens described in the classics, secondly on Genesis, and thirdly on lists of flowers, many of which he had used previously in *Lycidas*. Milton's description is therefore formal, and lacking in spontaneity. It can be beautiful, but rather in the manner of a stained glass window: the beauty is artificial, deriving firmly from the artist rather than from the object described. As is originality, spontaneity is perceived as a virtue in modern times, but would have been perceived as a failure in technique prior to the advent of Romanticism in the eighteenth and nineteenth centuries. We sometimes fall into the trap of believing that new, modern critical theories are the way to enliven and revitalise our appreciation of literature. Sometimes works from an earlier age do the job just as well, simply by the fact they are different.

## *Lycidas*

*Lycidas* was written in 1637, as a memorial to Edward King, a friend of Milton's at Cambridge who was drowned in the Irish Sea. The poem adheres strictly to the pastoral mode of writing (see Ch. 3). Whatever else may have troubled him, Milton never doubted that he was a great author writing for posterity. Thus *Lycidas* is not really a poem about the death of a close friend, in the sense that genuine personal feeling and a sense of loss do not really come into it: Milton is trying to write about life and death in general terms that will apply to all experience, rather than to write a poem on the life and death of one man.

Milton shows great skill in the poem with use of the pastoral mode, variations in tone and rhythm, and classical allusions. The artistic skill with which Milton manipulates his subject is a common examination question, but the clash of philosophies in the poem is also noteworthy. Milton is trying to blend the pastoral mode of writing, the classical deities and ideas of Fate, and the Christian belief in salvation and life after death. Some would argue that the poem starts from a classical base of despondency and despair at a sense of loss, and then moves onward into Christian exultation and hope of salvation. Others would argue that the classical despondency and the Christian hope sit ill-at-ease with each other, and that by combining the two Milton is trying to have his cake and eat it, producing thereby a clash of philosophies that can never be happily reconciled or blended.

Simply for interest and for purposes of comparison, the reader might care to glance at Alfred Lord Tennyson's much later long poem, *In Memoriam*, prompted by the death of Tennyson's close friend Arthur Hallam. Milton was very much writing in the classical tradition, Tennyson was a Romantic poet. The differences, and the similarities, between the two works are interesting in themselves, and interesting for what they say about the differences between classicism and romanticism.

## *Comus*

*Comus* was written in 1634, as 'A Mask presented at Ludlow Castle'. It was more poetic and less spectacular in its effects than the masques of Ben Jonson (see Ch. 8), but still relied quite heavily on special music and staging. As with *Lycidas*, a Christian belief in virtue and temperance develop from a classical base, though it is arguable that the marriage of the two elements is happier and more easy than it is in *Lycidas*. *Comus* has been described as a 'dramatic poem', but it can also be seen as a poetic moral debate. The blend between poetry, drama, and debate is well worth examining in the poem, as is the poetry itself and the blend of classical and Biblical elements in the work.

## Question and answer

**Question**

Discuss Milton's style and the manner in which he presents Adam and Eve in the following passage:

> Two of far nobler shape erect and tall,
> Godlike erect, with native honour clad
> In naked majesty seemed lords of all,
> And worthy seemed, for in their looks divine
> The image of their glorious maker shone,
> Truth, wisdom, sanctitude severe and pure,
> Severe but in true filial freedom placed;
> Whence true authority in men; though both
> Not equal, as their sex not equal seemed;
> For contemplation he and valour formed,

For softness she and sweet attractive grace;
He for God only, she for God in him:
His fair large front and eye sublime declared
Absolute rule; . . . the loveliest pair
That ever since in love's embraces met
Adam the goodliest man of men since born
His sons, the fairest of her daughters Eve.

**Answer**

Milton is at pains to stress in this extract the superiority of Adam and Eve to the men and women who followed them, without losing sight of their essential humanity. They are thus 'Godlike', but only in the sense that they are in God's image; it is clear that they are not gods themselves, but merely of Godlike appearance. The real emphasis is on the word 'nobler', implying figures who contain all that is best and most pure in humanity. Physical description is kept to a minimum, and their appearance is described in abstract terms much more than in concrete and physical terms. Words such as 'nobler', 'naked honour', 'looks divine', 'Truth', 'wisdom', 'sanctitude', and 'valour' associate Adam and Eve strongly with moral virtues, and add to the impression that their physical beauty is merely a secondary manifestation of their moral virtue and purity. Whilst appearing to describe them in physical terms ('fair large front') the passage actually describes Adam and Eve as moral and spiritual beings.

There is a clear division in attitude between the man and the woman, and Milton is straightforward about them. Adam is the boss, Eve not his 'equal'. Adam is 'for God only', implying that Adam is under only God's authority, whereas Eve must find her God in Adam ('she for God in him'). He has 'absolute rule', her task clearly being to serve Adam and thereby serve God. Milton does not go as far as to state the view held by some authorities that the fact that Eve was created by taking a rib from Adam's side showed her inferiority, and that had God meant Eve to be equal something would have been taken from Adam's head, but the subservience to Adam is nevertheless manifestly clear. On the other hand Eve is not damned for her later eating of the forbidden fruit; she is the 'fairest of her daughters', a leader and symbol in her way as Adam is in his.

As regards the style of this passage, the most obvious feature is that it is one long sentence in its entirety; long, rolling, and occasionally complex structures are a feature of Milton's style in all his work. His use of Latinate inversion is also marked, as in 'their sex not equal seemed' rather than 'their sex seemed not equal', and 'eye sublime'. Lines are balanced out and contrasted so as to highlight their effect, as in the comparison between Adam and Eve in, 'For contemplation he and valour formed/For softness she and sweet attractive grace,' in which 'softness' and 'valour' are deliberately contrasted and offset against each other. Milton's willingness to use a word in its Latin sense is also clear in 'front', which it is tempting to translate in its modern sense as meaning the whole view of Adam from the front. Milton is using it in the sense of 'forehead', a meaning derived from the Latin word *frons*. There is no example of the epic simile in this passage.

The characterisation of Adam and Eve is clearly based on Genesis, where in 1:27 it is stated 'So God created man in his own image'. Despite this close following of scriptural authority, there is no feeling of the author's being hemmed in or restricted in the scope of what he writes. He can, for example, make a clear reference to the fact that Adam and Eve enjoy a healthy sexual relationships, as they are, 'the loveliest pair/That ever since in love's embraces met'. Despite their nakedness there is no sense of shame in Adam and Eve, and the two-fold repetition of the word 'erect' is there to emphasise the superiority of Adam and Eve to beasts, who walk on four legs. They are not presented as lords in Heaven; they are presented as lords of Paradise and the earth in which they live.

## Further reading


- Cedric C.Brown, *John Milton. A Literary Life* (Macmillan, 1995)
- John Carey, ed., *Milton. Complete Shorter Poems* (Longman, 1997): excellent detail of modern Milton criticism on the shorter poems.
- Thomas Corns, *Regaining Paradise Lost* (Longman, 1994)
- Dennis Danielson, *The Cambridge Companion to Milton* (Cambridge University Press, 1998)
- David Kearns, *How To Study Milton* (Macmillan, 1993): a good basic text for A-level students.
- Annabel Patterson, ed., *John Milton* (Longman, 1992): excellent coverage of modern criticism.
- Lois Potter, *A Preface to Milton* (Longman, 1986)
- Christopher Ricks, *Milton's Grand Style* (Oxford University Press, 1978): one of the great works of Milton criticism.
- James Grantham Turner, *One Flesh. Paradisal Marriage and Sexual Relations in the Age of Milton* (Oxford University Press, 1994)
- J. A. Waldock, *Paradise Lost and Its Critics* (Cambridge University Press, 1966): another excellent older work, and still the standard rebuttal to those who dare to criticise Milton's standing.

CHAPTER TWELVE

# Restoration drama

Restoration drama is the term given to plays written after the restoration of King Charles II to the English throne in 1660, and up to the end of the century. It is probably less fashionable now than for many years, though the period and its work still appears regularly on syllabi.

## The literary and historical background

The Puritan government of Oliver Cromwell, which ruled from 1642 to 1660, was opposed to theatre in all forms. Charles II, who came to the throne in what was effectively a bloodless counter-revolution in 1660, had spent his exile in France, and there become familiar with, and devoted to, theatrical performances. With royal patronage and greater moral laxity it was clear that theatre was due for a strong revival. There were problems, however. Fourteen years of neglect had rendered the old Jacobean theatres unusable; the old acting companies had dispersed; developments in drama on the continent and changing tastes had given rise to a taste for more elegance, richness and show in drama. Even Shakespeare was considered barbarous, and had to be rewritten for the taste of the day.

The theatres therefore changed. There were only two for the first part of Charles's reign, at Covent Garden and Drury Lane. They cost a great deal more to build than the old Jacobean theatres, and were far more luxurious in concept. They were totally enclosed, and lit by artificial light. They had proscenium arches (see Ch. 3), and a whole series of sliding, painted flats to form a backdrop to the action. Women were allowed to act the female roles for the first time, there being no trained boys available to take over the parts. The plays and the audiences changed. The latter were now rich, often young, upper-class, London-based and orientated, cynical, and fashionable, at least until the end of the century, and the plays were written to match the audience.

The plays were roughly divided into comedies and tragedies, but the comedies have stood the test of time better than the tragedies. *All for Love* (1678) by John Dryden (1631–1700) and *Venice Preserv'd* (1682) by Thomas Otway (1653–85) are two Restoration tragedies that are still sometimes performed. The former is a version of the Antony and Cleopatra story, and so is often set if Shakespeare's *Antony and Cleopatra* appears on the same syllabus.

The comedies valued *wit* (see Ch. 4) above all other features, except perhaps those of high or noble birth. Certain stock characters and themes became common, the former establishing a link with Jonson's comedy of humours. There was the fop or dandy (the man obsessed by his appearance and social status, and frequently a fool as well); the young rake (fashionable, well-born, with plenty of charm, often very little money and a cheerfully cynical attitude to love and marriage); the country bumpkin (a rustic, rural figure made fun of by the sophisticated town folk); the pure young heroine; the licentious and immoral young woman-about-town; the sexually frustrated old woman; the funny servant; and the boring, tedious and usually ridiculous ordinary citizen or Puritan.

## Basic themes in restoration comedy

### The younger son

Membership of London society, and one's status in it, depended on wealth as much as birth, though someone who worked for a living was automatically excluded from top society. Money came from the rents and incomes of land ownership, or from money left by parents. The law of the time demanded that the eldest son inherit his father's whole estate, which meant that younger sons had to be produced and trained to handle the burdens of running an estate in case the elder son died. Young sons who did not inherit were often given a small annuity or pension and left to fend for themselves. The army and the Church offered some prospects for such people, but these were limited. Younger sons, with a taste for money but no way of achieving it, are often at the heart of Restoration comedies. A quick and easy way to achieve wealth was by marrying a rich woman. The law of the time gave all a woman's property to her husband automatically once they were married.

### Marriage

In Restoration times, marriage for upper-class families was as much a matter of economics as of love. Arranged marriages were the norm, and a means whereby a family's estates and holding could be increased. With no certainty of a loving relationship within marriage, it is perhaps inevitable that having a mistress or a lover would come to the fore, particularly as Charles II himself was not renowned for his moral rectitude. Sexual dalliance is also perhaps inevitable in a society where a group of rich and healthy men and women know each other intimately and have time and energy on their hands.

The attitude to marriage expressed in many Restoration comedies is cynical, with the assumption that husbands are there to be cuckolded, wives to be seduced. Although good or effective marriages are shown for form's sake, the action of many plays tends to emphasise a rake's progress through life. The frequently occurring marriage at the end is assumed to be virtuous, though rarely shown.

## Basic issues in restoration comedy

Marriage and matters of inheritance and money are stock themes of Restoration comedy, and as a result questions on them are commonly set in examinations. Other general issues are as follows.

### Morality

The issue of the morality or immorality of Restoration comedy is perhaps the one most favoured by examiners. The morally lax Stuart monarchy of Charles II, and the nature of the audience for the plays, encouraged drama of the time to develop what was, effectively, its own moral code. Good looks, wit, and the ability to adapt to the demands and conventions of upper-class London life came to count for more than the old and traditional virtues of sobriety and morality. This trend continued more or less unchecked until the accession of the much more puritanical, sober and cautious William III, in 1688. His accession marked a turning point, though this did not become clear for several years. In Charles's time the theatre had been for the rich upper classes; in William's time it became much more open to the middle classes, and this type of audience was much less willing to accept the degree of immorality in plays that the older audience had supported. Under the twin pressures of the monarchy and its audience, and aided by a society where Puritans were beginning once again to raise their heads, the theatre did what it has always done; it produced what the audience wanted, that is an altogether more quiet and less daring play. A pamphlet written by the Reverend Jeremy Collier (1650–1726) became the symbol for this change in taste. It was called *A Short View of the Immorality and Profaneness of the English Stage* (1698). This pamphlet roundly condemned the immorality of the English theatre. No two plays illustrate the change that came over the theatre better than *The Relapse* (1696) by Sir John Vanbrugh (1664–1726), one of the plays singled out for damnation by Collier, and *The Beaux' Stratagem* (1707) by George Farquhar (1678–1707).

### *The Relapse*

This was written partly to get a friend out of jail for debt, and partly to refute an earlier play which had shown a young London rake marrying a virtuous wife and proceeding to live in purity and contentment in the country. Vanbrugh did not believe in such easy conversions to virtue, and the 'relapse' of the title is the relapse of the hero in his play back to his old, immoral ways. From the outset, therefore, the play expresses a cynical view of morality, preferring to believe the worst of people.

*The Relapse* has two plots (see the discussion of plot and sub-plot in Ch. 6). In the first of these the supposedly reformed rake returns to London, decides to seduce a recently widowed young woman, and totally deceives his virtuous wife, Amanda. The one trace of conventional morality in the play is that Amanda is herself the object of a seduction, but refuses to give in. Nevertheless, no punishment is given to Loveless, the unfaithful husband, before this particular plot fades out. In the second plot another young rake, Young Fashion, returns penniless to England. His older brother, who has inherited his father's estate in its entirety, is not willing to help, and in any event has just paid out vast sums to buy himself a peerage and become Lord Foppington. (As such he is one of the most brilliant comic creations in the whole of Restoration comedy.) Being thus short of funds, Lord Foppington has contracted to marry a rich young country girl, Hoyden, through the agency of a 'sodomite' marriage broker, Coupler. Young Fashion decides to steal his brother's would-be wife and marry her. Once the marriage has happened no one can take his wife's property and money away from him. Young Fashion succeeds in his task, marries Hoyden, and carries off the girl and the money, again with every sign of approval from the author, and no punishment.

It is not merely the immoral actions that take place in the play that have aroused criticism and hostility, rather that the audience are intended, or asked, to sympathise with some of those who commit the worst sins. One response is that in the play's own terms there is a morality at work. Hoyden, the heiress, is a young animal, who will clearly be much happier married to Young Fashion than to Lord Foppington; the woman that Loveless seduces wants to be seduced, and is only happy when this takes place. No one is really hurt in *The Relapse*, and those who are, tend to be foolish and worse than those who fool them.

### *The Beaux' Stratagem*

Farquhar's play shows a major change from the more or less blatant immorality of *The Relapse*, although in plan at least the plot is equally immoral. Two penniless young men from London decide to chance their all on visiting the country town of Lichfield, with the express intention of finding a young woman, having one of them marry her, and sharing the proceeds. Naturally enough the only feature the woman has to have is wealth. This is cold-blooded, ruthless, and utterly cynical. One of the men, Aimwell, is younger brother to Viscount Aimwell. The plan is that he will pretend to be his brother in order to attract a wife, whilst Archer, the other man, will pose as his servant. Aimwell meets a suitable young girl, who falls in love with him. Archer seduces a servant girl (a rather complicated and hilarious sub-plot, featuring a highwayman and the landlord of the inn at which the two men are staying, surfaces at this point), and then sets out to seduce the unwilling wife of the local squire, who has made an appallingly unhappy marriage and wants nothing but out of it.

The difference from *The Relapse* is that at the end of the play it is as if a magic wand were waved and the huge potential immorality of the plot made to vanish. Aimwell falls in love with the girl he has set out to corrupt, confesses what he really is, and then, lo and behold, finds out that his brother has died and that he has inherited the title, thus becoming what he had pretended to be. Archer falls in love with the woman he sets out to seduce (he only fails because a robber enters the house as he is about to fall into bed with the woman), and equally suddenly finds he is able to marry her and get her fortune into the bargain. All ends on a note that even a bishop would hardly cringe at. The ending is not as unconvincing as this bald plot summary makes it seem to be; it is actually quite charming and very funny, but Farquhar has done a marvellous sidestep by cramming hugely titillating immorality into his play without ever letting much of it happen, and cleansing all consciences by making the ending a dream of holy married bliss, rather in the manner of a Shakespearean comedy. Farquhar manages to get all the fun of immorality, and hardly any of its consequences. In this sense – how to evade moral condemnation whilst still being thoroughly immoral – at least the play is a masterpiece.

The content of *The Relapse* and *The Beaux' Stratagem* is almost the same – money, marriage, seduction, high life – but the endings are different. *The Beaux' Stratagem* can offend nobody – unless, that is, they look at what almost happened, and note that it is only averted by a huge series of coincidences that lack credibility.

The whole issue of morality needs to be treated with great caution as it applies to Restoration comedy. Many of the objections to the plays' morality came from the Victorian period, when it was believed that immorality on the stage genuinely persuaded audiences to follow suit. A more serious complaint is one that will be familiar to those who have read Chapter 11 in this work, on Milton, which is that it is the bad characters who have life, vitality, and attractiveness in these plays, whilst the good ones appear lacklustre and lukewarm. The difficulty of making goodness attractive applies to all literature, not merely Restoration comedy.

## Satire

Restoration comedy frequently has a satirical base, in that it invites laughter at human vice and folly. The extent to which any Restoration comedy is genuinely satirical, as distinct from pure entertainment, is an interesting question. Beware of assuming too easily that lightness of touch and a desire to entertain an audience mean automatically that a play has no serious impact or meaning.

## *The Way of the World*

The play at the summit of achievement for Restoration Comedy is undoubtedly *The Way of the World* (1700) by William Congreve (1670–1729). It is generally held to be the classic work of Restoration comedy. Congreve was an artist, rather than just an entertainer, and was vitally concerned to write great art. His knowledge of the classics and his scholarship are clearly revealed in his work.

### Issues in *The Way of the World*

**The Plot**

The plot of *The Way of the World* is extremely complex. This is not unusual in Restoration comedy, but *The Way of the World* is more complex even than many of its contemporaries, so much so that the actors rehearsing it for the first performance were reported to have come to Congreve and asked him what was actually happening. Part of the complexity derives from Congreve's concern for symmetry of form and his classical leanings. It also derives from the fact that the play is about hypocrisy, so that it takes some while for the real villains to be distinguished from the heroes. The point about hypocrites, and why they are so dangerous, is that their evil is not visible at first sight, and this is how they harm people.

**Morality and marriage**

In one sense *The Way of the World* is a conventional Restoration comedy. A young man, Mirabell, who has committed sins in the past but is essentially a generous and warm personality, wishes to marry Millamant but is barred from doing so by his own lack of money and by an aunt, Lady Wishfort, who controls Millamant's inheritance and her power to marry. After much suffering, trial, and tribulation Millamant and Mirabell are allowed to marry. The conventionality of this plot conceals a far greater richness of characterisation and thematic concern than is usual in other plays of the type. Marriage is seen as capable of being a private hell, but also as a genuine and desirable relationship, as long as the two partners have genuine knowledge of themselves and of each other. In moral terms the play is impeccable, with generosity the most admired feature in a character, and with the good characters rewarded, and the evil ones punished and banished.

The law is used as a symbol in the play of how human relationships should be conducted. One of the most famous scenes in the play is the 'proviso' or 'bargain' scene, where Mirabell and Millamant lay their demands for marriage in front of each other, in the manner of lawyers in a court room. This is funny, but also serious. Human instincts and desires have to be tempered with rationality and businesslike control if they are not to run wild and destroy the people who hold them.

**Characterisation**

The characterisation of the play is one of its strongest areas, and is frequently examined. The effectiveness of the characterisation is greatly aided by Congreve's skill with dialogue; he gives a completely individual voice to each character. This voice is also variable according to circumstances. Thus Lady Wishfort has her moments of total honesty, as when she remarks that she looks like 'an old, peeled wall', her stumbling malapropisms, as in 'indigestion of widowhood', and her moments of raucous invective, as in 'go, go, starve again, do!'

The depth and variety of Congreve's characterisation is perhaps the main point of significance. He takes the stock figures of Restoration comedy and lifts them out and above the mould in which they were formed. Millamant is one of the greatest character creations in drama. She need only be the beautiful, pure, and rich young heroine whose sole purpose is to marry the hero. What Congreve actually produces is a woman of many parts, possessed of a wit the equal to any man in the play, and most of all a spirit of freedom that is determined to take on life on her terms and no one else's. She is deeply in love with Mirabell, but is determined to make him sweat before she will 'dwindle into a wife'. She has the sharpest satiric eye of any character in the play, and protects herself by hiding behind a glorious display of many of the vices she perceives in others. She hates fools, and her curtain of wit and elegance has barbs in it for any fool who tries to break through to her real feelings. Millamant hides behind a façade, which makes her extremely funny as long as the audience can see the real personality, and can accept that implicit in her facade is her capacity to laugh at herself and the society in which she finds herself.

*Lady Wishfort*, as her name implies, could simply be the elderly, widowed lady, sexually frustrated and desperate for a husband. That she is, but much more besides. She is shown to have a heart, and compassion, and, whilst being funny, Congreve never loses sight of her essential pathos and the unhappiness of her situation. She is laughed at but never condemned, because her 'sin' is in part simply a need for love and to be loved. Congreve is too magnanimous simply to laugh this out of court, and because she is shown as being capable of honesty and magnanimity an element of sympathy follows her throughout the play.

Both characters make statements about women that seem firmly in line with modern feminist thinking, allowing them to emerge and be accepted as individuals whilst shattering some gender and sexual stereotypes.

*Sir Wilful Witwoud* is, on the surface, another stock character, the rustic or country fool made to look a bumbling oaf by the side of the sophisticated town dwellers. Here again Congreve triumphs. Wilful is sometimes an oaf, but he also has a heart of gold, occasionally shows more sense than most of the other characters, and again has the saving virtues of generosity and magnanimity. Again his portrayal is funny, but leavened also by sympathy and, in the end, by a surprising degree of respect.

**Fools**
In his Introduction to the play Congreve stresses that it is not his intention simply to make people laugh at fools, who cannot help what they are, and are therefore objects worthy only of pity, not derision. Instead, he intends to show not 'natural folly', but rather 'an affected wit which at the same time that it is affected, is also false'. In other words, he wishes to satirise people who have chosen to be foolish. The problem is that this definition really only fits one character in the play – Witwoud – and that some audiences have taken his false wit for the real thing. A good essay title on the play is Pope's remark, 'Tell me if Congreve's fools be fools indeed'.

**Wit**
Another typical area of question in Restoration comedy is that which asks if the surface glitter of wit is all the characters have to offer, implying that the characterisation is superficial. This can be refuted quite easily with regard to *The Way of the World*. It is less easy with certain other plays. Modern, linguistically-based critical theory can be helpful on wit and the manner in which it operates on the reader.

## William Wycherley and *The Country Wife*

*The Country Wife* (1675) by William Wycherley is the other play, after *The Way of the World*, most commonly set for Advanced level. Its central character, Horner, pretends to be sexually incapable, as a device whereby he may lull husbands into a sense of false security, and seduce their wives. He finds little difficulty in overwhelming the 'honour' that is so marked a feature of Restoration comedy; it did not stop a woman sleeping with a man, but it did make both partners paranoid about that fact becoming known. Horner's part in the play is central. He avoids condemnation or punishment, and can thus be seen to render the play wholly immoral. A major factor on the other side of the argument is that Horner is not really a character at all, but more of a satiric exposer of other people's vice. In other words his importance in the play is not as a personality, but as a means whereby the author can reveal the features of other people.

It is also true that hypocrisy is condemned severely in the play, and that the vast majority of characters who suffer in it thoroughly deserve to do so. Otherwise the questions set on the play are very similar to those outlined above for other works. There is a tendency to ask about characterisation, with a quotation or leading statement to the effect that Wycherley's good characters are dull, and his bad ones full of life, but also corrupt beyond the level of normality.

## Goldsmith and Sheridan

Whatever the set text, the student should try to read *The Way of the World, The Country Wife, The Relapse* and *The Beaux' Strategem*. These sum up the main features of Restoration comedy.

Useful reading is also contained in the works of Beaumont and Fletcher. These Jacobean dramatists were more popular in the Restoration than Shakespeare, and reveal a lot about Restoration taste in drama.

After the Restoration period the initiative in literature passed from drama to poetry and the novel. In the theatres the fashion was for 'sentimental comedy', or rather light plays of conventional morality which avoided the unseemly, grotesque, or unsavoury elements of life. As a result drama is something of a blank spot for much of the eighteenth century, with Oliver Goldsmith (1730–74) and Richard Brinsley Sheridan (1751–1816) writing the only plays regularly set for Advanced level from this period.

## Question and answer

**Question**
In what sense does *The Way of the World* merit the description of being 'the masterpiece of Restoration comedy'?

**Answer**
If a work is to merit the description of 'masterpiece' it has to be shown to have outstanding features that render it superior to all or most other works of its style or genre. The fact that *The Way of the World* was not received particularly well by the first audiences who saw it is not a valid reason for dismissing it. In Shakespeare's own time *Titus Andronicus* was immensely successful, whilst *King Lear* appears to have been a relative failure. The more lasting verdict of history is almost the exact reverse of this, with the first play mentioned being consigned to obscurity, the second becoming one of the most highly regarded plays of any age or time. Contemporary judgement is not an accurate guide to the lasting value of any work, including *The Way of the World.*

The characterisation in *The Way of the World* uses the conventions of the time, but also rises above them, presenting a gallery of characters who are unmatched in any other single work of Restoration comedy; in this area the play can claim to be a masterpiece. In many instances Congreve's characters are based on the stock figures of the drama of the day, but each character has at least one other dimension. Mirabell is the conventional young rake, and Congreve shows his devil-may-care attitude and his sinful past. What Congreve also shows is a man who can genuinely fall in love, who has genuine regard for other people, and who most of all has the capacity of generosity that makes him much more than a conventional hell-raising young man:

> You are a gallant Man, Mirabell, and tho' you may have Cruelty enough, not to satisfy a Lady's longing; you have too much Generosity, not to be tender of her Honour.

Millamant is worlds apart from the conventional pure heroine, included in many Restoration comedies as a gesture to morality. She has the conventional features of such heroines. She is beautiful, well-bred, and rich, and is guilty of no sexual misconduct. As with Mirabell, it is the extra dimension added to her portrait that makes her an astounding success in the play. As well as the above features, she has vast intelligence, a capacity to change mood and direction that gives her almost total independence, and a magnificent defensive battery of wit and elegance that keeps out fools and allows her to preserve her independence. She will marry Mirabell, or 'dwindle into a wife' as she puts it, but she will give her man a run for his money and preserve her own dignity and independence whilst never failing in love or loyalty towards her husband. Lady Wishfort could be so easily the stereotyped, frustrated old lady, desperate for a man and a husband at any price. She has all the hilarity and ridiculous paraphernalia of such characters, and at times is presented as 'the Antidote to Desire', but she is also shown a degree of pity, and recognised by the end of the play as someone who cannot be simply dismissed because she has, at least in small measure, the prime virtues of generosity (when pushed to it!) and the capacity to learn from her mistakes. Sir Wilful Witwoud is the standard country bumpkin, bringing anarchy and manure in equal quantity into the elegant drawing rooms of 'the town', but he also has generosity, warmth and a very real insight into the hypocrisy, vanity, and self-worship of town life. As he says, 'The Fashion's a Fool'. Sir Wilful is as funny as any country bumpkin in any Restoration play. He is also warm, perceptive and altogether more complex than many other such figures. Even Witwoud, who could very easily be made into a comic butt for the other characters, is acknowledged as having something 'of good Nature, and does not always want Wit'.

The characterisation in the play does not only expand on conventional stereotypes. In certain instances it is inventive and original in presenting characters who have few equivalents elsewhere. A triumph in this sphere is Mrs Fainall. Her honour is far from unstained, and she has had affairs in the past, but she is also 'the Pattern of Generosity' and a character who refuses to be fitted easily into any convenient, one-dimensional category. Fainall and Mrs Marwoud are not original in the sense that many plays had their malcontents and mischief-makers. They verge on being original in having eminently convincing and practical reasons for what they do. The characterisation as a whole also benefits from Congreve's technique of gradual revelation. In real life villains do not declare themselves openly, even if they are as 'Bankrupt in Honour, as indigent of Wealth' as Fainall, or the 'mischievous Devil' of Mrs Marwoud. Congreve recognises this by only slowly revealing to the audience the depths of their villainy and the heights of the good characters' generosity.

The dialogue in the play could also be seen as qualifying for the description of a masterpiece. It is taut, sharp and immensely witty. Each character is given a distinctive style and mode of speech, from the elegance of Mirabell and Millamant to the finely tuned Wrekin accent of Sir Wilful, and the breathless, utterly memorable speech of Lady Wishfort. Two of the most famous lines from the play show in very different manners how memorable and evocative Congreve's style can be, as when in the example already mentioned Millamant confesses she will 'dwindle into a wife', and Lady Wishfort screams that she is like 'an old, peel'd wall!'. The proposal scene between Millamant and Mirabell has found its way into a host of anthologies, and is justifiably one of the most famous scenes in English drama. In this scene Congreve slips effortlessly into legalistic dialogue, adapting the language of the law court to a proposal of marriage in a manner that is at one and the same time very funny and yet sharply pointed and effective in conveying the need for checks and balances, and full understanding, in all relationships.

The morality and balance of the play are also very strong features. The fact that *The Way of the World* does actually have a moral structure is mildly remarkable. Congreve does not attempt to deny the existence of power, of cynicism, hypocrisy, greed, deceit, unfaithfulness, or mental blindness. Indeed, in many respects he provides the audience with a more exhaustive analysis of them than most other contemporary writers. His characters are largely mixtures of good and evil; what makes them thoroughly good or evil, and the yardstick by which moral worth is judged in the play, is the presence or absence in them of generosity. The philosophy here is similar to that found in many other works, one of which is Henry Fielding's *Tom Jones*. In *Tom Jones* and *The Way of the World* a man or woman can be forgiven the occasional bad deed (though they will always be punished for it); they cannot be excused a bad heart, or receive any credit at all unless they have the prime virtue of generosity.

The plot might be seen to confirm the play as a 'masterpiece', but this is a more uncertain area. The plot is very neat, very skilfully built up and structured, allows characters to be contrasted, and builds up to a resounding and satisfying climax. It is also immensely complicated, so much so that the actors in an early performance were reported to have gone to Congreve and asked him to explain exactly what was happening. As a technical exercise in plotting, the plot is a master-piece; as effective drama it taxes the concentration and understanding of the audience to a level that is not disastrous, but which might well be thought to place too much strain on them in the crucial opening scenes.

There is a depth and bite to *The Way of the World* that marks it out from most of its contemporaries. The evil in the play is real evil, and there is no sign that Fainall and Mrs Marwood have changed or been stopped from future acts of malice. If this is a strength, the play has weaknesses as well. The characters do not develop very much in the play, and whilst one relationship is examined in depth the theme of love in general is treated rather briskly and even superficially. Congreve's concern for realism precludes him to some extent from presenting a character as wildly excessive as Lord Foppington in *The Relapse*, and can lead to the charge that his play is lacking variety and range. His presentation of the comic, impudent, and witty servant in Waitwell is not particularly effective, and his desire not to laugh at natural idiocy of the type the character cannot help, but only to laugh at affectation or acquired folly, is laudable but can lead to a certain 'sameness' in the characters. All this being said, these are minor blemishes on a play that in its range, thoughtfulness and sheer dramatic skill has a genuine claim to be a masterpiece of its kind.

## Further reading

- Richard Bevis, *English Drama: Restoration and Eighteenth Century 1660–1789* (Longman, 1988)
- John Bull, *Vanbrugh and Farquhar* (Macmillan, 1998)
- Deborah Payne, *The Cambridge Companion to Restoration Theatre* (Cambridge University Press, forthcoming)

CHAPTER THIRTEEN

# Pope, Dryden and Swift: Classicism and the eighteenth century

## The literary and historical background

The eighteenth century is sometimes referred to as the Augustan age, a term meant to imply a comparison or similarity with the literary brilliance of Rome under the Emperor Augustus (27 BC–AD 14) when Virgil, Horace and Ovid flourished. The seeds of modern western European society began to be laid in the eighteenth century. The Restoration period had confidence, energy, and vitality. The eighteenth century cooled down some of the excesses of this period, and added its own brand of confidence and a belief in progress. Perhaps rather oddly in the light of this forward-looking element, the eighteenth century also tended to look back to the classical age for its inspiration in literature. Classical models began to exert a grip on literature that was initially beneficial and a force for discipline, but which then became a stranglehold, only broken by the force of the Romantic movement. Read the definitions given of 'classical' and 'Romantic' in Chapter 3 of this book.

There were other factors in the age that influenced writers. Pope was the first writer other than a dramatist to make a living out of his writing. He did this through the sale of his translations of the classics, rather than his own original writing. The importance of this for the critic is that authors such as Pope were no longer writing their poetry for reading out loud to a close circle of friends, but to be read by all who could afford a copy of the book. Pope's poetry is personal and impassioned, but the classical importance of form (or the manner in which something is said) is central to his work, and can act as a cloak for his more private vision of man. Authors such as Donne and Herbert, who were not writing for public consumption, had no need of any such disguise. The eighteenth century tends to direct its attention in literature outwards onto society, not inwards into the nature of the individual.

The writings of Alexander Pope marked a new style and approach to poetry, and one which has become associated with the eighteenth century. Some of Pope's best-known work is satirical. Satire attempts to take unwelcome or undesirable factors in life (individuals or wider social issues) and laugh them out of existence. Ridicule has a withering effect; satire is a caustic material that can burn off vanity and excess, piercing through their outer layer to reveal them for what they are. In order to do this one must have a tremendous certainty about what is right, or a belief that everything is rotten. Eighteenth-century satire sprang from the certainty and assuredness of the Augustan age; the satire of the Jacobean period or of the 1960s sprang from the opposite cause, a collapse of values and certainty. Thus satire tends to be the product of excess, excess of either certainty or uncertainty.

Pope's passion also gives a clue to the nature of eighteenth-century culture. Pope felt strongly on a number of topics, but his passion is not the same as that of Shakespeare or the Metaphysical poets. It is more formal, more social and more elegant, a deftly-wielded rapier directed largely against human weakness. Pope's concern is largely social, not so much about what people are as individuals, much more about what they contribute to society. Mankind in the eighteenth century is not an individual but a member of society, judged on and by his contribution to that society. As was mentioned above, this pattern is repeated in the literature of the day. The eighteenth century was above all the age of reason, an age which believed in the rational and intellectual side of man's nature, as distinct from the emotional, passionate side. A fuller discussion of the differences between Romanticism and classicism can be found in Chapter 15.

The strength of Pope's passions and his convictions made him a number of personal enemies, and their attacks on him did not stop short of physical, cruel abuse directed at Pope's physical deformities. Pope's own bitterness emerges in some of his work, and his well-publicised feuds and vendettas have tended to give the eighteenth century the image of an age in which such disputes carried on with such strength were normal. So they were, but probably so have they been throughout history. Bitterness is not a preserve of Pope's. Indeed, it is one of the most common features to be found in literary artists through the ages. Personal disputes between members of a close society were not new either, and the student would be wise not to get this aspect of eighteenth-century life out of proportion.

## Alexander Pope

Pope (1688–1744) is undoubtedly one of England's major poetic talents, and the colossus in literary terms of the Augustan age.

### Pope's works

Pope's first major work was his *Essay on Criticism* (1711), followed by his famous exercise in the mock heroic style, *The Rape of the Lock* (1712–14).

Pope then translated two of the great classical epic poems, the *Iliad* and the *Odyssey* of Homer, in 1715–20 and 1725–26 respectively. Pope also wrote *Eloisa to Abelard* (1717), *The Dunciad* (1728), *Epistle to Dr Arbuthnot* (1735), and the *Essay on Man* (1734). All these, except the translations from Homer and the *Essay on Criticism*, are commonly set texts, albeit not in their entirety; the most common text set is undoubtedly *The Rape of the Lock*. This poem, and the whole subject of the mock-heroic style, is the subject of a full answer at the end of this chapter.

## Issues in Pope's Work

### The Augustan background

Pope is sometimes seen as a problem poet by students because he seems to require study on three levels:

1. the poetry itself;
2. the general background against which it was written and from which it sprang;
3. a further layer of more detailed historical knowledge pinpointing particularly the specific objects of Pope's satire, be they individuals or institutions.

Pope also presents a problem to modern taste in a number of his attitudes, not least of all to women. The author of the line, 'Most Women have no Characters at all' (from 'To a Lady', in *Epistles to Several Persons*) will not recommend himself to a considerable body of contemporary opinion, even if satire and irony are never far away from anything that Pope said or wrote. However, modern criticism has also done good service to Pope. As will be discussed later, contemporary opinion hailed Pope as a master technician, leading to allegations that he was little else. New criticism has pointed out Pope's wit, his complex yet clear morality, the depth of passion he can achieve in its own right and through humour, and hopefully disproved once and for all (if anything is ever proved once and for all in criticism!) the theory that he is simply a clever versifier.

The idea that he requires more effort from the student than other authors is a fallacy. Primary knowledge of the text is essential for all authors, and Pope is easier to read than many. Background knowledge of the society and age in which an author lived is also essential for any author. It is true that the student needs to make an effort to find out who the original of Sporus or Atticus was in Pope's work, but he needs to make an equal effort to understand Chaucer's language, the mechanics of Shakespeare's theatre or Milton's biblical and classical allusions. Pope requires no more and no less 'extra' work than any other author. The only difference is that it is more obvious what needs to be done regarding Pope's work, and harder to cover up if it has not been done. Background knowledge does matter with Pope, because questions linking him to the Augustan age, or asking for an explanation of the influence of that age on his writing, are set. There is only one thing the student can do, which is read – in particular as much of Pope's work as is possible. Note down, as it is read through, the specific areas where Pope seems to reflect his own age and society. The eighteenth century is a period of marked preferences and tastes, and an authoritative introduction to the age itself must be read as well as Pope's own work. There are a number of well-written and readable books which introduce the eighteenth century, and are often interesting in their own right, as well as for what they tell us about Pope. Examples are given in the reading list at the end of this chapter.

One particular type of question comes as standard with Pope's satirical work. His satire is varied, but inevitably a portion of it is directed at specific individuals and issues of his time. Thus his character Atticus is a portrait of Joseph Addison the essayist (1627–1719). This raises the question of whether Pope's satire is dated and merely topical, and the extent to which it is irrelevant or out of its time. A knowledge of the Augustan age is clearly essential for an answer to such a question. Other areas for consideration are discussed below.

**Satire and Pope**

The question of whether satirical portraits of individuals or issues relating to a particular time can have lasting literary merit, depends almost wholly on whether or not the person or issue satirised is wholly individual and unique, or has failings that are universal and to be found in any age. Pope satirised vanity, hypocrisy, and affectation in his portrayals; he can locate them in one individual, but the folly thus presented can have a far wider application, provided we can recognise that folly in our own and other ages.

'Grub Street' scribblers are heavily satirised in *The Dunciad*, which as its title suggests contains more than a fair sampling of sub-standard humanity. Grub Street was the name given to signify hack or mediocre authors, grubbing out a living from literature in a way reminiscent of a parasite, rather than as an artist or craftsman. Though the term is not nearly as widely used nowadays, and the writers Pope is talking about are long dead, writers with no talent, no pride and a capacity to overrate themselves still exist, perhaps even more so than in Pope's day. If in doubt, read the average 'ghosted' biography of a soccer player, or listen to the script for a television comedy show which has run out of steam. All this suggests that every object of Pope's satire is universal. This is not the case. His instinct was not always accurate as to what was a lasting human folly, and, as a poet with a physical disability who sometimes received cruel personal abuse, Pope sometimes lashed out with an anger and intemperance that was wholly personal, and which clouded his objective judgement. Here the student must come to a reasoned but personal decision in deciding which areas of Pope's work remain firmly locked in an eighteenth-century closet, with no key available in the twentieth century.

Pope had high ideals about satire, though as the above suggests he did not always manage to adhere to them. He wrote that his satire was published to assist virtue and 'to mend people's morals', a justification that in one form or another has been made by most satirists. Pope certainly did have burning ideals of moral, social, and artistic behaviour, and the questions to ask yourself include some of the following:

- How varied is Pope's satire? Can it gently prod in some areas, and totally destroy in others, with a whole range of strength in between these two extremes?
- What are the issues on which Pope feels really strongly? Are they personal, moral, social, religious, artistic, or even trivial? Remember that Pope was a Roman Catholic, at that time something of an underprivileged minority.
- How much humour and comedy is there in his satire? Satire exposes vice and folly, which is serious, by means of ridicule and laughter, which are not: apart from moral lessons, how much straight humour is there in his satire?
- How does Pope set out to satirise people and issues? Is it by caricature, exaggeration, actions, putting words in their mouths that damn them and make them appear ludicrous, by wholesale use of irony, or by all these?

**Pope and originality**

The eighteenth century placed little value on originality in literature, for reasons already discussed in previous chapters. Pope's couplet 'True wit is nature to advantage dress'd/What oft was thought, but ne'er so well exprest' suggests that it is not what a poet says that matters as much as how he says it. This remark, the feelings of the eighteenth century, and his style (the heroic couplet is a neat, well-disciplined, and elegant mode of writing, but it can give the impression of superficiality) all lead to the question of whether or not Pope is a mere decorative artist, someone with very little to say that is new, but with a pleasant and skilful way of saying it. Most of his literary and philosophical ideas are not original, but derived from other authors, with a leaning towards classical sources. Any author who is a technical master in his field tends to have this question raised of his or her work, especially those with the capacity to write outstanding comedy. It is partly a reflection of the obsession in our own age with themes and 'meanings' in literature, partly a tendency to undervalue comedy as distinct from more 'serious' styles such as tragedy, and partly a belief that the entertainer cannot really at the same time become a creative and original artist. There is also a feeling, perhaps inevitable, that an author with great technical resources at his disposal can pass lead off as gold, and can dress up a thin content to make it seem better than it is. Pope can in fact do both: his technical skill, particularly with the heroic couplet, is outstanding, and he can be extremely funny.

Few examination questions ask specifically if Pope's work is 'glitter formed round dust', but some do use phrases such as 'surface brilliance', implying his work has a hollow ring to it. Here again the final decision is down to you. If Pope had not convinced you of the essential seriousness of what he has to say then you have a right to say so, given as always that you have specific evidence to prove your point.

**Pope's style**

Any discussion of Pope's style tends to be dominated by his use of the heroic couplet, or end-rhymed and stopped iambic pentameters. Pope makes this rhyming style look effortless; it is actually an immensely hard technique to master in English, a language which does not by any means always have a convenient rhyme to hand.

Ask yourself, what are the strengths and limitations of this style? It is in fact marvellously suited for epigrammatic lines, or for situations where the reader is to be lulled into a false sense of security by the first line of the couplet, with the main point being rammed home by a different style or content in the second line. It is disciplined, controlled, and musical, a pleasing exercise in technical mastery, and a marvellous way of giving a stirring climax to the end of a line. Does it have built-in weaknesses? The rhythm needs careful handling if it is not to become monotonous, and some way is needed for breaking out from the two-line unit and letting the poem become something more than a collection of two-line epigrams.

**Non-satiric poetry in Pope**

Pope did not always write satire. He wrote love poetry, some pastoral work, poems with a significant philosophical content, translations of the classics, poems of praise to men he liked and admired, and some verse which is plain funny without a hint of satire in it. The likelihood of being examined on these other aspects of Pope's work depends on the text chosen. If it is one or two books from a satirical poem such as *The Dunciad*, or *The Rape of the Lock*, it is unlikely that the candidate will be required to answer on the non-satiric elements in Pope. If the text is a selection of his work, then a non-satiric question might crop up.

To our taste Pope's nature poetry can seem rather artificial and overladen with classical references, but his instinct for imagery is sound, and as with Milton, a knowledge of the classical allusions adds a new dimension to the appreciation and understanding of the poetry. Whatever the set text, it is worth reading some of the poems Pope wrote in praise of those he admired. One of his most famous couplets was intended for Sir Isaac Newton (1642–1725), the great philosopher and mathematician: 'Nature and Nature's Laws lay hid in Night./God said, *Let Newton be*! and All was *Light*.' This couplet illustrates one of Pope's major skills, the ability to be utterly clear and simple, as well as highly economical in flashing a meaning and an image across in a condensed yet simple couplet. The poems in honour or praise of people are a necessary corrective to the occasional bitterness, and sometimes even malice, of the satirical poems. It is always easier to respect a satirist when one can see that not all in his world is open to ridicule. A simple poem such as 'To Mrs M. B. On Her Birthday' shows the warmth and sympathy that can flow through Pope's writing:

Let Joy or Ease, let Affluence or Content,
And the gay Conscience of a life well spent,
Calm ev'ry thought, inspirit ev'ry Grace,
Glow in thy heart, and smile upon thy face.
Let day improve on day, and year on year,
Without a Pain, a Trouble, or a Fear;
Till Death unfelt that tender frame destroy,
In some soft Dream, or Extasy of joy:
Peaceful sleep out of the Sabbath of the Tomb,
And wake up to Raptures in a Life to come.

The poet who could write the above, and write the savage, morally outraged 'The hungry Judges soon the Sentence sign,/And Wretches hang that Jury-men may dine' is a poet with a range and variety that arguably makes him one of the greatest of English poets.

## John Dryden

John Dryden (1631–1700) was appointed Poet Laureate in 1668, and whilst seen as a major literary figure in his own time is now far less highly regarded. He is best known for the play *All for Love*, his version of the Antony and Cleopatra story, and for *Absalom and Achitophel* (1681), a political satire. Dryden's bitter attack on the poet and dramatist Thomas Shadwell, *MacFlecknow, or a Satyr upon the True-Blew-Protestant Poet, T. S.* (1682) occasionally surfaces on advanced courses. Of particular note, and very well worth examination, are two pieces from the end of Dryden's life – *A Song for Saint Cecilia's Day* (1687) and *An Ode in Honour of Saint Cecilia's Day* (1697). They show a move away from the strict control of the eighteenth century in to irregular stanzas and a slightly looser form, and both have been set successfully to music.

Too much of Dryden's work is seen as being that of a spokesman for poetry, too little of it as a poet's work. There was a public element to Dryden's life that affects his work, and too much of it now seems either worthy or dated, or both. Yet he can write powerfully and well, and is recommended reading for any student looking on the eighteenth century in general and the work of Pope in particular.

## Jonathan Swift

Jonathan Swift (1667–1745) is probably best known for a book parts of which have become a children's classic – *Gulliver's Travels* (1726).

It has been said that Swift wrote 'to vex the world rather than divert it', and as a result he has always provoked strong critical responses. A clergy-man who was born in Dublin and spent most of his life in Ireland, nearly all his works were published anonymously, and *Gulliver's Travels* was the only one for which he received any payment. Swift was a member of the 'Scriblerus Club' in London, which numbered Pope among its members. He published a very large number of works, many political, many pamphlets relating to Ireland and a huge number of satirical and other writings, including various pieces detailing his complex love affair with Esther Johnson ('Stella'), the daughter or servant of his patron's sister. He suffered badly in his later years from what is now believed to be Ménière's Disease, and was thought by many of his contemporaries to be insane. This view has been challenged by modern biographies.

## Swift's Work

Swift can be ferocious, violent, coarse and apparently wholly intemperate in his satire, yet at other times shows remarkable sanity and common sense. He is becoming fashionable again for a variety of reasons, not least of all his ability to deconstruct existing ideas of literary form, and traditional literary values. There is a searing individuality to Swift that also makes him an attractive figure to write on. Whilst *Gulliver's Travels* looks set to be forever the work of his that is read and set, the interested student should turn at least to the famous *A Modest Proposal* (1729), one of the most savage pieces of satire ever written. Another very interesting piece is *Verses on the Death of Dr Swift* (1731, published 1739), in which Swift in effect writes his own obituary with some sentimentality but even more humour.

### *Gulliver's Travels*

*Gulliver's Travels* is divided into four books. In the first Lemuel Gulliver, a ship's surgeon, is stranded on the island of Lilliput, the inhabitants of which are six inches high, and everything in their world shrunk in proportion. Given their size, the pomp and pretension of the Lilliputians allows Swift marvellous opportunities for using them to satirise the pomp and pretension of his own world. Gulliver is then stranded on Brobdingnag, where the inhabitants are hugely tall and everything else big in proportion. The satire is therefore extended to Gulliver himself, fresh from thinking himself lord of all he surveys in Lilliput, but also again to his society, described by the King of Brobdingnag as 'little odious vermin'. These two books, in edited form, are the 'children's classics'; the reader who came to them in childhood is well advised not to judge them on this reading, but to go for the real thing. The third part takes place on the flying island of Laputa, where the satire is directed against researchers and those who pursue useless knowledge, and the fourth part in the land of the Houyhnhnms. These are horses who have all the gifts of civilisation and advanced powers of reasoning. They are contrasted with the Yahoos – coarse, brutal, dirty and all-too-recognisable as human beings. The Russian Formalist school of critics has written interestingly about Swift. For them it is necessary to 'defamiliarise' experience so the reader can come to it having removed traditional familiarities that make it acceptable. In effect, familiar experiences need to be made unfamiliar so that we can see them objectively and freed from clutter. By having the hero of *Gulliver's Travels* explain human society to an intelligent horse this is precisely the effect achieved.

The book was immensely popular in its time, partly because it catered for the vogue in travel books and partly because it is superb satire. Its adoption as a children's classic is ironic, as it is a very dark book indeed in its original form, so dark and violent that it has offended many readers and other authors. That violence and 'the darkness of Swift's vision' is a central topic, as is the effectiveness of Swift's satire: as with Pope, is he turning his fire against purely contemporary vices, or are the objects of his satire sufficiently lasting to give the book more than simply topical reference? It is now less common than it used to be to damn an author as an excellent technician but little else (Tennyson and W. H. Auden have suffered from this over the years, as have a number of other major authors), but it is still possible to find questions that ask if one essentially good idea (the contrast in size between Gulliver and the people he meets in the first two books) is not used to cover an essential thinness of material.

Swift's attitude to women has caused problems for a number of modern readers, as is the case with Pope. One of Swift's offerings was, 'A very little wit is valued in a woman; as we are pleased with a few words spoken plain by a parrot' (*Thoughts on Various Subjects*), but extreme care has to be taken with extracts from Swift, as with extracts from any satirist and expert at wielding irony. A good tip for student searching for an original subject for a project or long essay is the last book of *Gulliver's Travels*. It manages to be quintessentially eighteenth-century as well as extremely in tune with many aspects of current thought, and in the opinion of this writer at least is the most interesting and challenging of all four books in *Gulliver's Travels*.

## Question and answer

**Question**

'Slight is the subject, but not so the Praise,/If She inspire, and He approve my Lays.'

How would you defend *The Rape of the Lock* against the allegation that it is a 'slight' work?

**Answer**

The incident which inspired *The Rape of the Lock*, and round which it is based, is undoubtedly slight and trivial. Lord Petre snipped off a lock of Miss Arabella Fermor's hair, thus causing ill-feeling among the families concerned. This does not mean that the poem itself is slight. Indeed, to succeed in its aim of laughing the two families back into common sense the poem has to show exactly how slight the incident was, and thus if a part of the poem does not appear as slight and trivial it has failed in its main aim.

In technical terms *The Rape of the Lock* can be defended very easily against the charge laid against it in the title. The mock heroic style of writing depends for its effect on presenting the discrepancy between heroic passion and style, and trivial actions, treating the latter with all the glory of the former. This requires great skill. The style only works to full effect when the reader is made aware of the true heroic, epic style, and to do this the author has to write with something of the power and force of the original style. Many lines in the poem are near to true epic style. A line such as 'What dire offence from am'rous causes springs' could quite easily be the opening of a genuine epic poem on, say, Helen of Troy, or any of the great epic love stories of history. Once the poet has established an epic feel to the poem he must then handle very carefully the transition between epic and trivial. The line that follows the one given above (which is the opening to the whole poem) shows this transition working very effectively. When Pope follows his heroic opening with 'What mighty Contests rise from trivial things' the word 'trivial' sets up an immediate tension with the preceding matter, hinting at what is to come without destroying the force of the epic style. As well as moving subtly from the heroic to the mock heroic, Pope can also plunge the reader from one to another, milking the contrast for every last shred of humour. It takes a mere three lines to move from the epic conviction of:

> Mean while declining from the Noon of Day,
> The Sun obliquely shoots his burning Ray

to:

> The Merchant from th'Exchange returns in Peace,
> And the long Labours of the Toilette cease

Merchants, the Exchange, and the Toilette most definitely do not belong in epic poetry, and the humour carries all the more relish because learned readers would spot in the last line an echo of 'And the long Labours of your Voyage end' from the Aeneid. Pope has all the technical features necessary for the creation of a masterpiece. He knows his epic poetry extremely well, and can recreate its mood and feeling with great skill. He has an acute eye for the detail of trivial, high-society life, and can manage the transition from one to the other sharply or gently. The smooth, apparently effortless heroic couplets bind both elements together so that the transitions are never sharp or jagged, and the contrast is held permanently before our eyes.

For a slight poem, *The Rape of the Lock* has some very serious things to say. The poem, of course, is satirical in that it holds the stupidity of those involved in this squabble up to gentle ridicule in the expectation that this will laugh them out of their folly. However, the satire is not restricted to the incident in hand. A whole array of social weaknesses or follies is held up for gentle ridicule. The weakness of ladies for anyone of noble birth is well covered:

Say, what strange Motive, Goddess! cou'd compel
A well-bred Lord t'assault a gentle Belle?
Oh say what stranger Cause, yet unexplor'd,
Cou'd make a gentle Belle reject a Lord?

and the whole question of how deeply-held honour is in society is raised in the question of whether a lady will 'stain her Honour, or her new Brocade'. The suggestion is clearly that a stain on a dress is equal to a stain on one's honour. The poem also raises the question, throughout its length, of what it is in human nature that can permit so trivial an incident to get out of all proportion. Furthermore, high seriousness can make an appearance in the poem, as in the savage power of the famous lines:

The hungry Judges soon the Sentence sign,
And Wretches hang that Jury-men may Dine.

Lines such as 'When those fair Suns shall set, as set they must,/And all those Tresses shall be laid in Dust' stand fair in their own right as serious and powerful poetry; their expression in a mock heroic work is purely incidental. There is also the haunting suspicion throughout the poem that perhaps the loss of the lock is not such a trivial thing, and that the incident reveals in cameo some dark and dangerous depths of human nature.

There is also a magnificent realism in the poem, and an energy that again produces poetry that has a far greater relevance than the incident which prompted its authorship:

Oh! if to dance all Night, and dress all Day,
Charm's the Small-pox, or chas'd old Age away;

At times Pope is drawn into the imaginative world he has created so far and so deeply that his mock heroic devices attain a genuine beauty in their own right. His description of the Sylphs is funny and a parody of the epic style, but it has a beauty that is independent of this, with:

Transparent forms, too fine for mortal Sight
Their fluid bodies half-dissolv'd in Light.
Loose to the Wind their airy garments flew,
Thin glitt'ring Textures of the filmy Dew;

No description as evocative and powerful as this could ever be termed slight.

*The Rape of the Lock* is a masterpiece of the mock heroic style. It achieved its aim in bringing two families together, but did much more than this. It recreates the epic style as well as using it to create glorious comedy. It has a surprising range in both satire and seriousness. Its wit, its realism, its energy and its skill allow Pope to create from a slight incident a poem of lasting and superior worth.

# Further reading

## General

- James Sambrook, *The Eighteenth Century. The Intellectual and Cultural Context of English Literature 1700–1789* (Longman, 1993)
- W. A. Speck, *Literature and Society in Eighteenth Century England, 1680–1820* (Longman, 1998)
- James Sutherland, *A Preface to Eighteenth Century Poetry* (Oxford University Press, 1963): a classic text.
- Stephen N. Zwicker, *The Cambridge Companion to English Literature 1650–1740* (Cambridge University Press, 1998)

## Alexander Pope

- John Barnard, ed., *Pope: The Critical Heritage* (Routledge & Kegan Paul, 1985): rather detailed but very scholarly.
- Bonamy Dobree, *Alexander Pope* (Oxford University Press, 1963): positively ancient in terms of its date of publication, positively classic in its content.
- I. R. F. Gordon, *A Preface to Pope* (Longman, 1994): an excellent survey and introduction.
- Brean Hammond, *Pope* (Longman, 1996)
- Maynard Mack, *Alexander Pope. A Life* (Yale University Press, 1985)
- Donald C. Mell, *Pope, Swift and Women Writers* (Associated University Presses, 1996): covers feminist issues in the writing of Pope and Swift.
- Cynthia Wall, ed., *The Rape of the Lock* (Bedford Cultural Editions Series, Macmillan, 1998)
- Thomas Woodman, ed., *Early Romantics: Pope to Wordsworth* (Macmillan, 1998)

## Jonathan Swift

- Victoria Glendinning, *Jonathan Swift* (Hutchinson, 1998)

CHAPTER FOURTEEN

# The eighteenth- and early nineteenth-century novel: Defoe, Fielding, Austen and the Brontës

## The basic authors

The authors most commonly set from the range of early and relatively early novelists are Daniel Defoe (1660–1731), Samuel Richardson (1689–1761), Henry Fielding (1707–54), Tobias Smollett (1721–71), Laurence Sterne (1713–68), Sir Walter Scott (1771–1832), Jane Austen (1775–1817), Charlotte Brontë (1816–55), and Emily Brontë (1818–48). Of these, by far the most common as set authors are Fielding, Jane Austen, and the Brontë sisters.

## The literary and historical background

The novel is the youngest of the three literary forms, for reasons which are largely technical. The audience for drama does not have to be able to read; it simply sits, listens and watches. Poetry can be read out aloud, or circulated privately in manuscript form. A novel however, needs to be sold to a sufficiently large readership to make it profitable. Before the eighteenth century there were insufficient literate members of the population to provide an economic readership, and even had they existed, poverty and bad communications would have made it difficult for the readership to afford the copies. These problems facing the novel were considerably eased during the eighteenth century as the Industrial Revolution came to England. It brought with it a huge increase in population, an increasing tendency for that population to concentrate in urban centres, increased wealth (particularly among the middle classes), and increased standards of literacy. To all this could be added improved printing and communication systems for helping distribute books more widely and efficiently.

## Daniel Defoe

There were a number of works which could very loosely be described as novels before the eighteenth century, but with the arrival of Daniel Defoe there could be no doubt that the English novel had arrived. Defoe turned to novel writing almost by accident, a feature of many early novelists, and he was at various times a merchant, a journalist, a pamphleteer, and a spy, was made bankrupt, and at one time was pilloried and imprisoned. As well as all this he produced over five hundred separate works, though only a small fraction were novels. His best-known works are *Robinson Crusoe* and *Moll Flanders*, published in 1719 and 1722 respectively. *Robinson Crusoe*, based on the true story of one Alexander Selkirk, is about a sailor marooned on a desert island for many years. It has become a children's classic, often in edited form, the same fate as has befallen the first two books of Swift's *Gulliver's Travels*. *Robinson Crusoe* shows, among many other things, a man adapting very successfully first to life on his own, and then to life with another, subservient man. Both have made the novel interesting to critics of the feminist and postcolonial schools. *Moll Flanders* is the story of a woman who is a thief, a criminal and a prostitute, who finally makes her fortune and achieves respectability in the New World. *Moll Flanders* can very easily be seen as one of those books which was a feminist tract long before feminism was officially invented. Major areas of interest in Defoe are:

1. *Style*: Defoe narrates in a matter-of-fact, almost documentary style. The narrator does comment, but by and large characters are allowed to speak for themselves, and are judged by their actions. Narrative style and technique are frequently an issue of great interest to modern critical theorists, as well as to more traditional criticism.
2. *Plot*: The books are rambling and relatively disorganised, again quite a common feature of the early novel, but Defoe's humanity and compassion, his sense of humour and the sheer liveliness of his mind compensate for this.
3. *Optimism and human nature*: Defoe is an optimist, albeit a hardheaded one. The real Alexander Selkirk was in a semi-savage state when he was rescued, but Robinson Crusoe manages to build a small civilisation around him, and survives his experience very well. Moll Flanders also survives the horrors of her life, and finishes the novel as a stable and contented person. There is therefore an essential optimism about the novels, coupled with a realistic vision of the harshness of life. The 'Protestant Work Ethic', or the belief common in post-medieval and post-Reformation Europe that hard work was the answer to all social and moral problems, can be seen as influencing both *Robinson Crusoe* and *Moll*

*Flanders*, though in the case of the latter novel Moll's eventual success denies most conventional moralities. If what lets Moll succeed is indeed hard work then the term itself is being hugely and comically re-defined by Defoe.

4. *Morality*: See the comments above: Moll Flanders in particular is a very soiled figure who engages in a number of plainly immoral actions. There is thus an argument that she should be punished more than she is for her misdeeds. Defoe seems to be saying that we should judge people on their basic motivation and character, and not always on what they do. They are often victims of circumstances over which they have no control. Of course, if one sees Moll as a woman corrupted initially by a patriarchal, utterly hypocritical male society, and rescued simply by her own wit and character, then she has nothing to apologise for. Defoe sees the capacity for survival as a major virtue, something which perhaps surprisingly links him to some Renaissance writers.

## Samuel Richardson

Richardson is an author much talked and written about by critics, but rather less often read. He makes only a rare appearance on lists of set texts. Richardson was a printer who married his employer's daughter, and so came to own the firm. He was commissioned to publish and write a book of specimen letters for literate but badly educated people who did not know the correct forms to use when writing letters. From this developed *Pamela* (1740), a novel about a young maidservant whose mistress has just died, and who is subjected to an all-out attempt at seduction by her ex-mistress's son. She resists, and is finally rewarded by marrying the son. The novel is written in the form of letters. Basic questions on the novel are:

1. *Morality*: The lust that her would-be seducer shows towards Pamela is condemned, and then apparently made respectable by marriage, yet it is still the same feeling. This can be seen as a sham morality.
2. *Pamela*: Pamela can appear as a calculating, self-satisfied, and rather hypocritical figure, rather than the pure heroine she is presumably intended to be.
3. *Letter writing*: The technique has certain limitations, and the sheer number of letters written can appear ludicrous and impractical.

Whilst Richardson has never quite caught the reading public's imagination in the way that Dickens has, he has been fêted by parts of the academic establishment. In part this is because he is outwardly a far more modern writer than someone such as Fielding. By choosing to write a novel in the form of a letter, Richardson can go inside a character's head and give an internal monologue. Most other early novels described characters from the outside, as an observer might do, and did not feel free to dip in and out of characters' skulls at will. More modern novels have tended to place characterisation at a premium and demote plot to a lower level. Richardson's detailed, almost intimate insight into a character's mind, given by the letter-writing mode, thus brings Richardson closer to modern practice and priorities than many other eighteenth-century novelists. He also concentrates on women as his central figures, another feature which has added to his popularity in the feminist-conscious twentieth century. Richardson's second novel, *Clarissa* (1747–8), is altogether deeper and less smug than *Pamela*, and has attracted a great deal of critical attention.

## Henry Fielding

Henry Fielding is undoubtedly the examiner's favourite eighteenth-century novelist. Like Richardson he became a novelist almost by accident, when closure of the theatres in London stopped him from writing plays. He was a dramatist, a journalist, a lawyer and a campaigning magistrate, as well as a novelist. His early prose efforts were directed at satirising Richardson, whose morality he found unacceptable because it was simplistic.

Fielding's novels reveal another side of eighteenth-century life, a rumbustious, hell-raising rough-and-tumble approach somewhat at odds with the image of the age of reason and refinement. Neither Fielding nor Pope can represent wholly the eighteenth-century; taken together they can. Despite the harum-scarum nature of his heroes, Fielding's basic belief in progress, in the perfectibility of mankind and in the progress of civilisation is clear. What is also clear is his hatred of cant and humbug, something he shares strongly with Pope. Both poets hate a hypocrite more than anything else.

### The Picaresque

Fielding favoured the 'picaresque' style of writing. In the picaresque novel the central figure is known as the 'picaro'. Plotting is extremely simple. The central figure, normally given a friend and confidante (often a servant), is sent off on a journey on some pretext or other, and the plot of the novel consists of the various episodes and incidents the hero encounters. Traditionally these follow a see-saw pattern – an incident in which something good happens to the hero is followed by one in which something bad happens. Humour and episodes are frequently based on physical incident, even slapstick, and there is little continuity in the plot, with characters appearing only once in the whole course of the novel. The best-known and most influential picaresque novel is the seminal *Don Quixote* (1605–16) by Cervantes (1547–1616). Cervantes and Fielding manage to bring a remarkable degree of sophistication to this relatively simple model. A novelist such as Tobias Smollett (1721–71) is altogether more crude and simple. Modern thinking has tended to deride the picaresque novel, seeing in its limitations and emphasis on incident a dead-end for the novel. It was nevertheless used to great effect by Daniel Defoe.

Fielding made great play of using certain classical elements in *Tom Jones*. This can be seen as revealing considerable nervousness on Fielding's part about producing a 'new' type of writing in an age which did not value originality. Equally it could reflect the way in which most eighteenth-century authors turned automatically to classical models for their writing.

### *Joseph Andrews*

This novel begins as a direct parody of Richardson's *Pamela*, with Joseph (Pamela's brother) fleeing from attempted seduction by his employer, Lady Booby. This turn-about, with the man being seduced by the woman, is a good illustration of the occasionally riotous and earthy sense of humour evident in Fielding. Halfway through the novel Fielding seems to forget he is writing a satire on *Pamela*, and writes an excellent novel in its own right. Issues include:

1. *Parson Adams*: The hero of the novel, Parson Adams is a comic, but hugely appealing figure. He is also an outstandingly good man, a notoriously difficult thing to portray. Issues are therefore the subtle blend of gentle ridicule and admiration in Fielding's character study, and Adams' status as a truly good figure.
2. *Plot*: The plot of the novel is somewhat rambling, but still disciplined, and the techniques used by an author who had very little previous experience to go on in writing a novel (either his or other people's) are of interest.
3. *Morality*: Fielding was a realist, as was Defoe, and his morality is not prudish. He judges people on their heart or basic motivation much more than on their actions, though bad actions are always punished. Fielding's morality is warm and compassionate, though fierce when applied to true evil which hurts other people. The effectiveness and humanity of the book's morality is one of its most attractive features, as well as being significant in examination terms.
4. *Comic technique*: The novel is richly comic, and utilises a wide range of comic techniques, including irony, coarse physical humour, bathos, and comic set-piece situations.

### *Tom Jones*

Basic issues in this, undeniably one of the greatest novels in the English language, are these:

1. *The Narrator*: Each major section or 'book' in the novel is introduced by Fielding, and it is sometimes said that Fielding imposes his own personality too much on the reader. There is some truth in this, but it is also true that the authorial presence in the novel is often witty and amusing, and allows Fielding to point the reader gently in the direction in which he wants him or her to go.
2. *Characterisation*: Fielding's characters are described externally, by their appearance, actions and words. The conventions and style of the day did

not allow him to give internal psychological narrative, whereby a character's thoughts are described directly to the reader. In one sense this is closer to the manner in which we judge people in real life; after all, we never get a chance to hear what is happening inside anyone's head other than our own. In another sense it can give rise to slightly ludicrous situations, such as when Fielding has to have Tom quite literally tear out his hair to express extreme emotion. A further point is the statement that Fielding's minor characters are often much more than 'mere types', and have a real individuality all their own.

3. *Plot*: The plot of *Tom Jones* is highly organised, logical, and symmetrical. The skill and precision with which it is organised is frequently a question, but so also is the accusation that it is too elaborate.
4. *Morality and comic technique*: The same as was said above of *Joseph Andrews* could apply to *Tom Jones*. Fielding's use of irony in the latter novel is perhaps a more prominent area for examination than in *Joseph Andrews*, as is his use of the mock heroic style.
5. *Epic*: The phrase 'a comic epic in prose' is sometimes used as a peg upon which to hang an Advanced-level question. The novel does take some features of epic poetry and apply them to novel form, and the novel is also epic in the sense of being long, complex and fairly wide-ranging. Partly the epic structure reflects Fielding's nervousness about this new form of writing, and partly his desire to make his novel respectable by linking it with the epic form.

## Jane Austen

Jane Austen is much beloved of examiners and the reading public, a combination which is not always to be found. She published only six novels – *Sense and Sensibility* (1811), *Pride and Prejudice* (1813), *Mansfield Park* (1814), *Emma* (1816), and *Northanger Abbey* and *Persuasion* (1818). It is sometimes said that rivers have a juvenile stage and a mature stage. In terms of the eighteenth century, Fielding represents the juvenile or youthful stage. He has the respect for classical form and traditions, the belief in reason and the belief in society as a civilising agent, but he also has a wildness and joy in finding, for example, an elderly pedagogue with his trousers down in a whore's room or women fighting with old bones in a churchyard. This aspect of Fielding's work seems almost like a remnant of the wild Restoration days. None of the latter is visible in Jane Austen's work, altogether the mature form of the eighteenth century in prose. By authorial choice and by virtue of the age in which she lived Jane Austen shows a classical restraint and elegant awareness of form, yet she is also a superb satirist.

Jane Austen led a secluded life with her family, never marrying. Her novels deal with country landed gentry, and have a very narrow social range. It is a small sector of society, and her subject matter might also be seen as small in the sense that most of her novels have as their subject a young girl who is either about to be married, or ready for it. World events do not impinge on the novels, and a ball at a local country house is more important, or at least more relevant, than a great victory or defeat of Napoleon's. With this limited range it is perhaps surprising that her novels have lasted so well and proved so popular. Suggestions as to why this has been so, and outline answers to other major topics, are given below.

1. *Limitations and range*: A major question is this one of why and how these novels, dealing only with young girls, and firmly set in one particular time and place (and a restricted one at that) have lasted. One answer is that Jane Austen is a superb writer. By taking the reader into the minds of the characters, and by her acute observation that makes us really feel we know them, their trials and tribulations, limited as they are, become as important to the reader as they are to the fictional characters. Her use of irony (another favourite examination topic) is masterly, and she wields it like a delicate razor blade that can dissect a character such as Mrs Bennet in *Pride and Prejudice* in a seemingly effortless manner. She has a good ear for dialogue, and her characters represent universal failings and strengths, and so are instantly recognisable and interesting.

   Some of the more adventurous examination boards very occasionally set questions directed at another possible source of her popularity. Jane Austen's world, with its country houses, servants, ability to ignore the outside world and comforting absence of disaster and horrific suffering, is one to which the modern reader can escape, and find a certainty and tranquillity that perhaps his life does not offer. Even if this is true, it need not be made into a hostile criticism. Jane Austen's world impresses with its realism, nor is it devoid of harshness and suffering.
2. *Manners and morality*: Manners matter greatly in Jane Austen's world. Behaviour must be and has to be controlled, regardless of personal feelings, and it is the people who cannot exercise restraint who are condemned in her novels. This does not mean that people should be hypocritical, merely that one has a duty to other people to restrain and control one's own feelings. Effectively, good manners are a sign that a person considers others as important as himself, and is prepared to modify his or her behaviour for the sake of other people. Jane Austen admires love, generosity and compassion. She also admires common sense. Thus she does not object to people marrying for love – provided there is enough money in the marriage to help love along the way. She can sometimes be seen as callous, mercenary and heartless; actually she just has an element of prudence and caution to her. She does perhaps duck one or two issues. For example, she never really comes to grips with what would happen if one of her heroines did fall madly in love with a man who was penniless, and the depth of her morality and its complacency are sometimes probed by examiners.
3. *Style*: Clarity, economy, skilful use of dialogue and tight plotting are the main features of Jane Austen's style. There is a neat, rounded and rather satisfying completeness to her plots, and in an undemonstrative way she is an extremely competent story-teller.

4. *Other themes and topics*: Houses, estates, and family wealth run like an undercurrent through many of the novels, sometimes not so much as themes but as accepted issues of vital importance in the society of that time. Duty and decorum are terms sometimes used to describe what I earlier referred to as manners. Decorum is a sense of propriety, particularly on the part of young ladies. Jane Austen admires girls who can take a swipe at propriety and decorum when it is demonstrably stuffy, outmoded or plain silly, and she despises all that is pretentious, arrogant and proud. Equally her heroines must know where to stop, and when a character such as Lydia Bennett elopes scandalously in *Pride and Prejudice* she receives the full blast of Jane Austen's hostility for her gross breach of duty and decorum. Society is owed things in her novels, and the debt must be honoured. Rank and money matter greatly in the novels. They preserve the fabric of society, must be respected and carry with them rights and obligations. So also does marriage, which should be based on love, genuine understanding – and social suitability.

## The Brontës

Jane Austen and the Brontë sisters are complete opposites, the voice of restraint, reason and decorum opposed to the voice of violence, passion, and the emotions. New critical theory has responded to the Brontës with rather more eagerness than it has to Jane Austen. Charlotte Brontë's *Jane Eyre* in particular has become a favoured text of Anglo-American feminism, though modern critical work on the Brontë's is far from restricted to feminist critics. Lesbian and gay critics have seen in *Jane Eyre* a central text, with Jane nurtured and supported by a succession of females and female relationships, and betrayed by a succession of males and male relationships. The work of the two Brontë sisters is also firmly in the mould of Romanticism, and Romanticism has commanded a very great deal of attention from a wide range of modern critical theorists, not least of all because of the interest of those theorists in the way that language works.

In prose Jane Austen and the Brontë sisters illustrate the same opposed outlooks as do Pope and Wordsworth in poetry. Chapter 15 discusses the difference between the Romantic and the classical outlook in literature.

There were originally six Brontë children, brought up in the parsonage of an isolated Yorkshire village, with the moors on the one hand and their father's library on the other to encourage them in the invention of a bizarre and compelling fantasy world. Illness, violence and early death marred their domestic happiness, and helped make the family as attractive to Hollywood as to literary critics and examining boards.

### Emily Brontë and *Wuthering Heights*

*Wuthering Heights*, by Emily Brontë, was published in 1847, and was Emily's only novel before her tragic death from tuberculosis in 1848, when she was a mere thirty years old. It is remarkable for many reasons, one of which, its exceptionally mature plot and structure, is the subject of a full answer below. The novel is almost tragic in its scope, dealing in good and evil rather than in right and wrong, and is imbued with an elemental, primitive force that can hardly be matched in any other novel. At times it seems to generate its own morality, rising up above conventional morals and codes of behaviour and making them seem irrelevant to the great love affair that is at its centre. Its tragic element and its moral structure are both frequently examined. Psychologists have commented that the novel's power may be based on adolescent sexuality, moulded by innocence and repression. It is certainly true that there is immense violence and passion in the novel, created without a single reference to sexuality or the physical side of love. Critics also comment on the extent to which the novel was influenced by Shakespeare's *King Lear*, and the gothic novel (for the latter, see Chapter 16).

Examiners are also very keen on questions about the moorland setting, and the manner in which Emily uses natural descriptive detail to suggest and augment the power of passion present in her characters. A typical question might be 'To what extent does Emily Brontë's use of the moorland setting contribute to the atmosphere of *Wuthering Heights*?' The character of Heathcliff is also endlessly fascinating, to examiners and readers alike, with most questions concentrating on the extent and nature of his evil. He is described frequently as a devil in the novel, and questions tend to concentrate on this fiendish aspect of his nature, how it is made credible and sometimes if he is actually a credible character. Occasionally you might be asked if the novel could be described reasonably as 'poetic' or even 'dramatic'. The novel is also cyclic; one of the areas in which it has a link with tragedy is that it comes full circle, from relative peace and harmony to violence, destruction, and suffering, and thence on to final and conclusive harmony again.

## Charlotte Brontë and *Jane Eyre*

*Jane Eyre*, also published in 1847, is slightly less violent, passionate, and wild than *Wuthering Heights*, but still enough probably to send Jane Austen rushing for the smelling salts. The novel is autobiographical, in that it clearly leans on Charlotte's own experience as a governess and the feeling of humiliation it produced in her, but it is also wish-fulfilment on a grand scale, as the governess in *Jane Eyre* marries above her, and the man she loves. It is also quite moral, because both parties have to undergo suffering that, in the case of Rochester, the hero, goes as far as his being almost burnt alive. As in *Tom Jones*, the good people triumph and gain what they wish, but must be punished for their wrongdoing before they are allowed to do so.

*Jane Eyre* is at one and the same time a Cinderella, rags-to-riches story, a moral tract, a novel of passion, love, and mystery and, possibly, a feminist manifesto. The blend of these various elements is a possible examination question, as are the novel's weaknesses. Dialogue is not Charlotte Brontë's forte, if only because lack of experience forces her to imagine how upper-class people speak to each other, and she gets it slightly wrong, with the result that much of the dialogue is clumsy and weak. The plot also relies on one particularly unlikely supernatural incident and a lucky inheritance on the part of Jane, but sheer imaginative drive and power rescue the novel from melodrama. They do not rescue examination candidates from having to explain why the novel is credible and not melodramatic. Marriage, happiness, suffering, and the nature of duty, all feature in *Jane Eyre*, within the careful, episodic nature of the plot which follows Jane through the various stages of her life, and sees her grow morally and in stature with every new phase of her life. The impact of modern critical thinking on the novel is unlikely to appear, at least as such, on an A-level question, but will almost certainly do so at University level.

## Questions and answers

**Question 1**

'Nobility of heart is seen to matter a great deal more than nobility of birth in *Tom Jones*.' Discuss.

**Answer**

*Tom Jones* is almost a panorama of society. Its characters range from the noblest in the land, such as Lord Fellamar, to the lowliest, such as Black George, and the range and variety of characters is matched by the range and variety of settings, from the countryside to the heart of London. There are therefore numerous examples of both nobility of heart and nobility of birth in the novel, though 'noble' birth is here taken to mean good breeding and the families of land-owning gentry.

Being high-born is certainly no guarantee of purity or goodness in *Tom Jones*. Lord Fellamar tries to rape Sophie. Lady Bellaston is described by Squire Western as a 'fat a****b****!' or fat-arsed bitch, an entirely accurate description of a foul, selfish and venial woman. Blifil, possibly the most odious character in the novel, is of good birth, and Bridget Allworthy, of impeccable good breeding and a member of a highly influential and respected family, conceives and gives birth to an illegitimate child, concealing the fact until and beyond her death, which is certainly an act that is ignoble, base, and worthy of condemnation. This is not to say that the base characters of low birth do not equal or even exceed the immorality of the gentry. Blifil,

> tho' a prudent, discreet, sober young gentleman, was at the same time, strongly attached to the interest only of one single person; and who that single person was, the reader will be able to divine without much assistance of ours.

But Black George is his equal in selfishness, avarice and ingratitude, and actually owes Tom more than he himself is owed by Blifil. Envy, hypocrisy and self-interest dominate Mrs Waters, a servant, as much as they do Lady

Bellaston. These examples might suggest that nobility of heart is not associated with class in the novel, but this would be inaccurate. Nor would it be true to say that family, birth and breeding do not matter in the novel. There are certainly good-hearted people in the novel who are not of good birth, such as Mrs Nightingale, and even Partridge, who may be misguided and occasionally foolish, but manages to cling on to an affection for Tom that starts off with a selfish motivation but then gains more than an element of genuine affection and loyalty. However, the three characters whose hearts are undoubtedly in the right place are Tom, Sophie and Squire Allworthy, and all three have the benefit of being from the gentry. Nor can it be said that birth does not matter greatly in the novel. At the highest level it provides, rightly or wrongly, a permanent bar to Tom's marrying Sophie. On a lower level, the outward symbols of being well-born dictate how a character is treated in an inn, or whether or not he is likely to be press-ganged. Fielding shows us a society where birth does matter greatly.

Despite this, Fielding is wholly committed to the doctrine that nobility of heart, or the extent to which a person can behave with generosity, compassion and selflessness towards others, is the prime virtue in human beings. Tom is the hero of the novel because 'though he did not always act rightly, yet he never did otherwise without feeling and suffering for it'. In other words his actions may be wrong, but his intentions and his goodwill are never in doubt. He may sleep with women, but 'To debauch a young woman, however low her condition was, appeared to him a very heinous crime.' Clearly in the novel good intentions matter more than good birth.

Yet in the final count Fielding never really faces up to the question indirectly posed in his novel, of whether or not a truly noble and generous mind can be found in someone of low birth. The issue around which the main conflict is based, that the noblest of minds is found in a bastard, someone of the most ignoble birth, collapses when Tom's true birth is revealed. The reader can never know if Tom's frankness, his honesty, his generosity, and all his other noble features could be found in someone of low birth.

Nobility of heart is certainly what matters in Tom Jones, and it does matter more than nobility of birth. The implied moral of the novel is that whilst a well-born person can be as evil or misguided as a low-born one (though the higher the birth the more that person will be able to conceal their evil), birth and the character of a true gentleman will always be found together.

**Question 2**

How does Emily Brontë persuade the reader of the credibility of the events portrayed in *Wuthering Heights*, and to what extent is the plot of the novel one of its major triumphs?

**Answer**

The events of *Wuthering Heights*, when taken out of context, might well seem implausible. Civilised people are kidnapped, and dealt with violently. A man starves himself to death willingly and almost cheerfully for the sake of a long-dead lover. Babies are dropped over banisters, anvils thrown at people, a pet spaniel hanged from a tree by the man who is going to marry the dog's owner and a character beats his head against a tree in anguish until the blood flows.

A major technique in making these events credible is the style of narration used in the novel. Essentially the story is fed to the reader through the twin mediums of Lockwood and Nellie Dean. Lockwood is an effete, weak, almost sickening character – 'My dear mother used to say I should never have a comfortable home...' – but he is all too credible as a vain, pampered man, though he has been seen as a warm, mild and good-humoured man. Either way, he is a credible representative of the civilised world. Nellie is an enormously practical figure, down-to-earth, unimaginative, with a normal stock of virtues and defects. Having the story related to Lockwood by Nellie removes the reader from direct contact with the wild and improbable events described, and this slight distancing reduces them slightly, and so their improbability is reduced as well. Even more important is the fact that once Lockwood and Nellie are established as normal and credible people the reader can hardly help but accept anything they accept as being true. In one sense they represent the voice of normality in the novel, and represent therefore the reader. If they believe the events of the novel, it is all the more likely that the reader will do so as well.

The imagery of the novel and the moorland setting are also essential in establishing credibility. The wildness of the moors is a known, proven geographical fact. The wild passion of Heathcliff and Cathy seems merely an extension of nature when placed in this setting, an impression reinforced by the dialogue which talks continually of their love as a natural phenomenon:

> My love for Linton is like the foliage in the woods: time will change it, I'm well aware, as winter changes the trees. My love for Heathcliff resembles the eternal rocks beneath: a source of little visible delight, but necessary.

Furthermore, Emily Brontë provides the reader with more than a glimpse of normality in Thrushcross Grange, and deliberately places Wuthering Heights up the hill and away from the soft valley. The very emphasis of the fact that Wuthering Heights is a different world geographically makes it easier to accept that it is different in other ways, a place perched on the edge of the world where we cannot expect normality. On the other hand, relationships are described in terms of 'calm' and 'storm', perfectly natural events, and so natural in humans as well.

The novel starts when the tale of Heathcliff and his love is almost at an end. This provides both tension and a desire to find out more that can blanket out some of the unreality, or at least force it to the back of the reader's mind, but also gives finality to the whole story. This has happened, and therefore it is a fact. When the reader first meets Heathcliff his looks and manner are strange, but not unbelievably so, and Lockwood seems to feel he has Heathcliff summed up, and even feel a sneaking fondness for him. The extremes of Heathcliff's behaviour are built up to slowly. The reader is prepared for his extreme behaviour by continual references to him as a 'devil' or 'fiend', and by the fact that the humiliation and violence of his childhood are bound in all reason to provoke a strong response.

One of the most gripping and violent episodes in the novel is when Lockwood behaves in a manner apparently far removed from what we have seen of his gentle nature, when he 'dreams' of Cathy beating at his window in Wuthering Heights.

> terror made me cruel; and, finding it useless to attempt shaking the creature off, I pulled its wrist on to the broken pane, and rubbed it to and fro till the blood ran down and soaked the bed-clothes: still it wailed, 'Let me in!' and maintained its tenacious grip, almost maddening me with fear.

This episode is made credible by consummate skill on the part of the author. It has all the effect of a real episode, but the reader who feels its unreality can take consolation in the fact that it is probably all a dream. Yet Lockwood is described as 'dozing' rather than sleeping, and the incident is poised beautifully between dream and reality. Intellectually it is a dream; emotionally, we know it to be real. Almost the same technique, that of blurring the distinction between fiction and reality, is used with the vision of Heathcliff's and Cathy's ghosts walking the moors after their deaths. The incident is not baldly stated, it is merely seen by a boy, and reported at third hand. The reader can decide on the truth.

Narrative technique, plotting, and imagery all contribute to making the events in the novel credible, but the plot has other virtues that make it a major triumph. Despite an apparently confused time scheme that shifts back and forth, all the details of births, deaths, and events fit together chronologically and bear each other out. Information is withheld sufficiently to create suspense and interest, but never to an extent where the reader is hopelessly confused or lost. The plot has a magnificent symmetry, with the lives of the two Cathys sufficiently parallel to provide a sense of unity and echoes, but sufficiently divergent to bring the novel firmly back to normality and happiness at the end. The overall effect is to bring balance and unity to the events described and the novel as a whole.

## Further reading

### General

- Arnold Kettle, *An Introduction to the English Novel, Volume 1* (Hutchinson, 1967): a classic work of criticism.
- Richard Kroll, ed., *The English Novel, 1700 to Fielding* and *The Eighteenth Century Novel* (both Longman, 1998)
- John Mullan, *Sentiment and Sociability. The Language of Feeling in the Eighteenth Century* (Oxford University Press, 1990)

- Clive T. Probyn, *English Fiction of the Eighteenth Century 1700–1789* (Longman, 1987)
- John Richetti, *The Cambridge Companion to the Eighteenth-Century Novel* (Cambridge University Press, 1996)
- Ian Watt, *The Rise of the Novel* (Pelican, 1963): a discussion of the early novel which did much to promote the reputation of Richardson.


## Jane Austen


- Marilyn Butler, *Jane Austen and the War of Ideas* (Clarendon Press, 1987)
- David Cecil, *A Portrait of Jane Austen* (Penguin, 1980): a superb biography.
- Edward Copeland, ed., *The Cambridge Companion to Jane Austen* (Cambridge University Press, 1997)
- A. Craik, *Jane Austen: The Six Novels* (Methuen, 1968)
- Christopher Gillie, *A Preface to Jane Austen* (Longman, 1985)
- Vivien Jones, *How to Study a Jane Austen Novel* (Macmillan, 1987): an excellent introductory work for A-level students.
- David Nokes, *Jane Austen. A Life* (Fourth Estate, 1997): witty and perhaps rather more gossipy than normal.
- Tony Tanner, *Jane Austen* (Macmillan, 1986)
- Claire Tomalin, *Jane Austen. A Life* (Penguin/Viking, 1997): a detailed, serious biography.


## The Brontë Sisters


- Edward Chitham, *A Life of Emily Brontë* (Basil Blackwell, 1987)
- Rebecca Fraser, *Charlotte Brontë* (Methuen, 1988)
- Heather Glen, *Jane Eyre* (New Casebooks Series, Macmillan, 1997)
- Felicia Gordon, *A Preface to the Brontës* (Longman, 1989)
- Pauline Nestor, *Villette* (New Casebooks Series, Macmillan, 1992)
- Beth Newman, *Jane Eyre* (Macmillan, 1996)
- Patsy Stoneman, *Wuthering Heights* (New Casebooks Series, Macmillan, 1993)
- Brian Wilks, *Charlotte in Love. The Courtship and Marriage of Charlotte Brontë* (Michael O'Mara Books, 1998)


## Henry Fielding


- Martin Battestin and R. Ruthe, *Henry Fielding: A Life* (Routledge, 1989)
- Ian Bell, *Henry Fielding. Authorship and Authority* (Longman, 1994): covers the impact of modern criticism on Fielding.
- Harold Pagliare, *Henry Fielding. A Literary Life* (Macmillan, 1998)


## Richardson


- Terry Eagleton, *The Rape of Clarissa* (Basil Blackwell, 1982)

CHAPTER FIFTEEN

# Romanticism and the Romantic poets: Blake, Wordsworth, Coleridge, Byron, Shelley and Keats

## Romanticism and classicism

As often happens in literature, at the end of the eighteenth century the pendulum swung from one extreme to another, from reason to passion. The distinction between a 'classical age' and a 'Romantic age' is one of the most vexed issues of literature; what follows can only hope to scratch the surface.

It is possible to see two basically different ways of looking at life and experience, and tag these two different approaches as 'classical' or 'Romantic'. Pope's age was by and large a classical age, believing in reason and that the passions should be controlled. Mankind could reach perfection, but for this to happen basic instincts had to be conquered. Civilisation, as attained in Greek and Roman times, was also within the grasp of the 'modern age'. It is not difficult to see historical reasons for this attitude in the eighteenth century – perhaps it is even too easy to see the links. Reforms in medical care and farming techniques in the eighteenth century began to allow the rise in the population that was to be a major factor in the Industrial Revolution, the process by which Great Britain became the first nation in the world to move from a farming to an industrial economy. Discoveries were beginning to be made in the sciences, in engineering and even in the social sciences that were to change the face of British society. It must have appeared as if mankind was set on a new advance, and one which could only bring benefit to all. The huge commercial growth of the Industrial Revolution created an advanced economy, which in turn created vast wealth and allowed for a major population growth. In the Middle Ages literature had needed the patronage of wealthy members of the upper class; though an element of that continued, the Industrial Revolution created a wider wealth, and the possibility of authors earning their living through the actual sale of books.

The Romantic outlook, on the other hand, sees man's salvation as lying within himself. The Romantic believes in and trusts only himself, believing that society and civilisation corrupt humanity's natural innocence and instinct for good. Romantic literature, particularly poetry, often sees man in communion with the natural world, rather than with other men. It trusts instincts, the emotion and the heart, rather than reason, intellect and the head. The distinction is perhaps best illustrated by two examples. The concept of 'the noble savage' is specifically a Romantic one. It consists of the idea that man in his primitive state is in a higher state of purity than civilised, urban man, whose natural instincts have been ground out of him by the process of civilised life. The savage may appear primitive, but the truth is that he has an instinctive knowledge of himself and the world which is often superior to that gained by civilised man. The classical thinker would laugh derisively at this concept. To him the savage is just what the word states, a human in a savage state of primitive bestiality whose only hope lies in his being educated and brought up the scale of evolution by the application of civilised virtues. The savage represents crude, unrefined static man, a hopeless bundle of raw instinct and repulsive primitivism, and a denial of all progress in humanity. Only a Romantic would think of a savage as noble; to a classicist, he would be merely sad and regrettable.

Nowhere is this better seen than in the different attitudes to children shown in the work of poets influenced by the two different outlooks. To Pope a child is important only in as much as he will become adult, and a civilised being. As a child his instincts have yet to be trained, and he is too near the level of a savage to be a real person. Instead he is the raw, unrefined material than can be turned, with time and effort, into the sophisticated and civilised human being, in control of his instincts. Pope's attitude is that of the classical age. To the Romantic a child is in some respects a holier and purer object than an adult. The child is unspoilt by civilisation and uncorrupted, in a natural state that can mean he is even closer to God and the source of his creation than are his older fellows. Rather than being something to be hurried out of, childhood to a Romantic is a state to be envied, cultivated and enhanced, as well as admired. A Romantic author will usually use unkindness towards children as the ultimate damnation; a classical author is just as likely to use unkindness against adults, and to ignore children altogether.

In general, a classical author tends to turn his attention outward to the society in which he or she lives, whilst a Romantic exposes his own soul, directing the light of analysis and comment internally. This analysis, of course, indicates the two extremes, and most ages and types of literature share classical and Romantic features.

## The romantic movement

The Romantic movement is generally seen as starting around 1770. It affected all the arts and culture in general, but was essentially, as discussed, a reaction against the eighteenth century and the Age of Reason. It was often in open revolt against accepted social conventions. Romantic writers frequently alternate between peaks of ecstasy and depths of intense depression. Romantic poetry has become associated with Nature poetry, but as will be shown below it was by no means dominated by this. Some commentators have seen in Romanticism and Romantic poetry a reaction against industrialisation, creeping across Europe in the eighteenth century and threatening every aspect of society and the way people lived. There is a link between the Industrial Revolution and Romanticism, but it cannot be taken too far without detailed historical knowledge. The Romantic movement predated industrialisation in many instances, and reached its peak when for the majority of people industrialisation was a local phenomenon. The trigger for some of Wordsworth's finest work was the French Revolution, and to the Romantic authors themselves this revolution had more impact than the Industrial Revolution.

## Romanticism and modern criticism

Romanticism has proved very fertile ground for modern critical theory. The period between 1790 and 1830 saw Great Britain acquire an empire as well as an industrial base, and as a result Postcolonial and Marxist criticism can give valuable and sometimes surprising insight into the work of the major Romantic poets. New political and social structures have also been seen as determining factors in Romantic poetry. As one example, links have been shown to exist between the work of Wordsworth and Shelley and a number of far more avowedly 'political' poets, including those involved with radical protest movements such as Chartism. Challenging new views of gender and ambivalent attitudes towards femininity have concerned a number of authors. The romantic period saw the birth of several movements or schools of thought that have come either to dominate or exert a great influence on modern thought. Mary Wollstonecraft's *Vindication of the Rights of Women* is one of the very first feminist manifestoes. In politics this was also the period of Thomas Paine's seminal *Rights of Man*. Far from being poets locked in to their own vision of solitary nature, modern criticism has shown the Romantic poets to be at the heart of the development of the romantic age, developments which can be seen as marking the start of the modern world. One aspect of such modernity was the growth in the number of authors who earned a living from their writing and the resultant new relationships with the reader have all provoked intense discussion. Romanticism can, by one view, be seen as the 'deconstruction' of the rigid code and ethics of classicism, and so is attractive to post-structuralist theory. The intensity of the psyche in Romantic poetry, and the intensity of self-examination and a subjective approach, have also interested followers of psychoanalytic criticism. 'Utopian' theories have also been extensively examined with regard to all Romantic writing. The term derives from a political essay written by Sir Thomas More (?1477–1535). *Utopia* (1516) envisages an imaginary island on which is found an ideal society. Subsequently, books portraying 'Utopian' ideals have been very common, but modern criticism has pointed out the relevance of the ideal to Romantic poetry. Such criticism has sometimes taken as its starting point the social experimentation of such pioneers as Robert Owen, whose mills and factories were based on an 'ideal', philanthropic system of employment and management. Owen's experiments point to a society which was willing to tread new ground, and which recognised the death of an old social order by its attempts to create one which was truly new and in tune with the times. It is hardly surprising that poetry and literature in general reflect the wider social trends.

In summary, if Romanticism has not been reinvented by modern criticism it has been subject to searching new scrutiny in almost every one of its aspects. This makes it one of the most rewarding areas to view in the light of modern critical theories and approaches.

## William Blake

William Blake (1757–1827) belongs to no one school of poetry, and is one of the most individual poets of any age. However, certain features in his poetry are forerunners of Romanticism. Blake was an engraver whose art work was slightly hampered by the rather clumsy drawing technique that was taught in his age. He was a glorious eccentric, choosing to read *Paradise Lost* with his wife, the pair of them clothed only in two fig leaves in order to bring them closer to Adam and Eve. Blake held conversations with angels over breakfast, and when food and money had run out his wife was forced into reminding him of the necessities of life by placing an empty plate before him at the meal table. He achieved little fame in his own lifetime, but in the twentieth century has come to be hailed as a genius.

### The main features of Blake's poetry

Blake was a prophet and a mystic. By far and away the most commonly set of his books is *Songs of Innocence and Experience* (1789), a relatively early work. His later work became more and more philosophical, prophetic and mystical, and less and less related to poetry.

**Symbolism**

Blake wrote in and through symbols. He saw humanity in terms of a natural collection of virtues and innocence, held tyrannically in chains and destroyed by society, the Church and its own ignorance. Innocence is symbolised by children, flowers or certain of the seasons. Oppression and tyranny are symbolised by priests, the urban industrial landscape, or those in authority. Blake also sees the existence of a natural heroic and creative energy in life; swords, spears, chariots, the sun, and animals such as lions or tigers are used as symbols of this admirable and earth-moving energy, as in the famous poem 'The Tyger'. The power of Blake's symbols is immense. It can also be confusing, because the meaning of a symbol can change from one poem to the next, and because sometimes images are used in direct contradiction to their conventional meaning.

**Blake as prophet**

'Prophetic' and 'mystic visionary' are words often used of Blake, although sometimes their meaning is not stated clearly. What they amount to is that Blake puts all his yearning and desire for a perfect world into glowing visions of an innocent past, or a glorious future. At the same time he condemns, with an awful grandeur and prophetic insight, the evils of his own world, its attack on human freedom and its denial of basic liberties and the life of the imagination. The prophetic element in his work springs from his vision of the future and the past, and the dire warnings he issues about the downward path his own society was taking. He is a mystic because all his vision is wrapped up and contained in elaborate symbolism, the meaning of which is sometimes tantalisingly complex and even obscure.

**Industrial landscape**

All that Blake most loathed in life was summed up in factories, machines and analytical science. As always in his work these are not hated so much for what they are, but for what they symbolise about society's willingness to abandon imagination and humanity to machine-like, unthinking precision.

**The Bible**

The Authorised version of The Bible is required reading for any student interested in Blake's work. Its imagery and tone permeate his work. Blake's use of Biblical items is fascinating. He sees it almost in the same terms as he sees his own poetry, a vision rather than documentary truth. He can convert the words and symbols of the Bible to his own use, either expressing what he sees as the truth of their meaning, or adding to it with his own.

## William Wordsworth

William Wordsworth (1770–1850) is probably the most famous of the Romantic poets, and may be the best. He was born in the Lake District of the United Kingdom, in what was then Cumberland; his love of the wild, mountainous English Lakes never left him, and remained to the end of his life a major influence on all he wrote. He was greatly excited by the French Revolution (1789), seeing in it the chance for a whole new order in the world. Whilst in France he fathered an illegitimate child. When the French

Revolution turned towards tyranny, and England declared war on France, Wordsworth suffered mental anguish that brought him near to collapse. His ideals were divided between England and France, the collapse of a revolution that had seemed so noble and liberal tormented him, and his child and its mother were beyond his reach in France. Guilt and confusion threatened to engulf Wordsworth, and he was helped to recovery largely through the influence of his sister Dorothy. It is sometimes said that all great authors are at war with themselves, and that great literature is born out of internal conflict; Wordsworth suggests the truth of this idea. In his early years he wrote a significant amount of the poetry by which he is remembered, and although he lived until 1850 much of his best work was written by 1807.

## Issues in Wordsworth's poetry

### Simplicity and Style

Wordsworth stated explicitly some of his poetic philosophy in the various prefaces to his *Lyrical Ballads* (1798), which he wrote in company with Samuel Taylor Coleridge (see below). The *Preface* to the 1800 edition of *Lyrical Ballads* is essential reading for any student. A main plank of his philosophy was to move the language and the subject of poetry away from the clichés and stylised, elaborate fashion of the eighteenth century, prune it of excess and move towards the language of everyday speech and the life of ordinary people. Perhaps in expressing this desire Wordsworth sums up a central part of the Romantic movement, at least as it concerned himself, that is the simple man, living at one with the natural environment, is seen as mankind in its purest and therefore strongest form. Uncorrupted by society, the spirit of man shines through in these uncluttered surroundings, and his simple language reflects better than any poetic posturings the true basic essentials and beauty of life.

Wordworth's language, and whether or not he did use the language of ordinary men, is a standard issue in his work. The answer, as always, is not simple. Wordsworth can write very often with a beautiful simplicity and directness. He can also write so simply as to be ludicrous, and often his language is not so simple as his declared intentions would have us believe. Romantic poetry is at its strongest when it turns inward to the mind of the poet, not outward to observed characters. Everything Wordsworth wrote was, he claimed, based on life; he had no time for anything that he believed was unreal, and what was most real to him was the impact of what he saw on himself. It is these shared moments of insight and high passion that mark Wordsworth's highest achievements in verse. What he observes, be it simple people or nature, is often only an excuse to create and share these moments of sublime insight.

### Nature

Perhaps above all Wordsworth is associated in the popular mind with his vision of Nature. His poetry may contain a few surprises for the student who comes to him armed only with a general awareness of what his work is meant to contain. Wordsworth is perhaps not as good at describing the natural landscape as a number of other poets. As a purely descriptive poet he is highly capable, but his real genius lies in showing what happens when the innate power of Nature meets the power of perception of a human mind. It is as if the individual's perception of Nature, its awe, power and capacity to teach, is what matters, rather than Nature itself. It is the interaction of Nature and human nature that enlivens and stimulates him. The word pantheism is sometimes used in connection with Wordsworth. A pantheist believes that God is visible in everything, and that his nature can be ascertained from the nature of his creation, the Universe. In a restricted sense Wordsworth is a Pantheist. Nature is a store of truths about human nature, the world, and God, but that truth lies inert until a human being conjoins with Nature and draws that truth out.

#### The Sublime Egotist

Keats referred to Wordsworth (in a parody of Milton) as the 'egotistical sublime'; sublime because he was forever searching for a moment of transcendental insight and perception, a moment in which every fibre of the mind and the imagination caught light, egotistical because everything he wrote was based directly on his own personal experience and observation of life, or that of his sister. The extent to which his poetry is autobiographical is a standard examination question, though attention here should be diverted from a straight examination of his life and its influence on his work to the more rewarding study of the extent to which his poetry presents us with the landscape of an individual mind. The Romantic poets looked within themselves and then related that observation and its conclusion to life in general. Perhaps personal is a better word to describe what we find in Wordsworth, rather than autobiographical, but as with all great authors Wordsworth persuades the reader that what he sees has a universal significance.

### Wordsworth's poetry

*Lyrical Ballads* is a major work, containing 'Tintern Abbey', one of Wordsworth's most famous poems. Other poems which the student starting on Wordsworth should turn to are 'Michael' (1800), 'Sonnet Composed Upon Westminster Bridge', 'The Solitary Reaper', and 'The Daffodils' (1807). *The Prelude*, a long autobiographical poem not published until after his death, is generally regarded as Wordsworth's masterpiece. Finally, 'Intimations of Immortality' (1807) must be studied, not only as a fine poem in its own right, but as a major source of insight into Wordsworth's mind and sensibility.

## Samuel Taylor Coleridge

Coleridge (1772–1834) was one of the more remarkable personalities of a remarkable movement. He had one of the most brilliant minds of his age, and one which delved into all areas of human learning and experience. He was, arguably, among the most outstanding literary critics that England has produced; his marginalia (notes commenting on a text) on Shakespeare still provide some of the best insights available into Shakespeare's work. He attended the University of Cambridge, but left without a degree after a career that involved him joining the army under the name of Silas Tomkin Comberbacke. He was rescued from this by his family. He met Wordsworth in Somerset, embarked on a close friendship, and collaborated with Wordsworth by contributing to *Lyrical Ballads* (1798), though the majority of the poems were Wordsworth's. Coleridge married very unhappily, became addicted to opium and was later to fall out with Wordsworth. Though the quarrel was eventually patched up their relationship never regained its former strength. Financial, medical and personal problems beset him throughout his life. Coleridge was only intermittently successful in his poetry, and a comparatively small number of poems written by him have achieved lasting fame. Those which have are remarkable and unique.

**'The Rime of the Ancient Mariner'**

This poem was Coleridge's major contribution to *Lyrical Ballads*, and is justifiably one of the most famous poems in the English language. It tells in ballad form the story of a young man stopped on his way to a wedding feast and forced to listen to the story of an ancient mariner. This story-within-a-story tells of how the mariner kills an albatross, is punished and suffers for this deed, and then is finally rescued and redeemed by the power of love and generosity, which re-establishes the bond between him and nature.

It is almost impossible to do justice to this poem in a short space. It is nowhere near as realistic as Wordsworth's work, nor does it direct the attention of the reader inward to the poet's mind. Instead it uses the techniques of the medieval ballad and creates a world of intense symbolism, in which each image is crammed full of a significance that the reader can always feel but rarely understand in its entirety. In its simplest form the poem is a nightmare about what happens when a man offends the power of nature. His sin is followed by suffering and eventual expiation. What this description does not convey is the intense power that Coleridge can give to the narrative, partly through technical devices such as his use of metre, rhyme and symbolism, but partly through the contrast between stark narrative that describes in almost matter-of-fact terms the most outlandish events. Some of this stark simplicity is illustrated in the following extract:

Day after day, day after day,
We stuck, nor breath nor motion;
As idle as a painted ship
Upon a painted ocean.
Water, water, everywhere,
And all the boards did shrink;
Water, water, every where,
Nor any drop to drink.

The repetition, short verse lines, simple rhyme, stark rhythm and description through visual imagery are all features of the ballad, as is the heavy reliance throughout the poem on dialogue and the spoken word. It has been said that it is a crime to try to interpret this poem, and that one should simply experience it. Issues in the poem are its technique, its symbolism, and the extent to which it is a moral allegory. Perhaps it is best seen as a myth, a poem the success of which springs from the clarity and power of its symbolism, rather than from any specific meaning.

**'Kubla Khan'**
'Kubla Khan' is a fragment, reportedly composed whilst Coleridge was under the influence of opium, and unfinished because its composition was interrupted by a visitor, and when the poet returned his inspiration and memory of the lines in his head had vanished. The River Alph in the poem is a symbol for some destructive force, possibly Art itself, and the 'pleasure dome' described with such excited longing is as much a series of sense impressions as an attempt to produce an image with a controlled and understood meaning. The poem is a dream vision of vast intensity, and a dream in which the nightmare is never far beneath the surface. The yearning for a transcendental moment of beauty and insight, and the feeling of a moment of total spiritual insight that is always just beyond the perception of the poet, make this one of the most concentrated and powerful of English poems.

## 'Christabel', 'Frost at Midnight', and 'Dejection: An Ode'

'Christabel' is based on the romance and medieval ballad form, mixing excitement, enchantment, the grotesque and the sinister with compelling power. It is well worth reading 'Christabel' at the same time as some of Tennyson's poems which are similarly based on the romance ballad (see Chapter 18).

'Frost at Midnight' is a very different poem. Here Coleridge does turn into his own mind. Very exact and vividly realised observation of his surroundings are the bed-rock of the poem:

> . . . the thin blue flame
> Lies on my low-burnt fire, and quivers not;
> Only that film, which fluttered on the grate,
> Still flutters there, the sole unquiet thing.

but out of these Coleridge generates a quiet and reflective perusal of personal and universal issues, such as paternity and childhood (at the heart of the poem is the image of the poet's sleeping daughter).

'Dejection: An Ode' is about the failure of the poet's imagination, and perhaps even his whole life. At the start his tone is resigned, almost wry, but the poem moves to expressions of grief that are almost stark in their directness; the strain of the poet's misery cuts out and renders ineffective any attempts to philosophise or moralise about his position. Coleridge's imagery, the nature of his personal passion, his use of rhyme and metre, his ability to create universal significance out of personal reflections are significant areas in all these poems.

## Lord Byron

Byron (1788–1824) has arguably received rather less critical attention in recent years than some of the other poets covered here. He was the son of a wild and lawless family. He despised his mother and idolised his father (his parents split up when the father had spent most of his wife's fortune), and despised also the fierce, Calvinistic nurse who helped to bring him up. Under these circumstances it was hardly likely that he would have a happy childhood, and his being born with a deformed foot was a further major disadvantage. He inherited his title unexpectedly, and was launched to instant public fame by the publication of *Childe Harold's Pilgrimage* (1812), a partly autobiographical long poem based on his European travels. He married an heiress who was determined to reform him, left her after only a short while, and went to live abroad, eventually losing his life from a fever whilst fighting for Greek independence against the Turks. Before this he had managed to scandalise society by a relationship with his half sister.

### Byron's poetry

Byron's reputation is based on *Childe Harold's Pilgrimage, Beppo* (1817), *The Vision of Judgement* (1822), and *Don Juan*, which began publication in 1819, and which was never finished. *Don Juan* is generally regarded as his greatest work.

## Issues in Byron's work

There have been numerous debates on the essential value of Byron's work, and Advanced-level questions sometimes ask the candidate to consider his strengths and weaknesses.

Complaints about his poetry are that it contains no emotion and no intellect. He fell particularly foul of modern authors such as T. S. Eliot and W. H. Auden who, in their own work, were deliberately trying to install an intellectual spine into poetry to offset what they saw as the excessive triviality and sentimentality of pre-First World War poetry. He has also been described at various times as heartless, prejudiced, morally dishonest, and seen as lacking a perception of beauty. Byron made some of his name and much of his fortune by writing exciting adventure poems, and the traces of this style show through strongly in his major works. He is no great philosopher, and there is often a great deal more energy than thought in his work. His writing shows strong traces of the picaresque style, with an essentially rambling structure unified only by the presence of a central figure, and with excitement and incident outweighing characterisation and thematic coherence as virtues.

The virtues of his poetry are his immense skill at telling an exciting story; his awareness of, and capacity to write for, an audience; and his superb comic touch. Byron may have been amoral, but his poetry attacks hypocrisy wherever it can be found; sometimes his attacks are unfair, but they rarely fail to be amusing and witty. His narrator in *Don Juan* is a masterpiece, an amusing cynic with a wide range of tones at his disposal. The ideas in the majority of his poems are commonplace, but exceedingly well-expressed. His use of ottava rima (an eight-line stanza of iambic pentameters, rhyming abababcc) in *Don Juan* is unequalled by any other English poet, and within its confines Byron manages to develop a vibrant snappiness and some marvellously stinging satiric slaps. Byron has an acute ear and eye for the presence of hypocrisy, considerable technical skill, a wide range of tone and a highly developed narrative skill. He wrote stories with epic settings but no epic morality, and any lack of coherence and unity in his work is often offset by its huge and enjoyable energy. He could treat and recreate emotion seriously when the mood so took him, as the famous 'Haidee' love story of *Don Juan* proves.

### The Byronic hero

Byron gave this phrase to the language, and in doing so created a myth in the bargain. The concept of the Byronic hero is drawn from both heroes and narrators in Byron's poetry. He is a morose, enigmatic, cultured, bitter figure, gloomy, outwardly devil-may-care but full of dark secrets. All the controversy about Byron's life, as well as sometimes obscuring an accurate picture of his poetry, has made some readers see the figure of the Byronic hero and Byron himself as one and the same thing. As it is, the Byronic hero reflects aspects of Byron's character, but by no means the whole. Perhaps the safest thing to say about Byron is that, like all the Romantic poets, he was a man in search of a spiritual truth that for much of the time could be experienced only through the sensations; perhaps he found that truth, and his release, in Greece.

## Percy Bysshe Shelley

Shelley (1792–1822) was the son of a Sussex aristocrat. He was 'sent down' (expelled) from the University of Oxford for publishing a pamphlet advocating atheism. He married a sixteen-year-old girl in 1811, but left her after three years. Two years later she drowned herself. In 1816 Shelley eloped with and married Mary Godwin, who as Mary Shelley was the author of the famous *Frankenstein, or the Modern Prometheus* (1818); this is discussed in Chapter 16. Shelley was drawn to the Continent, and particularly the Mediterranean, and whilst in Europe he became friendly with both Byron and Keats. He died alone when the boat he was sailing foundered in a storm, and there were strange stories about the episode. In his poetry he had come near to prophesying his own death by drowning, and there were rumours and signs that he made no attempt to save himself.

Out of all the Romantic poets Shelley has perhaps received the most interest from modern criticism. Shelley's first major poem was *Queen Mab* (1813), and in it he displays many of the features that can be seen as typical of his poetry. Shelley was a revolutionary. He was obsessed by the manner in which society, institutions and conventional morality destroyed and corrupted mankind. A frequently quoted line, 'Power like a devastating pestilence/Pollutes whatever it touches', shows both the depth of his feeling and his loathing of conventional authority. Shelley had a strong belief in an absence of original sin, and that humanity could attain perfection. This, and his hatred of authority, society and conventional morality, may suggest that he was a far more accurate and precise political and social thinker than was actually the case. His beliefs when turned into poetry favour a soaring flight after beauty and truth, shrouded in mystic imagery and visions of Utopia or perfection; how to reach that perfection is less clearly stated. *Queen Mab* and many of his other poems have no logical structure to them, and sometimes little control or planning. He has been accused of self-centredness and of an excess of self-pity. His lack of structure is perhaps one reason why his short lyric poems are the most famous parts of his poetic output; his weaknesses tend to diminish with the length of what he writes.

*The Masque of Anarchy* (1819) was a response to the Peterloo Massacre in England. It is a stark, grim poem, in which Shelley, described by Matthew Arnold as 'a beautiful and ineffectual angel, beating his wings in a luminous void in vain', has his feet firmly on a ground that is filthy, and stained with the blood of oppression. In *Alastor, or the Spirit of Solitude* (1816) a more conventional Romantic outlook is used. The hero, in Shelley's words 'a youth of uncorrupted feelings and adventurous genius' (and clearly based partly on Shelley himself), is led out to search for a vision of beauty in a dream world, a search that is never to be fulfilled and which ends in the death of the hero. Beauty, yearning, a sense of mystery, and the search for some inspired moment that is forever just beyond; these are central features of much Romantic writing, and of Shelley's poetry. *Prometheus Unbound* (1820) is generally regarded as Shelley's most successful long poem. It is based on the Greek myth of Prometheus, who was punished for giving the gift of fire to mankind. The 'poem' is in fact a verse drama, which shows Prometheus redeemed through love. Shelley's search for a saviour, a yearning for freedom and an end to tyranny, his faith and belief in the power of love are all found in *Prometheus Unbound*, which though patchy contains some justifiably famous passages. The poem ends in joy, and offers fulfilment, whereas this fulfilment is merely a dream and an aspiring hope in much of his other work. Shelley's most famous poems are his short lyrics, most notably 'Adonais' (an elegy on Keats), written in 1821, 'Epipsychidion' (1821), one of his fullest statement on love, 'Ode to the West Wind', and 'To a Skylark', all written in 1820. 'Ozymandias' is also well worth reading. His *A Defence of Poetry* was written in 1821, but not published until after his death, in

1840, and is a fine prose work that shows clearly Shelley's own views on poetry.

### The poet as legislator

Shelley believed in the poet as a legislator, someone who could reform the world through poetry. He says that he sees poetry as subordinate to moral and political science, a suggestion that might be taken to mean that the poet is merely a sociologist who chooses to write his tracts in verse. Of course nothing could be further from the truth. Shelley believed that it is through the power of the creative imagination that the world and society will be reformed, and through the enhanced perception of beauty. It was Shelley above all other poets who saw the poet as a person with a mission, an actual leader in and of society who, by unleashing the creative power latent in the human mind, could become a new form of the Messiah for society. His idealism and perception of beauty are inspiring and uplifting; equally powerful are the moments in his poetry when he fails to reach that summit of beauty for which he is aiming. The full-throated idealism in his poetry, when linked to a startling awareness of the horrors of tyranny, makes for a very potent and startling mixture. His occasional technical carelessness, selfishness, and even childish fits of anger can be seen as merely making more human one of the warmest and most fascinating figures in English Literature.

## John Keats

Keats (1795–1821) came from relatively humble origins, but was able to attend private school and start training as a medical student, something he later gave up in order to write poetry. His early works were savaged in various influential journals, he underwent a tormenting and hurtful love affair, and finally died as a result of tuberculosis, an illness that had already killed his mother and brother. Despite these handicaps he has emerged as one of the Romantic poets about whose greatness there is little doubt. His letters are sometimes included for study in examinations, and they remain one of the most interesting and well-written collections available to the general reader. As well as being interesting in themselves they contain a great deal of information about Keats' thoughts on poetry, and are essential reading (whether or not they actually appear on the syllabus) for any examination candidate studying his work.

### The poetry of Keats

Keats published his first volume of poetry in 1817. It contained only one poem of lasting fame, 'On First Looking into Chapman's Homer'. His second volume was *Endymion*. The book was savaged in *Blackwood's Magazine* and in *The Quarterly Review*, not so much for its weaknesses as for the fact that Keats was seen as an associate of Leigh Hunt (1784–1859), an important sponsor of Romantic poets and a figure who for a variety of reasons was extremely unpopular with the magazines mentioned above. The political element in the criticism should not disguise the fact that *Endymion* does have various weaknesses. It was written in a hurry, and was described by Keats as a 'feverish attempt'. It has Keats' lush imagery, but this overwhelms the narrative, and the whole poem is rather breathless.

**'Isabella, or the Pot of Basil' (1820)**

'Isabella' is a transitional poem which goes some of the way to producing Keats' finest style, but which still shows traces of his immaturity. It matches an extremely grim story with an ottava rima metrical pattern which Keats fails to handle with the same skill as Byron, and the clash between a rather delicate tone and a grim story is not always effective. Keats was not a precise writer, and he lacked the ability to give a sharp dagger-point to the conclusion of an ottava rima stanza.

**'Lamia' (1820)**

'Lamia' is altogether more precise and controlled than 'Isabella', though still open to accusations of being loose and disjointed. It is remarkable for the ease with which Keats can create a sinister and ominous mood. In the poem Lycius falls in love with Lamia, a sorceress who has disguised herself as a beautiful girl. Lycius is therefore about to marry an illusion, but he is nevertheless happy. When a wise sage reveals the true identity of Lamia she vanishes, but so do all Lycius's dreams and hopes, and his happiness. Truth kills him, and the poem therefore poses some favourite questions of Keats', such as the relationship between emotion and reality, the possibility of happiness, and the search (so typical of Romantic poetry) for an elusive and all-satisfying beauty.

**'The Eve of Saint Agnes'**

'The Eve of Saint Agnes' is a love story told against a medieval backdrop. It is a masterpiece. It has colour and a vibrant sensuality together with stark descriptive powers, and an ability to 'paint' a scene in words and images so as to bring out a rich emotional and visual flavour. The narrative is taut and controlled, and the contrasts in the poem between the warmth and intimacy of the lovers and the threat and danger surrounding their love are used most effectively. Light and dark, warmth and coldness, passion and sterile old age are juxtaposed throughout the poem. Keats' narrative skills and his ability to tell a tale of high romance, but at the same time include quite complex characterisation, are common issues in his work.

**The Odes**

Keats' major achievement, and one of the major achievements in English Literature, is the sequence of odes that he wrote in 1820. In passing it should be noted that arguably no other English author has produced so much fine poetry in so short a space of time as did Keats in 1820–21. 'Ode to a Nightingale' and 'Ode on Melancholy' are the subject of a full answer below, and are generally held to mark the beginning and end respectively of the sequence of odes. 'Ode to a Nightingale' shows how an awareness of suffering and an awareness of beauty are inextricably linked, so that one cannot be shed without the other. 'Ode on a Grecian Urn' deals with the same themes of transience and permanence, beauty and life. At first sight the figures drawn or carved upon the urn are an ideal. Art and the artist have frozen human activity at its most beautiful, giving immortality to moments of happiness, preserving them against time.

This poem leaves a deep impression on anyone who has at one time felt moved and uplifted, and then realised that even the best and most pure of moments must die and vanish. The poem then moves on to the realisation of what happens when art preserves human experience. The price to be paid for making it timeless is also to make it lifeless. The figures on the urn are 'frozen'; it is pure beauty, deprived of the warmth and passion of humanity. It is too cold, too pure, too lifeless. As with 'Ode to a Nightingale', the price for our realisation of beauty is that it must pass, and perhaps this knowledge adds to its piquancy. To perpetuate a feeling is to remove from it the finer edge of its power; only in its transitory nature can it be fully experienced.

'Ode on Melancholy', and, to a lesser extent, 'Ode to Autumn' conclude the theme, by showing beauty at its purest, and revealing a capacity to enjoy them for what they are. The great gap between enjoyment and transience is bridged by the poet expanding the hints in the two odes mentioned above, and saying that true beauty is beautiful because it is transient and lacks permanence. The result is a pure and almost unalloyed vision of beauty, realised in Keats' most sensuous and richly descriptive language.

'Ode on a Grecian Urn' ends with the phrase that has fascinated critics, and those who set examination questions, ever since the poem was written – '"Beauty is truth, truth beauty – that is all/Ye know on earth, and all ye need to know."' It is often overlooked that the urn makes this comment, not the poet. It appears to suggest that the whole meaning of life can be summed up by the definition and expression of what is beautiful, and that real truth and real beauty are the same thing; where one is to be found, so will the other. It suggests also that beauty is what life has to offer, and that the search for it should be the spiritual aim of all men.

## Question and answer

**Question**

Compare 'Ode to a Nightingale' with 'Ode on Melancholy', commenting particularly on the treatment of the themes of beauty and death.

**Answer**

Keats rarely comes to any firm conclusions in his poetry, something which is at the heart of his doctrine of negative capability. This is where man is capable of being in uncertainty and doubt without any 'irritable reaching' after fact and reason. This does not mean that the two odes are mere open-ended statements of a passing mood; rather they recreate a mood and heighten its tension, allowing the reader to see into the meaning of an essential and puzzling gap. The gap is between an ideal vision of life, a heaven of the imagination symbolised in the nightingale, and a grim vision of life's realities.

> Where palsy shakes a few, sad, last grey hairs,
> Where youth grows pale, and spectre-thin, and dies;

'Ode to a Nightingale' shows the poet unable to exclude the real world. 'Ode on Melancholy' reconciles the two worlds, and shows how they are integrated, indivisible, and wholly necessary to each other.

In 'Ode to a Nightingale' beauty is transient.

> Where Beauty cannot keep her lustrous eyes,
> Or new love pine at them beyond to-morrow.

All round the poet is decay, but the nightingale's song stands for a new and different kind of beauty, one which has been heard through all the history of the world and therefore has a touch of eternity to it. The poet wishes to immerse himself totally in the song and the vision of beauty it suggests, and just as he seems about to achieve this total empathy he and the reader are hauled back into the real world by the word 'forlorn', which is 'like a bell/To toll me back from thee to my sole self!' The poet is imprisoned by his humanity. He is able to perceive the beauty of the bird's song by virtue of his life, but that same life brings also misery and pain. The mind that appreciates the beauty cannot fail to be as sensitive to the 'fever' and the 'fret'. Death is no solution. It stops the pain, but also the beauty, and puts the poet in a situation where he has become 'To thy high requiem . . . a sod'. The fact that the nightingale will be unaware even of the poet's death is a very effective device for bringing out forcibly the unbridgeable distance between the two worlds. The poet's mortality dooms him to a world 'where but to think is to be full of sorrow/And leaden-eyed despair', but does allow him to partake partially of eternal beauty. He is like the meanest stage-hand in a great theatre: he can comprehend and yearn after the power and beauty he sees on the stage, but knows he has neither the power nor the ability to take part himself. To rid himself of the pain he must also rid himself of the joy. In 'Ode on Melancholy' he says 'Ay, in the very temple of Delight/Veil'd Melancholy has her sovran shrine'. To banish the avalanche that has killed a friend we must also banish the beauty of snow-capped peaks, and to banish misery we must also banish delight. Indeed Keats comes near to saying that it is through melancholy that we come to appreciate delight.

In 'Ode on Melancholy' pain and delight are reconciled. Rather than try to escape from pain, as he does in 'Ode to a Nightingale', the poet in 'Ode on Melancholy' must experience beauty through it,

> But when the melancholy fit shall fall
> Sudden from Heaven like a weeping cloud,
> That fosters the droop-headed flowers all
> And hides the green hill in an April shroud,
> Then glut thy sorrow on a morning rose,
> Or on the rainbow of the salt-sand wave,

Melancholy falls from Heaven, and it fosters the flowers. It is therefore something cruel yet beneficial. As Keats said, 'Do you not see how necessary a world of pains and troubles is to school an intelligence and make it a soul?'

The conclusion from a reading of both poems is that beauty exists, must be aspired to, and is the highest reward that man can attain. Death is inevitable and painful, but the cessation of pain that it offers comes at too high a price: the loss of life and perception.

## Further reading

### General

- Marilyn Butler, *Romantics, Rebels and Reactionaries. English Literature and its Background 1760–1830* (Oxford University Press, 1981)
- Cynthia Chase, ed., *Romanticism* (Longman, 1993)
- Philip Cox, *Gender, Genre and the Romantic Poets* (Manchester University Press, 1996): an interesting examination for the degree-level student of gender issues in the poetry of the period.
- Elizabeth A. Fay, *A Feminist Introduction to Romanticism* (Blackwell, 1998)
- Peter J. Kitson, ed., Coleridge, *Keats and Shelley* (New Casebook Series, Macmillan, 1996)
- Sari Makdisi, *Romantic Imperialism* (Cambridge University Press, 1998): heavy going for the beginner, but an excellent example of a modern critical reading.
- Paul O'Flinn, *How to Study Romantic Poetry* (Macmillan, 1988): a good basic guide.
- Michael O'Neill, *Literature of the Romantic Period. A Bibliographical Guide* (Oxford University Press, 1998) is considerably more readable than its title suggests!
- J. R. Watson, *English Poetry of the Romantic Period, 1789–1839* (Longman, 1992): an excellent general survey.

### William Blake

- Peter Ackroyd, *Blake* (Minerva Paperback, 1996)

- Alexander Gilchrist, *The Life of William Blake* (Dover Publications, 1988): a reprint of a book first published in 1907, but still well worth reading.
- John Lucas, ed., *William Blake* (Longman, 1998)
- David Punter, ed., *William Blake* (New Casebook series, Macmillan, 1996): good examples of modern criticism.

### Lord Byron

- Harold Nicolson, *Byron. The Last Journey* (Prion, 1999)
- Leslie A. Marchand, *Byron: A Portrait* (Hutchinson, 1987)
- Frederick Raphael, *Byron* (Sphere, 1989)

### Samuel Taylor Coleridge

- Rosemary Ashton, *The Life of Samuel Taylor Coleridge. A Critical Biography* (Blackwell, 1997) is an excellent modern work.
- Richard Holmes, *Coleridge: Early Visions* (Harper Collins, 1997)
- ––, *Coleridge: Darker Reflections* (Harper Collins, 1998)

### John Keats

- Jeffrey C. Robinson, *Reception and Poetics in Keats* (Macmillan, 1998): a modern treatment of Keats but with much history in it.
- Cedric Watts, *A Preface to Keats* (Longman, 1985) is a very good introduction.

### Percy Bysshe Shelley

- Richard Holmes, *Shelley: The Pursuit* (Flamingo/Harper Collins, 1997): a stimulating modern study.
- Michael O'Neill, ed., *Shelley* (Longman, 1993): an effective collection of modern critical essays.
- Michael O'Neill, *Percy Bysshe Shelley. A Literary Life* (Macmillan, 1989): strongly recommended.

### William Wordsworth

- Kenneth R. Johnston, *The Hidden Wordsworth. Poet: Lover: Rebel: Spy* (W. W. Norton, 1998) details modern revelations about Wordsworth's life.
- John Purkis, *A Preface to Wordsworth* (Longman, 1986)
- John Williams, ed., *Wordsworth* (New Casebook Series, Macmillan, 1992)
- John Williams, *William Wordsworth. A Literary Life* (Macmillan, 1996): good value.

# CHAPTER SIXTEEN

# Gothic

Awareness of 'gothic' literature is not a new phenomenon – in the 1960s Penguin felt it worthwhile to bring out a book of three Gothic novels – but it has grown into a separate field of study more rapidly than almost any other *genre* or type. The reasons for this are various. Gothic literature has always translated easily into spoken or visual media, and so is a favourite with the relatively new field of media studies. Gothic writing is a cultural and spiritual creation, rather than a historical one, and so it is also of interest to another relatively new field, cultural studies. Gothic literature is also found across a wide time span and in a variety of different societies. More and more courses can be found that have a central theme at their centre, and which use that central theme as a core round which to group a wide variety and range of literature drawn from a number of different cultures and styles. Gothic literature is therefore very fashionable.

## The historical background

The Goths were a Germanic tribe which became associated in the popular imagination with the fall of the Roman Empire (and hence with the destruction of civilisation), and with the raw and uncontrolled exercise of physical power. The term then came to mean 'medieval', and was in particular applied to architectural style that produced some of the great architectural masterpieces of the world, in the shape of the great, soaring European cathedrals such as Chartres. There was a revival of 'gothic architecture' in the eighteenth and nineteenth centuries.

The use of the word 'gothic' as applied to literature first become common with regard to a number of novels published in the late eighteenth and early nineteenth century, which dealt with unbridled passion, violence and supernatural terror, usually in a medieval setting where the majestic height of oft-ruined towers was hidden by the overwhelming darkness of the setting. Famous examples are *The Castle of Otranto* (1764) by Hugh Walpole, *Vathek* (1786) by W. Beckford, *The Mysteries of Udolpho* (1794) by Ann Radcliffe, *The Monk* (1796) by M. G. ('Monk') Lewis and *Melmoth the Wanderer* (1820) by Charles Maturin. The fascination with the Middle Ages shown in many of these novels reflected a contemporary resurgence of interest in all things medieval. This can be linked on the one hand with the growth of the Romantic movement, of which the early Gothic novels are a clear part, and also with a reaction against the eighteenth century 'Age of Reason' in which everything could be explained even if the explanation was not yet known.

It was a novel that did not have a medieval setting that came for many to both typify and symbolise the Gothic novel – Mary Shelley's *Frankenstein* (1818). If this book forms one point on the great quartet of Gothic writing, Bram Stoker's *Dracula* (1897) forms another, and shows the growth of the movement into the late Victorian period. The third point has to be the work of the American author Edgar Allan Poe (see Chapter 24), whilst the fourth is Robert Louis Stevenson's (1850–94) *The Strange Case of Dr Jekyll and Mr Hyde* (1886).

If the early Gothic works were concerned in the main with gloomy medieval castles, more modern Gothic has changed the setting but kept the excess, the obsession with power, the explicit and implicit sexual agenda and the fear of an overwhelming anarchy that were present is much of the earlier work. That fear of anarchy and mob rule is in turn clearly identifiable with the events surrounding the French Revolution in 1798. The first phase of Gothic writing may well have been both a reaction against the Age of Enlightenment, and a vision of the negative side of Romanticism and its freeing of the human spirit. The more modern phase may be linked to two facts. One is declining religious belief in English-speaking culture, which some commentators believe has led those cultures to reinvent an equivalent to Satan. The second is the fear that in Science society has given birth to a monster that will destroy it. One view is that society needs to fear, another that it has plentiful cause to do so. In any event, it makes a fertile breeding ground for modern versions of gothic based on the old recipe of extremes of every type, of fear, of destruction and of power.

Gothic writing is now a very loose category into which almost any work of literature showing a fascination with the macabre, emotional and physical excess and the supernatural (usually in its most destructive and evil form) can be placed. The good thing about the interest in Gothic literature is that it has rescued some superb writing from a critical grave. The bad thing is twofold. It encourages readers to have as their first priority whether or not a book is Gothic, rather than have as their first priority an appreciation of the work itself. It is also a *genre* which has produced some truly appalling books. The critical bandwagon is rolling down the hill with regard to Gothic literature, and as is the case with all bandwagons its supporters can make extravagant claims for books deemed to be part of the *genre*. It is a busy market in Gothic literature, with some high quality merchandise on the stalls, and some rubbish.

## The Castle of Otranto

Walpole's *The Castle of Otranto* purported to be based on a 16th century Italian manuscript. Its plot is based on Prince Manfred who rules from the Castle of Otranto by means of his grandfather's usurpation of power. The story of the novel is based on the righting of that wrong and the return of power to its proper, youthful owners, but not before great violence and moments of terror. A vast helmet crushes Manfred's sickly heir to death. A sighing portrait saves the virtue of the heroine, Isabella. Ghostly chains clank, armoured ghostly giants walk dark corridors and the castle finally crumbles and collapses as virtue is restored at the end. The novel is heavy on plot and incident, light on characterisation and rarely raises the latter above stereotypes. The castle itself can be seen as a major character in the novel, almost with a life and certainly with a character of its own.

The novel also adopts a device not restricted to Gothic writing, whereby the author justifies all manner of horrors by tagging on a moral ending. Uncertainty of tone and style is a common issue with the novel, as is whether or not is stretches credulity too far. Its confused moral structure, or if indeed it has a moral structure, is also a common topic of interest. It is worth asking if the common Gothic issue of helplessness is simply a presence in the novel, or a theme. The novel can also be seen as being obsessed with violence and with its symbols, whilst appearing to reject it. The early picaresque novel rattled the reader through a breathless rush of plot ups-and-downs, moving almost frantically from one episode to another with an occasional dash of emotion catching up with the plot. This, the earliest recognisable Gothic novel, rattles the reader through a breathless rush of emotional highs and lows, with a plot attached and occasionally making an effort to keep up with the emotions.

Walpole himself was a social commentator as well as an MP and the son of a Prime Minister. One view of *The Castle of Otranto* is that it is all a vast joke at the expense of the reader who takes it seriously. Walpole's diaries and correspondence certainly suggest someone who could play such a joke on the reading public.

## Vathek

*Vathek* is the story of an eastern Caliph, a cruel tyrant who is both a sensualist and a magician and astrologer. It lacks the physical medieval setting of other Gothic novels, but has all the extremes of fear, of violence and, eventually, of destruction. Occasionally the Gothic novel appears like a bottle of carbonated emotion which the author has to shake up and then take the top off. What *Vathek* lacks in the darkness of its physical setting it makes up for in darkness of characterisation. Vathek is both what we the eader condemn but also what we secretly aspire to be, a potent recipe for a powerful book. As is often the case with Gothic novels, there is more than a trace in Vathek of the Faust figure – the man who strives for more power than the supernatural order or his place in the Universe will allow him. There s also another rather smug moral ending tagged on, emphasising how very much Vathek will suffer for all the sensual excess he has indulged in and we have so much enjoyed reading about. However, the novel has more complexity than a number of its counterparts, and its tone darkens considerably as it progresses, with a movement from buffoonery to real evil on the part of the main character.

## *The Mysteries of Udolpho*

Radcliffe's *The Mysteries of Udolpho* was a runaway success in her own time. As with *The Castle of Otranto*, and as with so many Gothic novels, a secret buried in the family past comes to haunt the present. The heroine, Emily St Aubert, is pursued through a number of decaying pieces of architecture with terrible threats surrounding her. She survives, just, with her honour and her virtue intact. Many of the supernatural elements in the novel are found to have 'sensible' explanations, and excessive emotion is again tied to a neat and moral ending showing the triumph of virtue. Radcliffe specialises in the description of landscape, and it is in this area that the novel presents some its best and most powerful writing.

## *The Monk*

*The Monk* caused outrage when it first appeared in 1796. It is an extraordinary book, capable of mocking itself and the whole *genre* of the Gothic novel whilst at the same time generating genuine terror and horror. *The Monk* is specific where its predecessors were not, but it also has a claim to be the first genuine horror story.

Hypocrisy in literature is often seen as the greatest evil because by definition it hides its threat: the hidden danger is more threatening than that which lies on the surface. The audience can like a character such as Shakespeare's Falstaff because for all his sin anyone with half an eye to reality can see what Falstaff is, and in any event Falstaff himself is likely to tell them. *The Monk* is a study in hypocrisy, and also of course a total contrast. The outer garb of sanctity covers a heart of total evil. Yet at the same time the Monk's evil simply reveals the evil that is within the characters in the novel and, by implication, within us all.

*The Monk* may have shocked its original readership so much because of its willingness to be specific, but part of the shock comes from the novel's refusal to paint over the horror it presents with a thin overlay of purifying and disinfecting sentimentality. The novel shocks because where one has become used to a sweetening flow of sentimentality coming at crucial moments in other novels little or nothing dilutes the stream of obscene excess in the book. Moreover, the book seems to criticise almost every institution – Church, state, justice, family, marriage – on which civilisation believes that it rests. It is one of the most purely anarchic of all Gothic novels, and pure anarchy, if portrayed honestly, can easily be formed in to pure terror. The challenge the novel presents to almost every aspect of Establishment life, and its compelling scenes of mob violence at its sequel, inevitably provoke comparison with the events of the French Revolution in 1798. Ambrosio, the Monk, bears comparison with a number of leading figures from Jacobean drama, such as Vindice in *The Revenger's Tragedy* and even Iago in *Othello*, as well as the malcontents in the plays of John Webster.

## *Melmoth the Wanderer*

Melmoth is a figure drawn from myth, the wanderer condemned to hell on earth until he can designate a successor to take over his role and thereby find a form of peace. Written at a time when the Gothic novel was in decline, *Melmoth the Wanderer* has many of the standard ingredients in mood and setting, but its central figure is a spirit who is somehow both human and supernatural, a demi-devil. He is a Faust-figure again, a tortured soul who finds only partial relief in the torturing of others and who is himself a victim. Human evil is inescapable in *Melmoth the Wanderer*, and the book's savage criticism of humanity and human institutions makes it a bleak work in which evil is so common as almost to be mundane. Viewed by many as the most compelling of the early Gothic novels, it is a complex, psychologically ornate work that transcends its basic material and setting.

## *Frankenstein*

*Frankenstein* has achieved a distinction earned by very few other novels: based on myth, it has itself become a myth. The story is of Frankenstein, a scientist who has acquired the ability to light the spark of life in matter. Seeking for perfection and beauty in the creature he makes, and for it to adore him, he creates instead a monster, sewn together from bits of various humans. Frankenstein's monster is monstrous only in physical appearance. In agony from the wounds that hold it together, the 'monster' inspires loathing in all who see it, despite it demanding little more from its creator than the life he promised it. Eventually Frankenstein's creation destroys him, his brother, his friend and his bride. Frankenstein pursues it to the Arctic, determined to kill it, but is himself killed as the monster appears to decide that Frankenstein will be his last victim, and he/it will kill himself.

The bare outlines do not do justice to the weight of the story. Frankenstein is an emblem for modern science, the lust for knowledge which creates a power for destruction which it cannot control, and which will eventually destroy the creator and itself. The monster is a symbol of the outsider, subject to fear, loathing and to being an outcast simply through its being different and through society's knee-jerk reaction to destroy anything that appears alien. It is also a version of the myth of the Noble Savage, where something essentially good is corrupted by so-called civilisation. There are also hints of the Faust myth, as there are in so many Gothic novels. Frankenstein is seeking to transcend the limitations of humanity, seeking to do what only God is empowered to do, namely give the gift of life. For this he must be destroyed, and in true tragic form that destruction will not be limited to him but also affect many innocent people and society in general. To that extent *Frankenstein* is also a tragedy, in the classical and neo-classical sense of the word.

The descriptions of nature are very powerful in *Frankenstein*, something which perhaps adds to the suggestion that in many respects the Gothic novel is the prose version of the Romantic movement in poetry. Narrative technique in the novel is also complex and effective, with the story in effect being told through the letters of Walton, a friend of Frankenstein's. The use of this 'epistolary' technique is a common one where the reader needs to be distanced from extreme events in order to believe them.

The novel does without many of the standard trappings of the Gothic novel, with ruined castles only appearing on faraway hilltops. It does contain some of the central features of the Gothic novel, most notably mob violence and riot, and a sense of a world teetering on the edge of total dissolution. Despite the gender of its author, it is essentially a novel dominated by men and their dreams and ambitions. Perhaps above all it is a novel about power and responsibility, or rather the abuse of power and irresponsibility. Frankenstein abuses his power to create life by denying responsibility for what he has created. His creature, in a cruel mockery of the Adam and Eve myth, demands from Frankenstein that he create a mate for it, to alleviate its loneliness. Frankenstein denies the entreaty, and 'the son' destroys 'the father'. This latter fact can be made into a terrible, cruel parody of the Christian ethic of 'God the Father' who gave his 'only Son' to die in the world so that mankind might be saved.

## *Dracula*

Between them *Frankenstein* and *Dracula* have become by-words for horror. They are two very different novels, separated by nearly 80 years, but share a number of thematic concerns. The setting of *Dracula* is closer to that of the traditional Gothic novel, featuring a semi-ruined castle and a lunatic asylum, as well as copious use of churchyards, cellars and tombs. The story is that of the Vampire, symbolised by Count Dracula, who is eventually destroyed by Van Helsing, in some ways the symbol of modern, rational man.

The origins of the vampire myth are quite complex. It is almost certainly linked to the plague and its virulence in the middle ages – an age which knew nothing of the virus or the link between hygiene and illness saw the plague as a 'nameless terror' a power for destruction beyond both the understanding and the control of humanity. This same 'nameless terror' typifies the response of normal mortals to the vampire. The concept of a creature that enslaves and corrupts its victim through the sucking of its blood is both sexual in its connotation and redolent of primeval rituals of sacrifice, in which survival and immortality are bought by the blood and the death of the innocent. The power of the Count, his ability to transfix his victims, can be seen as an expression of male dominance and even wish-fulfilment, in terms of the male drive for conquest, ownership and power. There are strong traces of the same myth that Hans Andersen uses in *Little Red Riding Hood*, where the child's fear of the adult who suddenly urns into a wolf is an emblem of the child's fear of adults, who can change in mood and personality without warning in a manner and for reasons that the child cannot understand. The urbane Count Dracula who meets the young lawyer Harker is the same supernatural creature of terror and blood-lust who enslaves and infects the humans he contacts.

Some critics have seen *Dracula* as simply an adventure story using terror for fairly superficial effects. The adoption of its central figure's name so quickly as a household word, the continuing popularity of the story and its derivatives and the seemingly endless fascination it seems to exert over a general readership and now over a growing number of critics all suggest that it taps more than one central nerve of the human condition.

The first moral of *Dracula* is that there are dark powers which the Age of Reason merely painted over, rather than destroyed. It is also an ironic novel. Dracula represents a primeval, violent and barbaric power which threatens the world of Victorian England, with its stability and its belief both in reason and in itself. As the novel progresses the violence necessary to kill the vampires increases progressively, until the violence used at the end to kill Dracula is on a scale with the violence he himself uses towards his victims. Hunter and hunted have become closer and more similar to each other than perhaps the outwardly more civilised party can bear to believe. What value is there in the destruction of the vampire if in destroying it the human becomes what he seeks to destroy?

*Dracula* is also a novel about evil. Unlike *Frankenstein*, its vision of evil is more straightforward. In Mary Shelley's novel, real evil is found in the socially acceptable and outwardly good figure of the scientist, whilst the monster, seen as evil by society, is in practice little more than an innocent suffering pain and anguish. In *Dracula*, evil is identified early on, and the issue is not its identification as such but rather its destruction. The arrival of the coffins in Whitby is the classical vision of evil being brought in to a society, from which it can only be purged by the death of the innocent as well as the guilty. In common with many other Gothic novels, *Dracula* is about the price of evil, as well as being about 'excess, horror, evil and ruin'.

## *The Strange Case of Dr Jekyll and Mr Hyde*

*The Strange Case of Dr Jekyll and Mr Hyde* is in large measure about the mixture of good and evil in the human personality. The split personality fascinated Stevenson, who laid claim to two different handwritings and who challenged his Calvinist upbringing and relative wealthy background by an early fondness for low life in the city.

The Dr Jekyll of the title is a physician who invents a drug that turns him into 'Mr Hyde', a distillation of all that is evil in his personality. The transformation back to Mr Jekyll becomes harder and harder as the novel progresses, with the evil personality increasingly taking over. After a terrible murder Dr Jekyll kills himself just before he is discovered. In this sense at least the novel follows the standard Gothic and part-tragic pattern whereby evil is introduced into society, destroys innocence as well as its own kind and only allows order to be returned to society by the fact that ultimately evil will destroy itself. The novel is also firmly in the Gothic mould because of its awareness of a terrible evil bubbling away just below the surface of even a moderate, educated man. Jekyll can also be seen as a scientist in the mould of Frankenstein, who uses his knowledge without responsibility and who cannot control the power that he unleashes. The Faust figure appears again, with Jekyll seeking to trespass in areas that are banned to humanity and being punished for seeking to know too much.

The novel does not have the medieval setting of earlier Gothic writing, but replaces this with the gloom of the city, a dimly-lit arena which increasingly seems to become its own jungle, indistinguishable from the real primeval jungle where threat lurks in every shadow.

As with so many other Gothic novels, nothing really ends with the suicide of the protagonist. The perpetuator is dead. The beast that was within him is still within us. The drug to call it forth can be reinvented. Even without it, we know that we carry our own Mr. Hyde in our heads. The most terrifying thing about the novel is that there is no suggestion of the drug *creating* anything when it allows Mr Hyde to walk abroad: it merely releases him.

Stevenson claimed to have written the novel when he had a nightmare brought on by indigestion. Bram Stoker claimed to have invented Dracula after a bad night resulting from eating crabs, whilst Walpole claimed the idea for *The Castle of Otranto* came to him in a dream. The link between sleep, dream, nightmare and the Gothic novel might seem merely an author's fancifulness, but is a pointer to the extent that the whole Gothic edifice depends on creating an awareness of a world as real as reality but somehow buried for the most part beneath it. Some parts of Elizabethan culture believed that humanity trod a thin layer of matter, with the four elements carved in to some form of order by God, above an abyss of conflicting particles which could never cohere and which formed the vision of Chaos. Modern science, and particle physics in particular, shows us layers of matter below those presently understood, behaving in a manner that seems to defy know laws of science. In between comes the Gothic novel, showing us a veneer of civilisation, reason, law and order, below which lurks the anarchy of lust, power and excess, threatening always to rise up and destroy.

It is interesting to note that two years after the publication of Stevenson's book the Jack the Ripper murders took place in London. Cruelty, terror, excess, horror, obscene violence; a sequence of events demanding that we redefine the definition of man as a civilised creature; horror linked in some incomprehensible way to sexuality, power, submission and dominance; a corrupt act of vengeance enacted against the innocent and the corrupt . . . if the reader is tempted to dismiss the Gothic novel after a giant helmet descends on a child or a heroine faints for the umpteenth time, it is worth remembering that a Gothic novel containing horrific events was followed shortly after its publication by events that match and exceed its fictional horror.

## Modern Gothic

Much of what might be seen as modern Gothic writing might seem to fall in to the category of horror fiction. This would to diminish it. Gothic is everywhere, in rock bands, in theatre, in a wide range of writing and above all in the cinema. Gothic's willingness to camp itself up and become burlesque can be seen in the theatre in *The Rocky Horror Show* (1975) or *The Little Shop of Horrors*. Alfred Hitchcock's *Psycho* (1960 and 1998) is pure Gothic as are the settings for the modern *Batman* films, and much of the content of a film such as Ridley Scott's *Blade Runner* or the *Alien* films. The *Gormenghast* trilogy – *Titus Groan* (1946), *Gormenghast* (1950) and *Titus Alone* (1959) by Mervyn Peake (1911–1968) bear strong resemblances to classic Gothic texts – and so the list could go on. Auschwitz, Belsen and Dachau showed the twentieth century that horror and excess beyond belief was actually entirely normal. In that world and that culture, Gothic must inevitably thrive.

## Further reading


- Chris Baldick, *In Frankenstein's Shadow. Myth, Monstrosity and Nineteenth Century Writing* (Oxford University Press, 1990)
- Fred Botting, *Gothic* (Critical Idiom Series, Routledge, 1996)
- D. Brewer, *English Gothic Literature* (Macmillan, 1983)
- Glenys Byron and David Punter, ed., *Spectral Readings: Towards a Gothic Geography* (Macmillan, 1998)
- Richard Davenport-Hynes, *Gothic. 400 Years of Excess, Horror, Evil and Ruin* (Fourth Estate, 1998)
- Maggie Kilgour, *The Rise of the Gothic Novel* (Routledge, 1995)
- David Punter, *The Literature of Terror* (Longman, Volume 1 1996; Volume 2, 1996): a survey from early times to the Edwardian period; recommended.
- Victor Sage, ed., *The Gothic Novel: A Selection of Critical Essays* (Macmillan, 1990)

CHAPTER SEVENTEEN

# Dickens, Thackeray and George Eliot

## Charles Dickens

After Shakespeare, Chaucer and Milton, Charles Dickens (1812–70) has been the author most commonly set for Advanced-level examinations. As such he is, of course, what some schools of American criticism might refer to, scathingly, as yet another 'dead, white European male'. As with the three other authors mentioned above, he has become a literary institution, at one time revered by schools, colleges and examination boards alike, and perhaps inevitably also selected for some rather less reverential treatment by criticism with an eye to deconstructing reputations as well as texts. Ironically, new critical theory has helped Dickens as much as it has hindered him, particularly because Dickens' use of language can be commented on at length by linguistically-based critical theories. His reputation at universities has sometimes had to be fought for, but is still secure, though perhaps less so than at Advanced level. Even here the fact that he is a superb writer does not stop some students responding in a negative manner to his work, just as we will sometimes decline to see a film or read a book because so many people tell us to do so. The situation is not helped by the fact that the choice of books set in examinations does not always reflect the true nature of Dickens' genius.

*A Tale of Two Cities* (1859) is a very popular Dickens novel particularly for use in schools, but it is hardly the book to reveal Dickens' real strengths. It is a historical novel based on the French Revolution, which gives it wider 'educational' value, but neither of Dickens' historical novels (*Barnaby Rudge* [1841] is the other one) is an accurate reflection of his greatness. He wrote most powerfully when dealing with areas and settings he knew intimately, and particularly when writing of London. *A Tale of Two Cities* is melodrama, and lacks the imagination, vividness, range and sheer power of much of his other work.

*The Pickwick Papers* (1837) is sometimes set; this was his first major novel. It suffered from neglect for many years, but increased interest in Dickens' journalistic writing has focussed more attention on his early work, and there are slight signs that *The Pickwick Papers* might be coming back into fashion.

The novels which are most commonly set are studied below. Of these *Great Expectations* (1861), *Our Mutual Friend* (1865), and *Bleak House* (1853) are probably the most popular. This, of course, varies from year to year, but anyone who wishes to gain a full appreciation of Dickens' genius would have to read at least these three novels.

## The biographical background

Charles Dickens was the son of a pleasant but wholly ineffectual clerk. When his father was imprisoned for debt, Charles was sent out to work as an odd-job boy in a blacking factory. This was an experience which totally humiliated and degraded him and left him with a permanent mental scar, the traces of which can be seen in the frequent appearance in his novels of lost, neglected or maltreated children. It can also be a starting point for approaches to his work by critics interested in the psychoanalytic approach. With a little education and a lot of hard work Dickens became a Parliamentary reporter, a minor journalist, and then a full-scale novelist. His publishing breakthrough came with his second book and first full-blooded novel, *The Pickwick Papers*, which after a slow start became something of a publishing sensation. The majority of his novels were published in serial form, in instalments, and at times he had three novels in progress at the same time, as well as being involved in a host of other activities. His sales figures dipped with some of the less successful novels, but his position as the dominant novelist of the time was never really threatened, and survived even the messy separation from his wife relatively late on in his life.

Dickens was never an intellectual (a critic has described the theme of all of his novels as being that 'people should be nicer to each other'), but he was always in close touch with his readers, who came from all sectors of society. He was an actor of some genius, with an interest in drama and amateur theatricals that at times was obsessive. The frantic energy he showed throughout his life took its toll, as did a near-fatal train crash in which he was involved. He began to give extremely successful public readings from his work, perhaps because he fed off the closeness and immediacy of a live audience and could always write for his readers as much as for himself, but these were also a great strain, and almost certainly contributed to his relatively early death. He was recognised as a genius in his lifetime. Later ages may have changed the vision of what is most valuable in his work; but none has been able to deny that he was a genius.

Dickens is sometimes referred to as a Victorian writer. Queen Victoria reigned from 1837 to 1901, but the term is hardly useful as a description of Dickens. His work spans two ages, and draws some of its strength from the differences and tensions between them. When Dickens was born, all the foundations of the great Industrial Revolution that turned England from a rural to an industrial nation had already been laid although many were not yet evident. In 1812, the year of Dickens' birth, Wellington and Napoleon were in command of armies that used breech-loading muskets, ships were powered by sail, and the stagecoaches were the fastest mode of inland transport. In 1870, when Dickens died, soldiers were beginning to experiment with machine guns; ironclads and steam were the order of the day in shipping; and the railways had revolutionised transport and industry.

With hindsight, the changes in this period from 1812 to 1870 do not seem as great as those faced by a man born in, say, 1912 and who died in 1970, but they were quite sufficient to change the face and the nature of England and its society. Great Britain began quite rapidly to reap the reward of its Industrial Revolution: wealth. At the same time, it began to pay the price. A huge explosion in population, the move from the land to the cities, and a society that at times seemed turned upside down, all served to produce appalling overcrowding, dissolution of family units, illness, poverty and confusion. Phrases that are rather tired in the present age – pollution, safety at work, slum dwellings, sewage – were newly born and screaming for assistance in Dickens' day. The Victorians rose to the occasion. They made very many mistakes, but they tackled the new age head-on and with great gusto. They built the town halls that still dominate English local government. They built (sometimes badly, but sometimes very well) a significant part of the nation's present housing stock, the sewers and reservoirs that clean and feed the great cities, the urban rail networks. They laid the framework for twentieth-century Britain. They failed to abolish poverty, hardship and inequality; so have we. It was the industrial revolution that created much of the social environment in which Karl Marx believed revolution could happen, in particular with the rise of the so-called 'middle-classes' who in Marxist theory start the revolution which can then be taken over by the working classes. Dickens' close involvement with post-industrial, urban society makes his work a rich ground for Marxist critics.

It is a fascinating and almost lifelong exercise to trace the way that Dickens' society permeates his novels. Perhaps one of the most surprising points to make about his novels is that very often they ignore the later part of the nineteenth century, and look back to the pre-1850s when the full effects of the Industrial Revolution were yet to be felt. There is a strong element of nostalgia for the old world of the stagecoaches in Dickens' novels. Equally, some of his novels deliberately stage confrontations between the old and the new, as when Sir Leicester Dedlock is brought face to face with the 'ironmaster' or industrialist in *Bleak House*. Dickens' attitudes can be cloudy.

He spots that the ironmaster is here to stay, feels he should like him, but actually shows more genuine affection (mingled with appalled exasperation) for the old nobility. At other times Dickens charges head-on into the new world, though a novel such as *Hard Times* (1854), based on the new industrial town of Preston ('Coketown') and very much concerned with industrial life, suggests he was happier with the London he loved and knew.

Dickens' involvement with his times is not really specific, in the sense that he catalogued social developments in the manner of a historian. Rather it is in his feelings and obsessions that his background shines through. A major example is the campaigning element that is immensely strong in much of his work, be it a specific and passionate plea for reform of such things as the law (*Bleak House*), the prison system (*Little Dorrit*) or the Poor Law (*Oliver Twist*). Dickens often campaigned for things that were changing anyway; the Marshalsea debtors' prison was long demolished when Dickens wrote *Little Dorrit*. It is not really the specific buildings and institutions of his novels that matter; they are often merely a springboard, even an excuse, to write about wider human issues that span all the ages and generations. Examples of other major themes are given below.

## Major topics in Dickens' novels

### Plot

The plot of any Dickens novel is liable to be an issue, and quite frequently (especially where the early novels are concerned) faults and weaknesses in plotting will be the centre of attention. Dickens wrote his novels in serial form, or instalments. The demands of the printing process required him quite literally to write a precise number of words for each instalment. The result of this is twofold. Firstly, it means that in some of his novels there is an inevitable tendency to work in relatively short episodes, rather than to write the novel as one coherent and organic entity; it has been said that *The Pickwick Papers*, his first major novel, is actually a collection of short stories and anecdotes, rather than a complete novel. Secondly, the demands of the printing and issuing process gave him relatively little room for manoeuvre, in that each instalment has to end on a climax and consist of a specified number of words. This can result in a tendency to 'pad out' a novel rather than write to any overall pattern or structure. Dickens was not perfect, but the most remarkable thing about his novels, given the way that they were written, is that the strains of periodical publication show up so little in what he wrote.

It is also essential to realise that the plots of the novels he wrote change quite dramatically as he gets older. *The Pickwick Papers* is episodic and anecdotal, though it also has a large number of features which link episodes and give them unity. A later novel such as *Little Dorrit* has an altogether different plot which is rigidly planned, very coherent and unified, and which shows very few of the tendencies seen in a novel such as *The Pickwick Papers*.

Dickens tended to rely on spontaneous improvisation in his early work, inventing an incident or a character when the novel appeared to be flagging, or simply because he delighted in variety. It is this feature which is progressively banished from his novels, although he never did lose his habit of doing startling things. *Our Mutual Friend* appears to start with the intention of being a detective story based round an inheritance, but half-way through changes direction completely and concentrates on a love story. Even more remarkable is that this is a resounding success.

Dickens' fascination with the detective story may have been a major factor in tightening up his plots, in that the style requires clues to be carefully laid ahead of revelations, and only a measured and limited amount of information can be passed on to the reader if suspense is to be maintained. The early novels concentrate on incident, perhaps to a greater extent than they do either characterisation or themes. When, in his later years, Dickens' plots primarily become the vehicles for his characterisation of thematic concerns, so the wildness and improvisatory element in his plots becomes less marked. He also becomes less reliant on the picaresque style (see Ch. 3) which favours rapid invention of incident, and as he became more experienced his command of material obviously grew.

**Characterisation**

This is a major feature in any Dickens novel.

1. *Development* Dickens is sometimes accused of writing characters who do not develop or change during the course of a novel. This criticism was also made during his lifetime, and regarding *The Pickwick Papers* he confirmed that Pickwick did not change during the novel, but argued that the readers did get to know him better.

   This alleged lack of development is a valid criticism, but as with so many other statements on his work a different set of standards have to be applied, depending on when the novel was written. In any case one might ask why a lack of development is such a bad thing: in reality people often refuse to change as much as we would wish them to. Dickens chooses to show the reader features that were there from the very start, but hidden. It is certainly the case that Dickens' characters never lose their capacity to surprise us. Sir Leicester Dedlock in *Bleak House* is shown to have virtues at the end of the novel that the reader was largely in ignorance of, and Eugene Wrayburn in *Our Mutual Friend* develops from a spoilt and selfish young puppy into a deep and wholly admirable young man.
2. *Caricature* Related to the above comments are the allegations that Dickens writes one-dimensional caricatures, linking his characters to one dominant feature and providing only superficial detail (often physical) about them. It is certainly true that Dickens delights in quick pen-sketches of characters where the character is seen in relation to only one dominant feature. It is also true that his skill in portraying these characters is unsurpassed, and that the huge gallery of minor characters that people a Dickens

novel are often one of its major delights. There is a huge energy and vitality in Dickens' characterisation, an acute eye for telling detail, and a rich sense both of humour and of the unsavoury element in human nature. His minor characters may sometimes lack depth but they often make up for this by sheer vividness: a primary colour can be as attractive and interesting as a more sophisticated shade. Quite frequently Dickens will invent a character to illustrate one particular theme or human weakness. At times also Dickens is presenting a character to show their superficiality, as with the Veneerings in *Our Mutual Friend*. Their name also points to another issue on Dickens, namely the use of 'label' names. The technique implies characterisation through one 'label' or characteristic.

3. *Female characters* Dickens is sometimes attacked on two fronts as regards his female characters:

   - One complaint is that he is very unfair to women, and that portraits of bad, offensive, or unsavoury women far outnumber portraits of decent women in his novels. Nagging wives, dominant matrons, hard and harsh ladies and stepmothers appear frequently in his work.
   - A second complaint is that Dickens rarely manages to portray good women convincingly. A number of Dickens' heroines are rather sickly and simpering to modern taste, and Dickens appears at times to be asking us to admire as perfection in woman a Victorian ideal of passivity and helplessness that is far out of line with modern ideas and tastes. Esther Summerson in *Bleak House* is frequently cited as an example of such a heroine. However, modern criticism, and feminist criticism in particular, can give a new slant on old debates such as this. For example, if one views Esther not as a sickly, simpering whitewash but rather as someone whose desperate desire for and need of approbation is an illness contracted from the way her society treats women it revolutionises the way the reader sees her. It also makes Esther a fascinating case study in subjugation.

The fact that modern criticism can defend what might before have been seen as failures on Dickens' part does not mean that you should deny the existence of failure, and mistakes, in Dickens' work. Great authors can make mistakes as well as lesser-known ones, and most great works of literature triumph despite their failings, not because they do not have any. For balance the student should look at characters such as Lizzie Hexham in *Our Mutual Friend* or Nancy in *Oliver Twist* as examples of how Dickens can portray goodness in a meaningful way.

**Humour**

Dickens is by no means exclusively a comic novelist, but the comedy in his novels and the techniques he uses to create it are major features of his work. As a very broad generalisation (and as such to be treated with some suspicion!) characterisation is the source of much of Dickens' humour. He can and does delight in great comic set-piece scenes, and in putting his characters into incidents that will provoke a comic response (look at the episode where Pip is taught table manners by Herbert Pocket in *Great Expectations*), but for a very great number of people comedy in Dickens means the characters he creates. Many of them are verging on household names, such as Mr Micawber, Sam Weller, and Uriah Heep. One of Dickens' greatest skills, and perhaps the great skill of all comic writers, is the ability to command a vast range of comedy in his approach, from the affectionate laughter directed at Sam Weller to the very bitter comedy springing from a character such as the Reverend Chadband in *Bleak House*. Dickens can make his audience laugh at a character or phenomenon or make them laugh with them, and his comic range varies from pure entertainment and comic enjoyment of life to the harshest and most biting of satire.

### Grotesqueness and the macabre

Dickens sometimes manifests a very macabre sense of humour, one that appears linked to the darker side of human nature. Grotesque characters, such as Bill Sykes in *Oliver Twist* or Krook in *Bleak House*, appear frequently in his work, and are often used to promote comedy. Very occasionally the term 'black comedy' will be used of Dickens' more extreme caricatures, and the humour they provoke. The student needs to be aware of this element in his work, and link it to the Victorian tendency in literature to mingle the sentimental and the grotesque, the unbelievably pure with the unbelievably horrific. It should also be noted, however, that Dickens' use of macabre and grotesque elements is balanced by a full awareness of the brighter side of life.

## Themes

### Benevolence

It is sometimes said that the theme of all Dickens' novels is that people should be nicer to one another. This is an oversimplification, but benevolence as a major virtue does appear in all Dickens' novels. At the start of his career in a novel such as *The Pickwick Papers* the central figure, Pickwick, is shown to have huge benevolence, equalled only by his naïvety and innocence. In the course of the novel he loses none of this benevolence and desire to do the right thing by people, but he does learn from hard experience to temper it with a degree of wisdom and worldly knowledge. As Dickens grew older and more pessimistic, benevolence was increasingly seen as something which, on its own, cannot alter the course or nature of things, with that course tending more and more towards a pessimistic outlook on life. Good usually triumphs in any Dickens novel, but in the later novels it has more of a struggle to do so, and the victory is less powerful and overwhelming. In *Oliver Twist* good-hearted men with a lot of money can rescue Oliver and send him happy into life with no scars showing from his previous experience. By the time Dickens writes *Bleak House* the benevolent man with wealth, in the form of Mr Jarndyce, is shown as being more helpless. He cannot protect his innocent nephew, Richard Carstone, from falling prey to the corruption of the law, and even the pure and innocent Esther must suffer smallpox before she is allowed to marry her man. In a very late novel, *Our Mutual Friend*, money has become a sin and an evil: it is recognised that in the right hands it can do good, but its power to corrupt is conveyed, if anything, more strongly. Indeed a prime symbol in the novel is the fact that much of the money in it comes from vast heaps of rubbish.

Dickens lost his faith in benevolence and the power of the charitable individual as the sole requirement if wrongs were to be righted, as his awareness grew that social pressures could and did outweigh the power of the individual. What he never lost was his admiration of the kind and benevolent man or woman. One of the simplest and most touching examples of this is the simple-minded but eternally kind Jo Gargery in *Great Expectations*.

**Children**

The lost, neglected or ill-treated child is a central figure in a vast number of Dickens' novels, and perhaps derived from his own childhood and its nightmare of shame and humiliation. The figure of the child is used to reveal Dickens' views on society, and people are judged by their reaction to the innocence and hope that childhood represents, just as corruption, sin and decay are measured by how they affect children. Dickens' outlook is that of the Romantic. He believes that children are unsullied and uncorrupted humanity, and the children in his novels are frequently those who cast the right judgements on the adults and the society in which they appear. Dickens is scathing and vitriolic about any parent who neglects their child, seeing in this a denial of all that is best in human nature, and a threat to the fabric of society, as symbolised by the family unit. This attitude can take him into sentimentality and an excess of rather oversimplified emotion, but it can also provoke some of his strongest writing. Given what is often seen as Dickens' neglect of his own children, it can also provoke cries of hypocrisy against him – one of many interesting areas that has provoked fruitful critical debate over the relationship between the actual, real life of an author and what he or she writes in their books. Not the first time, one could be forgiven for feeling very grateful that we know so little about Shakespeare's life.

**Prison**

The prison is the central image of *Little Dorrit*, but it appears in many other of his novels. Again links can be drawn with Dickens' childhood, when his father was imprisoned in the Marshalsea Prison for debt for a few months, but the power of the image as used by Dickens lives in its own right. Prison is a symbol of man's inhumanity to man and of an uncaring society, but also a symbol of the waste of human potential, a strong element also in the theme of childhood. The tendency of people to imprison themselves, locking up their inner soul behind walls of hypocrisy and deceit, springs naturally from the physical image of the prison. Dickens may occasionally oversimplify issues in his novels, but rarely does so where prisons are concerned. In *Little Dorrit* he recognises that some men are fit only for imprisonment, and that the safety of the greater number of society demands that they be kept there. In *Great Expectations* he describes in Pip's own attitude towards them all the natural revulsion that people feel for prisoners, and the bestiality and coarseness of some prisoners, at the same time showing how Pip conquers these feelings and comes to a realisation that even prisoners may have benevolence and goodness in them.

**The law**

The law comes in for its strongest blast of criticism in *Bleak House*, but Dickens rarely lets a novel go by without some scathing comment on the law and lawyers. Again, as with all the objects of his condemnation, the sin of the law is that it is run for profit and self-interest, not for the good of the people, and Dickens detests any system that is run for its own benefit, rather than for the benefit of the humans it was designed to serve.

**The social panorama**

Dickens' novels are sometimes described as social panoramas, or sweeping views of society from the very top to the very bottom. This issue requires careful study. Dickens can and does make sweeping comments about society, its needs and its failings; he often does present a huge range and scope of characters. However, Dickens is neither a social historian nor a campaigning politician. Politics are a theme in his novels but, as with his experience of the law, his experience as a Parliamentary reporter seems to have led him to decide that the majority of politicians sold humbug and nonsense, regardless of their party or allegiance. As with the law, he damns it where he sees that authority and power have become divorced from responsibility and a caring attitude towards others. Any institution that denies its responsibilities is damned by Dickens.

It is also true that what appears to be a social panorama sometimes turns out to be a panorama of London, the city Dickens knew to its core, and which is by far and away the most successful setting for his novels. When Dickens writes about society he does so from his heart rather than his head, and it is feelings that concern him more than policies. A number of Dickens' 'campaigning' novels were written when the object of criticism was already in the process of being reformed, as was the case with imprisonment in *Little Dorrit* and the law in *Bleak House*. This fact illustrates the folly of reading Dickens as if he were a social historian, and not rather a creative writer of fiction.

**General themes**

Wealth is increasingly criticised in Dickens' later novels, not so much as a sin in itself, but for the way it can produce a false judgement of people and become a false god to worship, as is the case in *Our Mutual Friend*. False philanthropy or charity is also criticised, as is the Church and clergymen who become lost in selfishness and self-adulation.

## Issues in specific novels by Dickens

***The Pickwick Papers***

The characters of Pickwick and Sam Weller are a favourite area for questions, and in particular whether or not they develop or grow during the course of the novel. The plot and whether or not it is too anecdotal is often examined, and the novel's themes of benevolence, innocence, the law and imprisonment are also often the subject of questions.

***Nicholas Nickleby***

Dickens' satire of education and exploitation of children are the major thematic areas in this novel. Again its plot is sometimes criticised as episodic and lacking in authorial control, and Dickens' improvisation is also sometimes set as a question. Sentimentality is another area often examined, particularly the sentimentality of the Cheeryble brothers as their character creation is sometimes seen as a failure to a modern taste.

***The Old Curiosity Shop***

This novel is famous for its central heroine, Little Nell, possibly the most sentimental portrait of all in Dickens' novels. Her death is highly examinable, a stimulating line of questioning being whether Little Nell's death is gross sentimentality or effective tragedy. The novel is also famous for its powerful caricatures, notably Quilp the dwarf. The debtors' prison appears in this novel, though it is rather less vividly realised than in many of his other works.

***Dombey and Son***

This is often referred to as the first of Dickens' great novels, and quotations to this effect can make effective examination questions. Its plot is tightly controlled, as are Dickens' flights of fantasy and anecdotal irrelevance, and its imagery is powerful, concentrated and precise.

***David Copperfield***

This novel is famous for its opening, which is more or less autobiographical, and contains a portrait of Dickens' father in Mr Micawber. Micawber is a very famous character, and a common subject in examinations. Another standard question concerns the narrative technique of the novel, and in particular its masterly use of the point of view technique. Uriah Heep and Steerforth are often the focus of questions, the former as a powerful caricature, the latter as a relative failure in the creation of an ideal vision of genteel society. Characterisation of women, and whether Dickens makes David marry the wrong person all along, can also come in for attention. Equally, the Peggoty family are a masterpiece, and show Dickens' imagination working at its most vivid, powerful and endearing.

### *Bleak House*

The law and Dickens' attack on it are at the centre of the novel's themes. The conflict between conservative traditionalism and an anarchic desire to overthrow and change society both in the novel and in Dickens' own attitudes are very noticeable, as is his attack on false or 'telescopic philanthropy'. Minor characters, Dickens' atmospheric descriptions and his ability to summon up atmosphere are significant issues, as are the themes of justice and the law, love and marriage, and irresponsibility. The technique of dual narration of the plot, and whether or not Esther Summerson is a successful characterisation, are essential to any complete picture of the novel. Standard questions on improbability, the macabre and the grotesque, and Dickens being unfair to women are also common on this novel. The part played in the novel by the detective story element, and the detective must also be understood.

### *Hard Times*

*Hard Times* was written after Dickens made a visit to the industrial town of Preston in the north of England. Two distinct critical views of it have arisen, and the novel is an obvious area for those influenced by or interested in Marxist critical theories:

(i) The novel was written, according to this view, in a hurry, with inadequate research. Dickens allegedly did not understand working people or trade unions, and as a result is unfair to both in his novel.

(ii) According to the second view, a story of social and industrial inequality is allowed to turn into a rather melodramatic and unsatisfying tragic love story that makes the central heroic figure, Stephen Blackpool, unrepresentative. As a result the social criticism in the novel is, allegedly, blurred and superficial, with no clear distinction between good and evil, and with his characters resembling puppets, mouthpieces for rather strained thematic concerns.

An alternative, less critical, view is that the hurry in which the novel was written gives its style a taut directness that is admirable, and has forced Dickens to prune his usual luxuriance. It deals savagely with the new industrial philosophy that sought to treat people as mere numbers and machines, puts in a heartfelt plea for fantasy and the life of the imagination, and shows the crushing burden of mental and physical imprisonment inflicted on society by the Industrial Revolution. Whilst this view admits that the novel fails in some of its characterisations, such as Stephen Blackpool and Slackridge, the union agitator, it also cites several other characters (Bounderby, Bitzer, Mrs Sparsit, Sissy Jupes) as successes, and suggests that the novel becomes the tragedy of one man, Thomas Gradgrind. Some critics have seen the novel as the start of a change in Dickens' style whereby he moved from criticism of individuals to criticism of whole societies. It is certainly true that away from his home ground of London Dickens' descriptive touch is less sure, and that he only dimly understood some of the problems of industrial life that he dealt with in the novel. Nevertheless it is also true that the novel marks a brave and determined attempt to come to terms with, and to make a decent human statement on, some of the worst atrocities inflicted on human beings by the new industrial society.

### *Little Dorrit*

Modern criticism has tended to haul *Little Dorrit* up into the front rank of Dickens' work, and to see in it the start of his later and more mature work. Like all such attempts at division this is rather too clean and simple a way of thinking to reflect accurately the changing pattern of his work. In a rather stimulating manner the novel has been variously described as 'a crowning achievement' and 'twaddle'. The novel does show all the features of Dickens' later work:

- It has a tightly controlled plot and structure, a sardonic and ironical mood and also contains fewer traces of the popular entertainer within it.
- It has a leading theme that dominates the novel, in this case imprisonment of the mind and of the body.
- It has a very closely woven plot, recurrent images, and heavy use of symbols.
- It has considerable depth and complexity of characterisation, with less use of caricature, fewer 'humour' characters and less comic content in both characters and plot.

The novel satirises and criticises imprisonment (the plot is centred for the majority of the book on the Marshalsea Prison in London, where Dickens' own father was imprisoned for a short time), wealth, snobbery, the Civil Service and secrecy. Minor themes are the Church, the English Sunday, slum housing, the law, and Parliament.

Amy Dorrit, the central figure of the novel and its eponymous heroine, verges on sentimentality in her portrait, but by and large escapes it. Possibly the dominant figure in the novel is her father, a weak man whose capacity for independence and humanity has been overwhelmed by imprisonment, the effects of which have gone beyond his body and into his mind. There is a brooding and oppressive quality in the book that is very powerful, and it has been noted that many of the episodes could transfer with the minimum adaptation to the stage, their use of dialogue and scene setting suggesting that live drama was influencing Dickens in his style.

### *Great Expectations*

*Great Expectations* was welcomed by some critics in Dickens' own time as a return to the cheerful style of writing associated with *The Pickwick Papers*. It is true that the novel does contain some elements that seem to hark back to the earlier novels, but it also has all the strengths of the later works. The novel is the story of Pip, who suddenly becomes rich after a childhood dominated by a terrifying aunt. Wealth and its effects on the individual are a central theme of the novel, which shows how wealth corrupts individuals and is a totally false base on which to judge people. The novel is heavily ironical, in that Pip's wealth comes from a convict, a man despised by Pip for all that he stands for. The novel shows Pip's progress through life, from poor waif to pampered rich boy and finally back to wise and mature adult. The characterisation in the novel is notable. Miss Havisham, who has sought to freeze time at the moment when her fiancé jilted her, is a classic and famous portrait, a symbol of decay and corruption. Herbert Pocket and the simple-minded, but eternally loyal, Jo Gargery are triumphs, showing that convincing pictures of goodness are possible in literature. The novel has a 'happy' ending, though Pip has to work and suffer to achieve his happiness, but there is a tidal surge of violence in the book that surfaces quite frequently, and a sombre vision that is typical of the later novels. It is more limited in themes than many of the other late novels, being centred on the issue of wealth and the growth to maturity of one person, but the complexity of the portrait drawn, and the sheer power of the descriptive writing, more than compensate for this. In what is generally held to be a mistake, Dickens altered the original ending of the novel so that Pip married his childhood sweetheart, Estella. The suitability of this ending is a clear issue in the book. Its style and narrative technique have also aroused the interest of a number of post-structuralist critics.

Note the importance of Estella, and the relationship between her and Miss Havishman, to feminist criticism.

### *Our Mutual Friend*

*Our Mutual Friend* is a giant of a novel, in length and in quality. It contains all the features of the later novels as listed in the section on *Little Dorrit*. It is essentially a novel about money, as in some ways is *Great Expectations*, but the concept of money as a disease and an illness, and a totally false god, is developed more strongly in *Our Mutual Friend* than in *Great Expectations*.

*Our Mutual Friend* starts off as a mystery story based round an inheritance. The influence of the detective story in its style and technique is an issue that can best be explored if the works of Wilkie Collins, a contemporary of Dickens, are also looked at. It is a fact that in Victorian times huge piles of rubbish could be sold at vast profit, sometimes for the valuables they contained, but sometimes also for building and other industrial work. This provides Dickens with a marvellous symbol for wealth and money in a corrupt society.

The novel is not without its weaknesses. It appears that Dickens veers off his main plot approximately half-way through the novel and becomes rather more interested in the feud between the schoolteacher Bradley Headstone and the upper-class Eugene Wrayburn, over their love for Lizzie Hexham. Equally that plot strand can easily be seen as the crowning success of the novel, as it produces characters and a relationship that are remarkably complex and effective. Bradley Headstone is a marvellous portrayal of an obsessive character. Sentimentality and a patronising attitude to women are present in the novel, and the treatment of Bella Wilfer by Boffin and John Harmon is frequently discussed. However, many great works of literature triumph despite their weaknesses, and in general *Our Mutual Friend* co tains in large measure all the strengths of Dickens' novels noted above. Anyo who reads *Great Expectations*, *Bleak House*, and *Our Mutual Friend* (pr ferably in that order) will be reading three of the finest and most commandir novels ever written in any language.

## William Makepeace Thackeray

William Makepeace Thackeray (1811–63) was in his own time one Dickens' greatest rivals, but in our own time, and as far as modern sylla are concerned, he is known for one novel, *Vanity Fair* (1848). This is a fran satirical and sometimes world-weary portrait of the top level of society (th 'vanity fair' of the title).

### Examination topics in *Vanity Fair*

**Becky Sharpe and Amelia**

Becky Sharpe is a girl with nothing but her good looks, intelligence and utt ruthlessness to see her through life. Amelia Sedley, on the other hand, something of a conventional, rather passive and pure good woman of th type the Victorian readership seemed to like and want to be shown. It ca be argued that the novel falls into one of the eternal traps of literatur in that it makes the morally despicable Becky a more vital, vigorous an attractive character than the sometimes tedious Amelia. Becky Sharpe is tremendously effective portrait. In defence of Thackeray it can be argue that Thackeray is deliberately pointing out the weaknesses of women suc as Amelia; that he makes her suffer in order to provoke sympathy for he and that it is perfectly possible to feel a degree of sympathy for Becky with out ever losing sight of who and what she really is. Becky has become som thing of an icon for feminists.

**A novel without a hero**

Thackeray said that *Vanity Fair* was 'a novel without a hero'. The obviou 'good' characters in it, Amelia and Dobbin, have their weaknesses empha ised by Thackeray as much as their strengths, and Thackeray goes to gre lengths with Dobbin in particular to show how unheroic he is in his clums ness and eternal loyalty. Neither Dobbin nor Amelia are shown as co ventional heroes. It can be argued that Becky Sharpe, evil though she is, the real hero of the novel, or even that a character such as Rawdon come near to being a hero at the conclusion of the novel. However, what Thacker says is not always what he means. It might be that in the novel Thackera is trying to adjust the reader's concept of what a hero actually is, saying th the person we should view as a hero is Dobbin, whilst society and its co ventions (and the conventions of literature) might make us look to Ameli or even George; both these have at least some conventional heroic feature

Or it might be felt that Thackeray was arguing that true heroism is not possible if we are shown a true insight into human nature: heroes simply do not exist in the real world.

**Puppets**

Thackeray also described his characters as 'puppets', a description that is sometimes used to introduce questions on the extent to which the characters in *Vanity Fair* have lives of their own, or are seen merely as creations and mouthpieces for the narrator. A puppet implies a lifeless imitation of a figure under someone else's control. An intriguing question is whether the characters in the novel are seen to be controlled by the author, or by the society in which they live. They may not be puppets at all; if they are puppets, they need not be Thackeray's, but could be dancing on a string controlled by a false and manipulative society.

**The narrator**

Thackeray actually appears in the novel as a character at the end, as well as making his presence felt throughout the novel by direct addresses to the reader. The effectiveness of this technique, its usefulness in directing the attention and feelings of the reader and its contribution to a lack of realism or an artificial presence in the novel, are all significant issues.

**Dark moral**

Thackeray wrote at some length on *Vanity Fair*. He said that Briggs and Dobbin were raised up above the level of the other characters because they had the power of love, that the majority of the characters were 'odious' (he reserved a specially vicious tone for George Osborne) and that there was a 'dark moral' in the novel. All these are intriguing areas. Love in *Vanity Fair* is perhaps the single redeeming point in what otherwise can be seen as a rather bleak attitude towards humanity; it redeems Rawdon Crawley for one, and points also to the importance Thackeray attaches to the family and parents carrying out their proper duties. This is, of course, a very obvious link with Dickens. Thackeray's comments also emphasise how repulsive many of his characters are, and lead on to the vexed question of whether or not the novel is pessimistic, or blighted by an excess of cynicism. The 'dark moral' could be a statement that human nature is basically flawed, perhaps a statement along the lines that those who are good are weak, those who are strong evil. Thackeray's attitude to human nature is as important an issue in the novel as his attitude to society.

**Themes**

Selfishness and the corruption of fashionable society are the central themes in *Vanity Fair*. Thackeray shows a society which bases its judgement of people on money and outward show, and which ignores the true virtues of love, generosity and loyalty. 'Vanity' sums up the features Thackeray most hates in the society. There is hope in the novel by virtue of the fact that the good characters prove one can live in vanity fair without being tainted. Als the children appear to be making better and more wholesome jobs of the lives than the adults, and some characters do change for the better. How ever, the ending of the novel is only diluted happiness, and as such shoul be compared to the ending of *Little Dorrit* by Dickens. It can be said th Thackeray fails to provide the positive ending the novel needs.

*The plight of women in Victorian society* is a theme. Just as *Vanity Fa* makes puppets out of people by depriving them of freedom (another poi of comparison with *Little Dorrit*), so the young woman of spirit and inte ligence can find no outlet for her talents or character, and is tied to a pas ive role. The Marxist interpretation of the novel sees it as showing a socie in which large numbers of parasites live and feed off the work of others.

**Irony**

Thackeray is a master of irony, which can range from gentle and no malicious fun to savage, flaying criticism. The range and nature of his iron should be studied in depth.

## George Eliot

George Eliot (1819–80) was the pen name of Mary Ann Evans. In her tim she was hailed as one of the greatest living novelists, but her reputation ha fluctuated since then. Her best-known novels are *Adam Bede* (1859); *Th Mill on the Floss* (1860); *Silas Marner* (1861); *Middlemarch* (1872); and *Dani Deronda* (1876).

Realism, ability to write accurate dialogue and knowledge of provinci life are strong features in her work, but it is perhaps characterisation th is her strongest feature as a novelist. She marks a major step forward a regards the Victorian novel in her ability to go into a character's mind an to draw that mind with all its complexity and depth. George Eliot lived life that was highly unconventional in terms of Victorian morality, bu despite her living with a married man quite openly for many years she gaine tremendous respect from those who knew her. Her morality, which is pe haps surprisingly traditional given her life, is another significant and inte esting feature in her work. There is a strong autobiographical element in he work. Some critics have seen her as being too intellectual, in that she trie to force her novels and characters into an overall thematic concept, and ca try unsuccessfully to turn her characters into rather unconvincing symbol As with Jane Austen the material for her novels is ordinary life, rather tha high and great events, but she succeeds in showing how normal life is live Her humour and understanding are marked features, and in her refusal t make savage judgements on her characters she opened the way for man modern novels.

Feminist criticism has tended to see George Eliot as one of the 'first phase of women writers, where an attempt is made to imitate the dominant mal culture of writing and fiction. The complexity of her characterisation makes one wonder if this judgement is not a little too simplistic.

## Further reading

### General

- Michael Wheeler, *English Fiction of the Victorian Period* (Longman, 1994)

### Biographies of Dickens

- Peter Ackroyd, *Dickens* (Minerva, 1990)
- Kate Flint, *Dickens* (Harvester, 1986)
- Fred Kaplan, *Dickens: A Biography* (Hodder & Stoughton, 1988)
- Una Pope-Hennessy, *Charles Dickens* (Penguin, 1970)
- Grahame Smith, *Dickens. A Literary Life* (Macmillan, 1996)

### Criticism on Dickens

- Steven Connor, ed., *Charles Dickens* (Longman, 1996): a collection of modern critical essays, revealing the impact of new critical theories on Dickens's work.
- A. C. Goodison, ed., *Dickens and New Historicism* (Macmillan, 1998): an excellent example of what happens when a relatively new critical theory is applied to a 'classic' author.
- Allan Grant, *A Preface to Dickens* (Longman, 1984)
- Michael Slater, *Dickens and Women* (Dent, 1983)

### George Eliot

- Rosemary Ashton, *George Eliot. A Life* (Penguin, 1997)
- Gillian Beer, *George Eliot* (Harvester, 1986)
- Graham Handley, *George Eliot: A Guide Through the Critical Maze* (Bristol Press, 1990)
- Kathryn Hughes, *George Eliot. The Last Victorian* (Fourth Estate, 1998)
- Kerry McSweeney, *George Eliot. A Literary Life* (Macmillan, 1996)
- Ina Taylor, *George Eliot: A Woman of Contradictions* (Weidenfeld & Nicolson, 1989)

### Thackeray

- Ann Monsarrat, *Thackeray: An Uneasy Victorian* (Cassell, 1980)
- Edgar F. Harden, *Thackeray the Writer. From Journalism to Vanity Fair* (Macmillan, 1998) is expensive enough to be obtained only from the library, but is an excellent modern work on Thackeray.

CHAPTER EIGHTEEN

# Victorian poets: Tennyson, Browning, Hopkins, Arnold and Hardy

## Alfred, Lord Tennyson (1809–92)

Tennyson is sometimes thought of as a Romantic poet, sometimes as a Victorian poet. He was actually both, and that fact says something about the often unnecessary urge to pigeon-hole authors into groups or schools. He is also a poet who has aroused strong feelings. He had an immense popular readership in his own time, and still does, but from then until now critics and intellectuals have worried over his work and not infrequently tried to reduce or diminish Tennyson's reputation. To an extent this has been true of many writers who have exerted a great popular appeal, and there is a strong tendency in criticism to believe that great popularity can only be achieved at the cost of intellectual truth. To describe Tennyson as 'popular' is therefore seen by some as damning him. Other areas of his work have also invited criticism. He was an immensely skilful technician, with a magnificent command of rhyme, rhythm and metre. This can be admired. It can also be used to suggest that his technical skill covers up a deficiency in thought and content, and that his technical skill allows rather inadequate poetry to appear much better than it actually is. Tennyson was a Victorian through and through. He was much admired by Queen Victoria, which fact alone is enough to damn him in certain eyes. He had a dogged, if sometimes troubled, faith in a middle-of-the-road Christianity, and can thus be accused of writing in the manner of a hymn book rather than a poet. He wrote some stirring and often patriotic verse about wars and conflict ('The Ballad of the Revenge' and 'The Charge of the Light Brigade' are well-known examples) and can thus be accused of being right-wing, warmongering, and unthinking.

Much of his poetry is very simple, and so he can be accused of being simple-minded. Very few Romantic poets seemed to have made much use of the waste-paper basket, and his copious outpourings can lead to his being accused of lacking discrimination and standards. The student must read the poems and make up his or her own mind on these issues. Whilst doing so it would be wise to remember that simplicity is often derided, but is also one of the most difficult effects to achieve in literature.

It is perhaps because the perception of Tennyson can be that of an Establishment figure that his work has profited less than many other nineteenth century authors from modern criticism. There are signs that this pattern is changing. It needs to change. Even one poem of his poems – 'The Lady of Shallott' – poses questions in three interesting areas – the whole nature of 'Victorianism' and its sense of having despoiled something fragile and beautiful, the nature of reality and the role of women. There is pervasive melancholy in many of Tennyson's earlier poems, a melancholy that sits rather ill at ease with the conventional image of a Victorian society entirely pleased with itself. It is tempting to tip Tennyson as a possible area for project or dissertation: the combination of an author of undoubted skill who has a capacity to surprise the reader with the sense that he is someone who has been relatively neglected is often a very successful recipe.

## Issues in Tennyson's work

Students are usually asked to read and study a selection of Tennyson's work, rather than one poem or book. As he wrote for over sixty-five years there is ample poetry to choose from, although his best work was written very early on in his career, much of it between 1830 and 1835. It is often unwise to date a poem by Tennyson from the year in which it was published, because he often included work written earlier in books published much later. 'Tithonus', for example, was written between 1830 and 1835, but not published until 1860, whilst one of Tennyson's most famous works, 'In Memoriam', was written over a number of years.

Tennyson was born in Lincolnshire, the son of a gloomy and melancholic country parson. He issued a volume of poetry with his brother, Charles, in 1827, and went up to the University of Cambridge in 1828. There he met Arthur Hallam (1811–33), who was to be perhaps the major influence on Tennyson's poetry. Hallam had a brilliant mind, became an intimate friend and was due to marry Tennyson's sister. Tennyson never completed his degree, but in 1830 published *Poems Chiefly Lyrical*, his first major book. Poems followed in 1833. By this time Tennyson had written many of the shorter poems that typify his work for many readers, such as 'Mariana', 'Claribel', 'The Lotos-Eaters', 'The Palace of Art', 'The May Queen', 'Oenone' and 'The Lady of Shalott'. Many of the above poems illustrate Tennyson's skill at using classical myth and medieval legend in his poetry. 'The Lady of Shalott' is typical, in that medieval legend is used to create a dreamlike world in which characters move with tragic inevitability towards a melancholic climax. It is an intensely musical poem, and in Tennyson's early work metre and rhythm are used with particular skill. 'The Lotos-Eaters' shows Tennyson's mimetic quality, his belief that language could recreate the sights, sounds and feelings of life. This in turn leads to the suggestion that Tennyson is much more concerned with conveying experience, rather than commenting on it. In other words, ideas matter a great deal less than sensations in his poetry. A musical quality is very evident in his verse. 'Tithonus' and 'Ulysses' are both highly regarded poems, and probably the best examples of Tennyson's use of the monologue form.

'Tithonus' starts with typical Tennysonian melancholy:

The Woods decay, the woods decay and fall,
The Vapours weep their burthen to the ground,
Man comes and tills the field and lies beneath,
And after many a summer dies the swan.

'Ulysses' was written soon after the tragic death of Arthur Hallam in Vienna. It is obviously based on classical sources, but its major inspiration is the feelings inspired by the death of Hallam. Ulysses in the poem is isolated, at the end of his life, and 'become a name'. The future is uncertain, the past only to be recalled in snatches and fragments, and so the scene is set for what would easily be a melancholic and despairing poem. As it is, Ulysses expresses a sombre, stoic resolution, and hope is mingled with despair. The poem has strong symbolic overtones, a standard feature of Tennyson's verse, and it is possible to see Ulysses as a symbol of the artist.

The publication in 1842 of *Poems* marked the start of Tennyson's lasting fame, and by 1850 he was financially secure enough to marry. In this same year he published *In Memoriam*, a long series of poems on the death of Arthur Hallam which inevitably lead on into speculation about the whole issue of death and mortality.

*In Memoriam* contains some of Tennyson's finest writing, and some of his worst. The basic scheme of the poem is a movement from despair through to hope and a form of acceptance. The religious statements in the poem tend to be conventional and unoriginal, and Tennyson can all too easily slip into cliché and conventionality when on a moral high horse. Despite this the poem remains a masterpiece. Dimly, sometimes even ponderously, the poem shows a man who is,

An infant crying in the night;
An infant crying for the light:
And with no language but the cry.

It is the quality of doubt, the painful search for meaning and reconciliation, that emerges as the poem's strongest feature. Again one is reminded that Tennyson was no intellectual, but equally one is reminded that he did have a mind and a vast sensitivity, and that his unwillingness to impose ideas on all experience makes him perhaps more relevant and more comprehensible to ordinary people. Victorian intellectuals and later critics may not have espected Tennyson's philosophy and thinking in *In Memoriam*, many people who have struggled with a sense of loss and hopelessness have recognised the poem's honesty, relevance and capacity to put extreme personal emotion and doubt into graphic poetic form. One of the most famous couplets from the poem, and the one which sums up its attitude, is ''Tis better to have loved and lost/Than never to have loved at all.' *In Memoriam* also illustrates a conflict that appears in Tennyson's other poems, between Tennyson as the prophet of his age, and Tennyson the man who saw doubt and uncertainty all around him.

Death is a major concern in Tennyson's work, and also an issue in much Victorian literature and an obsession of Victorian society in general. Trance or death-like states also feature heavily in Tennyson's poetry, but ironically the retreat into these states is often an escape from the realities of life rather than an end to life itself.

Scientific theory exerts a significant influence on Tennyson's work. It is easy in the present time to underestimate the pure shock of certain scientific developments on thinking men and women in Victorian times. One example is the growth of geology as a science – a science which proved that mountains, for centuries a symbol of everything that was fixed, immovable and immutable, were subject to erosion, change and decay as was every other thing in existence. So great was the shock of this new learning (an inevitable comparison can be drawn here with the Renaissance) that for years there were those who tried to pretend that fossils, which proved modern geological theory, were either the Devil's footprints, or left where they were found by the Devil to lead humankind away from the path of true belief. Occasionally, Tennyson makes a fool of himself. One reference to railways and 'grooves' makes it clear that he believed the wheels of railway engines ran in metal grooves, rather than overlapping a metal rail. On far more occasions Tennyson brings in modern learning to rattle the bars of conventional belief and to send a shiver of fear through the reader. The oft-quoted lines referring to the geological past in which 'A thousand types are gone' and where 'dragons of the prime . . . tare each other in their slime' strike a chord both with modern fears about extinction and modern interpretations of dinosaurs. It is this essential modernism in Tennyson, the manner in which he seems to stake out one of the first claims to have examined entirely modern concerns, that help make him so interesting. His dream-worlds, states of mind poised between life and death, cannot help but have a relevance to modern drug culture, the need for escape and the endless questioning about what it is society is seeking to escape from.

Tennyson became Poet Laureate in 1850, in succession to Wordsworth, and from this time one the 'official' side of his poetic personality became more and more marked. As with many Victorian authors his popularity and feeling for his readership did not always help his poetry. A poem such as 'Enoch Arden' (1864) is rather too concerned to preach the conventional moral that some of Tennyson's readers wished to hear, and not concerned enough with letting characters develop and flower outside the demands of morality. Tennyson recognised a duty to society in what he wrote. It is a limiting factor in his work sometimes, but a glance at 'Maud', written in 1855, shows that his occasional complacency and urge to oversimplify were offset by poems of genuine excitement and originality. 'Maud' is a particularly fine poem, one of the very few love poems which uses 'hate' as one of its first words. Whilst poems such as 'Morte d'Arthur' achieve undisputed excellence, his *Idylls of the King* (1859) is less satisfactory, being seen as using legend as a vehicle for simple Victorian moralising that is neither convincing in itself, nor suited to its subject.

### Basic issues in Tennyson

There are a number of well-trodden paths in studying Tennyson's work.

1. Does Tennyson's technical skill as a poet conceal a poverty of material, thought, and subject matter?
2. How skilful is Tennyson as a story teller?
3. How significant is Tennyson's use of classical and medieval legend?
4. Are the sentiments and truths expressed in his work commonplace, or simple?
5. Is doubt rather than certainty the main feature of his poetry?
6. How significant in his work is his ability to show people building up an elaborate artifice around themselves, and then showing it threatened or shattered?

As a final note it is worth remembering that Tennyson's poetry can take on a new dimension when it is read aloud when his musical sense and skill with rhythm and metre are heard most clearly.

## Robert Browning (1812–89)

### Browning's life and poetry

Robert Browning was born in 1812, the son of a wealthy banker. He published *Pauline* in 1833, anonymously. The book was heavily criticised, conforming to the pattern whereby a large number of Romantic or late-Romantic poets were damned when their earliest works were published. In 1846 he married and eloped with Elizabeth Barrett, a semi-invalid and at the time more famous as a writer than Browning. They lived in Italy until Elizabeth died in 1861. Browning wrote a number of unsuccessful plays, but it was the publication of *Men and Women* in 1853 that marked the start of his rise to fame, a fame which was to equal Tennyson's in his own lifetime. *Dramatis Personae* (1864) and *The Ring and the Book* (1868–69) are his two other best-known works, and the poetry which made him famous was largely based on the dramatic monologue form, of which he is still probably the most famous exponent in English Literature. He wrote a number of poems which are well-known to non-specialist readers, such as 'The Pied

Piper of Hamelin', 'How They Brought the Good News from Ghent to Aix' and 'Home-Thoughts, From Abroad'.

## Issues in Browning's poetry

*Men and Women* is the most commonly set of Browning's works for examination purposes, although *The Ring and the Book* has received more attention recently. As with Tennyson, it is possible to find an undercurrent of hostility to Browning's poetry. Some of the reasons for this are similar to those which apply to Tennyson, and hardly valid in strictly literary terms. He was very popular, and a skilful technician, features which often cause an occasional critical eyebrow to be raised. His work lacked some of the dark, brooding moral concern that typifies so much of Victorian literature. More serious complaints are that his work lacked an overall philosophy, that it was inconclusive, limited in scope, not worth reading a second time and buried in the past. The student might feel that it is all too easy to criticise an author for what he did not do, and that such critical judgement can reflect rather too strongly on the personal tastes and scheme for literature held dear by the particular critic.

What Browning did do he did very well. His skill is in the dramatic monologue form, and his greatest ability is that of flashing a complete picture of a personality through to the reader by using that character's own speaking voice. Attitudes to his speakers emerge in plenty, but there is little in the way of judgement. The absence of a clear authorial judgement, the placing of responsibility on the reader to decide between what is truth and what is fiction, the peeling back of layer upon layer of truth and falsehood do not make Browning a 'modern' poet, but they do help to make him a transitional author, one of those whose work points the way forward to modernist writing. There is plenty of sin and corruption in Browning's characters, but the joy of the poetry is that it lets the reader make his own judgement, or feel that he is doing so. Language and syntax in the dramatic monologues are carefully moulded to the speaker, and the techniques and vividness of characterisation in his dramatic monologues are the areas most frequently questioned in examinations.

*Love*, *religion*, and *time* are sometimes described as major themes in Browning's work, but an examination question on any of these needs to be treated with even more than usual respect. The term 'theme' suggests a concept which is explored by the author, but it can also suggest a concept about which some conclusions are drawn. Browning's work is short on conclusions. Love in his poetry is a lower rather than a higher passion, at times an animal instinct. Religious faith is not examined in depth, but examined as it manifests itself in a variety of people. It is dark, deep, passionate and opulent. The theme of time in his poetry consists largely of an awareness of things unfulfilled, but this rarely reaches the level of melancholy of a poet such as Tennyson.

Browning displayed the Victorian fondness for eccentric and grotesque characters in his poetry. In his later years his work became less effective and more garrulous, but this is rarely looked at or commented on in examinations. A poem which is well worth reading even if it is not on the syllabus is 'Childe Roland to the Dark Tower Came', a marvellous mystic vision of largely unspecified but very evocative horrors and triumphs. 'Browning spoke always through a mask' is one question that has been asked on his poetry; 'Childe Roland to the Dark Tower Came' suggests that he could adopt a symbolist mask, as well as that of another character, if he so chose.

## Gerard Manley Hopkins

Gerard Manley Hopkins (1844–89) was born into a prosperous middle-class family, educated at public school and Oxford, and joined the Roman Catholic Church, becoming a member of the Jesuit order in 1868. By his decision to join that order he effectively cut himself off from the literary world of the time. The Jesuits showed little interest in his talent for poetry, or even hostility. The world outside the order largely did not know of that talent. These facts do not explain his poetry. They can help the reader to understand it. His poetry, highly experimental for its time, was not published until long after his death, in fact in 1918, under the editorship of Robert Bridges (1844–1930) a poet himself and a lifelong friend of Hopkins. Less than fifty of his poems are seen as mature and finished products, but his influence on modern poetry has been out of all proportion to the relatively small number of poems he had published.

**The standing of Hopkins**

The brief summary of Hopkins' life given above might suggest that he was a latter-day Metaphysical poet. His poems were not widely known in his own lifetime, had a strong religious element in them and also a sensual and violent element. However, these links only go so far. Hopkins is generally regarded as a difficult poet to study at Advanced level. The Metaphysical poets are sometimes thought of as difficult because their language can be intricate, and the pressure of ideas in their work intense and very fast-moving. Hopkins' poetry has the intensity, the spirituality and the violence of the Metaphysical poets, but adds to it a whole new dimension of technical experimentation, and a new and highly individual theory of poetry. Some books pour cold water on the concept of Hopkins as a difficult author, and adopt a cheerful, commonsense tone suggesting that with a little work and effort Hopkins will fall under the control of the average student. This is simply not true. Hopkins *is* a difficult poet, and though the rewards of studying and understanding his work are great, so is the effort required to reach that understanding, perhaps more so than with any other author studied in this work.

The fact that Hopkins' language can be seen as 'difficult' and consciously literary has made him interesting to structuralism and any modern critical theory concerned with the nature of literary language. In some respects

Hopkins can act as a good tester of modern critical theories. The worst type of modern criticism invents a theme which has still to be proven and leaps on certain authors with gleeful lines to the effect that, 'Of course, this theory can be proven by reference to the works of . . .'. Hopkins was working to a scheme of language that took considerable thought. Quite a surprising number of critics who believe that authors were writing to schemes of language of which they were unaware steer clear of an author such as Hopkins who was writing to one of which he was aware. It is almost as if Hopkins plays the worst type of modern critic at his or her own game and calls their bluff. In developing his own scheme of language, for which he invented his own terms, Hopkins was in some respects a harbinger of much modern criticism. As such his work has also attracted some of the most intriguing responses from modern critics, as well as apparently striking others dumb.

**Hopkins and technical innovation**

In order to understand Hopkins' poetry it is necessary to understand what he was trying to achieve when he wrote it. He was an intensely spiritual man with a passionate belief in the value of a disciplined faith, but a man also with a strong sensual side. These two features are sometimes at odds with each other in his work, and help form it in extremes of high excitement and low depression. Most of all Hopkins is renowned for his techniques of writing, for which he developed his own technical terms. Hopkins believed that every object, event and experience had its own unique, intrinsic pattern and flavour, almost a mental fingerprint. The term 'inscape' is used by him to describe this uniqueness, and his poetry seeks to go inside every object and experience and draw its special nature. The energy for this uniqueness is generated by 'instress', a power that hails partly from God and partly from the relationship that every object and experience has with itself and with things around it. Hopkins attempts to show experience in a new light to the reader, thereby making the uniqueness of all things visible to us.

*Sprung rhythm* is another term often used by Hopkins and of his poetry. In its basic form it is a line of verse with a varying number of syllables but the same number of stresses per line. In its wider meaning it is the philosophy that diction, syntax, sound and rhythm are all geared to the nature of what is being described. It is onomatopeia on a hugely expanded scale; in onomatopeia a word is made to sound like the noise it describes. In Hopkins' poetry every single aspect of language and arrangement of words, rather than just sound, is used to create the same effect. Hopkins' verse has no conventional metrical structure; any structure there is, is dictated by the specific nature of what is being described. In a poem such as 'The Windhover' the rhythm mimics the movement of a flying bird, but also the mood of the poet watching it fly. To achieve his aims Hopkins invents new words (he was influenced in this by his knowledge of Welsh, medieval language and dialect), and combines words in surprising and original ways. He makes heavy use of the hyphen, alliteration and internal rhyme, and indeed the whole battery of sound effects available to the poet.

## Hopkins' themes

*Nature, God,* and *Man's relationship to both Nature and God* are strong themes in Hopkins' poetry. In common with many modern authors Hopkins appears more concerned to present and recreate experience than to comment on it. He can write in a richly sensual manner, and the effect of his poetry is not so much that of a stone dropping into a pond and causing ripples in our mind, but more a massive explosion of water, stone and rock in an experience that is at one and the same time emotional, sensual and intellectual – and highly concentrated. In one sense all Hopkins' poetry is religious, but in the poems with a very specific religious element to them there is a sense of tortured doubt and agonising after faith that is very marked. His so-called 'Dark Sonnets' were written between 1885 and 1886, at the end of his life, and are some of the most powerful poems ever written. In them the human soul is desperately searching for Christ and for the religious grace that appears to have vanished from the world. They are the voice of a man crying in the wilderness who has found that the wilderness exists not only outside, but inside his own nature as well.

## Issues in Hopkins' verse

Questions on *the complexity and difficulty of Hopkins' verse* frequently appear in examinations. The body of opinion which suggested that Hopkins was sometimes unnecessarily difficult is now more fashionable than it used to be. His control over what he writes is not always firm, he can appear appallingly long-winded at times and be led into a chronic excess of technical experimentation. Robert Bridges had a point when he said that Hopkins' poetry could sometimes verge on the ridiculous (the same could be said of Milton, Wordsworth and most great poets, without in any way diminishing their overall reputation or standing), and also when he commented that it was fair enough to expect the reader to expend effort on understanding complex themes or images, but not at all fair to expect him to expend this effort in overcoming difficulties of syntax. It is essential to distinguish between where Hopkins is making a complex point, and where his language simply lets him down, and he lacks the skill to communicate what he is attempting to say. Occasionally the examiners turn the coin round to face the other way, and ask whether Hopkins' verse is at its best when it is at its most simple.

*The conflict between sensuality and spirituality* in his verse is also asked about, and his use of language and technical devices are very frequent subjects for questions. Statements to the effect that terror rather than beauty is at the heart of his work are also to be expected, as are questions that enquire about his treatment of nature.

### Central poems by Hopkins

The following poems are central to any understanding of Hopkins' verse: 'The Golden Echo'; 'The Leaden Echo'; 'The Windhover'; 'The Woodlark';

'The Wreck of the Deutschland'; 'Spring and Fall'; 'Pied Beauty'; 'Carrion Comfort'.

## Matthew Arnold

Matthew Arnold (1822–88) was the eldest son of the famous Headmaster of Rugby School, Thomas Arnold. He spent nearly 35 years as an Inspector of Schools, but wrote a great many books of criticism and social commentary during his lifetime. He became a hugely influential critic, and was a marked influence on some of the first 'modern' authors such as T. S. Eliot and the critic F.R.Leavis. Increasing interest in literary theory has led to a resurgence of interest in his critical writing, partly for its literary and theoretical content but partly because of what it reveals about late-Victorian attitudes and thinking. His role as a Schools Inspector meant that travelled the country and acquired a first-hand knowledge of it granted to few people.

Arnold's poetry is effective but occasionally rather heavy-handed. He is probably best known for 'Dover Beach' (1867), and 'The Scholar Gypsy' (1853). Arnold thought his age was lacking in 'moral grandeur', and some of his criticism of Victorian society is quite savage. He makes an excellent choice for a project or dissertation, but the student would be advised to stick to either his poetry or his prose writing, rather than take on both.

## Thomas Hardy

Thomas Hardy (1840–1928) was the son of a master mason from Dorset. After training and working as an architect he became a writer, gaining fame firstly as a novelist and then later in his life as a poet. Three lasting influences on his life were a feeling of social inferiority that never quite left him, a troubled and erratic first marriage to Emma Gifford and the death by suicide of his close friend and advisor Horace Moule. The first two influences may have been reasons why he made a conscious and determined effort to hide certain features of his life from later generations, and only in recent years have parts of the smokescreen he tried to erect round his life been blown away by modern researchers and critics. Privacy is a privilege that few great writers in the past century have been allowed to keep.

### Hardy the poet

Hardy said that he considered himself a poet rather than a novelist, and in recent years increasing significance has come to be attached to his poetry, even to the extent of some critics seeing Hardy as the major influence on the development of modern British poetry. He did not start to publish poetry until 1898, possibly as a result of the limitations imposed on him by novel-writing and his dissatisfaction with the reception his novels received. He had however been writing poems for many years previous to this. His first volume, *Wessex Poems*, was not well received, but his epic verse drama, based on the Napoleonic Wars, *The Dynasts* (1903–8) was nationally acclaimed. He published ten more volumes of poetry after this – a huge output, by no means all of which is of a high quality. The student coming to Hardy's poetry for the first time needs to be selective in his reading if he or she is to see why Hardy is often regarded as one of the towering geniuses of English poetry.

## Themes in Hardy's poetry

### Nature

Nature is mentioned and described a great deal in Hardy's poetry. Antithesis, or the presentation of opposites, is a central feature in Hardy's poetry, seen at its strongest in his presentation of Nature. Thus Nature can be shown in either a sweet or a wild mood, or at any point within these two opposites. It can be full of cruelty to man, supportive of and sympathetic to him, or simply ignorant of his presence and wholly uncaring. At the same time there is such a thing as a 'natural impulse' in Hardy's poetry which is worthwhile. Man and Nature are frequently shown as suffering together, both victims of a ruling power in the Universe which scorns or ignores all living things. Nature and natural description are frequently used as emblems either for the state of the world, or for the mental state and mood of the author, as in 'The Darkling Thrush'.

### Humanity

Humanity in Hardy's poetry is also composed of opposites. Human beings can be 'breathing and passionate', but in a poem such as 'The Dynasts' humanity is a collection of puppets, dancing on strings pulled by an unknowable and unreachable force. Pessimism in Hardy's work is a major issue, both for poems and novels. Whilst he can be pessimistic about humanity, he also shows a vast love for it; it has been said that he is pessimistic about humanity because he loves it so much. There is a marvellous vein of cynical, graveyard humour in Hardy's poetry, seen at its best in a poem such as 'Voices from Things Growing in a Country Churchyard' or 'Ah! Are You Digging On My Grave?' He is a delighted and amused observer of country people, their speech and their idiosyncracies.

### Destiny

Phrases such as 'The Immanent Will', 'Unconscious Cosmic Will', 'Cosmic Will', and 'Destiny' abound in and of Hardy's poetry. Be careful with all these phrases. They express something central to an understanding of Hardy's work, but are not technical terms in the sense of having a precise and exact philosophical meaning. Essentially they are all terms which express Hardy's belief that there is a force which controls human lives and destiny, but that this force is ignorant of humanity and all living things. It is an unconscious force that rules our lives and this world, and is all the more terrifying for this. The poem 'The Convergence of the Twain' is as good an example as any of this idea at work in Hardy's poetry. The mighty ship the *Titanic* is sunk by an iceberg. This is not an accident, in that 'The Immanent Will that stirs and urges everything' has 'grown' the iceberg so that it can meet and sink the *Titanic*. Equally the sinking is not a conscious act, but an automatic, instinctive response. It is the response of a machine that registers threat to the balance of nature. Man has pushed that balance too far in his favour by building this mighty vessel; the Immanent Will ensures its destruction in a totally unthinking way, similar to the way that white blood-cells will surround and try to kill any foreign body in the bloodstream. Man is therefore crushed into submission for life to a system that takes no heed or cognisance of him, and is actually unaware of his existence in any meaningful sense. Put another way, the machine still works like a computer program that has been set to run, whilst the controlling intelligence or programmer has gone away, or is unconscious.

All this leads to the presence of a strong tragic element in Hardy's work, both novels and poetry. The struggle against a hostile fate, the virtues of courage and endurance, the questioning of the nature of existence and the fierce hope that the human spirit can be unvanquished even though its physical container can be destroyed, are all tragic features, and are all present in Hardy's poetry. The presence of a tragic element in his work should not hinder the student from seeing how important small issues are in Hardy. He believed firmly that an incident on a small scale could reflect a much larger truth. There is also a rich vein of ironic humour in his work.

**Other issues**

Love is a common theme in Hardy's work, as a subject for both exultation and depression. A prophetic element is frequently present in his writing, and what has been described as a 'controlled nostalgia' for the past. He is very aware of time, both as a haven for the troubled mind and as a threat to mortality. Animals are common in his poetry. In general he treats them with the same sympathy and understanding that he affords to humans.

## Hardy's technique

Hardy frequently uses unusual metre and rhythms in his poetry. Sometimes this and his fondness for dialect, uncouth language or words that he has invented himself ('darkling' and 'madding' are two examples) work exceptionally well; sometimes they make his poetry appear clumsy or even ridiculous.

His tone is often that of a man musing alone. It has been said that his verse shows signs of being written by an older man, but this needs to be treated with some caution, if only because some of his poems were written in relative youth, and it is rather difficult to generalise about what old men adopt in the way of tone. Irony is a central technique in his work, and the incidents he writes about are rarely as important as the comments made on them by the author.

## Hardy's novels



Many of the comments made above on Hardy's poetry could apply to his novels. Hardy bases his novels in the invented country of Wessex, which to all intents and purposes is the Dorset that was always his spiritual home. Of his novels five have come to be seen as the foundation of his worth and the source of his reputation.

*Far From the Madding Crowd* (1874) has many of the features that have come to be seen as typical of his novels. It sets individual humans with their desires, hopes and frustrations against the ruthless power and imprisoning force of the seasons, which, like the Immanent Will, dominate human existence without being answerable to those so dominated. In this novel the ending is more or less happy; in later work it becomes uncompromisingly pessimistic. The novel was published in serial form. Hardy was less happy than many another authors with this form of publication, and throughout his novel-writing career found the limitations of Victorian morality a stifling and almost unbearable influence. The novel is also typical in that one of its central characters is a woman. The brunt of the story and its thematic concerns are often carried by a woman in Hardy's novels.

*The Mayor of Casterbridge* (1886) develops one of Hardy's strongest themes, the decline of farming and rural life in the face of Britain's growing industrialisation. It is a dramatic novel, markedly less optimistic than *Far From the Madding Crowd*. It is an interesting novel from a feminist viewpoint, with its central issue of a wife sold as a piece of property. Hardy's female heroines are often more impressive than their male counterparts. Hardy shows women as an amalgam of extremes – is Tess, for example, seducer or seduced? The social values of the time condemn her as the former, natural feeling sees her as the latter. One of the greatest achievements of Hardy's novels is their willingness to allow for the emergence of a new concept of femininity, the 'modern' woman, whilst at the same time refusing to categorise those women, and to show the confusion inherent in the clash of ideologies that the emergence of anything new to society provokes.

*Tess of the D'Urbervilles* (1891) is generally regarded as Hardy's crowning achievement in novel form. Tess herself is a young country girl who is destroyed by a society that cannot bend or flex sufficiently to allow a courageous and even heroic person to exist happily. Hardy's hatred of unthinking efficiency, his concern for the individual and his bitter awareness of how a cold and cruel society can waste and destroy human endeavour and spirit are magnificently expressed in this novel. It has weaknesses as well. Victorian morality and Hardy's perhaps exaggerated concern for the feelings of his readers allow for ludicrous incidents. Hardy originally intended that Tess be carried by a man over a patch of wet ground. Moral conventions (in effect, censorship) of the time dictated that this had to be changed so that Tess is conveyed by a wheelbarrow over the ground. This way the man is not in physical contact with the woman. . . . Similarly Tess's seduction is so hedged round with non-specific description that the reader could at times be forgiven for thinking that she had simply fallen asleep, rather than been seduced into intercourse. Tess can be accused for being too passive, a common failing in all Victorian heroines, but perhaps this is inevitable in a novel that seeks to show so clearly how human desires and wishes are destined to be crushed underfoot by unthinking and unfeeling authority, be it human or natural.

*Jude the Obscure* (1895), *The Return of the Native* (1878) and *The Woodlanders* (1887) carry forward themes seen in the earlier novels. In both novels agricultural life and the dominance of the seasons and tradition are seen as both an imprisonment and a strength. On the one hand they offer security and certainty, on the other a total unwillingness to change in the light of human desires. Hardy shows a rigid society in a rigid world, and that rigidity can very easily break the fragile human spirit, even if it is seen as admirable that such a fragile spirit should seek to challenge the system.

*Jude the Obscure* is so obsessed with a pessimistic view of human nature, and so concerned to impose this thematic load on the reader, that at times the whole success of the novel is threatened. In Hardy's other novels the countryside can be cruel but also kind. In *Jude the Obscure* even that haven is denied. Humanity exists in chains of convention, tradition and class-consciousness, and Hardy's characters are sometimes so wrapped round in these chains that they themselves are hardly visible. The pessimism in the novel, despite the fine writing it can contain, is so oppressive that it can be seen at different times as strangling it, or simply making its characters appear ludicrous. As a necessary antidote to authors who tell students what to think when they are perfectly capable of making up their own minds, it might be a good idea to write an immediate justification of *Jude the Obscure* as a more effective novel than *Tess of the D'Urbervilles*; it can be done!

## Hardy and the Church

The Church of England, in the form of its buildings and people, feature heavily in Hardy's novels and also in his poems. The Anglican Church, established at the time of Henry VIII's break from Roman Catholicism, had together with the State become the twin pillar of English society for hundreds of years. The Church appears in Hardy's work as a physical and a social presence, not as something with anything of spiritual significance to say. The grand buildings, the sonority of the liturgies and the social status remain: the real meaning of the Church has withered and died. It is as if the Church is a great beast with a shell or carapace. The shell – what one actually sees – remains, whilst all the living flesh inside it is dead. Even hinting at the spiritual death of the Anglican Church was outrageous in Hardy's time. We might now see the Church as a symbol for all Victorian society – outwardly impressive and massive, inwardly rotting from within and torn by doubt.

## Question and answer

**Question**

Comment on the themes contained in the following passage:

*The Darkling Thrush*

I LEANT upon a coppice gate
When Frost was spectre-gray,
And Winter's dregs made desolate
The weakening eye of day.
The tangled bine-stems scored the sky
Like strings of broken lyres,
And all mankind that haunted nigh
Had sought their household fires.

The land's sharp features seemed to be
The Century's corpse outleant,
His crypt the cloudy canopy,
The wind his death-lament.
The ancient pulse of germ and birth
Was shrunken hard and dry,
And every spirit upon earth
Seemed fervourless as I.

At once a voice arose among
The bleak twigs overhead
In a full-hearted evensong
Of joy illimited;
An aged thrush, frail, gaunt, and small,
In blast-beruffled plume,
Had chosen thus to fling his soul
Upon the growing gloom.

So little cause for carolings
Of such ecstatic sound
Was written on terrestrial things
Afar or nigh around,
That I could think there trembled through
His happy good-night air
Some blessed Hope, whereof he knew
And I was unaware.

*31 December 1900*

**Answer**

Thomas Hardy is reputed to have written this poem on New Year's Eve, 1900, at the dawn of a new century. It commences in the personal, subjective mode, but the poet's feelings and mood are suggested by his observations of nature, rather than by any direct statements. The bitter hopelessness of a cold winter's evening are stressed by the imagery: 'Frost', 'spectre-gray', 'dregs', 'desolate', 'weakening', 'broken' and 'haunted' are unified and strengthened by their suggestion of cold, weakness, and death or ghostliness. The 'strings of broken lyres' is a classic image of disharmony.

The second stanza continues the mood of the former, if anything in even stronger terms. The whole past century is a 'corpse', and the imagery in this stanza continues and enlarges on the motif of death contained in the first. Despite the personal, subjective start of the poem, by the end of the second stanza Hardy has made his mood an emblem for all life upon earth, and he even suggests that the very life force is 'shrunken hard and dry', that life itself is near to exhaustion and death. This is achieved in an undramatic, almost quiet manner, with a slow build-up to a terrifying vision of death, driven largely by natural images.

The sudden hurling out of its song by a thrush might be seen as the injection of a rather fatuous optimism into the poem. The 'full-hearted evensong/Of joy illimited' is certainly a cause for hope, but Hardy stresses in the third stanza that the thrush is 'aged . . . frail, gaunt, and small', as well as being 'blast-beruffled'. The phrase 'fling his soul/Upon the growing gloom' suggests almost a vain, futile gesture, though heroic and courageous at the same time. In the final stanza Hardy is careful not to be sentimental about the thrush. Hardy can see no cause for joy, but he can hope that the thrush can see something he himself is unable to perceive. The poem is thus finely balanced. It suggests there may be hope, and the very sound of the thrush and its defiance of the prevailing moods shows at the very least the existence of a tragic hope; life may be threatened, its physical existence at risk, but its spirit is indomitable and cannot be crushed. Equally, Hardy does not deny the hopelessness that exists around him in the very fabric of nature; he merely shows it as co-existing with the hope expressed by the thrush.

The poem is typical of Hardy's work in that it shows life on Earth, human as well as animal, existing under the iron grip of an unsympathetic controlling force, in this case Nature. In praising defiance and the unconquerable spirit it is also typical, and in its firm unwillingness to state a clear conclusion, balancing hope and pessimism, it could stand for Hardy's poems and his novels. The musing tone, use of natural imagery to create and represent human moods and feelings and the simple rhyme scheme are unobtrusive and powerful. The tight rhyming gives strength and authority to the poem, but the metre is more relaxed, giving a natural and free-flowing feeling to the lines.

## Further reading

- J. B. Bullen, ed., *Writing and Victorianism* (Longman, 1997): a good general survey.

## Tennyson

- Robert Bernard Martin, *Tennyson: A Biography* (Faber/Oxford University Press, 1983)
- Christopher Ricks, *Tennyson* (2nd edn, Macmillan, 1989)
- Rebecca Stott, ed., *Tennyson* (Longman, 1996): a selection of some of the most interesting modern treatments of Tennyson.

## Browning

- J. R. Watson, ed., *Browning: 'Men and Women' and Other Poems* (Casebook Series, Macmillan, 1974)
- John Woolford and Daniel Karling, *Robert Browning* (Longman, 1996): modern critical writing on Browning.

## Hopkins

- Margaret Bottrall, ed., *Gerard Manley Hopkins: Poems* (Casebook Series, Macmillan, 1991)
- Graham Story, *A Preface to Hopkins* (Longman, 1992)
- Norman White, *Hopkins. A Literary Biography* (Oxford University Press, 1995)

## Hardy

- Robert Gittings, *Young Thomas Hardy* (Penguin, 1978) and *The Older Thomas Hardy* (Penguin, 1980), are required reading for all those interested in Hardy's work, and classic texts.
- James Gibson and Trevor Johnson, ed., *Hardy: Poems* (Casebook Series, Macmillan, 1979)
- Trevor Johnson, *A Critical Introduction to the Poems of Thomas Hardy* (Macmillan, 1991)
- Robert Langbaum, *Thomas Hardy In Our Time* (Macmillan, 1997): an excellent introduction to modern views of Hardy.
- Charles P. C. Pettit, ed., *Reading Thomas Hardy* (Macmillan, 1998)
- Martin Seymour-Smith, *Hardy* (Bloomsbury, 1994)
- Peter Widdowson, ed., *Tess of the D'Urbevilles* (New Casebook Series, Macmillan, 1993)
- ––, *On Thomas Hardy. Late Essays and Earlier* (Macmillan, 1998) is highly individual.
- Merryn Williams, *A Preface to Hardy* (Longman, 1993)

CHAPTER NINETEEN

# Victorian drama: Ibsen, Chekhov, Shaw and Wilde

## Background

The middle of the nineteenth century saw the breaking of the monopoly of the only two theatres allowed by law in London, Covent Garden and Drury Lane. In fact, other, unlicensed theatres had been ignoring or evading the law for many years, and so the effect of this was not as dramatic as might have been expected. The ending of the monopoly came at a time of growing demand for the theatre, in both Britain and Europe. English theatre was able to respond with quantity, and spectacle, but not with quality. Spectacle, high drama and sentimentality were commonplace, and the latter part of the nineteenth century failed to produce any new dramatist of real and lasting merit. The revolution was to start with two non-English dramatists, Henrik Ibsen (1828–1906) and Anton Chekhov (1860–1904).

## Henrik Ibsen (1828–1906)

Ibsen's influence on drama was immense. A Norwegian, his best-known plays are *Peer Gynt* (1867), *A Doll's House* (1879), *Ghosts* (1881), *An Enemy of the People* (1882), *Hedda Gabler* (1890) and *The Master Builder* (1892). Ibsen was vastly influential. He wrote social drama, often based in small towns, and stripped out from his plays the excessive Victorian effects and backdrops. By simplifying plays in this manner he made them all the more pointed and stark. He was able to create tragedy out of the lives of ordinary people. He saw himself as more of a poet, but many commentators have seen him as a social philosopher.

In common with a number of dramatists whose work he influenced, there is a move over the whole period of his life from very naturalistic drama to very symbolic works; it is the enduring quality of this symbolism, as well as Ibsen's ability to observe ordinary people, that have been responsible for his lasting fame. Ibsen's 'reality' was in his choice of subject matter, rather than in his treatment of that subject or his characters' language, and he is not to be compared with the French naturalists who viewed the aim of drama to present man on stage as he was in reality, wholly and totally. Ibsen was an excellent technician; his plays are usually superbly constructed. Comedy is not his strength, and there is an element of Nordic melancholy pervading his work. The latter is powerful, but lays him open to mimicry.

### Topics in Ibsen's plays

The issue of Ibsen's true nature – social philosopher or poet? – rarely goes away when questions are asked on Ibsen. This is also one of those most irritating questions, in that the answer is so clearly that he was both that the question is sometimes not worth the asking. Optimism or pessimism in his work is another common topic for questions, as is whether or not his work can really claim the accolade of being termed 'tragedy'. This is a common question for certain other dramatists; the obvious link is with Miller's *Death of a Salesman*, where students are perpetually being asked if it is possible to write modern tragedy and with lowly and low-born protagonists. Symbolism in Ibsen's work is a fruitful question area, particularly the manner in which he can run a strong symbolic content alongside naturalism. For wider-ranging courses such as those found at degree level the question of Ibsen's status as 'the father of modern drama' is a popular topic, particularly now that cross-cultural courses give many students more than one country on which to base their answers.

'Immorality' is not a word that will spring to mind first of all when one sees an Ibsen play. Yet when they were first produced in London Ibsen's plays produced outrage and condemnation, being seen as morally 'putrid'. Some of the outrage felt by contemporary playgoers had to do with Ibsen's willingness to show women in a new light, as victims rather than mere passive recipients of the sterile role society sought to afford them.

## Anton Chekhov (1860–1904)

Chekhov was a Russian doctor who wrote short stories, and then four plays towards the end of his life on which his reputation as a dramatist rests. These are *The Seagull* (1895), *Uncle Vanya* (1900), *Three Sisters* (1901), and *The Cherry Orchard* (1904). As with Ibsen, there is a blend of naturalism and symbolism in Chekhov's plays, which remain very popular in the commercial theatre to the present day. Chekhov specialised in showing an upper-class society somehow under threat, and in danger of suffocating through its own inactivity and boredom. In this respect Chekhov was one of the first writers to create the sense of terminal decline and sterility that reached a peak in T. S. Eliot's *The Waste Land* and which has echoed down through modernist writing ever since.

Chekhov's major skill is his ability to blend tragedy and comedy. The plot and characters in his plays are frequently tragic, but also so inherently absurd and credible as to be funny. The inhabitants of E. M. Forster's *Howard's End* would recognise their counterparts in a play by Chekhov: both are privileged, both exist in dim memories of a satisfactory past and both are threatened. However, where some at least of Forster's characters are destroyed simply because they do not have the imagination and depth to cope with a world that does not operate on straight steel lines, those in Chekhov's work do have a depth, albeit unrealised or repressed by themselves. It is that depth that gives rise to the poignant tragedy and comedy of Chekhov's best work. It was almost as if Chekhov's artistic imagination presaged the Russian Revolution and the First World War, the events which brought to an end forever the style of life of his characters and all those like them. Chekhov's skill lies in persuading us that we are like them, and, by association, that we too will be destroyed, gently or otherwise.

### Topics in Chekhov's plays

The tragi-comic nature of Chekhov's work is commonly examined, and his techniques of characterisation. The nature of the malaise that affects his characters is an excellent area for discussion, and, as with Ibsen, the relative weighting in the plays given to poetry and social comment. Modern criticism has made the perception of women a crucial feature in his work, and Marxist criticism does not have to work very hard to show the plays as testimony to a society destroyed by its own lack of powerful principles.

## George Bernard Shaw (1856–1950)

Shaw was the first genuinely original dramatic talent to make itself heard in many years. He was a notable critic as well as dramatist, heavily influenced by Ibsen and totally full of a sense of his own importance and rightness.

Surprisingly, though this makes him controversial, his sense of humour stops him from appearing a smug and arrogant bore; one never quite knows with Shaw whether he is saying something because he believes it, or because he knows it will stir up and outrage those people and those ideas in society which deserve it. Shaw's best-known works are *Mrs Warren's Profession* (written in 1893 but not staged until 1902, because its honesty about prostitution was unacceptable at the time it was written); *Arms and the Man* (1894); *The Devil's Disciple* (1897); *Major Barbara* (1905); *Man and Superman* (1901–3); *Pygmalion* (1913); *Heartbreak House* (1920); *Back to Methuselah* (1918–20); and *Saint Joan* (1923).

Shaw appealed to the intellect of his audience as much as to their emotions. He was a great admirer of Chekhov, but never managed to create in his own plays the depth of characterisation and warmth that Chekhov produced – something which Shaw may himself have recognised in some of his comments on the relative worth of Chekhov's and his own plays.

## Topics in Shaw's plays

Characters are mere mouthpieces for the author's views is a description often applied to Shaw's characterisation. Shaw was a fiercely didactic writer; he has something very firm to say in all his plays and by the end of them the audience have been left in no doubt as to what it is Shaw wants to tell them. Shaw's characters are mouthpieces for what he wants to say, but they are also painted in very strong colours, are frequently comic and very rarely lack interest. Shaw shares at least one feature with a more modern writer, Tom Stoppard: both can make lengthy discussions of serious issues dramatically entertaining and convincing. Fluency, wit and precision are the features of his style that allow him to achieve this, coupled with an instinctive, showman's 'feel' for an audience, how to manipulate them and how far they can be taken.

Realism and his treatment of social issues are significant topics. Shaw is often thought of as left-wing; sometimes he is merely unconventional, and his ideas rarely become bogged down in political issues, but rather go on to a much wider sphere of moral issues. Thus in *Major Barbara* there is an armaments manufacturer and a member of the Salvation Army. In conventional social terms the armaments manufacturer is a villain, but Shaw suggests that by providing employment to thousands of people he should be seen as a saviour, whilst the girl from the Salvation Army is seen as a canting and ineffectual hypocrite. The explosion which eventually disrupts the armaments factory is an interesting symbolic twist to the play, but it is worth asking if in many of his plays Shaw's apparent certainty about his themes and his preaching on them is not sometimes tongue-in-cheek, and designed to disturb as much as to preach.

The blend of comedy and serious intent is a common question on Shaw's plays. Shaw can be savagely yet comically critical of society. *Mrs Warren's Profession* examines the hypocritical attitude society takes to prostitution, and *Pygmalion* is a hilarious examination of class attitudes and behaviour, where a working-class girl is groomed into presenting herself as upper class; it is typical of Shaw that this is done not for moral reasons as much as to win a bet and prove a personal point.

Shaw often damns ignorance; the candidate might ask if what Shaw is really damning is any group which does not totally accept his viewpoint. Shaw's dialogue is highly examinable. He is not a poet, but his grasp of conversational tensions and his capacity to write in a concise, highly economical and yet fluent style is notable. His characters may be mouthpieces, but they can still talk in a personal voice and with great power.

*Saint Joan* appears more regularly than any other play on examination syllabuses. Its historical framework is sometimes examined, not as a history play but rather to see how Shaw takes, manipulates and changes historical material to suit his purposes. By seeing what he chooses to show and what he chooses to leave out the reader can gain an insight into his basic aims in the play. The variety of characterisation in the play, the character of Joan, the effectiveness of the Epilogue, the play's realism and its blend of comic and tragic elements are some of the questions most often asked.

## Oscar Wilde (1854–1900)

Oscar Wilde was an Irishman educated at Oxford, and a leading figure in the Aesthetic Movement (see Ch. 3). He dabbled in poetry and poetic drama, but his fame is based largely on one novel, *The Picture of Dorian Gray* (1891), and on four plays: *Lady Windermere's Fan* (1892); *A Woman of No Importance* (1893); *An Ideal Husband* (1895); and *The Importance of Being Earnest* (1895).

Wilde's relationship with Lord Arthur Douglas led to him being imprisoned for homosexual offences in 1895. He was declared bankrupt. His letter to Lord Alfred Douglas whilst in prison was published in 1905 as *De Profundis*. He was released in 1897 but the social stigma of homosexuality was so strong that he was forced to go to Paris, where he wrote the justifiably famous *The Ballad of Reading Gaol* (1898).

Wilde was an immensely witty person, and any Dictionary of Quotations will be full of his sayings and aphorisms. Many of these were beautifully staged, as when he declared in answer to the American Customs' question whether he had anything to declare, 'Only my genius'. To borrow the phrase used by Bernard Levin of Mick Jagger, the persecution of Wilde can appear to be a case of a butterfly being broken on a wheel. Examining boards and universities have traditionally been nervous about Wilde's work, there being a strong feeling that it is light, popinjay stuff not worthy of serious attention. His relatively new status as a gay icon has changed much of that.

Wilde's work can be seen as trivial, but even in the lightest of his work there is epigrammatic brilliance and some very shrewd social observation. A kinder view of Wilde might see him as a precursor of the Drama of the Absurd school of dramatists; in the face of the absurdity of upper-class society the only sane response is laughter. Furthermore, sentimentality and melodrama are far less evident in *Lady Windermere's Fan* than in his other plays, and this work in particular has all the elegance, structure and wit of a play by Congreve.

Above all Wilde delights in provocation, his wit and savage irony activated by any ideology or belief whose central concept is that it cannot be challenged. In being willing to challenge everything and suggest that nothing can be treated as seriously as it might wish, Wilde ironically creates an alternative system of morality where the freedom to challenge is the ultimate moral value. His work can be seen as having a strongly feminist streak, the women in his plays usually being far more impressive than the men.

It is impossible to drawn a clear dividing line between Wilde's life and his work, simply because he is one of those authors whose life turned out to be as dramatic as anything he wrote. His life does help point out a significant feature in his work, the theme of difference. Phobic attitudes to homosexuality in Victorian times forced Wilde to be the outsider. His nature challenged basic assumptions of Victorian society, made him 'different', and his plays are almost obsessive in their need to challenge what is acceptable and what is accepted. An extra level of irony is added by the fact that it is often Establishment figures in Wilde's plays who come out with the most outrageous statements. The surface glitter and wit of a Wilde play can be deceptive, a layer of reflective ice over very deep waters.

Wilde's homosexuality and the savage punishment of his sexual inclination have inevitably made him something of an icon for gay, lesbian and queer schools of criticism.

### Topics in Wilde

Wilde appears with sufficient rarity for examination to make this section a question more of what should be asked about Wilde than what is asked about him, although there are signs of a major change in this respect. The nature of his social satire and whether his work supports or opposes the upper-class society of his day is a valid area, as is the structure of his plays. The overriding question must be his worth as a dramatist. There does seem to be increasing critical interest in Wilde, suggesting he is a good choice for a project or dissertation.

## Further reading

### General


- Jean Chothia, *English Drama of the Early Modern Period 1890–1940* (Longman, 1996)
- A. Jackson, *Victorian Theatre* (A. C. Black, 1989)


### Shaw


- A. M. Gibbs, ed., Shaw: *Man and Superman and Saint Joan* (Casebook Series, Macmillan, 1991)
- Sally Peters, *Bernard Shaw. The Ascent of the Superman* (Yale University Press, 1998)
- Christopher Innes, *The Cambridge Companion to George Bernard Shaw* (Cambridge University Press, 1998)
- Margaret Morgan, *File on Shaw* (Methuen, 1989)

## Wilde

- Richard Ellman, *Oscar Wilde* (Penguin, 1988)
- Montgomery Hyde, *Oscar Wilde* (Methuen, 1990)
- Peter Raby, ed., *The Cambridge Companion to Oscar Wilde* (Cambridge University Press, 1997)
- John Stokes, *Oscar Wilde. Myths, Miracles and Imitations* (Cambridge University Press, 1996): an advanced work, but contains stimulating information on Wilde's contribution to modern literature.
- Anne Varty, *A Preface to Oscar Wilde* (Longman, 1998)
- William Tydeman, ed., *Oscar Wilde. Comedies* (Casebook Series, Macmillan, 1982)

CHAPTER TWENTY

# War literature

This chapter differs from others presented in this book because based as it largely is around the First World War and other modern conflicts, it does not describe a literary period or school, but rather a time in history. The reason for making it the subject of a separate chapter is the increasing emphasis given at Advanced and degree level to works which trace their origin back either to the First World War, or other wars. These fall into a number of categories. Firstly, there is the work of the so-called 'war poets'. Secondly, there is the work of the numerous novelists who based their novels on the First World War. Thirdly, there are the women poets whose writing was inspired by or based upon the same war. Fourthly, there is the work of populist poets writing in the First World War who are coming in for increasing critical attention after years of neglect. Fifthly, there are the dramatists whose writing was based on the war. Sixthly, there are the modern or contemporary novelists who have used the war as their inspiration. Seventhly, and perhaps riding on the back of the popularity of the First World War authors, there has been increasing interest in the poetry of the Second World War. Eighthly, and largely beyond the scope of this book, there is the work of European writers in verse and prose with either the First or the Second World War as their subject.

All this makes up a vast canon of writing and one which increasingly the student cannot ignore. The period is also interesting because it allows full expression to one of the healthiest developments to have been spawned in the United States and crossed over to Europe, namely the willingness to blur the lines between the traditional academic disciplines of English Literature and History, and even the newer ones of Sociology and Economics, and write about literature in its widest possible context, and not merely as lines upon a page. Various new words have been coined to describe this 'interdisciplinary' tendency, which is actually the reinvention of an old approach.

When E. M. W. Tillyard wrote his famous book *The Elizabethan World Picture*, many years ago, he was doing little more than stating that a study of a work of literature cannot be disentangled from a study of the time and the culture within which it was written. The 'literature' of the First World War was provoked by a specific and identifiable historical event, namely the war that broke out between European powers and which lasted from 1914 to 1918.

A third reason why this area has become so significant in recent years is that it allows for comparison of works with a shared theme or setting across the conventional literary genres of novel, poetry and drama. It also allows for comparison between works which also share a theme and setting but are separated by nearly a century in terms of when they were written.

## The literary and historical background

The First World War was a defining moment in British culture. Prior to 1914, the United Kingdom, or Great Britain as it was then more commonly known, had (as a colonial power) fought its wars at a distance. Britain had last been invaded in 1066. The last battle fought on English soil had been hundreds of years previously. Britain had evolved a small standing army, core elements of which were posted overseas and numbers made up by locally recruited 'native' soldiers. The Royal Navy, by far and away the most powerful naval force in the word in 1900, policed the Empire, fired its guns on demand at rebellious natives and kept the trade routes open. Both army and navy required relatively small number of personnel, and recruited these from a relatively narrow range of society. War was therefore a matter of prestige, influence and taxation for the average English person at the turn of the century. It was not, as it had been for very many inhabitants of the European mainland, a matter of losing one's son, husband or father, or one's wife and daughter to troops marauding through one's back yard or fields. The British had been protected from the reality of war through an involvement in it that was colonial, far away and restricted either to an 'officer class' or a low ranking sector of the working class. As a result British society glamorised war more than the majority of its European counterparts, and far more so than American society for whom the memory of appalling Civil War was too loose either for comfort or for sentimentality. 'Jolly Jack Tar' became the symbol of the Royal Navy, the equally cheerful 'Tommy Atkins' the symbol of the infantry soldier.

This cheerful naiveté about the reality of warfare was shattered by the First World War, where for the first time in its history Britain had to mobilise a massive army and engage in what we would now call total war. The modern poet Philip Larkin, writing about the lines of men queuing up patiently to enlist in the army in 1914, said much about the experience of the war when he wrote, 'Never such innocence again . . .' The First World War, in which nearly every family had a relation die or be injured, stopped Britain from ever being innocent about war again. The blitz (the bombing of civilian targets in the Second World War) and the same war's Holocaust rammed the message home.

Why did Britain go to war? A complicated system of treaties and alliances existed between the great European powers in 1914, designed ironically to stop war happening. These treaties were effectively a form of bluff, and that bluff was called in 1914. The reasons would be comic if they were not so tragic. Europe in 1914 consisted of an unstable mix of three 'types' of country. Great Britain saw itself as a colonial power, and by choice not a direct player on the European stage. It was politically stable and prosperous, and was joined as such by countries such as France and Belgium. Russia and the old Austro-Hungarian Empire were rotting from within, decaying and unstable. Germany and Italy were new countries, whose existence in a recognisable form only dated from the middle of the nineteenth century. Germany in particular had its civilian government dominated by the military, was aggressive and had tasted military success in conflict such as the Franco-Prussian war. When a Serbian student assassinated the Archduke Ferdinand, heir to the Austro-Hungarian Empire, that Empire decided to teach Serbia a lesson. Serbia had for a long time been a flash-point between the Empire and Russia, and when the Empire started to move against Serbia Russia objected and began to mobilise her forces. The Empire called on its ally, Germany, to support it.

This is where farce begins to creep in. Germany and France were traditional enemies, with France on Germany's western boundary. Russia was also a likely enemy in the event of war, on Germany's eastern boundary. Germany was fixated by the prospect of having to fight a war on two fronts in the event of a European conflict, against France in the east and Russia in the west. Germany assumed that if war broke out with one of its traditional enemies, be it France or Russia, then the other country would take advantage of this and invade in its own right. To contest this possibility it had come up with one, and only one, military plan of action in the event of a war in Europe. It was called the Schlieffen Plan, after the General who wrote it. When war looked likely Germany would invade France, bypassing its defences by hooking through Belgium on France's north-east boundary. Taking the French by surprise the Germans would first deliver a knock-out blow to France, then regroup and direct all their forces against Russia. They would thus be able to avoid having to fight a war both on their eastern and their western frontiers. Russia was not only a vast country, but also far slower to mobilise than France, so seemed the best choice for the second strike on all counts. Deciding that European war was inevitable, Germany launched an unprovoked attack on France, invading Belgium to do so. Britain was allied to Belgium and a treaty of mutual protection, and so was dragged into the war, albeit reluctantly. Thus in a space of weeks most of Europe was at war.

However, what no-one realised was the effect technology had had on warfare. Warfare tends to go in cycles. Someone invents a weapon that allows one side a huge offensive advantage, then after a while a defence to this weapon is invented and the advantage goes back to the defenders. In 1914 technology hugely favoured the defender. Barbed wire was simple, cheap and highly effective in blocking access for infantry soldiers. Bombardment and explosives tended merely to tangle it rather than destroy it. A soldier in 1914 using a bolt-action rifle could deliver 15 lethal and accurate rounds a minute up to half a mile away – put another way, the ordinary soldier armed with such a rifle could kill 15 of his enemy as they advanced towards him. His counterpart in the Napoleonic wars only 100 years earlier would have been lucky if he fired two grossly inaccurate rounds a minute. The soldier in 1914 could kill many more with the machine gun, easy to set up in defensive emplacements but impossible to fire from the hip. The defender could also direct exploding artillery shells on to his advancing enemy. If the defender also dug himself into a trench, only a direct hit from artillery could kill him yet he remained largely invisible to his attacker. As a result of this total dominance of defensive technology the war in Europe soon bogged down in trenches, with opposing armies sometimes dug in only a few metres away from each other. Vast artillery bombardments of the enemy 'line' followed by wave after wave of troops advancing 'over the top' lost millions of lives often for no advantage on the ground, or merely a few miles gained. Technology had the last laugh here again. An advancing solider could only move at walking speed. Reinforcement could be brought up to any area by railway engine at 70 or 80 miles an hour. For most of the war it was far easier to block a gap with new defenders than to fill it with advancing soldiers – the railway lines were in place behind the trench lines but were inevitably blown up in front of a line of advance by the preliminary artillery bombardment.

The result was a dreadful war of attrition. Technology eventually produced the means to break through the stalemate. Tanks could crush barbed wire and cross over trenches. Aircraft could bomb and machine-gun trenches and blow holes in a trench line for the infantry to walk through, as well as blowing up the trains bringing reinforcements. Radios could keep soldiers in contact with each other once they had left their own trenches, whereas for much of the war the only electronic communication was by telephone which needed an actual wire laid between those communicating, a wire which rarely survived a bombardment for long. However, it took four and a half years and millions of lives lost before that situation was reached.

The war was a particularly shocking experience for Britain, but was also a shattering experience for every country which fought in it. In terms of literature, the war spawned contemporary poetry and prose in very large measure, but has also continued to provoke a very significant amount of writing right up to the present time, with no sign of it diminishing. It has also created an interest in Second World War writing.

English poetry prior to 1914 was dominated by the Georgian poets (see Chapter 3). The Georgians were essentially a Romantic movement, and though in their decadent, post-war phase they appear as lacklustre nature enthusiasts their pre-war work was highly innovative in content, albeit conventional in form. Pre-war poetry could be simplistic and jingoistic, but it was also popular and accessible.

# The war poets

Poets and other writers have been writing about war for hundreds of years, but in English Literature the term 'war poets' is usually taken to mean the poets who wrote during and about the First World War. There are a number of reasons why this war of all wars produced a coherent and strong body of poetry. Firstly, English poetry in 1914 was a very *popular* medium, in that it was widely read and widely written. The First World War required vast armies, far in excess of the volunteer force that was traditional in England before 1914. The result was that vast numbers of young men who under normal circumstances would never have become soldiers enlisted in the forces, thus producing an army with a far greater number of authors in it than would normally have been the case. Poets such as Rupert Brooke, Robert Graves, Siegfried Sassoon and Isaac Rosenberg would almost certainly not have been called on to fight in any war prior to 1914, or felt that they had to volunteer.

Secondly the First World War was a static war, with the great European armies facing each other sometimes across only a few hundred yards of barbed wire, and this lack of movement made it far easier, in purely practical terms, to write poetry.

Thirdly, the experience of the war was so horrifying and so intense – and for many of the poets so utterly new to their experience – that it provoked an intensity of desire for self-expression unequalled by almost any other single event in history. There are fine war poets of other nationalities than British, and who wrote about other wars. It is only the British poets who are studied below.

Major changes are coming over the way in which the poetry of the war in particular is viewed. Some of these are provoked by new historical research which suggests, for example, that the soldiers at the Front retained their patriotism whilst it was those at home who lost it and became bitter. This is a reversal of the view that held sway for many years, and it makes poets such as Owen representative of the civilian population rather than representative of those who fought.

Are Owen and the other war poets writing about one war, or about all war? The distinction is crucial, and was the one first raised by W. B. Yeats in his controversial condemnation of the war poets. If we are to believe that the 'war poetry' is poetry limited to and about one war that took place in Europe between 1914 and 1918, then it is possibly excellent journalism but possibly not good art. The counter argument is that the war is simply the excuse for these poets to examine what are in effect some of the great themes of all time - life, death and the basic instincts that prompt and define the human spirit.

## Wilfred Owen (1893–1918)

Wilfred Owen held Shelley as one of his models, and he had Shelley's sense of mission and his vision of the poet as a prophet and legislator. The son of relatively poor parents, and dominated by his mother, Owen considered a career in the Church before enlisting. His early work is overloaded with Romantic luxuriousness, but when he was admitted to hospital in 1917 for chronic nervous shock ('neurasthenia'), brought about by dreadful experiences at the Front, he met Siegfried Sassoon (see below). This meeting, together with his own natural inclination to write more realistic poetry, led to a year in which he produced most of his finest poems. He was killed in 1918, right at the end of the war, so close to the cessation of hostilities that the telegram telling his parents of his death arrived at the family home as the church bells were ringing out to celebrate the end of the war. Owen had chosen to go back to the front, when he did not have to do so.

Owen is probably the most highly regarded of the war poets and, if this is so, it is partly because he could master very many of the different styles used by the war poets. For example, he very quickly mastered the *realistic, colloquial* and *satiric* style of much of Sassoon's work, in which a realistic poem ends with a 'hammer-blow' final line that throws the whole poem, and its meaning, into relief. 'The Letter', 'The Chances' and 'Dulce et Decorum Est' are good examples. However, Owen branched out into an *elegiac and intensely moving vein of poetry*, seen in poems such as 'Strange Meeting', 'Anthem for Doomed Youth' and 'The Send Off'. In these poems and others like them he can evoke an overwhelming sense of pity and loss, and combine the power of a personal lament with the strength of a universal complaint. 'Strange Meeting' is probably Owen's most famous poem, but a number of critics feel that 'Spring Offensive' marks the real summit of Owen's achievement.

*Pity* is often seen as the major feature of Owen's work. He was able to publish only a handful of his poems in his lifetime, and in his papers after his death an embryonic Preface and Table of Contents for a book of his poems was found. 'Pity' emerges from it as a major concern. Caution needs to be exercised here, as this has become almost a critical cliché about Owen. *The growth of an increasingly objective style* in his work has obsessed a number of critics. There is a movement in his work towards a less subjective style and tone, but the tendency to see this as an early move in the direction later taken by T. S. Eliot and the modernist movement in poetry (see Chapter 21) is not necessarily correct. Earlier poets such as Hardy had shown a capacity to write in the first person but reach an objective, distanced tone. An interesting issue in Owen springs from this, as to whether or not his work is an enforced flowering of a late-Romanticism or an early flowering of the poetry that became fashionable after the war.

Owen was a technical innovator who was very aware of sound in poetry, and he is perhaps most famous for his use of *half or para-rhyme* (see Ch. 4), and to a lesser extent for his use of *alliteration*. W. B. Yeats refused to include Owen and other war poets in an anthology he edited. One of the reasons he gave was that the poets of the First World War merely presented 'passive suffering', and that this on its own was not 'a fit subject' for poetry. A standard examination question asks to what extent *pity is the only feature in Owen's work*.

The issue of whether or not Owen was homosexual was glossed over for much of this century, not only through moral prurience but also because of family objections to any highlighting of this area of Owen's life. It is a perfectly valid question to ask whether any artist's sexuality actually matters. In Owen's case, it probably does. Just as a number of Donne's poems can be seen as love poems, with the poet being in love with God, so many of Owen's poems can be read as love poems to the young soldiers with whom he served. It is not a reading that diminishes either Owen, the subjects of his poetry or the poetry itself. In any event, *comradeship*, the bonding between men that took place under the shared stress and trial of war, has now been established as a major feature in many of the war poets. It is a crucial concept. It is perhaps the only way to explain why men such as Owen, essentially pacifist in their nature and opposed to the war, could face returning to the front line and a situation in which they knew that they would be called upon to kill the enemy. For many people, it was comradeship, the overwhelming sense of love and duty towards those left fighting, which drew them and men such as Owen back to the front.

It is not Owen's homosexuality that makes him (and many of the other war poets) so vitriolic towards women, but rather lack of experience. It is only very recently that Owen has been criticised for his attitude to women, as has Siegfried Sassoon (see below). In both men's poems women are seen as egging on the men to fight, even glorying in a war that they should condemn. Owen, Sassoon and the majority of the other war poets were young men, unmarried and without children of their own. Only someone who has never been a parent could believe that a father or a mother would sent their son off to fight without sending a part of their heart (or at least their dreams) along with him. The sense of total loss felt by women has been rediscovered as the women poets of the war have gained more and more prominence, but it is ground that poets such as Owen and Sassoon never occupied in their lives or showed in their poetry. The mothers, the lovers, the fiancées, the wives, the sisters and the daughters are increasingly coming to be seen as equal victims of the war to those who died and fought in it. The absence of any such realisation in Owen's work, and that of Sassoon and many others, reveals the extent to which this poetry was written by young men who underwent the one experience of warfare with frightening intensity, but whose sheer youth never allowed them access to the emotional hinterland occupied either by women, or by parents.

## Siegfried Sassoon (1886–1967)

Siegfried Sassoon became famous for his bitter, satirical poems with their harsh 'hammer blow' final line, already referred to above. 'The General', 'Blighters', and 'The One-Legged Man' are good examples of this style. He also wrote a number of fine poems in the *dramatic monologue* style, and these are sometimes neglected very unjustly. Few poems are as moving as his 'To Any Dead Officer' and 'Repression of War Experience'. Sassoon's novels

*Memoirs of a Fox-Hunting Man* (1928) and *Memoirs of an Infantry Officer* (1930) are also extremely famous, as are his personal exploits in the war. Known as 'Mad Jack', Sassoon was a brave and sometimes foolhardy officer, who was so pained by the war that he deliberately, and in full knowledge of the possible consequences, attempted to disavow the war and discredit it. This at least is the conventional view. There is some evidence that Sassoon was 'set up' by a particular group of people to become a martyr for the cause of pacifism, a group which took advantage of his extreme naiveté. In any event, the army was not prepared to let Sassoon make himself a martyr, and got itself and Sassoon out of what might have been a very tricky situation by declaring him a 'shell shock' victim, and hospitalising him, at which time he met Owen. He already knew and was extremely friendly with Robert Graves (see below), although the two later fell out. Sassoon is referred to in Graves's famous autobiography, *Goodbye To All That*.

Sassoon's homosexuality was widely rumoured long before it was written about, and it seems so central to his sensibility that a balanced judgement of his work is hard to come by. Sassoon is not widely set either at A-level or degree level, but he cannot be ignored by those who wish to understand better the authors who do receive more attention at Advanced-level.

## Isaac Rosenberg (1890–1918)

Isaac Rosenberg is one of the cult figures of the First World War. He was Jewish, and came from an émigré, working-class background, and as the only major poet of the war who was not an officer he occupies a unique position. It remains something of a mystery as to why he joined up, as he made a most unlikely soldier with his perennial disorganisation and lack of identification with colonial Britain. He was killed in April 1918. His platoon had been helping to resist the German spring offensive. They had left the front line but were called back to repel a breakthrough. Rosenberg was never seen again. His only publications in his lifetime were private and paid for either by himself or by sponsors, and recognition of his worth probably took longer than for any other war poet. It was not until the 1970s that he began to be recognised as a genuine and original talent. The publication of three biographies of him within months of each other in the 1970s turned him overnight from an undiscovered genius to one of the most discovered in twentieth-century literature.

To an extent attempts to make him a working-class hero are ill-founded. He was not working-class but rather a Bohemian, someone eking out a meagre living in the style of an artist and in the company of other artists. He was a painter of some distinction, although in his art and his poetry he was never able quite to bring his talents to a full realisation of their power. His poetry has a *visionary, symbolist power and fervour* that makes him unique among war poets, and which invited comparison with another London artist-poet, William Blake. His *form* is sometimes *anarchic*, and he has little control over narrative, rhyme or metre, but his *symbolic imagery* and his capacity to see the war in the *Judaic tradition* as merely another cataclysmic event in an ever-hostile and threatening world give some of his poems great power and strength. He can be appallingly obscure, and obtuse, but 'Returning, We Hear the Larks', 'Dead Man's Dump', 'Louse Hunting', 'Break of Day in the Trenches' and 'Marching' are extraordinary and outstanding poems. His *obscurity*, his use of *symbolic imagery*, his *Biblical tone* and his *objective view of war* are standard issues.

## Other poets

**Robert Graves** (1895–1985) has become a major figure in twentieth-century literature, as both a poet and a novelist. In terms of the war he has been best known for his autobiography, *Goodbye To All That.* Part of the reason is that until his death he suppressed much of his war poetry, but this is now available. As a war poet he is something of an enigma. We are denied knowledge of what many other war poets would have achieved after the war by the tragic fact of their deaths. Siegfried Sassoon, in a long post-war career, never quite managed to write in a way that captured the imagination as had his war poems. Graves went in the other direction. He has achieved a major reputation as a poet, but his war is often disappointing. 'Goliath and David' is an effective parody of a Biblical story turned to the First World War, but much of his other war poetry lacks certainty of tone. It can be argued that some of his post-war poetry, as in 'The Pier Glass', should be viewed as war poetry. It lacks the landscape and the language of the war, but has all the violence and the themes that other poets expressed in poetry more outwardly rooted in the war.

**Rupert Brooke** (1887–1915) was an extremely promising young poet and symbol for many people of all that was hopeful and promising in English letters. For many years he was remembered more as a symbol than as a poet. When he was remembered as a poet it was as a simplistic patriot, and the author of sentimental verses about England. He became exceedingly famous when he published his *Patriotic Sonnets* and died a tragic death (in uniform but not whilst actually fighting) off a Greek island. Brooke was far from being the golden-haired epitome of English manhood that was at times made out to be. He was a deeply troubled intellect of confused sexuality and a personality who was capable of tearing himself to pieces. He hardly qualifies as a war poet in that the vast majority of his poems were written before he had seen active service. His reputation as a war poet springs from the five 'patriotic sonnets', and from the fact that he was one of the first and very high-profile casualties of the war. He also had friends in high places, not least of all Winston Churchill.

Brooke may not qualify as a war poet, but he has been subject to a major revaluation in recent years and can no longer be dismissed as an apologist for patriotism. The criticism of his patriotic sonnets is that *they are not actually about England, but about Rupert Brooke*. The truth about them is that they capture a mood better than almost any other poetic writing of the time. Rather than condemn Brooke for writing self-glorifying poems about a war whose horror he ignores one can recognise that he catches a mood and expresses it with consummate skill. His other work also repays close study, not least of all the oft-maligned 'The Old Vicarage, Grantchester'. There is a resonance in Brooke's best poetry that defies its external lightness and glitter. The satiric 'Heaven' and the descriptive 'Clouds' are good examples.

**Charles Hamilton Sorley** (1895–1915) wrote a minute number of mature poems (well under forty), but included in these are some of the most mature and chilling poems written about the war. His *Letters* are also amongst the finest written by any serving soldier. He repays close study by any student working from an anthology, and is perhaps the most neglected poet of the whole war. Robert Graves described him as one of only three truly great poets killed in the war. Anthologies usually print three or four of Sorley's poems. It is well worth searching out the modern edition of both his letters and his poems.

**Edmund Blunden** (1896–1974) was the most *pastoral* of the war poets, only grudgingly altering his vision to take account of the war, but in so doing producing some magnificent reflective verse. Together with Edward Thomas (see below) Blunden has come in for renewed critical attention, not least of all because he both survived the war and continued to write compelling poetry. In surviving and continuing to write he begs comparison with Robert Graves. And another point of comparison is that both men wrote autobiographies based on the war. *Undertones of War* is discussed below. Blunden presented a problem to post-war critics. His poetry, though far from the simple and sentimental nature dirge preferred by the weakest of the Georgian poets (see Chapter 3), was based on nature, was outwardly subjective and within an unfashionable pastoral mode of writing. In addition, much of it failed to use the landscape of the war or even its language. It was about the war, yet in some ways apparently trying to avoid it. To that extent it can be compared with the poetry of Edward Thomas (see below). Much more of Blunden's 'war' poetry is available now than has previously been the case. It can be tangled, intense and tortured – but also immensely rewarding and far from simple.

**Edward Thomas** (1878–1917) was a major poet, but wrote only a very few poems with war as their specific subject. He only started to write poetry in the last two-and-a-half years of his life (he was killed in 1917), turning prose notes into verse at the suggestion of the American poet Robert Frost. Thomas's work has always commanded a near-fanatical following, but it has taken many years for it to win critical acclaim. It is deeply-rooted in a vision of English nature, and is deceptively simple. Thomas's landscape blurs past and present, producing from nature a vast canvas that can sometimes reflect human experience but more often than not dwarfs it. Nor is Thomas's work without controversy. No less an authority than *The Short Oxford History of English Literature* can cite Thomas's superb poem 'As the Team's Head Brass', and other works, as showing the war in terms of 'severances'. An alternative view is to suggest that Thomas's ruthlessly realistic view of nature makes the one point that certainly post-war society, reeling under the shock of the war, could not face or accept – that the war and its violence are nothing more or less than a recent reminder of the endemic presence of violence in nature, a violence that far from being exceptional is in fact part of the pattern of nature. There is a vast sense of loss in Thomas's poetry. This can be seen as a lament for the passing of rural England. It can be seen as a lament for the fragility and brevity of human life. 'Adlestrop' is a much-anthologised poem by Thomas.

**David Jones** (1895–1974) wrote *In Parenthesis* (1937), a prose and poetry account of the Great War centred round one Private, and considerable amounts of Welsh mythology. Something of a cult work, it has received a mixed press, but is certainly worth studying for anyone interested in the period.

Students looking for mainstream poets who have not yet found their way on to the examination syllabi in any large measure, but who are excellent material for projects, long essays or dissertations, might consider the poet and musician Ivor Gurney (1890–1937), the 'Georgian' poet Wilfrid Gibson (1878–1962), a close friend of Rupert Brooke's or the Canadian poet Robert Service (1874–1958).

## Women's poetry in the First World War

Until 1981 even many of the scholars who specialised in the poetry of the First World War had little or no realisation of the wealth of poetry written by women during, on or about the war. Then came Catherine Reilly's anthology *Scars Upon My Heart* (Virago, 1981), which brought the poetry to public attention often for the first time. This book alone dispels the view found in Owen and Sassoon's work that women during the war were idealistic and ignorant. What they *are* is harder to define than is the case with many of the male poets, because women's poetry of the period is not based nearly as heavily as the men's on a relatively small number of authors. The male poets had an element of conformity forced upon them by the shared landscape of the war, and the shared experience of being at the front line. The women wrote on a far looser basis of shared experience, and are thus more individualistic. At the same time an overwhelming sense of loss is probably the predominant impression in much of the poetry.

The student coming to this poetry needs to exercise some caution and some selectivity. There is some very weak writing from the women poets, as there is from the men. Giggly lyrics about girls doing men's work and gushing trips through a litany of the less-interesting flowers and birds are the equivalent of patriotic tub- and ego-thumping from the men and sentimental recollections of an England that never existed except in a rose-tinted imagination.

Margaret Postgate Cole (1893–1980) is one of the best-known women poets, with particular reference to 'The Veteran', 'Afterwards' and 'Praematuri'. Her poetry deals with the loss of innocence, an appalling sense of waste and the feeling that the war has brought people to the edge of the known world, facing them with an abyss of loss and horror from which there is no turning back and into which a whole generation has been hurled. May Wedderburn Cannan's (1893–1973) 'Lamplight', comparing the dreams of a young married couple, their hopes and their ambitions with the solitary fact of the man's death in war, is a classic poem of the period. Her 'Rouen' makes an interesting comparison with Owen's 'Anthem for Doomed Youth'. Cannan has technical control superior to many of the male writers of the war. The peculiar balancing act visible in some of her poetry, whereby the war is condemned by implication but not specifically, is a dual revelation. It describes the plight of those at home who felt torn apart by the war but committed to supporting in case by not doing so they let down their loved ones at the front. It shows also women straining against the passive role society afforded them at the time, achieving a tone which is emotionally rebellious yet not overtly political. Charlotte Mew (1869–1928), Alice Meynell (1847–1922) and Fredegond Shove are three other poets whose work has found its way into several anthologies, even if their worth is not recognised in enough individual volumes of their work even now. Rose Macaulay (1889–1958) can mix whimsicality with toughness, and challenge the conventions of her time whilst appearing to accept them. A major voice on the war is Vera Brittain (1896–1970), whose prose writing and in particular her *Testament of Youth* (1933) is now coming back into fashion after immense popularity in the 1930's and 1940's. She is a powerful writer, capable of being sardonic and emotional at the same time, and with a sorrowing capacity to put herself in the minds of the men who died that marks her out.

## Lesser-known and otherwise-known poets of the war

The First World War, and war literature in general, is a marvellous treasure house for those seeking subjects for long essays, projects or dissertations. Two categories of author remain largely ignored on examination and degree syllabi, but are both powerful and interesting enough to make excellent subject areas for research, with only one warning note: the student who chooses them will need access to a good library, as the one problem with this field is the occasional non-availability of texts.

This is less of a problem with the first group. These are poets, authors or personalities who achieved fame other than through writing war poetry, but who nevertheless did write some excellent war poems. One of the most obvious is Rudyard Kipling. Kipling was a fierce advocate of the war who encouraged his son to enlist. The son was last seen alive running away from the battlefield, shrieking in agony with half his face torn away. The poetry which Kipling wrote about the First World War is relatively small in terms of quantity, but powerful and sometimes searing in quality. It can also be most interestingly compared with his earlier, pre-war poems about soldiers and soldiering. A. P. Herbert (1890–1971) became famous for his work with the law, his prose work and his musicals. He wrote some outstanding war poems, a few of which are sometimes anthologised, most of them contained in *Half Hours in Helles* (Blackwell, 1916) and *The Bomber Gypsy* (London, 1919). G. K. Chesterton (1874–1936) is best known as the author of the *Father Brown* stories. His 'war' poetry is written from the viewpoint of a civilian, and whilst elliptical is very powerful and savagely satirical. J. C. Squire (1884–1958) was for many years seen as an Establishment figure and purveyor of jaded nature poetry. Again a civilian, he could exercise caustic satire as well as very effective powers of observation. Herbert Read (1893–1968) became known as a scholar and poet, but his war poems, largely contained in *Naked Warriors* (1919), are often ignored except for a few heavily-anthologised poems.

An area where texts are hard to come by but the effort is well rewarded is that of the 'popular' poets of the war, who often sold hundreds of thousands of copies of their work at the time but who have since sunk almost without trace. One example is John Oxenham (1852–1941), whose small pamphlets of poems had massive sales. Oxenham writes from a Christian stance, but he had a son at the front and whilst his poetry is clearly populist, and attempts to bring comfort to those suffering from the war, he is too good a writer for a real sharp edge not to show through in much of his work. The main pamphlets are *All's Well* (1916), *The King's High Way* (1916), *The Vision Splendid* (1917), *The Fiery Cross* (1917), *Hearts Courageous* (1918) and *All Clear!* (1919), all published by Methuen.

A very different figure is the Rev. Studdert-Kennedy (d. 1929), who wrote as 'Woodbine Willie'. Studdert-Kennedy was an Anglican padre or vicar who insisted on serving right in the front line with his men, and whose ready supply of cigarettes for his parishioners earned him his nickname, under which he published. His poems are written for the ordinary soldier and often attempt to imitate the soldier's language. A major question over his work is whether it was read by the soldiers who knew the truth about the war, or read by civilians who thought that in reading the work that was what they were reading.

## Contemporary prose works

For a number of years four prose works were identified above all others with the First World War. Henri Barbusse's *Le Feu* (1916) was translated into English in 1917 as *Under Fire*. The German Erich Remarque published *Im Westen Nichts Neues (All Quiet on the Western Front)* in 1929. Both are vivid, almost documentary accounts of the suffering of war, as written by front-line soldiers.

In English, two semi-autobiographies achieved early fame. Siegfried Sassoon's *Memoirs of an Infantry Officer* (1930) became a standard text on the war. It was itself the sequel to the very successful *Memoirs of a Fox Hunting Man* (1928), and was followed by *Sherston's Progress* (1936). All three books were published together in 1937 as *The Complete Memoirs of George Sherston.* The term 'semi-autobiography' has to be used of *Memoirs of an Infantry Officer* because the hero, George Sherston, is clearly based on Sassoon, but leaves out all mention of his poetry and his artistic endeavours and achievements. The book shows the progress of a young man brutally thrust into adulthood by the experience of serving as an officer in the war. It has suffered the fate of being relegated to a GCSE or equivalent set text, and is now far less fashionable than used to be the case. This does not mean that it has become any less valuable as a book! Part of the problem with all three George Sherston books is that they can appear relatively insipid by the side of the three 'real' autobiographies that Sassoon later produced – *The Old Country and Seven More Years* (1938), *The Weald of Youth* (1942) and *Siegfried's Journey* (1945). A comparison between the two sets of autobiography makes an interesting project.

Robert Graves's *Goodbye To All That* (1929) is also less popular than it used to be. Partly this is because Graves's reputation as a poet has grown over the years and *Goodbye To All That* has been seen something of an irrelevance in the development of Graves the poet, and a work which bears little relationship to his later successful novels such as *I Claudius* and *Claudius the God*. *Goodbye To All That* has been shown to contain as much fiction as fact, and the issue of the extent to which it is a 'true' record leads on to the far wider (and more interesting issues) of the division between fact, autobiography and fiction on a general level. Many of the prose works contained below are neither pure autobiography nor pure fiction, but blur the supposed divisions between the various forms of writing.

The good news for the student wishing to plough a relatively new furrow, or just read and write on something different, is that there are a number of other outstanding prose works of the war. Richard Aldington's *Death of a Hero* (1929) has as its theme the awful, despairing transformation wreaked on its central figure by the war, and the book catches very powerful the twin feelings of inevitability and despair found in so much war literature. In one reading the 'Hero' of the novel is society itself, the death that of civilisation by suicide. It can be argued that the book summarises the mood not so much of the war years, but rather of late 1920s and 1930s, when the Great Depression induced an almost total pessimism about the future among many writers. The novel is sometimes strongly, perhaps even too heavily, satirical, and its form had aroused some comments. Outwardly loose, and based on musical notations, it is more structured than a first reading might suggest. There is a strong authorial presence in the book. It can be criticised for being too didactic, too intense in seeking to preach a single doctrine. It can also be criticised for showing rage, and little else.

One of the most interesting novels to come out of the war is Frederick Manning's *The Middle Parts of Fortune.* It was first published anonymously in 1929 in an edition limited to 520 copies, and then an expurgated edition was published in 1930 as *Her Privates We* by Private 19022. Even in this neutered version it was a great success, the full version not being reprinted until as late as 1977. It tells in the most vivid possible detail of the life of an infantryman on the Western Front. It is written from the viewpoint of a private who is neverthless officer-class, and contains a superb social commentary as a result. The dialogue between the central figure, Bourne, and an officer about the nature of comradeship among the ordinary soldiers is outstanding and comes as near as anything to describing the intense power of comradeship that bound the army together. Manning has the balance that Aldington lacks. He can see the horror of war, but also recognise that as roses grow out of dung, so the very stress of war can produce in humans things that are beautiful and worthy. One hesitates to use the word 'unique' of any book, but *The Middle Parts of Fortune* comes very near to justifying that description.

A relatively neglected but extremely powerful book is Guy Chapman's *A Passionate Prodigality* (1933), viewed with *The Middle Parts of Fortune* by a number of commentators as a masterpiece. As with Manning's book, *A Passionate Prodigality* is not so much about war but about people. It has suffered at the hands of some modern criticism because of a displaced sense of guilt, a feeling that somehow any book that does not show its characters totally overwhelmed by the experience of war is glorifying war.

Edmund Blunden's *Undertones of War* (1928) makes an interesting comparison with *Memoirs of an Infantry Officer* or *Goodbye To All That.* Blunden, Sassoon and Graves all fought as officers in the war, all survived it and all went on to achieve distinction as poets and, in Graves's case, as a novelist. All three wrote autobiographical or semi-autobiographical prose works about their war experience. Blunden's central character is a version of Blunden himself, rather than the whole story. It is very much a work written by a poet with a deep, abiding love of nature, unsentimental and always unwilling to reach an easy conclusion. It is perhaps most interesting in its ability to present experience as it effects a young man without preaching about the outcome.

Very neglected and almost impossible to obtain nowadays is 'Charles Edmonds' (pen name for Charles Carrington) *A Subaltern's War* (1929). The book is unusual in its refusal to submit to any of the clichés of war. It portrays better than many other works the sheer excitement of serving at the Front, an excitement springing from the combination of naiveté and a belief in one's own immortality that typified so many very young officers.

Ernest Raymond's *Tell England* (1922) is in one sense typical of many post-war books, attracting the accusation of being sentimental and papering over the horror of the war. In some respects it is a prose equivalent of Rupert Brooke's patriotic sonnets. Its tone and sentimentality may not be what we as a culture have decided we ought to think about the First World War, but it is a powerful evocation of what how many people at the time chose to see the war. It is also well-written with a surprising capacity to move the reader.

The student looking for a fresh slant might turn to George Coppard's *With a Machine Gun to Cambrai* (1969). This is a prose memoir written by a working class man who was heavily engaged during the war as a machine gunner. It is not fiction and makes no attempt to be, and is an interesting comparison with many of the other prose works written during or about the war.

## Modern prose works

A significant number of modern works have used the First World War as their setting. Three of the most highly-regarded form Pat Barker's *Regeneration* trilogy: *Regeneration* (Penguin, 1992); *The Eye in the Door* (Penguin, 1995); *The Ghost Road* (Viking, 1995). The flood of novels published in 1929 or shortly thereafter often found difficulty in raising themselves above the sheer horror of the physical surroundings of the war, and often found it impossible to rise above the immediate to make any lasting statement except revulsion. Barker's books suffer from neither failing, using the background of the war almost as an emblem for the state of modern times. Her characters rise out of the experience of war, instead of simply being its victims. At the same time, there is a powerful commentary on both the First World War, and the experience of war.

Sebastian Faulks' novel *Birdsong* (1993) and Susan Hill's (1942– ) *Strange Meeting* (1973) are two highly-acclaimed modern novels based on the war. The former has yet to make the jump from GCSE to A-level syllabus with regularity, whilst the latter is still too 'popular' to have found its way on to the lists for A-level or degree courses. That should not stop the student from considering a comparison of Barker, Faulks and Hill, or a comparison between any one of them and the earlier authors noted above. Less well-known but very interesting is the *Loss of Eden* trilogy by John Masters (1914–1983): *Now, God Be Thanked* (1979); *Heart of War* (1980); *By the Green of the Spring* (1981).

## Drama

Two plays in particular have come to symbolise the dramatic response to the First World War – *Journey's End* (1928/1929) by R. C. Sherriff (1896–1975) and Joan Littlewood's *Oh, What A Lovely War!* (1963). *Journey's End* is the more conventional of the two. Set in a dug-out prior to an assault, it is a realistic, low-key anti-war play, suggesting the huge canvas of suffering by concentration on a few characters. The fact that these characters are now verging on stereotypes – the young officer brought near to breakdown by his experiences, the naïve young officer, the elderly father-figure, the traitor – are not the fault of Sherriff, but testimony to the success of books about the war. The play also manages to triumph over this, retaining its popularity over the years through taut plotting, vivid characterisation and character delineation, allied to a universal theme of loss and destruction. *Oh What a Lovely War!* is very different, an avowedly left-wing production using the pre-war 'pierrot' or clown-show as the basis for a series of sketches pouring satire on the war and its essential folly. The use of clowns is a variation of Brecht's 'Alienation Effect' (see Chapter 3), designed to keep a distance between audience and play and thus preserve both from a descent into sentimentality or pathos. Yet the distance between audience and play is reduced by the use of slides giving a historical commentary, and songs and music of the time. *Oh, What a Lovely War!* can be intensely moving as well as bitingly satirical. However, it can be argued that the play tells us more about society and culture in the 1960s than about the war itself, and the play is a useful stepping off point for a discussion about the distinction between literature and history. Works of literary art are just that, not history books. Distortion or misrepresentation of history can make as good art as it can bad history, something Shakespeare showed in *Henry IV Part 1* and *Part 2*.

## Literature of the Second World War and war literature

### Poetry

The poetry of the Second World War faced a welcome revival in the 1980s, and is now established on a number of courses. It is still sufficiently 'undiscovered' to be attractive to students searching for a long essay or dissertation subject. It differs from First World War poetry in several crucial respects. For the poets of the Second World War, war was far less of a shock than it had been to the soldiers of 1914. The experiences of the First World War had been disseminated, remembered and talked about over war memorial and school assembly hall, as well as being widely expressed in poem, novel and play. There was less of a divide between fighting men and those back home than had been the case in 1914–1918, if only because those back home were subject to German bombing and appalling loss of life as were those in the front line. Hitler was a simpler enemy than the Kaiser, simpler because Hitler seemed to symbolise raw aggression and commanded united opposition. The Second World War shattered fewer preconceptions because the First World War had left fewer preconceptions to shatter. Poets in the Second World War ranged across the class barriers more widely than their World War One counterparts. Many of them were well read, and brought up on poetry that was increasingly as complex and 'difficult' as the equivalent poetry for those in World War One had been simple and willing to give up its meaning at first glance. Finally the emphasis of war was different for many of the combatants and writers in the Second World War. There was less mass slaughter, less impersonal bombardment. Death in World War Two came more often from an aimed anti-tank round directed into the belly of a tank, the aimed bullet or the bomb delivered by the single pilot, the torpedo fired by the hand of the one commander. Death appears more personal in the writing of many Second World War poets, a conscious act as well as an accident.

Two of the best known poets of the Second World War did not survive it: Keith Douglas (1920–44) and Sidney Keyes (1922–43). Douglas felt the weight of the World War One poets press quite heavily on him. His work is ambitious, philosophical and concerned to place the war experience in a wider context. Sometimes his more immediate, front-line poems have been relatively neglected in comparison with his more reflective and sometimes consciously intellectual work. Douglas was clearly influenced by T. S. Eliot and W.H.Auden (see Chapter 21). Sidney Keyes has also a conscious 'literary' element in his work, shown by poems addressed to William Wordsworth and Virginia Woolf among others. His work will surprise those familiar with poets of the earlier wars. There is an *insouciance* and devil-may-care attitude to it, an acceptance of violence allied with a dread of it and an obsession with landscape that mark out his work as being very different.

Alun Lewis (1915–1944) was a Welsh poet, also very concerned with landscape. He may have died by his own hand. He is comparable to Edmund Blunden, in that both give the impression of being nature poets and civilians to the core, for whom service in war is an irritant and an absurdity, a dislocation from normality that at one and the same time disturbs life as well as summing it up. Lewis himself appears to have felt more of an allegiance to Edward Thomas, and there is an interesting comparison to be made between the two poets as well as with Blunden. His early work can be marred by vast abstractions. Many commentators rate Lewis as the finest poet of the war.

## Prose

Very few novels or memoirs of the Second World war have made their way on to examination courses as yet. An exception is the American author Joseph Heller's *Catch 22* (see Chapter 24). Other American war literature includes the early novel *The Red Badge of Courage* (1895) by Stephen Crane (1871–1900), and Ernest Hemingway (1898–1961) *A Farewell to Arms* (1929), the story of an ambulance driver in World War I.

Evelyn Waugh's *Sword of Honour* trilogy comprises *Men at Arms* (1952), *Officers and Gentlemen* (1955) and *Unconditional Surrender* (1961). It was published as a single work in 1965. The books are satires of English upper-class life, and illustrate the major difference between novels of the First and the Second World War. The former are usually about the war and the individuals within it. The latter are more often about individuals and wider society, with the war as a backdrop. Waugh's novels often feature an empty-headed society, with not so much a 'heart of darkness' at their centre but rather a vacuum. The individual central figure is on a pilgrimage of sorts, a search for both meaning and contentment, with an unusual emphasis on the latter. The interested student should also read *Brideshead Revisited* (1945). It is a novel based on the Second World War, but in some respects uses this as a lament for the passing of a golden age, and can be read as an account of the disillusion and bitterness that overcame British society in the aftermath of the First World War.

A popular novel that is well on the way to classic status is *The Cruel Sea* (1951) by Nicholas Monsarrat (1910–79). Those interested in personal memoirs of semi-autobiographies of the First World War might turn for comparative purposes to John Masters' *Bugles and a Tiger.*

Other modern novels with the Second World War as their base include J. G. Ballard *Empire of the Sun* (1984), Len Deighton, *Bomber* (1970), Patrick Hamilton *The Hangover Square* (1972) and *The Slaves of Solitude* (1972), Nigel Balchin *The Small Back Room* and Sebastian Faulks *Charlotte Gray* (1999). This is only a small sample from the available titles. Christopher Wallace, *The Pied Piper's Poison* (1998) is a first novel which ties in the Second World War with the European Thirty Years War, and is an interesting example of the use of the theme of war in prose.

### Drama

*This Happy Breed* (1942) by Noel Coward (1899–1973) is beginning to emerge from the opprobrium of being a patriotic pot boiler, just as Coward himself is starting to receive more and more serious critical attention. Other plays with war as either a subject or a theme are David Hare (1947– ) *Plenty* (1978), Charles Wood (1933– ) *Dingo* (1967); *No End of Blame* (1980) by Howard Barker (1946– ) and *The Long, the Short and the Tall* (1958) by Willis Hall (1929). Though not strictly about war, Arnold Wesker's (1932– ) *Chips with Everything* (1962) uses national service (compulsory enlistment in to the Army) as a means of discussing social distinctions and the class system in England.

## Further reading

There is a vast bibliography relating to war literature. This is not only because the area has received increasing critical attention over the years but also because there are so many individual authors involved. What follows is therefore biased far more than other similar entries towards 'classic' texts in the field of war literature.

## General

- A. D. Harvey, *A Muse of Fire. Literature and War* (Hambledon Press, 1998)

## Biographies

- Joseph Cohen, *Journey to the Trenches. The Life of Isaac Rosenberg* (1975)
- Eleanor Farjeon, *Edward Thomas. The Last Four Years* (Oxford University Press, 1997): an extraordinary mixture of biography and personal memoir.
- Pippa Harris, ed., *Songs of Love: The Letters of Rupert Brooke and Noel Oliver* (Crown, 1992)
- Christopher Hassall, *Rupert Brooke* (Faber, 1986): an early biography, reprinted.
- Michael Hurd, *The Ordeal of Ivor Gurney* (Oxford University Press, 1978)
- Jean Moorcroft-Wilson, *Siegfried Sassoon. The Making of a War Poet 1896–1918* (Duckworth, 1998): the only biography of Sassoon.
- Mike Read, *Forever England: The Life of Rupert Brooke* (Trafalgar, 1998)
- Miranda Seymour, *Robert Graves* (Bantam, 1997)
- John Stallworthy, *Wilfred Owen* (Oxford University Press, 1988): an award-winning and classic text.
- Barry Webb, *Edmund Blunden. A Biography* (Yale University Press, 1991)

## Anthologies

- Brian Gardner, ed., *Up the Line to Death* (Methuen, 1964)
- Catherine O'Reilly, *Scars Upon My Heart* (Virago, 1981)
- Martin Stephen, ed., *Poems of the First World War: Never Such Innocence* (Everyman/Dent, 1993)

## Criticism

- Bernard Bergonzi, *Heroes' Twilight* (Macmillan, 1980)
- Paul Fussell, *The Great War and Modern Memory* (Oxford University Press, 1975): a pioneering work.
- Dominic Hibberd, ed., *Poetry of the First World War* (Casebook Series, Macmillan, 1981)
- Samuel Hynes, *A War Imagined. The First World War and English Culture* (Bodley Head, 1990)
- John H. Johnston, *English Poetry of the First World War* (Princeton University Press, 1964): one of the first critical studies of the war poets.

- Jon Silkin *Out of Battle* (Oxford University Press, 1997)
- Martin Stephen, *The Price of Pity. Literature, History and Myth in the First World War* (Leo Cooper, 1996)

## First World War Prose

- Hugh Cecil, *The Flower of Battle. British Fiction Writers of the First World War* (Secker & Warburg, 1996)
- George Parfitt, *Fiction of the First World War. A Study* (Faber, 1988)
- Suzanne Rait and Trudi Tate ed., *Women's Fiction and the Great War* (Oxford University Press, 1997): covers an area not examined in this book.

## Second World War

- *Chaos of the Night: Women's Poetry and Verse of the Second World War* (Virago, 1984)
- Brian Gardner, ed., *The Terrible Rain. The War Poets 1939–1945* (Methuen, 1987)
- Phyllis Lassner, *British Women Writers of World War II* (Macmillan, 1998): covers work not discussed in this chapter.
- Erik de Mauny, Ian Fletcher and Norman Morris ed., *Poems of the Second World War. The Oasis Selection* (Everyman/Dent, 1985)
- Adam Piette, *Imagination at War. British Fiction and Poetry 1939–1945* (Macmillan, 1995)

CHAPTER TWENTY-ONE

# Modern and contemporary poetry

## W. B. Yeats (1865–1939)

Yeats is one of the founder-figures of modern poetry. He was both a Romantic and a modern poet. He was an Irishman with a lasting love for his country, and his early work was full of melody and decoration, luscious poetry in the Romantic and late-Romantic style. His style then began to change to something leaner, more refined and more austere. His third and final period culminated in the poem 'Under Ben Bulben', which is an epitaph for the poet written by himself, and which firmly proclaims his Irishness as a man and a poet. Yeats was also a vastly influential figure in Irish drama, although his work as a dramatist is rarely set for examination purposes.

### Issues in Yeats' poetry

#### The development of Yeats' style

Yeats' poetry falls into three readily definable categories or phases. His first period, sometimes known as the 'Celtic Twilight', is often based on Irish myth and folklore, and has a strong, mystical and dreamlike element in it, together with rich descriptive passages and a certain lack of structure. 'The Lake Isle of Innisfree', very often anthologised, is one such poem.

His second period dates roughly from 1914 to the late 1920s. In it his style tightens up considerably, and dreams are increasingly banished in favour of psychological reality and politics. His philosophical and political beliefs take the place of orthodox religion in his work.

His third and final period takes and reconciles elements from both his earlier periods, but adds something new. Poetry from this period is less public than earlier work, and often highly personal, but it also develops Yeats' theories of anarchy, violence and tragedy in human history.

It is important not to be dominated by the concept of three distinct phases in his work, much of which profits from being read as a whole. The progression of Yeats' work is much more unified than many critical discussions suggest.

**Magic, myth and folklore**

Yeats made heavy use of magic, myth and folklore in his work, frequently using figures from Irish history when he wrote. He became fascinated with spiritualism later in his life, and developed a family of symbols and recurrent images in his poetry. Full details of these are given in all good texts of Yeats' poetry. Critical opinion tends to be divided on the extent to which Yeats' interest in magic, the occult and what might now be called alternative religions helped or hindered his poetry. His metaphysical and philosophical insights are sometimes too complex or personal to be understood, and his poetry can circle downwards into nothingness as do the 'gyres' that are one of his most-used symbols, but the imagery provoked by his mysticism has a power that can operate independently of any clearly-defined meaning.

**Anarchy and joy**

Yeats came to believe in a cyclical theory of history, and in conjunction with this comes a belief in his poetry that civilisation was on the verge of collapsing into a new primitive era dominated by the simple values of strength and aristocracy. 'The Second Coming' (1921) is a chilling vision of impending death and dissolution. However, Yeats' vision is a very complex one. The anarchy and violence of dissolution is recognised and faced up to, but there is also fierce joy in the work, firstly for the power of love and generosity that life can give, and secondly because the dissolution is all part of the great cycle, a cycle which ensures growth and fulfilment even as it promises death. It is oversimplifying Yeats' complex thinking to say that he sees human life as being like the four seasons, whereby what is good returns again and again, and the winter has to be endured to ensure that return, but there is a similarity. For new life to flourish the old life has to be destroyed. In addition the inevitability of destruction creates a form of stoicism, whereby endurance and calm acceptance become major, and admirable, virtues. There is a fascination with strength and power in Yeats' work, as in 'Leda and the Swan'. Those who see this poem as 'phallocentric' have at the same time been unable to deny its power. There is gaiety in Yeats' later work, as well as terror and the fear of anarchy.

**Heart and soul**

There is a continuing concern in Yeats' poetry with physicality and spirituality, the eternal clash between man as a passionate, sensual animal, and man as a rational, aesthetic being. He can deal directly with sexual matters, and one of the reasons for the richness of his verse is the strength it draws from the clash and unity of physical and spiritual man.

**General features**

Yeats very often wrote poetry for people he knew, or about them, using these people as a starting point and often moving off from them to wider and more symbolic issues. His technical skill and his use of irony are notable.

Perhaps the most lasting features of Yeats' work are its passion and its total commitment. This makes Yeats a useful figure for the student who wishes to examine irony and its effect on modern literature, as irony is often seen as a feature that undercuts and diminishes passion and commitment to a theme or topic.

## T. S. Eliot (1888–1965)

T. S. Eliot has been seen as the most influential poet of the twentieth century, and his poem *The Waste Land* (1922) one of its most influential poems. For many years Eliot was deemed to have rescued poetry from banality, sentimentality and artificiality, and brought it into the twentieth century. There are now the occasional sounds of pick-axes chipping away at Eliot's throne from those who wonder if Eliot's values were entirely healthy for poetry in the twentieth century.

**Eliot's life**

Eliot was an American who travelled and worked in Europe, came to live in England, and eventually took up British nationality and adopted the Anglican faith. Before achieving literary fame he worked as a schoolmaster and as a bank clerk. He had a troubled personal life in his early years, and some of his early and most famous work was written when he was on the edge of complete nervous collapse. The first landmark in his career as an author was *Prufrock and Other Observations* (1917). The book was slightly ahead of its time, and received little contemporary acknowledgement, but it is an excellent point of first contact for the student coming to Eliot's works for the first time. Eliot was an excellent and still very relevant critic, and his early book *The Sacred Wood* (1920), a volume of criticism, is still worthwhile reading. His real breakthrough came with the publication of *The Waste Land* in 1922. In it Eliot pioneered a new style, a new approach and a whole new outlook, thoroughly opposed to the essentially optimistic and late-Romantic poetry that was typical of the pre-war era.

*The Hollow Men* (1925) marks the start of a strong religious element in Eliot's work, carried on in *Ash Wednesday* (1930). His verse play *Murder in the Cathedral* (1935) was explicitly religious, and his four other tragi-comic plays all have a religious element in them.

*Four Quartets* (1936) is his most complex and advanced work, and is sometimes seen as his masterpiece. These four long poems are all meditations on some of the eternal questions of human life.

## Issues in Eliot's works



### Eliot as the modern poet

Poetry before 1914 and the First World War had tended to be simple, pastoral and unadventurous, a decadent Romanticism rapidly losing momentum and the capacity to surprise. The First World War was possibly the greatest cultural shock Europe had received in hundreds of years. The appalling horror, waste and destruction of the war bred cynicism and loss of faith as avidly as crowded urban slums bred the influenza virus that was to kill almost as many people as the war in post-war Europe. Eliot reacted, possibly through a personal loss of faith, by writing poetry that was as firmly rooted in the city and modern civilisation as the Romantics had been rooted in the Lakes and the countryside. In so doing he became a spokesman for a whole generation. His early poetry in particular shows an urban civilisation in the process of an utterly sordid collapse. The extent to which Eliot's work is sordid is a favourite topic for examiners. It is as if Eliot has a driving desire to force his reader's attention down onto that which is sordid and revolting, and to debunk their expectations. A well-known example is the opening of 'The Love Song of Alfred J. Prufrock', where a conventional Romantic opening is savagely let down by a blunt modern image: 'Let us go then, you and I,/ When the evening is spread out against the sky/Like a patient etherised upon a table'. In 'Prufrock' the 'yellow fog' and 'soot' dominate the city, people have 'measured out my life with coffee spoons', and humanity is 'pinned and wriggling on the wall'.

### Loss of faith

In Eliot's early work humanity has lost heart, direction and faith in itself and what it does. His views reflect those of a society whose confidence had been shattered by a global war and suffering. He shows society as rotten, sterile, corrupt and hollow, a society with a past but no future, peopled by 'hollow men'. In his later poetry Eliot gains a faith, that of Christianity. His poetry moves from almost abject despair to the acquisition of this faith. Such faith may be stoic, bleak and occasionally bitter, but it is faith and it does offer hope and security. This movement from despair to belief is an essential topic for the student to grasp. In common with many other religious poets, Eliot can persuade us of his belief without letting us lose sight of the misery and horror which first provoked his loss of it.

### Objectivity

Pre-war poetry was largely subjective, limited to the views and outlook of one person, usually the poet, and often expressed by the poet using the 'I' mode in his work. Eliot reacted strongly against this, and said firmly that poetry should be objective, a statement culled from the poet's own observations but at the same time expressed as a universal statement that applied to all men. Figures appear in Eliot's early work, such as Prufrock, but they are not T. S. Eliot himself, and they do not monopolise the poems. Eliot therefore sought deliberately to make his poetry impersonal, and the use of irony was both a means and an end in this pursuit.

However, there is critical debate over the extent to which Eliot lived up to his avowed intentions, and some critics feel that Eliot's work shows a spiritual pilgrimage, and is far more intensely personal than either Eliot or some of his admirers admit. Certainly some of the specifically religious work, notably *Ash Wednesday*, seems to provide ammunition for this argument.

**Wilful obscurity**

Eliot believed that pre-war poetry had become too simple, and as a result was not able to express truth adequately, truth usually being complex. As a result Eliot made his poetry deliberately more difficult for the reader to comprehend. Images are thrown at the reader, as are strands of apparently unrelated dialogue, with no linking narrative and no clear thematic statement. Eliot believed that poetry did not have to be understood in order to communicate, a view that can sound ridiculous but which contains a large element of truth. Allusive and difficult are words frequently applied to Eliot's work. His reputation is being questioned somewhat nowadays, and so any candidate can expect a question on Eliot that the 'wilful obscurity' of his poetry is actually an affectation and a tedious ritual. It is worth noting that contemporary imagery lessens in his work as he gets older, and is replaced by images with more universal and recognised meaning.

**Myth**

Eliot used myths in his poetry, and also frequently alluded to other great works of literature. His own notes on *The Waste Land* are notoriously unhelpful in this respect. He believed that it was possible to draw in on the reader a whole battery of impressions by referring to other evocative works of literature and to lines within them. Thus when Eliot writes 'The Chair she sat in, like a burnished throne' he is making a reference to Shakespeare's *Antony and Cleopatra* and the famous speech in which Enobarbus describes Cleopatra's sensual magnificence, and the reader who knows the original is able to graft onto Eliot's lines at least some of the power of Shakespeare's. This can be seen as a type of literary shorthand, though of course it rests on the reader's awareness of the original for its full effect.

Eliot uses the Holy Grail legend and the myth of the Fisher King as a basis for some of his poems. The way in which these myths relate to what Eliot wrote and their effect on his work require detailed study, which is available in many of the dissections of Eliot's poetry that are available in bookshops.

**Sexuality**

A common theme in Eliot's work is that of sterile sexuality, as a symbol of fertility turned sour and of a society that has ceased to breathe and grow, and which has lost its capacity for passion and excitement.

**'Objective correlative', 'dissociation of sensibility' and 'fruitful ambiguity'**
These phrases, the first two of which at least are Eliot's own, are sometimes found in discussions of Eliot's work. The idea of an 'objective correlative' is, in its simplest form, the finding of an outside, exterior object that will sum up and suggest a given feeling to the reader. In other words choice of imagery or the 'chain of events' will produce an exact and precise response from the reader, an external provoker of a specific and predetermined inner feeling and response. 'Dissociation of sensibility' is little more than another word for objectivity, and 'fruitful ambiguity' is the concept that an ambiguous image or phrase can profit from the wealth of associations it can create.

**Motifs**
Eliot is also well known for the motifs in his work, that is the running images which recur time after time throughout a long poem, or sometimes over several poems and books.

## Other modern poets

A wide range of other modern poets are set by examination boards, of which some of the most popular are studied below. Degree-level courses tend to range further and wider, and dabble rather more adventurously in the work of living poets.

## W. H. Auden (1907–73)

Criticism still seems unsure of Auden's status. He produced no major, dominating work such as Eliot's *The Waste Land*, and it has been suggested that he 'dried up' and failed to write effectively after 1940. Auden was a brilliant poetic technician, and as always this has been used to suggest that he covered up slight content with great technical skill. However, he seems to be making a comeback in popular readership, something which usually presages a critical revival.

**Auden's early work**
There is a strong influence in Auden's early work from the great psychologist Freud who was becoming fashionable and well-known in the 1920s and 1930s, and a considerable Marxist influence is also visible. Auden became a Christian in his later life as did Eliot, though, unlike Eliot, Auden moved from England to America, rather than the other way round. With Auden's conversion comes a declining and eventually vanishing interest in Marx and Freud. The Marxist influence leads to a great feeling of change and destruction in his early poetry, much use of the frontier as an image and a fascinated and loving attachment to what is being destroyed. Above all a feeling of change permeates the early poetry.

**Later poems**

In his later poetry more humility is visible as his religious beliefs become more pronounced. As was the case with many of his generation, and generations before him, Auden seems to set out on a moral and spiritual quest, a search for roots, and a political, social and psychological answer is replaced by a religious one, and by the surrender of the poet to a greater being in God. His poetry becomes more reflective, urbane and discursive, leading to suggestions that in his later years he lost impetus and gained complacency. Questions are sometimes asked on Auden's sterile period, dating from 1940 onwards.

## General points

Conflicts abound in Auden's earlier work, and images of violence and destruction. He has been criticised for what some readers see as heavy moralising and a tendency to lecture the reader. He has a tendency to create his own words (as did Thomas Hardy), and to re-use lines from one poem in another. The majority of his ideas are not markedly original, and a sense of uncertainty is present in much of his verse.

**Suggested poems**

A good introduction to Auden's work is contained in the following poems: 'The Watershed', 'Ode (Which Side Am I supposed to be On?)', 'O What Is That Sound', 'As I Walked Out One Evening', 'Roman Wall Blues', 'Musée des Beaux Arts', 'In Memory of W. B. Yeats', 'A Walk After Dark', 'In Praise of Limestone', 'The Shield of Achilles', 'Bucolics (Lakes)', 'Cave of Making', 'Geography of the House', 'Enconium Balnei', and 'Vespers'. A number of the above poems show Auden's use of the ballad technique, a notable feature of his work.

## Philip Larkin (1922–85)

Philip Larkin represents a development in British poetry of the 1950s, namely the rise of an anti-heroic, 'all illusions gone' school of thought. Truth is emphasised at all costs, and a deliberate attempt made to remove all glamour from situations and people. The Church, childhood and Nature are presented in a manner that shows them without any sentimentality or illusions, and the approach is dry and matter-of-fact.

Larkin wrote two novels, *Jill* (1946) and *A Girl in Winter* (1947), and a volume of essays on what was a lifelong passion, *All That Jazz* (1970). His reputation rests on four volumes of poetry: *The Less Deceived* (1955), *New Lines* (1956), *The Whitsun Weddings* (1964), and *High Windows* (1974). His output is remarkably small, its quality remarkably high. From the outset Larkin delighted in the use of colloquial language, but he has a remarkable skill of blending this in with 'bitter lyricism', and, though a first reading might not suggest it, he is a superb technical craftsman. He has a capacity to write about what is normal and everyday and infuse it with both melancholy and insight. One of his best-known poems, 'Toad', describes work as a toad squatting on his (and our) lives, but in the poem and the later 'Toads Revisited' Larkin's anger is negated by an acceptance of what is and must be. His envy of gypsy families, their freedom and their capacity to flout the conventions is brought to heel by his own realisation that he has neither the courage nor, in the final count, the desire to break free. Indeed, the attraction and security of the mundane both reassures Larkin by its removal of the necessity for action, but also frightens and even disgusts him.

**Sociological comment**

Larkin has been accused of snobbery, and *The Whitsun Weddings* in particular wrinkles its nose up at working-class vulgarity, cheap jewellery and loudness. Those who see snobbery in this fail to realise that Larkin's disgust for middle-class values is no less strong. He perceives all that is cheap and not lasting and is offended by it, yet at the same time he accepts its inevitability. He can afford things such as the wedding parties in 'The Whitsun Weddings' some little dignity, as humans at least trying to pretend to have a degree of happiness and control over their lives. The mixture of defiance, bitterness and a lyrical yearning for what might have been, implied but rarely directly stated, gives Larkin's work great power.

**Death**

Larkin's later work is more obsessed by death, both as something which will inevitably affect the writer, and also as a symbol of transience. Transience as a theme runs throughout Larkin's poetry, linked to a search for what is valuable and meaningful in life. Larkin's capacity to ask very profound questions and his courage in not pretending to have answers give his work a distinctive flavour.

**Cynicism**

Larkin can be very cynical, but his approach does not mean an automatic denial of anything good or valuable existing in the world. Sometimes the true worth of an object or institution emerges once its superficial appearance has been stripped away. Larkin refuses to be romantic about life, or to put down views that are more attractive and comforting than true.

**Humour**

Larkin can laugh at himself, and this helps stop the poems from becoming too cold and analytical. A distancing irony is often visible when the poet appears to be speaking in his own voice, though often the poet is used simply as a recorder of experience rather than the presenter of one person's view of it. The poet emerges as more normal than heroic, and it is the object being described that matters, not the poet. Where the author's subject is his own inadequacy it can be said that the poems lose energy and bite. He uses the traditional metres and stanza forms of English poetry.

Those hostile to Larkin's work point out that it can be seen as' poetry of disillusion', and that Larkin has a remarkably capacity not to be excited by anything.

## Ted Hughes (1930–1998)

Ted Hughes, erstwhile Poet Laureate, was a poet very concerned with the forces of Nature and their interaction with man. A terrifying sense of the violence of Nature emerges in poems such as 'Pike' or 'Thrushes', and his vision of Nature is totally without sentimentality. It is possible, though not always productive, to link this violence to the growing concern with violence of the twentieth century.

Ted Hughes was married to the poet Sylvia Plath when she committed suicide. After years of silence about his marriage, during which Plath became something of an icon and Hughes something of a villain to Plath's supporters for his role in her suicide, Hughes published a sequence of poems about his relationship which received great critical acclaim and went immediately on to the best-seller lists. It seems likely that Hughes allowed the work to be published knowing of his impending death.

### The natural world

The elements in Hughes' verse have a mindless strength, not directed with any personal animosity against man, but perhaps all the more terrifying because, like Hardy's Immanent Will, they are unaware of man's existence. The violence in animals impresses Hughes because it is given strength and power by the single-mindedness of the animals. Unlike human beings they have no conscience or rational thinking capacity to hold them back from action. They are perfect in their simplicity and their design for survival, and therefore in a strange and disturbing sense more fitted for survival than man, and more powerful. Hughes can also see this single-mindedness as a limitation or narrow-mindedness, as in 'Hawk'.

### Time

Hughes is very aware of the length of time which animals and the forces of nature have had on Earth. Their vast legacy of history also gives them an advantage over man, and sometimes causes in Hughes a feeling of alienation (one of the most common themes in twentieth-century literature). Man is a newcomer.

### Realism

As with many modern poets, Hughes' outlook is totally unsentimental, and his concern is to show the reader a situation as it really is, not as the reader or poet might like or wish it to be.

### Myth and 'Crow'

In his later work Hughes has become increasingly involved with myth and legend, seeking to retell the Creation story from the predatory, bloody viewpoint of Crow, a potent and major symbol in his work. He has also experimented with an invented language in a play, *Orghast* (1971), and written a number of works for children. Hughes' work is almost at odds with the urbane, gently despairing bitterness of a poet such as Larkin. Some rather unconvincing attempts have been made to link Hughes' work and its popularity with the growing significance of green movements and concern with ecology. Equally, he has been attacked for the violence in his work, and for what has sometimes been seen as brutality.

## The Liverpool poets

The Liverpool poets were a group who came to prominence in the 1960s, at the same time as the rock music revival was peaking in what was seen as its originating town, Liverpool. The Liverpool poets were in part a move away from the academic, obscure and drily private work of poets such as T. S. Eliot. For them poetry was a performance art, frequently funny and very public. It was also primarily urban, often scurrilous and anti-establishment.

**Roger McGough** (b. 1937), **Adrian Henri** (b. 1932) and **Brian Patten** (b. 1946) are the poets most commonly associated with the group. McGough is frequently very funny, with an excellent sense of rhythm and an eye for the unusual or the bizarre. Some of his poetry revolves round the twin pillars of pathos and bathos, both usually well under control. Henri is rather wilder, marginally more academic and seeking a profundity and depth which his technique does not always allow him to achieve. Arguably the most interesting of the three is Brian Patten. Coming from a working-class background and with what would generally be regarded as a poor education, straightforward lack of vocabulary led his early work to be extremely simple as regards diction and structure. This, combined with real lyric passion and a very shrewd eye for details of imagery, produced poetry that was as approachable as that of his colleagues, but more firmly in a classic, Romantic vein of English writing. Patten's work has continued to grow in strength and maturity.

## Seamus Heaney (b. 1939)

At first sight Seamus Heaney bears comparison with Ted Hughes. Heaney's early work was concerned with rural matters, animals and the frequent violence of Nature, though in his case from an Irish background. However, the comparison is in part misleading. Heaney's work is strongly evocative of the physical environment, and his imagery is superb in its power and brevity, but there is a warmth of characterisation in Heaney's poetry, an awareness of humanity as rather more than a trembling witness of Nature's power.

Heaney's reputation was established with the publication of *Death of a Naturalist* (1966). It is a feature of Heaney's early work that the title of a poem frequently provides a key to its meaning. Thus the poem 'Death of a Naturalist' is about a young child whose vision of Nature is drastically altered by the sight of young animals being drowned, the 'death' referred to in the title. Heaney's later work has become obsessed with language and words, become darker and more forbidding and also harder to read. Notable books are *North* (1975) and *Field Work* (1979). Culture, politics and anthropology are all woven together in Heaney's writing, to powerful if occasionally obscure effect. The Irish influence in Heaney's work is significant, though stated with varying degrees of strength. Politics and other surface themes in Heaney's work are, however, rarely ends in themselves, and more often an excuse to explore basic aspects of the human condition.

Part of Heaney's success is down to the fact that, in common with many other modern poets, he is a superb performer and reader of his own work. Of all the poets who tour with their work Heaney has the highest reputation. This is not only because of his natural ability, but also because some of Heaney's work takes on an extra dimension when read aloud.

## John Betjeman (1906–1984)

John Betjeman was appointed Poet Laureate in 1974, and is a quintessentially English poet. He can be dismissed rather too easily as a light satirist and commentator on the social scene; he is far more. His command of rhythm, metre and rhyme is exceptional. He is a satirist, but also a poet of place with a powerful capacity to evoke atmosphere. Nostalgia in his work can become something more than remembered sentimentality, and verge on a lament for dying glory. Mortality is a major theme in his work, rather like a long, bass line played on a 'cello beneath the main melody.

## Tony Harrison (b. 1937)

Tony Harrison contains in the one body of work two apparent contradictions – the voice of the 'classical', educated and informed poet, and the voice of local, working-class verse. His work has a huge energy which sometimes spills over into anarchy, excess or sentimentality, but it is an energy which through public performance as well as the written word allows him to reach a mass audience. His conviction that poetry is public art does not stop him from writing, on occasion, intensely personal lyrics.

## Other poets

**R. S. Thomas** (b. 1913) is another poet concerned with the harshness of Nature. In his case this awareness springs from working as a clergyman in isolated rural communities, stripped of warmth, love or vigour. The result is powerful verse that interweaves images of physical rigour and harshness with religious symbolism, though he lacks the ability that Heaney has to send a symbol right through to the heart of the subconscious. Thomas is interesting in his own right, but also useful for students searching for a topic on which to write a project or dissertation: Hughes, Heaney and Thomas are an obvious triumvirate for study, similar enough to be linked but also interestingly different.

**George Macbeth** (1932–92) was another excellent performance poet, sometimes macabre and violent but more and more thoughtful in his later years. He wrote experimental work in 'sound' poetry, but his work became less comic and experimental as he grew older.

**Geoffrey Hill** (b. 1932) is an academic poet writing deeply symbolic and tightly packed poetry; violence, history and religion are his themes, and he has a deeply committed following in academic circles.

**Stevie Smith** (1902–71) has a cult following, but criticism seems unable to decide whether her calculated childishness is naïve art, or simply naïve.

Other poets include **Donald Davie** (b. 1922), **D. J. Enright** (b. 1920), **Elizabeth Jennings** (b. 1926), **Andrew Motion** (b. 1952), Poet Laureate in 1999, **Peter Porter** (b. 1929) and **Thom Gunn** (b. 1929). This brief selection is not all-inclusive, and does not cover a large number of younger poets who have yet to make their way on to examination or university syllabuses.

## Further reading

### General

- Neil Corcoran, *English Poetry Since 1940* (Longman, 1993)
- Cary Day and Brian Docherty, *British Poetry from the 1950's to the 1990's Politics and Art* (Macmillan, 1997)
- R. P. Draper, *An Introduction to Twentieth-Century Poetry in English* (Macmillan, 1998)
- A. E. Dyson, ed., *Three Contemporary Poets: Thom Gunn, Ted Hughes and R. S. Thomas* (Casebook Series, Macmillan, 1990)
- David Perkins, *A History of Modern Poetry, Volumes 1–2* (Belknap Press, 1987)
- Anthony Thwaite, *Poetry Today: A Critical Guide to British Poetry 1960–1984* (Longman, 1996)

### Auden

- Ronald Carter, ed., *Thirties Poets: 'The Auden Group'* (Casebook Series, Macmillan, 1984)
- Richard Davenport-Hynes, *Auden* (Mandarin, 1996)

## T. S. Eliot

- Peter Ackroyd, *T. S. Eliot* (Penguin, 1993)
- Bernard Bergonzi, ed., *T. S. Eliot: Four Quartets* (Casebook Series, Macmillan, 1969)
- C. B. Cox and Arnold P. Hinchliffe, ed., *T. S. Eliot: The Waste Land* (Casebook Series, Macmillan, 1969)
- David A. Moody, *Thomas Stearns Eliot, Poet* (Cambridge University Press, 1994)
- Tony Sharpe, *T. S. Eliot. A Literary Life* (Macmillan, 1991)
- B. C. Southam, ed., *T. S. Eliot: Prufrock, Gerontion, Ash Wednesday and Other Shorter Poems* (Casebook Series, Macmillan, 1978)
- Ron Tamplin, *A Preface to T. S. Eliot* (Longman, 1987)

## Tony Harrison

- Neil Astley, ed., *Tony Harrison* (Bloodaxe Critical Anthologies, Bloodaxe Books, 1999)
- Sandie Byrne, *H, v, & O. The Poetry of Tony Harrison* (Manchester University Press, 1998)

## Seamus Heaney

- Michael Allen, ed., *Seamus Heaney* (New Casebook Series, Macmillan, 1997)
- H. Cocorran, *Seamus Heaney* (Faber, 1986)
- Thomas C. Foster, *Seamus Heaney* (O'Brien Press, 1989)

## Ted Hughes

- Paul Bentley, *The Poetry of Ted Hughes. Language, Illusion and Beyond* (Longman, 1998)

## Philip Larkin

- Stephen Regan, ed., *Philip Larkin* (New Casebook Series, Macmillan, 1997)
- Terry Whalen, *Philip Larkin and English Poetry* (Macmillan, 1990)

## W. B. Yeats

- Keith Aldrett, *W. B. Yeats. The Man and the Milieu* (John Murray, 1997)
- Elizabeth Cullingford, ed., *Yeats: Poems, 1919–1935* (Casebook Series, Macmillan, 1984)
- R. F. Foster, *W. B. Yeats: A Life: 1. The Apprentice Mage* (Oxford University Press, 1997)

- A. Norman Jeffares, *A New Commentary on the Poems of W. B. Yeats* (Macmillan, 1984)
- Alasdair D. F. Macrae, *W. B. Yeats. A Literary Life* (Macmillan, 1994)
- Jon Stallworthy, *W. B. Yeats: Last Poems* (Casebook Series, Macmillan, 1968)
- Deidre Toomey, *Yeats and Women* (Macmillan, 1997)

CHAPTER TWENTY-TWO

# The modern and contemporary novel

## Rudyard Kipling (1865–1936)

Rudyard Kipling invented the phrase 'the white man's burden', using it to describe both the strain and the duties of Empire. Born in India and sent over to England for seven years to be educated (to his great unhappiness), Kipling was a prolific poet, short story and novel writer. Many of these works had aspects of the Empire at their heart. In his own time he was seen as being cynical about the Empire and its consequences. Until recently he has tended to be seen as jingoistic and prone to a simplistic sentimentality about colonialism, and the military paraphernalia that feeds Empire. He is now often revalued, and his work seen for the complex entity that it is – a part of Empire, an objective and often critical observer of it but also moved by it. A radical view is that Kipling does not comment on Empire, any more than many of the war poets comment on the First World War. It is simply too large and overwhelming an experience, the result of which is that Kipling observes the experience of Empire through its victims and its leaders, its servants and its masters. One might ask if Kipling's work is about Empire, or if it simply uses Empire to discuss the lasting features of human life.

In novels, Kipling is best known for *Stalky and Co.* (1899), based on his own school experiences, and *Kim* (1901), about an orphaned child who serves two masters – a Tibetan Lama and the British Empire. His short stories have achieved even more fame. *Departmental Ditties* (1886), *Plain Tales from the Hills* (1888) and *Soldiers Three* (1890) are collections of his journalistic writings. His collection of tales for children – *The Jungle Book* (1894) and *Just So Stories* (1902) – are justifiably famous. His book of poems, *Barrack Room Ballads* (1892), was an immediate success.

# Joseph Conrad (1857–1924)

Kipling makes an interesting contrast to Conrad. Both produced works based on Empire and the exercise of power, but Conrad's awareness of the extent to which power corrupts, and the sense of corruption in his work, far exceeds that found in Kipling.

Joseph Conrad's father was a Polish writer and nationalist who was exiled in Russia. Joseph was orphaned at eleven years of age, and did not learn English until he was twenty. He spent a number of years at sea in various merchant navies, eventually obtaining his master's certificate after a maritime career that included gun-running and an attempted suicide. His novels show that his knowledge of the sea, and his service in Africa, were a lasting influence. He was dogged by ill-health for most of his life, and did not begin to achieve real fame until as late as 1913, with the publication of *Chance*.

Conrad's work Conrad's most famous novels are *The Nigger of the Narcissus* (1898), *Lord Jim* (1900), *Heart of Darkness* (1902), *Nostromo* (1904), *The Secret Agent* (1907), *Under Western Eyes* (1911), and perhaps *Victory* (1915). It is generally agreed that his earlier work is tentative, and that there was a marked falling-off in standard in his last years. There is considerable disagreement over the quality and standing of *Chance* and *Victory*.

## Issues in Conrad

Many of Conrad's novels are based on the classic adventure story, but they rarely end at that. He is a master of complex narrative techniques and such devices as time-shifting or flashback, and the presentation of changing viewpoints.

Conrad has a fascination for situations that are extreme and which test humans to their uttermost limits. His characters do not always survive that test, one of the most famous examples being Kurtz in *Heart of Darkness*, who is found to be 'hollow at the core' and thus crumbles under intense pressure. Conrad stated that fidelity is one of the prime human virtues, though it is open to debate whether or not this is always carried through into his novels. It is certainly quite easy to see the genesis of Conrad's interest in his early life. When he was young, Conrad had to fight both himself (witness his attempted suicide) and an external force, namely the violence of Nature known to every seafarer (and, one might add, the violence of the relatively primitive societies to which he was exposed as a sailor). This feature of a twin battle runs strongly through much of Conrad's work, and his characters have to fight themselves as well as external forces. Depending on one's viewpoint, there is either a clash or a fruitful blend between two outlooks in Conrad's work. He is a Romantic author in his search for inner truth, certainty and insight within a man, in his belief that in the final count what we all rely on is what we carry within us, and in his fondness for mystery. A distinctly modern sensibility emerges in the uncertainty that is prevalent in his novels, the sense of corruption and the feeling of a society that has lost direction and purpose. There are obvious comparisons to be made here with another modern author, T. S. Eliot (see previous chapter).

Conrad's weaknesses are a tendency to present a rather vague, wordy and insubstantial Romanticism, his inability to present effectively love relationships and women and a slight tendency to oversimplify. His strengths are the taut control he can wield over a novel, his penetrating and mystic insight into the heart of modern man and the sheer power of the vision he can create. It is interesting to note that he is becoming increasingly admired for the political insight of his novels. Regardless of the specifically political element in a work such as *Heart of Darkness*, in which the colonial system is rigorously examined, the feeling of incipient and ever-present anarchy that permeates a novel such as *Under Western Eyes* is noteworthy and remarkable. There is a hint in this of the fear expressed by W. B. Yeats, and even W. H. Auden (see Chapter 21), but in the early novels it is compensated for by an awareness of some men's inherent strength. Postcolonial critics have pointed out Conrad's horror of Empire allied to complicity with it on the part of many of his characters. It is perhaps this duality in Conrad's vision that helps to make betrayal such a strong theme in his work.

## D. H. Lawrence (1885–1930)

David Herbert Lawrence was the son of a coal miner and a woman who had once been a schoolteacher. With the help of scholarships he worked his way to becoming a schoolteacher himself, eventually giving this up in order to become a full-time writer. His mother, a strong influence on his work, died in 1910 and in 1912 he eloped with and married the wife of a professor at Nottingham University College. He travelled widely with his wife, but was forced to leave England in 1916 in the middle of the First World War, because of his anti-war views and the fact that his wife was a German. His later years were spent mainly in Italy.

Lawrence was a poet as well as a novelist, but he is still most widely known for his prose work. The novels most often set for examination purposes are *Sons and Lovers* (1913), *The Rainbow* (1915) and *Women in Love* (1921). Another famous novel was *Lady Chatterley's Lover* (1928), a novel which contained explicit description of sexual acts, and equally explicit language. This novel was the centre of a famous law case in the 1950s, and the winning of that case by the publishers marked an effective end to censorship of the arts in Great Britain. The question asked of the jury by the prosecuting counsel in the case, to the effect of whether or not the jury would like or permit one of their wives or servants to read such a novel, has also become famous, as a symbol of an age that was already past in the 1950s.

Lawrence was a man on a self-confessed mission to liberate society from its social and moral chains, with sexual liberation a particular concern. One of very few major English authors to achieve lasting fame from a working-class background, Lawrence is a fascinating subject for that part of modern criticism which is interested in social and political issues, but Lawrence has provided more of a meal for feminist criticism. A man dedicated to a form of liberalisation for the sexual urge and women who also held views which saw the male spirit as typified by 'movement' and the female by 'inertia' is challenging all those with a view on gender, whatever their stance.

## Topics in Lawrence's novels

### Sexuality

Lawrence saw sexuality as a driving force in human relationships. He believed in love as a passion and a force that was both releasing and inexorable, but also believed that love must be felt and created on an instinctive level; as a passion it cannot answer to rationality or reason. It has been said that there was sexual tension in Lawrence's family, as a result of the blend it contained of working-class and middle-class attitudes to sexuality. Tension in sexuality is certainly a feature of Lawrence's work, and the whole movement in his work is towards a wholeness of personality that has at its heart the free expression of sexual desires. However, a concern with sexuality can, in one sense at least, be a misleading description of Lawrence's aims and ideals. He operated on a wider scale which took into account and presented the whole nature of the relationship between man and woman, physical and spiritual.

Lawrence's concern for this area of human experience can lead him into relatively ineffective writing. Sometimes his search for a mystical union in sexuality leads to writing that is incomprehensible and tedious. Sometimes his use of sexual symbolism and imagery is heavy-handed to a modern eye, as is his whole attitude. Lawrence was pioneering freedom of expression in this field, but now that the pioneering has been done and victory, if that is what it is, won, Lawrence's insistence on the importance and almost religious significance of sexual relationships can appear strident and even monolithic.

### Industrialisation

Just as Lawrence was against sterility in relationships so was he against it in society. The area of Nottinghamshire in which he was brought up was a close and harsh contrast between industrial and rural life, with the two side by side. The coal miner on his short walk home from the pit could, and still can, be walking through relatively unspoilt countryside only a few minutes after having left the tips, waste and filth of an industrial site. Like many authors before and after him Lawrence noted the contrast between lifestyles in the old and the new industrial order, and saw industrialisation as a threat to natural, fulfilled life. In this sense he was involved in a search for regeneration, a feature very familiar to anyone widely read in twentieth-century literature.

**The working man**
Lawrence saw the working or lower classes as having a more natural, stronger and fulfilled attitude to life than that held by fashionable society. The working man has his roots and his attitudes firmly placed, is more attuned to the realities of life than the fashionable middle or upper classes. The realism of Lawrence's novels is often noted, and his presentation of working-class life. In his later years his frustration with the established order led to a belief in strength that some authorities have seen as fascist, though this is best seen as an interpretation rather than an established fact. Lawrence's novels blend industrial and rural settings magnificently. He has excellent descriptive powers, both of character and setting, a feel for history, and a passionate, Romantic search for an ideal that can be inspiring, and only rarely tails off into excess.

**Frustrated desire**
The frustration of desires is another strong theme in Lawrence's work. Its sexual application is obvious, but it has a far wider application than that, leading to Lawrence's passionate yearning for a new, purer and more simple order.

## E. M. Forster (1879–1970)

E. M. Forster was educated at public school and Cambridge, and though he lived to 1970, the novels on which his fame is largely based were written before the First World War. These are *Where Angels Fear to Tread* (1905), *A Room With A View* (1908), *Howard's End* (1911), and *A Passage to India* (1924). He is also the author of the highly acclaimed critical work, *Aspects of the Novel* (1927). His homosexual novel *Maurice* was finished in 1914, but at his insistence not published until after his death, in 1971.

### Issues in Forster's novels

Forster was once memorably described as 'a guerrilla in a pin-stripe suit'. He has an urbane, intellectual and ironic style that blends interestingly with a rebellious attitude to Christianity and European inhibition. His homosexuality may well have spawned some of his feelings about English inflexibility.

Forster is something of a puzzle for those who seek easy answers. There is a reforming passion in his work, but also a shrewd capacity to observe and be detached. Thus in *A Passage to India* he can admire the Hindu attitude with its emphasis on mental and physical freedom, at the same time as spotting that the inflexible approach of the British at least has the virtue of producing decisions and a grip on power. He refuses to idealise. His heroine in *A Passage to India* recognises the freedom in India, but her response to it brings trouble and disaster in its train. Life is rarely simple in Forster's novels. Forster is the third novelist in this chapter whose work reveals the clash and battle between English culture and the culture of colonised nations, testimony if nothing else to the significance of Empire in English writing and the validity of postcolonial critical theories.

*Howard's End* looks from a different viewpoint to that of D. H. Lawrence at encroaching urbanisation. Howard's End is a house in the country but threatened by, and within sight of, the encroaching tide of suburban, anonymous housing. Its theme is voiced by its heroine; 'Only connect'. The heroine has her roots in the country rather than in the shallow, brash and angry world of the town, and in Forster's work, as in so many twentieth-century writers, there is a feeling of fear and impending doom created by the onward march of 'civilisation'. Civilisation is, to Forster, a state of mind and an attitude, not a telephone or automobile.

## Virginia Woolf (1882–1941)

Virginia Woolf shared at least one feature with E. M. Forster, which was membership of the 'Bloomsbury Group'. This was a collection of individuals who met or lived in the London district of Bloomsbury to exchange ideas, and it was a haven for intellectuals who otherwise found little support in English society between 1918 and 1939.

Virginia Woolf's 'modern' ideas, her suicide by drowning in 1941, and the strange isolation of her life have made her both an enigma and a figure of considerable attraction for modern writers. Her best-known and most frequently set works are *Mrs Dalloway* (1925), *To the Lighthouse* (1927), and sometimes *The Waves* (1931).

### Issues in Virginia Woolf's novels

**Victorianism**

The Bloomsbury group were in deliberate and knowing revolt against Victorian literature and its taboos, among which, of course, were the restrictions it placed on the discussion of sexuality. Victorian novelists often examined society; Virginia Woolf examines individuals. The Victorian novel was sometimes rumbustious and painted in broad strokes of characterisation and incident: Virginia Woolf's novels are delicate, finely shaded portraits of individual personalities. A comparison between a late Dickens novel and *To the Lighthouse* shows more effectively than any critical commentary just how far Virginia Woolf had moved away from Victorian ideals and style.

**Streams of consciousness**

Virginia Woolf is famous for her use of the stream of consciousness technique (see Ch. 3). *Mrs Dalloway* presents one day in the life of Mrs Dalloway, and attempts to recreate the stream and pattern of her thoughts and feelings from a totally internal viewpoint. The focus on the inner working of one woman's mind makes Mrs Dalloway a central character and a central novel for a number of feminist critics. Past experience, and hence a broader picture, is brought in by flashbacks and reference to past experience. A denial of chronological time could be seen as an emblem of the Bloomsbury Group's willingness to challenge all form and convention: time is, arguably, the most binding form of all.

**The individual and communication**

Virginia Woolf's novels show a feeling for privacy, a need for the mind to exist within its own parameters and to be freed of intrusion into that private world. They also show the need and sometimes the driving desire to communicate, and the desire for the type of certainty that can only be brought to a mind through its relationships with the outside world and other people. Thus communication in all its forms is a significant theme in her work, as in that of many twentieth-century writers. In many instances the issue of communication becomes a theme of non-communication, the inability of humanity to 'only connect' in the manner urged in Forster's *Howard's End.*

**Symbolism**

As a writer who rarely has a secure vision of reality and the external world, the ambiguity, suggestiveness and uncertainty of symbols are an obvious attraction to Virginia Woolf, particularly as each symbol can take on a different meaning for the person who looks at it, thus emphasising the uniqueness of each individual and the distance that can exist between them, even when gazing on external and shared reality. The lighthouse in *To the Lighthouse* shows this symbolism at work.

**Coarseness and narcissism**

Virginia Woolf has been criticised for her over-refined sensibility, and her capacity to ignore coarse and hard-grained reality in her novels. Some readers see her as too delicate and subtle, too concerned with fine shading and too little concerned with the broad spectrum of colours. She has also been seen as self-indulgent, a figure so wrapped up with the workings of her own melancholic psychology that the whole world and its experience is seen in her terms, in a manner that can become cloying and self-adulatory. Some of these criticisms deny the fine sensitivity she can display, and her genuine insight into the workings of the female mind in particular. They can also ignore the fact that, as with the Romantics before her, she turned inward to her own experience only when society failed to offer clear and unequivocal guidelines about behaviour and morality.

The period between the two world wars was one in which uncertainty, indecision and adventurousness in the arts vied with each other. It would be wrong to underestimate Virginia Woolf simply because others have followed in the paths she trod, and some have done so with considerably less skill than she did. She may work in minute detail and show the intricate workings of a mind, but a painting of one tree can be as great a work of art as one of a whole forest.

# James Joyce (1882–1941)

T. S. Eliot's *The Waste Land* and Samuel Beckett's *Waiting for Godot* are arguably the works that carried the most significance in their respective spheres of poetry and drama for the twentieth century. It is possible to argue that James Joyce's *Ulysses* holds the equivalent position in the novel, but it has failed to make the examination syllabuses to anything like the same extent as its two compatriots. This may be because *Ulysses* is a 'difficult' book, or because despite critical acclaim *Ulysses* has failed to gain quite the measure of popular support that has been true of Eliot's and Beckett's work. This appeared to be denied by a millennium survey which suggested *Ulysses* was the most popular novel of the 20th century. It would be cynical to suggest that, along with Professor Stephen Hawking's *A Brief History of Time, Ulysses* is praised in inverse ratio to the frequency with which it is read through from cover to cover. Those who give up on the novel after the first fifty or so pages miss a treat. Joyce's language requires a degree of acclimatisation from the first-time reader, but the initial effort is repaid by the rewards.

### *A Portrait of the Artist as a Young Man* (1916)

Joyce's first major work was *Dubliners*, a collection of short stories published in 1914. He followed this with *A Portrait of the Artist as a Young Man*. The novel is semi-autobiographical, telling the story of the early life of one Stephen Dedalus, an Irish boy and intellectual who eventually rejects the Roman Catholic Church and faith.

The novel is not told in the purest form of the stream of consciousness technique, but it is told wholly and solely from the viewpoint of Stephen Dedalus. The tone in which this viewpoint is expressed varies as the central character becomes older; an example of the 'baby talk' used when Stephen is very young can be found in the full answer in Chapter 6 of this work. Style and technique dominate examination questions on the novel, though its comic and ironic tone and its picture of a mind searching out the route to artistic expression are perhaps of equal significance. In *Dubliners* and *A Portrait of the Artist as a Young Man* the feeling of being trapped, by Irish society and by the Church, is also strongly felt and expressed. In the scrutiny of Joyce as a technician his comic skills can also be overlooked, although these are easier to see in *Dubliners* than in *A Portrait of the Artist as a Young Man*.

### *Ulysses* (1922)

*Ulysses* is a remarkable novel, but also something of a culture shock to a reader brought up on a diet of Victorian novels and modern thrillers. It takes the figure of Stephen Dedalus, seen in *A Portrait of the Artist as a Young Man*, and shows him to the reader slightly later on in his life. The novel is concerned with one day in the life of Stephen, and, to provide contrast, the same day is studied from the viewpoint of Leopold Bloom, almost the antithesis of Stephen. Joyce attempts to create the sound, feel and pattern of these characters' thoughts as they pass through their minds on this one particular day. The novel is a technical tour de force, because as well as the stream of consciousness technique it brings in a wealth of other styles, including a famous parallel with Homer. Both characters face a crisis, Stephen's being a mental and spiritual one, Leopold's the rather more simple matter of his wife's planning to sleep with another man. The two dilemmas are poised against each other, sometimes comically and sometimes with a depth of feeling that is tragic in its intensity if in nothing else. The novel offers no answers. After the two central characters meet at the end of the novel, Leopold goes off to bed and Stephen goes off to an unknown future, his decision still pending.

*Ulysses* is a kaleidoscope of impressions, thoughts and different literary styles, and as such is a difficult book on which to ask neat and concise questions. It offers no conclusions, merely explorations, fits in to no recognised style or pattern, blends wholly disparate elements and takes huge delight in technical innovation and experimentation. At its heart it carries many of the features that are central to twentieth-century literature, and as such it should be attempted by all candidates who study the twentieth century, regardless of whether or not it appears on a syllabus.

T. S. Eliot became in effect Joyce's publisher in later years, thereby creating the irony of a man who believed Ireland to be in a state of cultural paralysis being helped to publication by another who had written of Europe in the grip of sterility. Comparisons between two outwardly very different authors often prove very fruitful.

## Aldous Huxley (1894–1963)

Aldous Huxley was born into a privileged English family and went to Eton and Balliol College, Oxford. It was therefore from within that circle that he wrote a number of novels satirising the upper-class literary circles of his time. His better-known works include *Crome Yellow* (1921), *Antic Hay* (1923), *Point Counter Point* (1928) and *Eyeless in Gaza* (1936). However, Huxley's reputation and standing rest largely on one novel, *Brave New World* (1932). Critics seem uncertain about Huxley's other work. It is in some respects an awkward compromise between levity and seriousness, and can appear smart and superficial.

### *Brave New World*

There is no such doubt about *Brave New World*, which portrays a world where all birth is controlled and administered through the test tube, society rigidly planned and organised to afford 'happiness' for all, and sex and drugs are used as social palliatives to ensure an absence of rebellion. The novel is the story of a higher order member of the New World Society and the Savage an unreformed and unprocessed man. Tragedy for both protagonists is inevitable. The novel is superbly plotted, very funny and very poignant. It brings to a head Huxley's long-standing concern with psychological conditioning, and it is free by and large of the long 'essays' in which characters in the earlier novels, and some of the later ones, lecture the reader with philosophical points. The essential irony of the novel is that it portrays a world in which everyone (or almost everyone) is happy, and in so doing makes its central theme the huge guilt felt by 'modern' society.

Of all Huxley's novels, *Brave New World* is the one which outwardly shows the least sign of strain as a result of Huxley's intense desire to be 'modern'. Was Huxley excited by new ideas, or excited by being seen to have new ideas? 'Modernism' is a complicated concept that will never be satisfactorily defined, and a concept entirely at home with the parallel concept of deconstruction. By definition, modernism deconstructs itself with every passing moment, which makes yesterday's modernism obsolete in the face of today's and tomorrow's modernism. At a student union debate modernism was defined as any work of literature that makes sex appear as if it is boring. The reader must decide if Huxley fits into this entirely unofficial category.

In later life Huxley became heavily involved with mysticism and with drugs as a means of mental release, and his work is generally held to have deteriorated, with some of his later work being seen as sensationalist. As a footnote, his novel *Point Counter Point* contains a picture of his friend D. H. Lawrence, as Rampion; Huxley was by no means the first writer who lost popularity among his friends and social circle by including them very obviously in his writing.

**Topics**

The perennial question about *Brave New World* is the reason for its relative immortality. Futuristic novels are notoriously prone to being proven wrong, yet Huxley's work has weathered very well, perhaps because it is set so far in the future as not to impinge on practical contemporary reality. As a novelist associated with the production of ideas, a rather thin emotional commitment and a relative weakness in characterisation, these problems can be highlighted with reference to either *Brave New World* or the other novels. There is a central irony in *Brave New World* that makes a good question. The novel implies that the psychologically controlled new world is a horror and a nightmare, Shakespeare being used as the symbol of the unordered creative man destroyed by the new society. Yet at the same time the filth and decay of the unregulated world is also made very clear. *Brave New World* may not be what humans were designed for, but the Savage Reservation is a good reason why mankind should move to the clinically clean new world. This clash where neither the past nor the future is satisfactory gives the novel some of its power, but also leaves a gaping question in its middle: what is the world that Huxley sees as ideal, and can it ever exist?

## George Orwell (1903–50)

George Orwell was also a member of a privileged class, though less so than Huxley. Born in India, he went to Eton and then returned to India as a member of the Imperial Police. From this privileged, colonial background he developed strong left-wing views, though his politics did not fit into any particular grouping, and he is best seen as an opponent of totalitarianism and of domination of man by man. He was in effect a democratic socialist, increasingly disillusioned by communism and the Fascism prevalent in the 1930s. He fought and was wounded as a Republican in the Spanish Civil War, having left the Imperial Police Force in 1927 to pursue a career as a writer.

Orwell is known above all for two novels, *Animal Farm* (1945) and *1984* (1949). The former uses the example of a small farm on which the animals rebel against their human owners as an emblem for the corruption of communism and totalitarianism, and the urge of man to dominate his fellows; the animals are not animals at all, but recognisable human figures, many of them based on figures from the Communist Revolution in Russia. Dobbin the horse and Napoleon the pig have become household words.

### *1984*

*1984* is all the more noteworthy because despite the date of its title having been passed it has lost none of its power. It is a novel based on signs and tendencies visible in the Europe of the 1930s and 1940s, but it needs no understanding of these to succeed. It is a vision of totalitarianism, remarkable in that its lessons can be applied to extreme left or right-wing government. Its logical conclusion is that totalitarian regimes must seek to wipe out the individual consciousness altogether, and all individuality. Orwell brings to life with remarkable vividness the appalling seedy decay of the world of 1984. Every member of the Party can be observed and heard at any time of day or night through the telescreen. Religion and sex are rigidly controlled as both offer an experience potentially more powerful than that offered by the State. Big Brother watches all the time. The world is permanently at war, the war being used as an excuse to justify privation and to rally the masses. History, biography and language are plastic in the hands of the State, to be moulded and changed at will. The hero of the novel, Winston Smith, makes a pathetic rebellion; his torture and his failure make *1984* rank among the most powerful literary works written in the twentieth century.

### Orwell's other work

It would be a pity if the success of *1984* stopped the student from reading Orwell's other work. *The Road to Wigan Pier* (1937) is an examination of unemployment, but in it Orwell shows his total individuality by attacking left-wing intellectuals as well as the right-wing thinking that he believed produced poverty and deprivation. Well worth attention also are *Burmese Days* (1935); *Keep the Aspidistra Flying* (1936); *Inside the Whale* (1940).

## Evelyn Waugh (1903–66)

Some of Waugh's work is covered in Chapter 20. He is probably best known for *Decline and Fall* (1928) and *A Handful of Dust* (1934), in addition to the novels covered in Chapter 20. Waugh is a savage satirist, but also a prophet of the same spirit of disillusion that can be seen in the poetry of T. S. Eliot. He shows the divorce between old and new values in his own society, and reveals in stark clarity a society and a culture rotting from within. He is also highly amusing, never quite losing his journalist's eye for telling detail and always possessed of a vast sense of incongruity.

## Graham Greene (1904–91)

Graham Greene, a prolific author and writer, is seen primarily as a novelist, and one with a very particular and personal style. He exists on the cusp between being an academic's novelist and someone beloved of the general public, and part of his success lies in his having satisfied both. His first major novel was *Stamboul Train* (1932), and he followed this with, among other novels, *The Power and the Glory* (1940); *The Heart of the Matter* (1948); *The Quiet American* (1955); and *A Burnt Out Case* (1961). Greene was rather dismissive about others of his novels, describing them as 'entertainments'. It is arguable that these novels are at least as great an achievement as his others, and they include *Brighton Rock* (1938); *The Confidential Agent* (1939); *Our Man in Havana* (1958); and *The Third Man* (1950).

### Themes in Greene's novels

Greene became a Catholic, and elements of that faith colour much of his work, though never dominate it. Indeed, it could be argued that sin, corruption, justice, mercy and the nature of Creation are universal themes and do not need Catholicism to explain their presence in his work. Above all Greene is concerned with 'moral dilemma'. The dilemma can be political, religious or simply personal, but it is rarely absent from his novels or his central characters. Greene is known above all for the seediness of his characters. It can sometimes appear that salvation in Greene's world can only be obtained through sin, and in an ironical vision Greene can show that proximity to sin matters less than a capacity to judge whether one is good or evil: the awareness of the two separate concepts and a capacity to judge and distinguish between them is all-important, and a central quality necessary for heroism in his novels. Betrayal and innocence recur as themes time and time again in his work.

### Issues in Greene's work

The quality that defines heroism in Greene's central characters and the influence of Catholic doctrine are central topics, as is Greene's adoption of popular literary forms (the thriller, the detective story and the spy story). Greene's technique is interesting, and its 'cinematic' nature often asked about. Greene tends to write as if preparing a screenplay, with a strong visual element, carefully plotted movement and action, and a setting and duration that are akin to a film shot or scene. The famed seediness of his characters and setting and the extent to which he is optimistic or pessimistic are sometimes examined, as are the themes of betrayal and innocence.

## Other modern novelists

A novelist who has been fêted by the media and by critics is Anthony Powell (b. 1905). Powell produced his first novel in 1931 (*Afternoon Men*). His sequence of twelve novels *A Dance to the Music of Time* started in 1951 and ended in 1975. It is a masterpiece. Its humour has perhaps tended to obscure the dark, even sinister, seriousness it contains, which is particularly evident in the later novels. The central figure of the sequence, Kenneth Widmerpool, has become a seminal figure in the later twentieth-century novel. Widmerpool is comic yet threatening. He believes he can shape his life by the exercise of will; in so doing he denies the value of and loses love and sensitivity. He is eventually destroyed by a greater will, but not before his success leads the reader to suspect his own comic response to Widmerpool. Powell is a superb social observer who persuades us of the reality of that which he surveys, at the same time as persuading us that there is no single explanation of human nature or existence. Most of all he has a personal voice, even though his works distance author from reader by use of a narrator.

### Kingsley Amis (b. 1922)

Amis has been a source of confusion to critics. His first great success, *Lucky Jim* (1954), showed his talents to excellent advantage. Its hero could be seen as an 'angry young man', in tune with the times, but also as a pathetic example of a society drifting away from all wholesome roots. Amis excels at social comedy, but his denial of contemporary virtues gives his work a right-wing, conservative and thoroughly hostile view of modern society. Social comedy and conservatism are not marketable commodities with many contemporary critics, but Amis's success with the reading public provides them with a challenge that cannot be ignored. Amis's work may be comic; it has always been realistic, and the combination has made him a major force in the modern British novel.

## V. S. Naipaul (b. 1932)

Critical opinion has also been divided on V. S. Naipaul, who was at first seen as a minor talent. His novel *In a Free State* (1971) won the Booker Prize, though some have wondered if melancholia and his concern with violence, race and alienation have made him fashionable rather than worthwhile. Such views are almost certainly unfair, but have given rise also to seemingly endless comparisons with Conrad, another author concerned with a hollowness at the heart of modern life. In Naipaul's work culture is being shattered, violence and barbarity rising to take its place. It remains to be seen whether he is an author who catalogues the nightmares of the twentieth century, or concerns that are more lasting and less topical.

## William Golding (1911–93)

Golding achieved lasting fame with his novel *The Lord of the Flies* (1954), a novel which achieved school 'set text' status in a remarkably short time. Golding's work features man in his basic, elemental form, and his novels often consist of a plot form chosen to show man stripped of civilised excess and reduced to his basic essentials; that essential man is often shown to consist of cruelty and savagery. Golding won the Booker Prize in 1980 for *Rites of Passage* and the Nobel Prize in 1983.

## Salman Rushdie (b. 1947)

Of even more modern writers it is impossible not to mention Salman Rushdie, originally a minor if promising talent in the 'magic realism' school of novelists, thrust to notoriety by the Islamic death threat resultant on his *The Satanic Verses* (1988). The critic Alan Massie has pointed out that Rushdie's work can sometimes be glittering, sometimes be disgusting and sometimes be trivial.

## Peter Ackroyd (b. 1949)

Rather more promising is Peter Ackroyd, whose canon includes the remarkable *Hawksmoor* (1985) and *Chatterton* (1987). Ackroyd is obsessed with the past, and in his novels it acts on the present with an immediacy that mocks the distinction between past and present. He is also a novelist who has surprised critics, firstly by the development of sensitivity and compassion, secondly by a move away from pastiche and a London setting.

## Ian McEwan (b. 1948)

McEwan moved from 'macabre and disturbing' short-story writing via writing for television and cinema into novels. Alienation, disgust and despair are strong in his work, though some consider he was 'spoilt' by his immature early work receiving too immediate praise and recognition. This would seem to be denied by his prizewinning *Amsterdam* (1998), and a canon of work that is building up to very impressive heights.

## Martin Amis (b. 1949)

Amis is possibly a better bet for lasting fame. His early novels were excessively topical and have dated, but he struck a note of lasting values with *Other People* (1981). Amis has an adolescent desire to shock, but later works have developed this into something far more compelling. He can be verbally brilliant, and his style is, at its best, luxuriant and compelling. *Money* (1984) is essential reading for anyone interested in the modern novel.

## Other novelists

Second-guessing which contemporary novelist will survive and which is simply a short-lived meteor on the contemporary horizon is a dangerous game, so dangerous that few commentators make any serious attempt at it. What follows is simply one person's guess as to who will be on the examination syllabi in years to come, and a recommendation for those who might be read by students free to choose their own dissertation or project.

**Alan Garner** (b. 1934) was at one time best known for his children's book *Elidor*, and has even been branded as a 'fantasy' writer. His most recent writings, and in particular the novel *Strandloper* (1997) have commanded increasing critical attention and respect. Garner's best work hovers on the borderline between different realities, and his work is showing increasing signs of having the indefinable quality that makes works of lasting merit. The whole area of authors known for their children's work, and books which have become famous as children's books when they are far more, is an interesting area for research. Readers of the list below will not fail to notice the domination of the list by women writers.

**Margaret Drabble** (b. 1939) and **A. S. Byatt** (1936) are outstanding social commentators and creators of vividly-realised characters. The latter won the Booker Prize with *Possession* (1990). **Rose Tremain** (b. 1943) is widely-admired, with *Restoration* (1989) a particularly fine example of her work. The Canadian **Margaret Atwood's** book of short stories *Bluebeard's Egg* (1996) is an excellent introduction to a prolific and powerful novelist. **Kate Atkinson** is a name to watch. Her first novel *Behind the Scenes at the Museum* was the 1995 Whitbread Book of the Year. A brilliant first novel is often no guarantee of anything decent with the second, but her *Human Croquet* (1997) received ecstatic reviews. **Ruth Rendell** (b. 1930) has written a number of highly-regarded novels under the psuedonym of **Barbara Vine**. **Peter Carey** (b. 1943) is an Australian who won the Booker Prize with *Oscar and Lucinda* (1988). He has sometimes been described as 'escapist', perhaps part of a bias against those who set novels in the past. He is increasingly present on degree-level courses.

## Further reading

### General

- R. B. Kershner, *The Twentieth Century Novel. An Introduction* (Macmillan, 1997)
- Alan Massie, *The Novel Today. A Critical Guide to the British Novel 1970–1989* (Longman, 1990)

### Joseph Conrad

- Ross C. Murfin, ed., *Heart of Darkness. Joseph Conrad* (Macmillan, 1996). One of the best collections of modern critical essays on this book. In the same series is Daniel R.Schwarz, ed., *The Secret Sharer* (1997)
- Elaine Jordan, ed., *Joseph Conrad* (New Casebook Series, Macmillan, 1996)
- Zdzislaw Najder, *Conrad in Perspective. Essays on Art and Fidelity* (Cambridge University Press, 1997). Written by a Polish academic and biographer of Conrad, this is one of the few works to come to Conrad from the viewpoint of his nationality; a good insight into modern critical views on Conrad.
- Andrew Michael Roberts, *A Preface to Conrad* (Longman, 1993)
- Brian Spittles, *Joseph Conrad* (Macmillan, 1992): an effective biographical and critical introduction.
- ––, *How to Study a Conrad Novel* (Macmillan, 1990)
- J. H. Stape, ed., *The Cambridge Companion to Joseph Conrad* (Cambridge University Press, 1996)
- Cedric Watts, *Joseph Conrad. A Literary Life* (Macmillan, 1989). A straightforward and workmanlike biographical introduction.

### E. M. Forster

- Christopher Gillie, *A Preface to Forster* (Longman, 1983)
- Nigel Messenger, *How to Study an E.M.Forster Novel* (Macmillan, 1991)
- Mary Lago, *E. M. Forster. A Literary Life* (Macmillan, 1994): a straightforward and workmanlike biographical introduction.
- Jeremy Tambling, ed., *E. M. Forster* (New Casebook Series, Macmillan, 1995)

### Graham Greene

- Cedric Watts, *A Preface to Greene* (Longman, 1997)
- Norman Sherry, *The Life of Graham Greene. Volume 1 1904–1939; Volume 2 1932–1955* (Penguin, 1990 and 1996)
- W. J. West, *The Quest for Graham Greene* (Weidenfeld & Nicolson, 1997)

## James Joyce

- Derek Attridge, ed., *The Cambridge Companion to James Joyce* (Cambridge University Press, 1990)
- Morris Beja, *James Joyce. A Literary Life* (Macmillan, 1992). A straightforward and workmanlike biographical and critical introduction.
- John Blades, *How to Study James Joyce* (Macmillan, 1996)
- Sidney Bolt, *A Preface to James Joyce* (Longmans, 1992)
- James Fairfall, *James Joyce and the Question of History* (Cambridge University Press, 1995). A book for the advanced student, but one which gives a view of Joyce from the vantage point of several modern critical schools.
- R. B. Kershner, ed., *A Portrait of the Artist as a Young Man. James Joyce* (Macmillan, 1993). An excellent collection of modern critical essays on this book.

## D. H. Lawrence

The following three-volume biography is highly recommended:

- John Worthen, *D. H. Lawrence. The Early Years 1885–1912* (1991); Mark Kinkead-Weekes, *D. H. Lawrence. Triumph to Exile 1912–22* (Cambridge University Press, 1996); David Ellis, *D. H. Lawrence. Dying Game 1922–1930* (Cambridge University Press, 1998)
- Rick Rylance, ed., *Sons and Lovers* (New Casebook Series, Macmillan, 1996)
- Gamini Salgado, *A Preface to Lawrence* (Longman, 1983)

## George Orwell

- Bryan Loughrey, Graeham Holderness, and Nahem Yousaf, ed., *George Orwell* (New Casebook Series, Macmillan 1998)

## Virginia Woolf

- Rachel Bowlby, ed., *Virginia Woolf* (Longman, 1992): a collection of recent critical essays on Woolf.
- Juliet Dusinberre, *Virginia Woolf's Renaissance. Woman Reader or Common Reader?* (Macmillan, 1997)
- Jane Goldman, *The Feminist Aesthetic of Virginia Woolf* (Cambridge University Press, 1998). Heavy going, but a clear statement of the feminist dimension in Woolf's work.
- Mitchell Leaska, *Granite and Rainbow. The Hidden Life of Virginia Woolf* (Macmillan, 1998)
- Nicholas Marsh, *Virginia Woolf. The Novels* (Macmillan, 1998): detailed analysis of text from Woolf's novels – a good idea, well carried out.
- John Mepham, *Virginia Woolf. A Literary Life* (Macmillan, 1996): an effective biographical and critical introduction.

- Roger Poole, *The Unknown Virginia Woolf* (Cambridge University Press, 1996). One of the classic treatments of Woolf and her work.
- Sue Reid, ed., *Mrs Dalloway and To the Lighthouse* (New Casebook Series, Macmillan, 1993)

## Contemporary Novelists

- Catherine Cundy, *Salman Rushdie* (Manchester University Press, 1997)
- D. C. R. A. Goonetilleke, *Salman Rushdie* (Macmillan, 1998)
- Coral Ann Howells, ed., *Margaret Atwood* (Macmillan, 1995). A good title in a very useful series.
- Bruce Woodcock, *Peter Carey* (Manchester University Press, 1997)

CHAPTER TWENTY-THREE

# Modern and contemporary drama

Mention has already been made of the effect on British drama of Ibsen and Chekhov, and in particular their effect on the work of Shaw. The first two decades of the twentieth century saw a vogue for verse drama, though most of the works written as a result of this change in fashion are no longer known or performed. T. S. Eliot's *Murder in the Cathedral* is one exception.

Drama lay in a relatively fallow state until the mid-1950s, when it paid for the peace and quiet it had enjoyed for many years by a double explosion. On the one hand there was the 'kitchen sink' drama vogue, on the other the Theatre of the Absurd. Within a very short time British drama was enjoying a new power and success, and the sudden eruption of artistic theatrical talent needs some explaining. As with many literary phenomena, part of the explanation is sociological and economic. The 1950s saw many young men and women given the chance of an education at the universities of Oxford and Cambridge who would not have made it there in an earlier generation. The creation of Grammar Schools and rising affluence and expectations both contributed to this factor. These universities exerted significant influence on what took place in the world, particularly of the London theatre, and as an injection of directorial, acting and writing talent this rush of new blood was a powerful force for good. In addition, increased affluence and a policy of subsidy for the Arts saw the growth in theatre building and theatrical activity. If there was a power of new talent at the younger end of the theatrical world, so at the top a clutch of outstanding senior actors were coming into their prime, headed by the triumvirate of Olivier, Gielgud and Richardson, and superb work was being done at the Royal Shakespeare Company and the Royal Court Theatre.

## T. S. Eliot and *Murder in the Cathedral*

T. S. Eliot has already been examined as a poet in Chapter 21, but he was also instrumental in an attempt to revise *poetic drama*, and his play *Murder in the Cathedral* is frequently set, and is one of the very few plays from the 1930s which are afforded this treatment.

*Murder in the Cathedral* is based on the story of Saint Thomas à Becket, murdered in Canterbury Cathedral on 29 September 1170, on the orders of King Henry II. Henry had made his friend Thomas, Archbishop, but then found that instead of a playboy he had a tiger by the tail, and his murder by men in the service of the King was part accident, and part plan. The story has been the basis of several plays.

*Chorus* is a frequent object of attention in the play. The Greek tragedies used a Chorus on stage to comment on the action. In Eliot's play the Chorus are a group of women, and they are there partly to comment on the action, but also to amplify it. They are very emotional, and Eliot's full poetic power is unleashed on and in their lines. They are a form of emotional and spiritual thermometer, registering the temperature and mood of the play at any given moment, but also raising and lowering it.

*Becket's character* is another central issue. As a friend of Henry's and a man who before being made Archbishop was sinful, ambitious and worldly, he is a very credible figure, but this credibility comes about as a result of Eliot's careful blending of the man as he was and the man as he is. Eliot knows the lesson taught by most of the great religious and spiritual writers, perhaps most notably the poet George Herbert, that an audience or readers can believe in saintly men all the more easily if they can see them as humans who have a genuine *struggle* to achieve and retain their faith.

*The Tempters* are an essential element in this creation of credibility, and also of dramatic tension. Becket is tempted on four fronts. He is offered luxuries and wealth; power and a renewed friendship with the King; and power by means of joining with the nobility in open rebellion against the King. The fourth temptation is Becket himself; is he facing death because he wants to die a martyr, and glorify *himself* rather than God by so doing? In defeating all these temptations Becket proves himself a saint; he dies for the *glory of the Church*, not the *glory of himself*, but the battle to reach that state is exciting and convincing.

It is also worth studying the question of the *tragic status* of Becket; it has been argued that because his death is a fulfilment of his wishes and so much the right thing to happen he cannot be seen as a true tragic hero.

*Murder in the Cathedral* is a spiritual odyssey, but also gripping drama with a superb sense of atmosphere and tension. Its themes of regeneration, faith, hope, and the personal struggle against ambition and worldliness are sufficiently close to the themes of Eliot's poetry to make the latter essential reading for any student studying the play.

## Kitchen sink drama

John Osborne (b. 1929) and his play *Look Back in Anger* (1956) marked the start of a new type of play, and added two new phrases to the language: *kitchen sink drama*, and *the angry young man*.

*Look Back in Anger* has as its hero Jimmy Porter. For almost the first time (unless one includes *Hamlet*!) a major play chose to show a young man, an archetypal 'student', and to give credence to his views. Jimmy Porter represents a whole generation of angry young men, angry because they feel they have no say in the running of a society that is corrupt, rotten and run by the older generation entirely for their own benefit, and on the basis of outmoded principles. Despite its language and its setting being rooted in the 1950s the play has been revived successfully, if only because its central theme of disillusioned and frustrated youth set against the older generation is as old as literature itself. However, Jimmy Porter does not have it all his own way, and the older generation are not shown as being totally without sense or a point of view. The play's *themes* are obviously significant, as well as its attitude to the old, the young and society in general. It is interesting to compare the strength and nature of the disillusion felt in *Look Back in Anger* with that expressed after another and different war by T. S. Eliot in *The Waste Land*; the major difference perhaps is that the play acknowledges youth. The play can be seen as one of the first salvoes fired in the battle to gain youth a voice and a culture of its own, a battle which climaxed in the 1960s.

*Technique* is an essential area to be understood in the play. Its language is colloquial and rough, the setting naturalistic and its voice of protest strident in the way that it rubs its audiences' noses in seediness. Previously many plays had been based in the drawing rooms of fine houses, and hence the description 'kitchen sink drama', implying a movement away from refinement and elegance and into harsh reality.

*Complaints* about the play are that whilst it is made clear that Jimmy is angry, it is not always made clear precisely what he is angry *at*. Perhaps that is itself a theme. The play can also be seen to lack *variety*, and the issue of its *topicality and whether or not it has 'dated'* is always worth examining. The manner in which Osborne's play is hailed as 'new' needs to be treated with some caution. He does reflect a modern voice of protest, an anti-heroic mode and a concern for gritty realism that were unexpected and novel in the 1950s, but the newness and relative restraint of the play can appear rather quaint and old-fashioned nowadays, whilst some of its themes are universal.

## Drama of the absurd

If kitchen sink drama moved towards greater realism, then drama of the absurd appeared to move in the opposite direction. The first performance of *Waiting for Godot* (1953) by Samuel Beckett (b. 1906) was a tremendous shock, so much so that many of the audience walked out in disgust, and Beckett was either treated by the majority of critics with derisory contempt, or called a theatrical fraud (a phrase which occasionally crops up in examination questions on his work). It was hardly surprising. The play opens with two tramps alone on stage. Vladimir and Estragon are filthy, destitute and bored. They are waiting for a man called Godot. There are two acts. In both acts a man called Pozzo and his slave Lucky appear, and so does a boy sent by Mr Godot to say that he will not be able to come today. There are minor differences between the acts; in Act 1 Pozzo is healthy and his slave speaks, whereas in Act 2 he has gone blind and his slave is dumb. The tree which is the only set grows a few leaves in Act 2. Otherwise 'nothing happens'. This was not calculated to appeal to audiences brought up on a diet of elegant drawing room comedy and classic revivals of Shakespeare. For a definition of *drama of the absurd* the student should turn to Chapter 3 of this work. A discussion of *Waiting for Godot*, arguably the most influential play of the twentieth century, follows below.

## Topics in *Waiting for Godot*

### Comedy

The first and most important thing to note about the play is that it is comic. This humour is not always apparent from a first reading of the play, and much of it is based on the play's dialogue, which in turn needs excellent comic timing to make it funny. The humour springs from an extremely skilful mixture of straightforward clowning (Vladimir and Estragon can be traced back as having their roots in circus clowns and in a number of famous comic dual acts), shrewd observation of essentially ludicrous speech and behaviour patterns and the eternal ironies and self-deceptions that the two tramps (and, by association, we ourselves) involve themselves in.

### Nihilism and absurdity

The two tramps can be seen as representatives of all humanity. They are cold, bored and useless, living in an absurd world which does not recognise, acknowledge or care for them. Nothing has happened to them, nothing will happen, and their continued existence is a mockery made possible only by humanity's endless ability to deceive itself and hide from the truth. The truth (that we live in a meaningless world) is too appalling to face, and too *uncomfortable*; it must therefore be ignored at all costs, and thus much of the humour and the poignancy of the play comes from the sight of two men studiously walking round an obvious truth and pretending it is not there. Habit deadens sensibility and awareness, and so the habits of casual social intercourse, the basic needs of food and drink and dreaming about the future are used to keep the world and reality at bay. *Communication* comes into this; words can be used to stop real thought and to avoid communicating harsh truth. Until humanity can face up to the truth about itself and the Universe it will continue to live a totally false and *absurd* life, absurd because what we do and how we behave is based on a totally false conception of reality. Indeed in *Waiting for Godot* it could be said that reality has been ignored for so long that it has receded beyond recall. This view of the play as a *vision of nothingness* is a very tempting one, but it does not quite account for the peculiar attractiveness of the two tramps and the sympathy they can arouse in the audience. At the very least they have the virtues of many figures in tragic or semi-tragic plays, that of *stoic endurance*. This leads on to another common question on whether the play is a *tragedy* or a *comedy*. The answer that it is a tragi-comedy can only be used if the candidate thoroughly understands the manner in which tragic and comic elements are blended in the play.

**Time**

Time is a major concern in all Beckett's plays, and can be seen as a cancer. We are powerless in the grip of time, which creates and destroys us at its will and without our consent. Life is seen as merely an extended journey to the grave, a relentless progress towards nothing (*nothing* is the most common word in the play). Time can only destroy, and Pozzo's cry of 'On!' is one of the most tragic and moving in the play; we can only go 'On!' even though we have nothing to go on to.

**Religion**

It is very tempting to see the play as a straight satire on religion. Vladimir and Estragon are the gullible humans who spend their lives waiting for 'Godot' who will never appear. They wait not because he exists but because they need to believe that he does. This view is slightly clouded by the fact that the Boy does come (he can be compared to the Messiah), which suggests that someone must have sent him. Issues in Beckett are rarely simple.

**Occupation**

It has been said that the play draws its inspiration from German-occupied France in the Second World War, with its endless waiting, the threat of violence, uncertainty, a bleak vision of the future, pretending ignorance when questioned, Pozzo as a Gestapo officer and Lucky as a slave or concentration camp labourer. The atmosphere may be linked to France in the war, but it is oversimplifying the play to see it as a simple allegory.

**Conclusions**

Very few modern works of any sort operate solely on one level. Beckett's plays profit from their huge ambiguity and ability to be and to mean different things at different levels and to different people. Remember the aim of many modern writers is to stimulate thought on a wide range of issues, not to preach neat morals or conclusions.

## Harold Pinter (b. 1930)

Harold Pinter is sometimes hailed as the greatest living British dramatist, a fiercely-contested claim. The best-known plays are *The Birthday Party* (1958), *The Caretaker* (1960) and *The Homecoming* (1965) from his earlier period, and *Old Times* (1971), *No Man's Land* (1975) and *Betrayal* (1978). Pinter's later works have become more overtly political. Pinter has also written a number of screenplays, including *The French Lieutenant's Woman* (1982). His work has increasingly diversified in recent years.

### Topics in Pinter

Pinter's early plays tend to show characters (usually weak or failed in one way or another) trying to live or hide in a small and secure area, with the feeling of a hostile world ready to break in on them at any moment. The security is always destroyed, and the phrase *comedy of menace* has been coined to describe the powerful mixture of comedy and menace that exists in his work.

**Dialogue**
As with Beckett, Pinter is superb at recreating dialogue, so much so that the term 'Pinteresque' has been coined to describe the dialogue in his plays. Pinter's plays are also famous (and sometimes mocked or parodied) for the use they make of silences between characters. Pinter believes that characters can often communicate by silence more effectively than by words, and that language is more often than not used either to project a completely false vision of reality, or to stop people from realising the truth by filling the air with meaningless noise. Thus the theme of *communication and the inadequacy of language* is central to an understanding of his work.

**Questions**
Pinter is sometimes accused of being a hollow shell, a writer who can use the resources of the live theatre to summon up an atmosphere of great comic menace, but with no essential and coherent theme or philosophy of life to expound. *Violence* is a strong presence in his work, sometimes an undercurrent, sometimes open, but ever-present. The plays have been described as *wilfully mystifying* and *a succession of riddles*; it is as well to remember that they are also often marvellous theatre.

## Tom Stoppard (b. 1932)

A writer manifestly influenced by Beckett, but with a voice very much his own, is Tom Stoppard, although it should be noted that his plays have now moved away from his early absurdist mode of writing. Stoppard first became famous through his play *Rosencrantz and Guildenstern Are Dead* (1967).

This is often set by examining boards as a contrast or comparison with Shakespeare's *Hamlet*. Stoppard's play examines the lives of Shakepeare's Rosencrantz and Guildenstern from *Hamlet*, while the action of *Hamlet* swirls around them. The links with *Waiting for Godot* are obvious: both plays are tragi-comedies, and both have two rather amiable but weak central figures lost and wholly confused in a world they do not understand, cannot influence and which seems hostile to them. Other plays by Stoppard which are sometimes set are *The Real Inspector Hound* (1968), *Jumpers* (1972), *Travesties* (1974), *Professional Foul* (1977) and *Hapgood* (1988).

## Topics in Stoppard's work

*The blend between comedy and tragedy* is very marked in Stoppard's work. His interest in *philosophy* is also a strong presence in a number of plays. Stoppard tends to have some sympathy with professional and amateur philosophers who try to explain the mysteries of life, as well as being aware of the absurdity of trying to explain the inexplicable.

Stoppard is a great entertainer and hugely funny. This appears to confuse both examiners and critics, who sometimes find it hard to believe that someone so entertaining can also be so profound. Hence a large number of questions are set on whether Stoppard's work is *pure showbiz*, or a *hollow shell*, mere entertainment with no serious purpose. Sometimes the question is extended to one of the great debates on Stoppard, whether or not the comedy and showmanship of his work threatens, compromises or destroys the serious intent of his work. Stoppard delights in upsetting the audience's expectations. His *comic techniques* are a central issue in questions on his work, or, put at its simplest, how he makes his audiences laugh.

At the heart of Stoppard's plays is an *intense sympathy for the underdog*, a huge affection for ordinary people and a strong awareness of life's absurdities. *Death* can be a theme in his work. In *Rosencrantz and Guildenstern Are Dead* Guildenstern sees death as the only certainty, but even this security is removed from him by the Player, who shows that death is actually more convincing when it is acted.

A recurrent figure in Stoppard's work is the pragmatist, best seen perhaps in the Player from *Rosencrantz and Guildenstern Are Dead* and Archie from *Jumpers*. By wilful and total denial of any morality except that of survival, these characters achieve a degree either of success or of survival in the world, and as such represent a threat to a world which whatever its complexities must rely for happiness on basic human decency and responsibility. *Morality* is a major issue in Stoppard's plays, and whether or not there is any absolute morality that can always be applied to human behaviour. The answer can be seen as consisting of a statement that even if moral absolutes do not exist, they should.

The candidate studying Stoppard should check up on definitions of *farce* and *theatricality* (the latter term generally meaning a writer's ability to use the resources of live theatre to full advantage).

## Arthur Miller (b. 1915)

Arthur Miller should more properly be in Chapter 24 on American Literature, but his influence on British drama and his popularity in Britain make it more logical to include him here.

Miller is sometimes known by one play in particular, *Death of a Salesman* (1949). The two other plays of his most commonly set are both early works, *All My Sons* (1947) and *The Crucible* (1953). The latter is a parable of America in the days of the McCarthy persecutions, using as its starting point the infamous Salem witch trials of 1692. It can be used as a basis for discussion of the vexed issue of modern tragedy, and whether such a creature can exist.

### Issues in *Death of a Salesman*

*Death of a Salesman* examines the life and death of Willy Loman, an American travelling salesman, killed by a mixture of his own inadequacies and the values of the society around him.

#### Tragedy and social drama

One view of the play sees it as a *social drama*. In this view Willy is living in a capitalist society which offers success as the ultimate virtue, but which undermines its inhabitants and so stops them from achieving success. Willy is destroyed by the false values which society imposes on him and which he is powerless to refuse. Problems with this view are that Willy is clearly quite inadequate and can be seen as needing little help from society in his own destruction, and that the 'boss' or 'capitalist' figures in the play are presented with some sympathy.

Another view sees the play as a *tragedy*. Here again there are problems. The play is intensely sad, but it may lack the final dimension that would give it tragic status. Willy is perhaps too flawed to be truly tragic, too weak and too defenceless. Willy lacks grandeur and stature, and does not have a real moment of self-recognition, though he does have many tragic flaws. It can be said that the social drama element and the tragic element in the play sit uneasily side-by-side, each reducing the impact of the other.

#### The American Dream

The term 'The American Dream' refers to the early days of American society when the country was still being explored and settled, and when for many years there was an exciting land of danger and opportunity in the frontier. In an idealised way the frontier was seen as an environment in which the traditional virtues of independence and initiative could thrive and flourish; it was a land in which a man could make his own way. Willy tries to plant flowers in his backyard, but they are stifled by the tower blocks; so his own capacities are stifled and killed by urban, social life. The life of a salesman is taken by Willy rather than the life of the pioneer, offered by 'Uncle Ben', but what he has chosen is a suffocating, lonely and wholly sterile path which can only cripple him.

**Dreaming**
Willy says that a salesman has to dream, perhaps as his only escape from the futility of his job. The problem is that Willy's dreams come to interfere with reality, and actually replace it, a feature he passes on to his son and which cripples him also.

**Technique**
The play is famous for its set, a 'cutaway' house in which the front wall has been stripped off and all the rooms are visible to the audience. It also has a remarkable plot, in which the primary action takes place in the period shortly before Willy's death, but what has gone on before (much of which actually explains the state and situation he is in) is shown in a series of flashbacks, suggested by changes in the lighting. The play is a technical masterpiece. It is remarkable on a far more minor level because it gave the author of this work a sharp reminder of one of the warnings issued frequently throughout this book. He went to see a performance of the play at the English National Theatre, with Warren Mitchell playing the part of Willy Loman, after having spent a year teaching a class that the play was not pure tragedy. He emerged having witnessed a performance that was more purely tragic than almost any other work he had seen. The moral of this story is that healthy open-mindedness is a far better attitude to literature than narrow dogmatism; never let a critic (including the author of this work!) make your mind up for you.

## Other modern dramatists

### John Arden (b. 1930)

John Arden has a high reputation with critics despite the fact that his work has had nowhere near the commercial success of the authors covered above. His most frequently performed works are probably *Sergeant Musgrave's Dance* (1959) and *Armstrong's Last Goodnight* (1964). Arden's early plays mixed prose and verse, and were clearly influenced by the example of Bertolt Brecht. They were renowned for not coming to conclusions about the issues they presented, although in later years his work has adopted a more conventional left-wing outlook, though often in unconventional form. Arden has frequently been the centre of controversy and has diverted his attention rather towards fringe theatre and amateur productions.

### Joe Orton (1933–67)

Orton was the author of *Entertaining Mr Sloane* (1964), *Loot* (1966) and the posthumously produced *What the Butler Saw* (1968). Orton, a homosexual, was battered to death by his friend and companion, who then committed suicide. Orton's plays are black comedy, replete with sexual innuendo contained in stylish dialogue. Opinion differs as to his real worth. His reputation declined after his death, but is now in the ascendant again.

## Peter Shaffer (b. 1926)

Peter Shaffer has produced a string of extremely successful plays: *Five Finger Exercise* (1958); *The Royal Hunt of the Sun* (1964); *Black Comedy* (1965); *Equus* (1972); *Amadeus* (1979). There is great variety in Shaffer's work, from the middle-class family life observation of *Five Finger Exercise* to a tempestuous and tragic study of creativity and artistic relationships in *Amadeus*. Shaffer's capacity to write comedy and tragedy reflects his overall strength as a playwright, and his eye for dramatic situations and the tension of personal relationships.

## Arnold Wesker (b. 1932)

Wesker is probably best known for the 'Wesker Trilogy', three linked plays entitled *Chicken Soup with Barley* (1958), *Roots* (1959) and *I'm Talking About Jerusalem* (1960). The trilogy is based round a London Jewish working-class family and a family in rural Norfolk. It shows Wesker's concern with political and social hopes, from a left-wing viewpoint, and with class struggle. *Chips with Everything* (1962) took National Service in the RAF as an excuse to examine class attitudes. Economic and social reality loom large in Wesker's work, with both a sense of excitement at the freedom individuals have to break free, and a sense of depression at the difficulty of rising above the imposed drudgery and self-fulfilling prophecy of class expectations. Wesker has a rumbustious and gritty eye for comic detail, and innovatory technique.

## Edward Bond (b. 1934)

Edward Bond is perhaps best known for his play *Saved* (1965), which aroused a storm of protest and official censorship by its depiction of a baby being stoned to death in a pram. Bond writes in condemnation of capitalism, believing it provokes intense violence as a result of its injustice. A very powerful depiction of this theme is *Lear* (1972). Bond is required reading for anyone with an interest in left-wing theatre, or the use of violence in contemporary literature. Critical and public opinion is divided on the lasting worth of his plays. In addition the heavily politicised, radical drama of the 1970's and 1980's made an impact, particularly with Howard Brenton (b. 1942), Trevor Griffiths (b. 1935), David Hare (b. 1947) and David Edgar (b. 1948). Brenton's *The Romans in Britain* (1980) caused uproar when it was first performed. Among the best-known plays of the other authors are Hare's *Plenty* (1978) and Griffiths's *Comedians* (1975).

## Alan Ayckbourn (b. 1939)

Alan Ayckbourn has achieved immense popular success. He does not innovate, has no overt political agenda and as a result has tended to be dismissed as that most awful of things, 'middle-brow'. Yet he has a superb eye for characterisation, an excellent comic touch and a capacity to express central human dilemmas in a manner that is instantly recognisable and telling.

# Further reading

## General


- Martin Esslin, *The Theatre of the Absurd* (Penguin, 1987): a classic text.
- John Russell Brown, ed., *The Oxford Illustrated History of Theatre* (Oxford University Press, 1997)
- Christopher Innes, *Modern British Drama 1890–1990* (Cambridge University Press, 1992)
- Theodore Shank, *Contemporary British Theatre* (Macmillan, 1996)
- John Russell Taylor, *Anger and After* (Methuen, 1988)
- Michelene Wandor, *Drama Today. A Critical Guide to British Drama, 1970–1990* (Longman, 1993)


## Samuel Beckett


- Mary Bryden, *Samuel Beckett and the Idea of God* (Macmillan, 1998)
- James Knowlson, *Damned to Fame. The Life of Samuel Beckett* (Bloomsbury, 1997)
- John Pilling, ed., *The Cambridge Companion to Beckett* (Cambridge University Press, 1994)


## Edward Bond


- Michael Mangan, *Edward Bond* (Writers and Their Work Series, Northcote House/British Council, 1988)


## Arthur Miller


- Christopher Bigsby, ed., *The Cambridge Companion to Arthur Miller* (Cambridge University Press, 1997)
- Dennis Welland, *Miller the Playwright* (Methuen, 1983)


## John Osborne


- John Osborne, *A Better Class of Person* (1981)
- ––, *Almost a Gentleman* (1991)

## Harold Pinter

- Raymond Armstrong, *Kafka and Pinter* (Macmillan, 1997)
- Martin Esslin, *Pinter: A Study of His Plays* (various editions, Methuen)
- Ronald Hayman, *Harold Pinter* (numerous editions, Heinemann)
- Martin S. Regal, *Harold Pinter. A Question of Timing* (Macmillan, 1995)
- Michael Bullington, *The Life and World of Harold Pinter* (Faber, & Faber, 1991)

## Tom Stoppard

- Ronald Hayman, *Tom Stoppard* (various editions, Heinemann)
- Jim Hunter, *Tom Stoppard's Plays* (various editions, Faber)

CHAPTER TWENTY-FOUR

# American literature

## The literary and historical background

This chapter does not concern itself with contemporary American writing. Any detailed study of that would require several books. Its aim is to give an introduction to the major American writers who have found their way on to English A-level and degree-level courses.

The United States of America declared independence from their colonial master Great Britain in 1776. Between then and the outbreak of the Civil War in 1861 American Literature established its own identity and achieved something of a golden period in the years immediately prior to the war. American Literature can quite logically be set on *English* Literature courses as it is written in English, but the cultural background is wholly different from that of Europe.

### The early days

There were various major influences on American culture in the early days. America was founded in its modern form by religious refugees. The Pilgrim Fathers who settled in New England in the seventeenth century were Calvinistic Puritans. They believed that man was inherently evil, that only a chosen few would achieve salvation. Puritanism was repressive, fiercely distrustful of sexuality, excess and frivolity, and capable of engendering brooding guilt and an obsession with orthodoxy within a culture. Puritanism in its bleak and basic form lost adherents as time went on in America, but it left its mark on the society it had helped create. The declining interest in the Puritan church also helped the series of evangelical religious revivals that took place in the years after the break with Britain. This input was fervent, excitable and highly emotional, in sharp contrast to the original Puritan ethic. To this rather uneasy combination was added a strong influence from what was known in Europe as the Enlightenment, or the Age of Reason. The Enlightenment taught that all things, men and women included, were answerable to reason, held up science and rational thought as the path to a new Utopia and generated a new optimism that whatever a man wanted to achieve could be achieved by hard work. This latter view was given strength by the Protestant Work Ethic, mentioned in the section on Daniel Defoe in Chapter 14. It is also clear that all three of these influences – Puritanism, Evangelism and Rationality – were at war with each other. The second was a reaction against the first, and the last tended to denounce religion as superstition, an unnecessary ritual in a world which could be explained perfectly well by means of reason and humanism. An additional influence was Romanticism, flourishing in Europe and attractive to embryonic American culture through its insistence on the primacy of the individual.

## The Frontier and the American Dream

From these primary ingredients two further appendages grew: the concept of the Frontier and the so-called 'American Dream'. For many years in American history the frontier was a potent symbol. Men had come to the New World to find freedom from oppression. The frontier was the new land, the land where basic human values ruled, where man was close to Nature and where success or failure depended on one's skill, one's courage and one's determination, not on office politics, the wealth or the social standing of one's family. It was probably never true, but it was marvellously attractive. For many years, until the nineteenth century when East and West met, the railway lines joined the whole continent and the Indians were banished to reservations, the frontier was always there. The office boy in San Francisco or the bank clerk in New York was very unlikely to chance his luck and go West – but the realisation that he *could* do if he so wished, that the land of the clean start and new horizons beckoned, was a strong factor in American culture. That culture breathed a rather sad collective sigh when the frontier finally became civilised. Wild West shows were really no substitute. From this and from a host of other features came the twentieth-century concept of the American Dream, basically a vision of a world where the individual could reign and reap his just reward. The dream is a complex one, and is seen influencing two very different works discussed elsewhere and in this chapter – Miller's *Death of a Salesman* and Steinbeck's *Of Mice and Men* – and a host of other major American works.

Just as in American football the principle of 'blocking' another player operates, so the fact that so many disparate and even contradictory elements were present in American culture resulted in a blocking of constraints, a remarkable freedom, a freedom not found in European culture to nearly the same extent. Underlying and perhaps powering this freedom was enormous economic potential and expansion, a depth of wealth-making that in the twentieth century rose to a level which made that of Great Britain in the nineteenth century appear almost puny in comparison. American economic expansion was restless and powerful. It helped give rise to a triumph of individuality and an overwhelming belief in progress, whilst at the same time encouraging a questioning of the consequences and direction of that progress.

### The lost generation

If there was a belief in progress in American culture there was also the story of the 'lost generation'. These were the artists and intellectuals who were embittered by American involvement in the First World War, and who in turn were disgusted by the materialism, extravagance and narrow-mindedness they perceived in American society, and which they believed dominated it. In particular they hated what they saw as the smugness and unquestioning obedience to outdated codes of behaviour that seemed to typify much of American society. Large numbers of American writers and artists went to Paris and formed an expatriate colony there. The lost-generation writers were hostile to American society, satirical and rebellious. Ernest Hemingway (see below) was deemed a member of this group, and William Faulkner and John Steinbeck may have been influenced by it.

As this work concerns itself only with those authors who appear regularly on examination and degree-course syllabuses, a large number of significant American writers are not included. The most numerous body to have demanded the attention of European examiners are undoubtedly novelists.

## The American novel

### Edgar Allan Poe (1809–49)

Poe has become a central figure in the study of 'Gothic' as a literary form and style, and any student interested in his work should refer also to Chapter 16 in this book.

Poe was the son of wandering actors; his father left his mother, and his mother died young, leaving Poe to be brought up by a merchant, with whom Poe had a tempestuous relationship. A start at a legal career, gambling debts, time in the army and time as an editor contributed to a stormy life, which ended tragically early as a result of alcoholism.

#### Poe's work

Poe could be seen as a greater poet than prose writer, but is included here under a prose heading because it is as a writer of macabre stories that he has achieved his greatest fame. Among these are 'The Fall of the House of Usher' (1839), 'The Masque of the Red Death' (1842) and 'The Pit and Pendulum' (1843). In his poetry he emphasised the qualities of 'music' and 'indefiniteness', and he produced well-argued theories of poetry to back up his work. His poetry is highly lyrical and atmospheric; the criticism levelled at it is that it is *all* atmosphere and nothing else. His capacity for sustained melancholy and a transcendental Romantic imagination are clear, but occasionally the lyricism rings hollow.

His short stories fall into two categories, the horror stories and detective stories. The former in particular are powerful expressions of a morbid imagination, capable of powerful symbolism, whilst the latter inject an intellectual sharpness into the genre. Poe was also a highly effective critic, and it is possible that this side of his writing has been wrongly ignored in favour of his more dramatic stories and even more dramatic life style.

Opinion is still mixed on Poe's lasting worth, although the huge increase in the popularity of Gothic writing has helped his critical credibility very significantly. He may have suffered in the past because the combination of popularity, sensationalism and a certain vulgarity is one that unsettles the critical establishment. Dickens has these features (with many others), and they have hampered his critical reputation. There is, however, much more to Poe than this, not least a unique quality to Poe's imagination that no other author has ever quite emulated.

## Herman Melville (1819–91)

If Poe's life was dramatic then Melville's was truly remarkable. The son of a bankrupt who died young, Melville took himself off to the sea, serving in whalers, merchant vessels and the American Navy. He used this experience as the basis for his early novels, which earned him great popular success. His most famous novel by far, *Moby Dick* (1851), marked the end of his period of popularity. Thereafter followed a period of steady decline, culminating in an obscure death as a minor customs official, and it was not until 1920 that Melville was resurrected and elevated to his present position. Melville wrote a great many books and stories – *Typee* (1846), *The Piazza Tales* (1856) and *Billy Budd* (1891) are particularly worthy of note, but it is *Moby Dick* that has won him lasting fame.

### *Moby Dick*

*Moby Dick* has suffered the same fate as Swift's *Gulliver's Travels*, in that it has been severely cut to act as a children's story. Many a child has returned to the uncut version of the book and found the metaphysical content a considerable surprise. It is weighty stuff. The whaling vessel the *Pequod* represents American and all society. The search for the great white whale, Moby Dick, is the search for universal truth and self-discovery, and Ahab and Ishmael are emblems of tragedy and survival. Even this cursory survey does minimal justice to the novel, whose various symbols echo and reverberate in a manner similar to the effect Coleridge achieves in 'The Rime of the Ancient Mariner'. *Moby Dick* is quite clearly a novel about good and evil, though as with many highly symbolic works the exact nature of the statement it makes on that subject is not always clear.

## Mark Twain (1835–1910)

It is a feature of early American novelists that they are known by one work, or, in Poe's case, one series of works. Mark Twain, whose real name was Samuel Clemens, is another such figure. Though his novel *Tom Sawyer* (1876) was and is immensely popular as a boys' story, it is the novel *Huckleberry Finn* (1884) for which Twain is best remembered.

### Themes in Twain's work

In one sense the high point of Twain's life was his time as a Mississippi River steamboat pilot. At that time the pilot was, in Twain's eyes, almost a God, 'the only unfettered and entirely independent human being that lived in the earth' (his *nom de plume*, 'Mark Twain', was a call used on riverboats to signal depth). This comment in itself reveals Twain's closeness to a part of American culture, the *denial of all authority* and the *fierce belief in the individual*, 'unfettered' and allowed to roam free, answerable only to himself. Twain's career was brought to a halt by the Civil War, which stopped all river traffic. After various adventures he became a writer. His novel *Tom Sawyer* is a boys' adventure novel, but in it he fails to hide his admiration for the free spirit of the boy and all it represents. *Huckleberry Finn* was planned simply as 'a kind of companion' to *Tom Sawyer*. It is far more than that.

As his life progressed Twain became more and more disenchanted with life and with America, following a well-trodden artistic path from optimism to depression. In his case bankruptcy added to his bitterness, something also true of England's Sir Walter Scott (1771–1832). Twain had to write to buy himself out of debt. That too left its mark. Family tragedies, disenchantment with the new, post-Civil War industrialised America and his own honest awareness of the hypocrisy of the idyllic, pre-war South all contributed to increasing melancholy, hidden beneath the facade of the humorist and extrovert. Twain wrote many books in the Southern–humorist style, and a number of travel books, often with an element of satire in them. It has been argued that his marriage into Eastern, genteel company spoilt his aggressive, Western satirical style. In any event, his skill as a satirist should not be overlooked. In his later life he came to see mankind as hypocrites and victims, the middle ground between them becoming thinner and thinner. His capacity to write as a child but somehow at the same time to create an adult perspective in that vision is a major force in his work. Of his other work, *Life on the Mississippi* (1883), *A Connecticut Yankee in King Arthur's Court* (1889) and *Pudd'nhead Wilson* (1894) best repay study.

### *Huckleberry Finn*

*Huckleberry Finn* is the story of a white boy and his journey down the Mississippi with his friend Jim, an escaped Negro slave. 'Huck' is about twelve years old, son of a jailbird and wastrel father. Part cheated out of his inheritance of significant wealth, part bludgeoned out of it by the fact that it brings his father's rapacious attention onto him, Huck Finn consciously rejects money and all the virtues of civilised life. The freedom he thus obtains is suddenly circumscribed by his meeting with Jim, a friend but also a runaway slave, and someone who is in dire need of Huck's help. This conundrum in itself acts as a symbol for part at least of the human condition. Freedom can only be obtained if moral and personal obligations are ditched. We respect Huck Finn for the fact that he chooses Jim, but his act is an emblem for humanity, an entity that yearns for freedom but which will at the same time lock itself in a dungeon and throw away the key for the sake of another human. In that fact lies both the tragedy and the reward of human existence: few have stated it more succinctly. The journey down the river is an education in hypocrisy, manipulation and human greed, but somehow from it Huck and Jim emerge unscathed, albeit much the wiser. The last chapters of the novels are usually deemed a failure. In them Tom Sawyer reappears, and the style and content of the novel revert to the rather silly game play of *Tom Sawyer*. Some argue that as a companion to *Tom Sawyer* it is only fitting that the novel should end back with the rather superficial tone of that novel; others see it as a wasted opportunity.

The novel is about *slavery*, *friendship* and *chicanery*, but it is also part of a wider tradition whereby life described through a child's eyes is shown in stark reality for what it is. One of *Huckleberry Finn's* great triumphs is that neither the reader nor Huck Finn ever becomes soured by what is revealed. There is an *optimism* in the book that does not conflict with its ability to show the *real world*. That world is partly the world of the magic river, the great Mississippi, partly the world of small-town America and partly a love story. The love is not for women, who hardly appear in the novel except as irritants or objects of pity. That love is summed up by the image of Huck and Jim moored up at some island on the great river, their raft tucked away out of sight, their food cooking on the camp fire and the two people snugly secure in the warmth of the companionship. It is love of the river, love of the outdoors and love of boyhood, *boyhood as a symbol of a simple, free self-sufficiency*. Twain has the strength of some of the great Romantic writers: dwarfed by Nature, in his case the river, he knows he will never find all the answers. He finds enough to make *Huckleberry Finn* a great book.

## Henry James (1843–1916)

There could be no greater contrast than that between Mark Twain and Henry James – the great outdoors and the privileged intellectual. James came from a wealthy background and went to law school, but soon concentrated on writing, coming increasingly to live in Europe. He wrote a vast number of books, among which some of the best known are *Washington Square* (1881); *Portrait of a Lady* (1881); *The Aspern Papers* (1888); *The Ambassadors* (1903); and *The Golden Bowl* (1904).

### Henry James' work

James saw himself as a detached observer of life, increasingly interested in the differences between American and European culture. Many of his novels use the gap between these two cultures as their springboard, presenting the reader with the American facing the complexity of European culture, with varying degrees of success. His novels are set against a background of affluence; they study manners, conversation and the refinements of civilised life.

It is conventional to divide James' career into three sections. The first, culminating with the publication of *The Portrait of a Lady*, is typified by psychological reality, examination of the growth of one individual's moral consciousness and the interplay between two civilisations and cultures. James does not express a preference for European or American culture. If anything the hope is that something stronger than either will emerge from the strain and stress of cross-fertilisation. In his second period, from the mid-1880s to the mid-1890s, his subjects become more specifically English, and he experimented with drama. The third period is the one which has aroused the most critical disagreement, it being argued that in this period James' work became over-refined and too highly stylised; supporters argue that this is merely the ultimate refinement in James' subtle portrayal of every aspect of a personality. Novels such as *The Ambassadors* and *The Golden Bowl* can be rather intense reading. It is sometimes overlooked that James in his later period wrote his novels by dictation; a different slant on his work can be given when it is heard read aloud, in one sense that being the way it was written.

James' criticism was very influential. His insistence on the importance of form, his emphasis on intricate psychological portrayal and his objective, distanced observation of the clash of two cultures have also exerted significant influence on the development of the modern novel. His weaknesses – over-elaboration and refinement, inability to write dialogue (all James' characters seem to speak with the same voice) – have not seriously challenged his position as a great novelist.

## William Faulkner (1897–1962)

William Faulkner left school early, joined the Royal Flying Corps in Canada in the First World War but never saw active service and then settled down to a life as a writer. He was a prolific poet, short story writer and novelist, several times winner of Pulitzer prizes and a Nobel Prize winner. His first novel to achieve lasting fame was *The Sound and the Fury* (1929). Later novels included *As I Lay Dying* (1930), *Intruder in the Dust* (1948) and *Requiem for a Nun* (1951).

### Faulkner's novels

Much of Faulkner's best work recreates life in north Mississippi, renamed for prose fiction purposes Yoknapatawpha Country. Faulkner has been criticised as merely a regional novelist, but few doubt the wide-ranging nature of his symbolism, or that his books have a relevance far beyond the physical confines of the country he recreates with such vividness. Faulkner has been seen as one of the 'lost generation', but the world-weariness that typified this group is only a small element in his work, though visible. There is a brutal, almost sadistic element in his work, a very great idealism about the *essential perfectibility of man* (something he expressed succinctly when accepting the Nobel Prize) and a tragic sense of *unfulfilled potential*. This latter theme is associated in much of his work with the South in the United States and its failure to avert its own destruction or recognise human values in the Negroes it enslaved. Failed humans in Faulkner's work are those who cannot love, and this inability dooms them. Sometimes they rise to near tragic status when it is perceived that their potential for love (and hence salvation) is stopped not by their own weakness but by the prejudice and malformed thought of the (Southern) society around them. Faulkner is equally opposed to the quest for self-aggrandisement, the non-idealistic human who cannot conceive of the finer emotions. *Love* and *racial prejudice* are the two main themes in Faulkner's greatest work, even if he never quite comes to terms with the inheritance of prejudice.

Faulkner's *technique*, sometimes aggressively modernist, has also attracted attention. Deliberately confused narrative lines, stream of consciousness, numerous narrators and intricate and elaborate style are common in his work. In some areas critics have sought to justify this experimentation. Time and chronology are rarely straightforward in a Faulkner novel, but it has been said that this merely reflects Faulkner's thematic belief that past and present flow in to each other, and do not exist in neat, separate compartments.

## Ernest Hemingway (1899–1961)

Hemingway was a reporter who saw service and was wounded in the First World War, as a member of a volunteer ambulance unit. His first great success was *A Farewell to Arms* (1929). Other well-known novels were *Death in the Afternoon* (1932), *To Have and To Have Not* (1937), *For Whom the Bell Tolls* (1940) and *The Old Man and Sea* (1952). He was awarded a Nobel Prize in 1954. He committed suicide by shooting himself, having been seriously ill for some time prior to his death.

## Hemingway's novels

Hemingway symbolises the 'lost generation' mentioned above. These were the men who had fought and served in the First World War and lost all faith and hope, both in themselves and in the institutions that went to make up society. All that was left was acceptance, and a retreat to what is sometimes referred to as a primal state, a state where only the basic emotions and attitudes are recognised, basic being defined as necessary for survival. The extent of this influence on Hemingway is arguable; the fact that he was obsessed with violence and brutality is not. He had spent much time hunting when he was young, and violence fascinated him. He sought to cauterise his own *fear of death*, brought about by his being wounded in 1918, by confronting physical danger whenever possible. His espousal of *primitive virtues* – fighting courage, resistance to pain, oneness with the natural environment – leads to what can be seen as an idealised portrait of what a true Romantic might recognise as a noble savage. Yet in Hemingway's best work there is far more than a portrayal of *macho* man. The lean, spare style of the 'lost generation' novels tends to hold emotion at arm's or rifle's length, but Hemingway can create a rich emotional pattern within the clipped, factual style he adopts. *The Torrents of Spring* is a very surprising novel, richly comic and in the final count self-mocking and heavily satirical on the cult of American masculinity.

What gives Hemingway his lasting value is his *nihilism*. His fear of death is partially also a fear that at the centre of life and death is Conrad's 'heart of darkness', a blank nothingness. That is what awaits us, the alternative being a cruel and rough world of violence and struggle. Hemingway is sometimes clumsy, but he confronts a fear at the heart of modern living, the fear that after all there may be nothing worth doing and nothing worth living for. It is the vision of the drama of the absurd, wrapped in fiercely realistic writing. It explains his love of richly physical experience, this giving at least some meaning to the passing of time, and it explains his conviction that we have only ourselves to rely on, and the recurrent theme in his novel of *unfulfilled love*. For Hemingway's characters to share their loneliness would be an easing of pain that he dare not admit to very often, for fear of wanting it too much. Both life and death are terrifying for Hemingway, and war often a potent symbol of life. A distinguishing feature is his ability to hold onto a certain faith in humanity, despite the fullness of his knowledge of its horrors.

## John Steinbeck (1902–68)

John Steinbeck came from a humble middle-class background, and attended Stanford University to study marine biology. He left without graduating, intending to be a writer, and faced quite severe hardship in his early days until he found success with *Tortilla Flat* (1935). He followed this with the equally successful *Of Mice and Men* (1937). His most famous work, for which he won a Pulitzer Prize, was *The Grapes of Wrath* (1939). Three later novels that are still widely read are *Cannery Row* (1944), *East of Eden* (1952) and *The Winter of Our Discontent* (1961). A modest but lonely man, usually dismissive of his own work, he was married three times, and won the Nobel Prize for Literature in 1962.

### Steinbeck and the critics

Steinbeck's reputation has been preserved by the fact that his books have continued to sell in large numbers, although in the past he has been viewed with some uncertainty by the critical establishment. He has been accused of superficiality, sentimentality, uneven style, melodrama and muddled thinking. He has also been called a 'regional novelist', in a manner that suggests his work is parochial and limited in meaning and scope. Conservatives have criticised his work for being communist, communists criticised it for not going far enough and for ignoring the obvious need for a revolution that his work suggests.

Many of these supposed criticisms suggest indirectly the strengths and lasting qualities of his work. There are no great intellectual surprises in what he writes, and he had few pretensions to being a critic or great thinker. There is a deep and abiding sympathy in his work for ordinary men and women, and immensely *powerful descriptive skills*, particularly when it comes to evoking and recreating atmosphere and place. He is a *master of dialogue*, with an unerring ability to present colloquial and vernacular speech. He can describe nature superbly and wholly without sentimentality, and use those descriptions to powerful symbolic effect. He has a consistent eye for the creation of tense and dramatic situations, and for intimate description of the relationships within a tightly knit group of people. The epic migration of the Joad family in *The Grapes of Wrath* is not only a poignant picture of the depression in the United States but also a symbol for the search for values.

## Other novels and novelists

### *The Great Gatsby*

One of the great classics of the twentieth century is *The Great Gatsby* (1925), by F. Scott Fitzgerald (1896–1940). It catches exactly the rotten–sweet blend of extravagance and corruption in America in the 1920s. It is a novel about futility, and based round a theme central to much American writing: a man and a woman seem to contain between them all that is needed to attain a dream of happiness and fulfilment, but that happiness and fulfilment are brutally snatched away from them as their own past, their own present actions and a hostile society destroy them and their dream. The poignancy is all the stronger because, as with a tragic hero, the source of their undoing is themselves, just as they are the source of their potential strength. At the same time, the hero of *The Great Gatsby* is not great at all, but a Prohibition bootlegger and criminal. The glamour of Gatsby's lifestyle is shown as a sham, a futile illusion.

Two other novels which are almost symbols for and of twentieth-century life are *The Catcher in the Rye* (1951) by J. D. Salinger (b. 1919) and *Catch 22* (1961) by Joseph Heller (b. 1923).

### *The Catcher in the Rye*

*The Catcher in the Rye* tells the story of the adolescent Holden Caulfield, convinced that all around him is 'phony' and desperately trying to preserve his innocence and essential goodness in a world where even his old English teacher makes homosexual advances to him and the prostitute he did not sleep with gets him involved in a fight for more money. The novel shows the adult world as almost wholly hypocritical, and respects Caulfield's search for something better, something he is hardly allowed to find.

***Catch 22***

Heller is an author who has been described in turn as paranoid, decadent, outstandingly clever and outstandingly funny. *Catch 22* is prose of the absurd. Its hero, Yossarian, is part of a bomber crew in the Second World War, condemned to fly ever more and more missions as his commander increases the number which each crew has to undertake. The novel shows Yossarian's attempt to cling on to sanity, a sanity which given Heller's vision of the world is really rather an ambitious desire. *Catch 22* is a magnificent satire, likely to last as an example of that genre as well as because of its implicit condemnation of the twentieth century.

## American poetry

### Walt Whitman (1819–92)

The son of a Radical and free-thinker, Whitman was schoolteacher, printer and journalist in turn. Something of a dandy, his image and his life changed dramatically in his very early thirties when he took on a vocation to become a 'prophetic bard' speaking for America and its ideal future. Whitman made myths in his poems and outside of them. The rough, sensual 'eating and drinking and breeding' image he sustained may have been at odds with what some critics have seen as his homosexuality. In any event the first version of *Leaves of Grass* appeared in 1855, and Whitman added to this throughout his life. He lost a great deal of money in the 1850s and tended the wounded in camp hospitals during the Civil War, from which he may have contracted the illness that bedevilled him for the rest of his life.

***Leaves of Grass***

The poems in *Leaves of Grass* are very varied. Their form is a major area of interest, as most of them are written in what would now be termed '*free verse*', the phrase or unit of meaning taking over as the basic structural unit, instead of conventional metre, rhythm or rhyme. Whitman's work celebrates procreation, the energy and diversity of Creation and the cyclical flow of energy that locks Creation into its vast cycle of death and rebirth. Whitman's poetry seeks to identify the unifying factors in Creation. Above all it celebrates energy. Democracy, love and religion were three key methods by which mankind might achieve the transcendental freedom that Whitman believed it capable of. The physical and highly sensual nature of his verse shocked many contemporaries and seriously harmed Whitman's career prospects, but from the outset he was recognised by many as a major and serious voice in American literature.

### Emily Dickinson (1830–86)

Emily Dickinson was born into a privileged family who helped provide her with a remarkably wide-ranging education. It is possible that she may have developed schizophrenia. In any event as she got older she became more and more of a recluse, never leaving her house and refusing visitors or contact with other people. It was only after her death that the full body of her poetry became available and was published, and that publication gave her a major and lasting reputation.

**Techniques in Emily Dickinson's verse**

Emily Dickinson's technique is bizarre. She makes heavy use of the dash, preferring it to the full stop, and uses capital letters at the start of words in defiance of grammar, but in line with her desire to emphasise certain words. Her diction (choice of words) is simple, but she chooses words with extensive connotations, producing at times what is almost a string of symbols and images, a network of meanings and suggestions that have a complexity and resonance rather at odds with their surface simplicity. *Condensation* of words and images is a key to her style. Her metrical form is very simple, usually based on that of a hymn – a four-line verse patterned in alternate lines of eight and six syllables.

**Themes in Emily Dickinson's work**

Emily Dickinson took her favoured verse form from Puritanism. An intense *spirituality* underpins all her work, but whilst she believed fervently in the presence of God in each person, and in His existence, she was unable to accept any conventional creed or belief. She saw God particularly in Nature and in the physical world, a feature which links her firmly to Romantic poetry.

*Transcendentalism* also influenced her, the belief that Truth could not be explained simply by rational thought and through the senses, but required an imaginative insight, an intuition that 'transcended' mere reason. The self-reliance and self-sufficiency encouraged by the movement were what attracted Emily Dickinson, and the results can be seen in her verse. Her overriding aim is to find and express truth, usually through the medium of metaphor. *Death* and the *isolation of the soul* are also common themes in her poetry.

## Ezra Pound (1885–1972)

Ezra Pound exerted a tremendous influence on modern verse. University-educated, he was unable to tolerate the restrictions of academic life. He lived largely in Italy and France, and became a leader of the *Imagist school* of poets, a school opposed to what was seen as the excessive sentimentality and subjectivity of prevailing European poetry, and aiming at hard, objective expression through the medium of imagery. He championed many new authors, including T. S. Eliot and James Joyce, and was heavily involved in promoting all modernist work. His most famous work was his *Cantos*, produced over a long period of time and finally collected in 1970. Pound was opposed to capitalism, but his anti-Semitism and other feelings prodded him towards support for Fascism. The wartime broadcasts he made for the Italians resulted in his being arrested after the war, but he was declared of unsound mind, released and returned to Italy, where he died.

**The 'Cantos'**

From relatively early in his career Pound developed a fondness for highly esoteric law and for complex theories that at times only he seemed capable of understanding. His *Cantos* and his work in general are very uneven. The statements they make are on every aspect of human life - politics, economics, religion and culture - and the materials used by Pound to illuminate his views are drawn from almost every culture known to mankind. There are moments of surpassing beauty in his work, and of great insight, but also long stretches where the work seems to die in its own complexity. Pound's influence was vast. His experiments with metre follow on from Whitman's revolution and have for many poets helped to rewrite the rule book, or throw it away completely. His determination that poetry should be intellectually demanding, his optimism and searching intellect and his restless urge to experiment make him as important for those he has influenced as for what he himself wrote.

## Other poets

**Robert Frost (1874–1963)**

Frost has always been popular in England, where he lived from 1912 to 1915. He spent many years farming, and that and his conscious simplicity pervade much of his poetry. He perceived art as something that cut away the outer and deceptive layers of experience to reveal the heart of the matter, and his lean style, operating through suggestion rather than by direct thematic statements, produces an interesting lyric realism, with a strong sense of the individual.

**Robert Lowell (1917–77)**

Lowell has themes that can be seen as typical of many American writers: *rebellion, images of decay and corruption* and the *search for spiritual truth* within a religious setting typify his early work, with interesting changes visible when he later became agnostic. The intensity and elaboration of his work is in contrast to the work of Robert Frost.

**e. e. cummings (1894–1962)**

Cummings developed his own typography and words somewhat in the manner of Emily Dickinson. A very gifted satirist with more than a hint of the anarchist in his cheerful hatred of authority and repression, he too was influenced by transcendentalist thought, but the major plea in his work is for the heart and soul of humanity and against those who live by mind alone.

**Henry Longfellow (1807–82)**
As a parting shot, the work of Longfellow deserves the attention of the student seeking a subject for a long essay, project or dissertation. Longfellow was immensely popular in America and in Great Britain in his day, but suffered savage criticism when fashions changed and his particular form of high Romanticism fell into disrepute. His poetry is simple, rather benign and sweet and distanced from the restless passion of, say, Cummings or Lowell. It can still be surprisingly effective.

## American drama

The relative success of British and European drama in recent years has perhaps contributed to a rather low level of interest being shown in American drama in Europe. The leading figure has been Arthur Miller, whose work has been discussed in Chapter 23.

### Thornton Wilder (1897–1975)

Wilder is best known in Britain for *Our Town* (1938). Primarily a satiric and comic writer, he has at the same time a gentle and popular touch. An underlying optimism and faith in humanity can take the edge off his work, which includes a number of excellent novels.

### Tennessee Williams (1911–1983)

Tennessee Williams is known for *The Glass Menagerie* (1944), *A Streetcar Named Desire* (1947), and *Cat On a Hot Tin Roof* (1955). He has been seen at times as a sensationalist. The violence, sexuality and physical horror of some of his work were more shocking when the plays were originally produced than they are now, and always in his work the violence and elements of the horror story are used to a purpose, and are not gratuitous. More often than not that purpose is to describe and portray the figure of a lone woman tortured by the present but sustained by a vision of the past or the future. The insecurity that is rampant in this figure is smashed by the arrival of the young male intruder, rather similar to the destruction from outside that typified the early plays of Harold Pinter. Violence in his plays cuts through social and personal pretence and is almost a primitive, motivating force in the Hemingway style.

### Edward Albee (b. 1928)

Albee is best known for *Who's Afraid of Virginia Woolf?* (1962), a play in which a middle-class supper party turns into a session of verbal torture and cruelty, with a redeeming resolution at the end when the violence is seen to lead to understanding and release. Albee is an absurd dramatist (see

Chs 3 and 23) who increasingly adopts a symbolist, wilfully obscure mode of presentation.

## Further reading

### General

The *Cambridge History of American Literature* so far runs to three volumes, all of which are edited by Sacvan Bercovitch: *Volume 1: 1590–1820* (1997); *Volume 2: Prose Writing 1820–1870* (1995); *Volume 8: Poetry and Criticism 1940–1995* (1996). Unfortunately only volume 1 is available in paperback. Don Wilmeth, ed., *The Cambridge Guide to American Theatre* (Cambridge University Press, 1996) is an excellent detailed survey, as is Malcolm Bradbury, ed., *The Modern American Novel* (Oxford University Press, 1992). Douglas Tallack, *Twentieth Century America. The Intellectual and Cultural Context* (Longman, 1991) is one of the best cultural histories of America. Richard Gray, *American Poetry of the Twentieth Century* (Longman, 1990); Brian Lee, *American Fiction 1865–1940* (Longman, 1988); Tony Hilfer, *American Fiction Since 1940* (Longman, 1992) and Gerald M. Berkowitz, *American Drama of the Twentieth Century* (Longman, 1992) are all very good value.

### Ralph Waldo Emerson

- Joel Porte and Saundra Morris, ed., *The Cambridge Companion to Ralph Waldo Emerson* (Cambridge University Press, forthcoming)

### William Faulkner

- Frederick Karl, *William Faulkner: American Writer* (Faber, 1989)
- Philip M. Weinstein, ed., *The Cambridge Companion to William Faulkner* (Cambridge University Press, 1995)

### F. Scott Fitzgerald

- Ruth Prigozy, ed., *The Cambridge Companion to F. Scott Fitzgerald* (Cambridge University Press, forthcoming)

### Robert Frost

- Robert Faggen, ed, *The Cambridge Companion to Robert Frost* (Cambridge University Press, forthcoming)

### Ernest Hemingway

- Scott Donaldson, ed., *The Cambridge Companion to Hemingway* (Cambridge University Press, 1996)

## Henry James

- Leon Edell, *Henry James. A Life* (Flamingo/Harper Collins, 1996)
- Jonathan Freedman, ed., *The Cambridge Companion to Henry James* (Cambridge University Press, forthcoming)
- Kenneth Graham, *Henry James. A Literary Life* (Macmillan, 1995)
- Sheldon N. Novick, *Henry James. The Young Master* (Random House, 1996)
- N. H. Reeve, ed., *Henry James: The Shorter Fiction* (Macmillan, 1997)

## Herman Melville

- Robert Levine, ed., *The Cambridge Companion to Herman Melville* (Cambridge University Press, 1998)

## Ezra Pound

- Ira Nadel, ed., *The Cambridge Companion to Ezra Pound* (Cambridge University Press, forthcoming)
- Peter Wilson, *A Preface to Ezra Pound* (Longman, 1997)

## John Steinbeck

- Thomas Fensch, ed., *Conversations with John Steinbeck* (University Press of Mississippi, 1988)
- Jay Parini, *John Steinbeck. A Biography* (Minerva, 1994)

## Mark Twain

- Forrest G. Robinson, ed., *The Cambridge Companion to Mark Twain* (Cambridge University Press, 1995)

## Walt Whitman

- Ezra Greenspan, *The Cambridge Companion to Walt Whitman* (Cambridge University Press, 1995)

## Tennessee Williams

- Matthew C. Roudane, ed., *The Cambridge Companion to Tennessee Williams* (Cambridge University Press, 1997)

CHAPTER TWENTY-FIVE

# Literary and critical theory

From time to time various academic disciplines have been subject to periods of introspection and self-doubt, their practitioners anxious to define what is being studied and the effectiveness of the tools being used for the study. Some subjects have been more prone to this than others, a classic example being Geography. To merit a degree being awarded, a Geographer clearly had to do more than make a map and list the industrial or agricultural produce of a given country. But almost from the outset Geography was challenged by other subjects which seemed to be about to invade its territory. Economics, Geology, Anthropology and a host of other subjects all appeared to be nibbling at what had been seen as the preserve of Geography, so that at one stage it looked as if nothing would be left. For this reason large numbers of undergraduates in the 1960s spent a disproportionate amount of time gazing into mirrors and asking 'What is Geography?' Someone somewhere clearly provided an answer, as the subject thrives to the present day.

English Literature was a subject poised some way between the apparent certainly of a subject like Mathematics and the seeming fragility of Geography. From time immemorial humanity had been responding to literature, and as a major concern of the human situation it was an obvious candidate to be included among the canon of new degree subjects. Its aim, in rather more simple days, was clear. A large element of it consisted of *scholarship*. Scholarship was the dry bones of critical study. It went into great detail about the classical antecedents that *might* have influenced Shakespeare in a certain line in a certain play. It waxed euphoric about the presumed confines of the Globe Theatre or charted the textual variants in the surviving manuscript of *King Lear*. Dull some of it may have been, but it provided the essential information in understanding what authors wrote and why.

At the same time, various famous names sought to define, almost by accident, the nature of criticism. A. C. Bradley wrote a book at the turn of the century which treated Shakespeare's characters as if they were real, breathing human beings, and in so doing contravened most of the regulations drawn up for undergraduates in the twentieth century. His marvellously warm, human book, *Shakespearian Tragedy*, has become an irreplaceable classic. So have the works of E. M. W. Tillyard, F. R. Leavis and I. A. Richards, despite the fact that on close examination these invigorating and rewarding works reveal strongly opposed theories of what the proper job and function of the critic is to be. Seminal figures in the history of twentieth-century literature such as T. S. Eliot wrote critical works, and in so doing defined explicitly or implicitly the nature of criticism and the function of literature.

However, it was not until the 1920s and 1930s that systematic attempts began to be made to draw up specific, codified theories of the nature and function of both literature and criticism. Some of these attempts were the result of applying to literature thought patterns and ideas which had a far wider currency, such as Marxism and Feminism. Others sprang out of research into linguistics and patterns of consciousness. Others were simply attempts to carve out a special niche for the critic and define his job and the material with which he worked. No one can doubt that such attempts are essential if literary studies are to continue to justify their existence, but they have brought major problems with them. Certain of these theories are of interest only to specialist academics. The language in which they are discussed and written about is often very difficult and tangled, the issues complex and sometimes confused. Internal squabbling at the University of Cambridge over Structuralism did little to enhance the public image of criticism, particularly as during the short period in which the media interested itself in this hitherto unknown phenomenon it failed to find a single academic who could explain satisfactorily to the ordinary man in the street what Structuralism actually was. There is much interest and stimulus in literary theory and criticism, but also much obfuscation, much confusion and a fair number of red herrings.

There are five reference points in literary and critical theory:

- language and the mechanics of literary language
- the work itself
- society and the historical background to a work of literature
- the author
- the reader.

Most schools of literary and critical theory can be defined by their attitude to one or all of these factors.

What follows is a rough chronological account of modern developments in literary and critical theory, though Historicism, to name only one example, has been around in different forms for many years.

## Archetypal criticism

Archetypal criticism sprang from two sources. The first was the School of Comparative Anthropology at the University of Cambridge and the book which came to symbolise some of its views, J. G. Fraser's *The Golden Bough* (1890–1915). This book traced 'elemental' myths and rituals which, it claimed, could be proved to run through and recur in very many diverse cultures. This tied in naturally with the theories of C. G. Jung, who believed that human life gave rise to types of experience that repeated themselves again and again, regardless almost of the historical and cultural background. This repetition built up 'primordial images', best seen in myths and dreams, that become part of the 'collective unconsciousness' of the human race, and which become images and symbols of great power when called upon by literary artists. Taken together, both views could be made to argue for a set of archetypal patterns in literature, patterns based on the central experiences of human life and which because of their eternity and lasting relevance achieve profound meaning.

Although a relative sideline in the flood of modern critical theories, it would be wise not to ignore Archetypal criticism, for all that it tends to oversimplify complex issues. The significance of myth in literature cannot be ignored, and some of the major myths that have been delineated are the death–rebirth cycle, the search or quest for healing and regeneration, the Promethean rebel–hero saga, the Beowulf or defeat of the monster myth, the Frankenstein myth, the Faustian myth and a host of myths about women and sexuality. The critic Northrop Frye even went so far as to see a series of equivalents or correspondences, with four great myths corresponding to the four seasons, and in turn corresponding to the four great literary genres of tragedy, comedy, romance and satire. T. S. Eliot based part of *The Waste Land* round *The Golden Bough*. A very different but equally famous work, J. R. Tolkien's *Lord of the Rings*, was based firmly on myth. Robert Graves's work was heavily informed by Archetypal criticism, as was the inspirational critical writing of G. Wilson Knight.

## Russian Formalism

Russian Formalism originated in Russia in the 1920s, was suppressed in the 1930s and moved as a result to Czechoslovakia. Its best-known exponents are probably Roman Jakobson, Jan Mukarovsky and Rene Wellek, all originally members of the Prague Linguistic Circle, and with Jakobson and Wellek exercising considerable influence as professors at American universities. As a movement, Russian Formalism ceased in the 1930s, but its supporters and its principles have had a major effect on literary and critical theory.

The Russian Formalists were concerned that literary studies had no life or meaning of their own, and were becoming simply a rag-bag consisting of remnants and ill-digested remains of other academic disciplines, such as history, philosophy, psychology and sociology. What was needed was for literary studies to stand up proudly in a suit of clothes that was entirely their own. Formalists sought therefore to define literary studies as an independent and intellectually rigorous discipline in its own right.

They started by trying to define what the subject matter of literary study actually was, and as is often the case with such attempts they found it easier to say what literature was not. It was not, in their opinion, *expressive* or *mimetic*. Expressive criticism treated literary work in terms of its author: the work sprang directly from the author's imagination, and could therefore best be understood and appreciated by reference to the nature and personality of that author. As all literature was an expression of the author's vision of the world, he or she was the key to any understanding of that view. Mimetic criticism saw literature as a reflection or representation of the world and of reality, to be judged therefore on the accuracy and truth of that representation. In much the same manner one might judge a painter on his ability to produce a painting that looked convincingly like its subject did in real life.

The Formalists concentrated on language, and decided that normal, everyday language had a wholly separate function from language found in literature. Put at its very simplest, literature consisted of language that was made strange or *defamiliarised*. The process of defamiliarisation suggested that by its very difference from ordinary language literary language refocused the reader's attention onto whatever was being written about, and let the reader rediscover his capacity for lost sensation. 'Literariness' and defamiliarisation apply a sharp, bitter-sweet poultice to jaded palates, forcing a new awareness by means of strangeness. In one sense this was hardly a new idea, as the Romantic poets had seen one function of language as being to refresh and renew our vision of life and show us in an unfamiliar light things to which we had become accustomed. It is easy to see that poetry adapts to Formalist study more easily than other mediums because it has techniques of moulding and adapting language (rhyme, rhythm, metre, diction) that clearly distinguish poetic language (in some authors at least) from normal language. Formalists did not believe that individual books were the proper study of literature; instead, *literariness* was the proper aim of literary studies, the definition of that which makes a given work a literary work. Formalism has exerted a considerable influence on **Structuralism**, both movements being greatly concerned with the structure of language.

## Marxist criticism

Marxist literary theory bases its outlook on the philosophy and principles of Karl Marx and Friedrich Engels. It is not a formal school in the manner of some others discussed here, but rather a loosely-knit group of theories and individuals which, whilst retaining a central unity, has tended to bend, shape and flex itself into a variety of reassessements and new models. It shares this at least with **Feminist criticism**, and there are a number of Marxist–Feminist or Feminist–Marxist critics.

Marxists believe that literature can only be understood by being viewed in context with history and society, both of which are and have been dominated by the class struggle and by the ownership of the means of production. In any age humans work to an *ideology*, a *superstructure* of ideas which they erect themselves to explain the way society works. In our present age every possible aspect of society is riddled with the *bourgeois* mentality, the bourgeoisie being the class which owns the means of production. The bourgeoisie are distinct from the *proletariat*, the wage-earning and working class. A 'vulgar' Marxist critic treats all literary works of art as being dominated by the bourgeois mentality, and demands a literature that will present social realism, meaning more often than not the triumph of Marxist ideals. This branch of Marxist theory has become somewhat discredited because of its association with the production of officially-approved art in communist states. More commonly, a Marxist critic can allow for the individuality of works of literature, and their ability to rise above bourgeois constraints. Thus a truly great author will be so accurate an observer and so powerful a presenter of social reality that they will be unable to avoid showing class conflict, the brutality of bourgeois oppression and the alienation of the individual under capitalism.

In an interesting link with Russian Formalists, the German Marxist Bertolt Brecht produced a theory of drama which saw its purpose not as reflecting life and truth and aiming at gathering the audience's sympathy for the protagonist, but instead as producing an *alienation effect* (see Ch. 3) which provoked estrangement in the audience, and hence shocked them out of their placid acceptance of capitalist norms and into a new awareness of social reality. The best-known of Marxist critics is the Hungarian Georg Lukács, whilst in England the leading contemporary figures have been Raymond Williams and Terry Eagleton. Their research has concentrated on *literary modes of production*, namely the social and material factors affecting the production of literature. If a major body of literature is produced as a result of upper-class patronage, it is inevitable that this fact will influence the nature of what is written. It is in a way typical of Marxist criticism that Eagleton's work has taken on board elements of **Deconstruction, Freudian Psychoanalysis** and **Feminist** criticism, illustrating the healthy catholicism that typifies the best Marxist work. Another view of the manner in which some modern writers have shifted emphases and jackdaw-picked at various branches of modern criticism is that it reflects too great a concern on the part of writers to be fashionable or to create a new fashion. In any event, Marxist criticism is anti-Formalist, and relatively little interested in linguistics.

It is crucial that the student is not put off by the labels attached to a number of critical schools. Marxist critical writing can enhance one's perception of a text regardless of one's political views, just as feminist criticism can do the same without the reader being in any meaningful sense a feminist. These are not political or doctrinal labels, but simply offer different perspectives on literature.

## Psychoanalytic and psychological criticism

Psychoanalytic criticism deals with a work of literature as the expression of the inner psyche or character and personality of the author. It is no new thing to link an author and his work very closely, although this approach is an anathema to a number of modern theories of criticism, such as Formalism and Structuralism. What was new was the influence of Sigmund Freud (1856–1939), who developed psychoanalysis as a method of dealing with mental illness, but then helped it to expand to cover a very wide number of other areas, including literary criticism.

Freud's basic contention was that humans have desires, largely sexual in nature, that are denied either because the lifestyle of the person does not allow them to take place, society bans them or the individual himself feels crippling guilt at the possibility of their enactment. The 'libido' prompts these desires in the mind, whilst the 'censor' is the name given to the internal faculty which represses these desires into the subconscious. Repression is not destruction. The desires do not go away. In the case of a patient harmed or crippled by neurosis these repressed desires exert an indirect but terrible pressure on the conscious mind, pressure which can change personality and stop a human from functioning effectively as a member of society.

Literature provides a form in which the mind's censor can permit the repressed desires to be expressed and released indirectly. The conscious mind or ego does not see what is written as the expression of these repressed desires, and therefore allows it through into print. However, these disguised fantasies carry tremendous strength in their coded, hidden form, strength both for the author and for the reader. Thus the author will 'condense' repressed desires into one, powerful whole, 'displace' it so that what was socially unacceptable becomes acceptable in a disguised form, and produce 'symbols' that can represent what is usually a sexual object without seeming to do so. In the latter category, the great white whale in *Moby Dick* and the lighthouse in Virginia Woolf's *To the Lighthouse* are both seen by psychoanalytic critics as a condensation, a displacement and a symbol of forbidden sexual desires.

Psychoanalytic criticism seeks to reveal the 'true' content of a work, and to explain its effect on the reader. The outward form of a work is translated back into its real form, as it exists in the unconscious. Freud believed that the literary artist, far from being mentally ill, was someone who possessed a power to take subliminal, unconscious fixations and communicate them with great strength. Understanding what the author has done is at the same time a gateway back to reality, back to the basic urges that govern our mentality. Psychoanalytic criticism can be applied to an author, his motivation for writing and his real meaning; to characters within a book; and to the eader and his response to a given work, the latter giving rise to **Reader Response criticism** in part. Psychoanalytic criticism has made a major contribution to literary studies. It does not demand total blind allegiance from those who are aware of it, and a significant number of critics have learnt from it and adapted part of its tenets in their own approach. It is not dogmatic, and by and large its major supporters have followed the lead of Sigmund Freud by writing clearly, logically and with considerable conviction. It carries within it the danger of becoming dominated by one theme, sexuality, and an additional danger is the inherently comic nature of both fanatical single-mindedness and sexuality. However, and unlike some other critical schools, Psychoanalytic criticism has managed to retain its own sense of humour, and avoid some of the excesses to which other schools have been prone. To those interested in this field of study there is no better introduction than *Hamlet and Oedipus* by the psychoanalyst Ernest Jones, first published in 1949.

## New Criticism

New Criticism took its name from *The New Criticism* by John Crowe, published in 1941, but the real founder of the movement was I. A. Richards, and in particular his book *Principles of Literary Criticism* (1924). The critical essays of T. S. Eliot are often associated with this movement. Cleanth Brooks and Robert Penn Warren's *Understanding Poetry* (1938) was a seminal work for the movement, doing much to establish it as the dominant critical school in American teaching for nearly thirty years. The work of the famous English critic F. R. Leavis is also associated with this movement, as is that of William Empson.

The New Criticism was in part a reaction against criticism which placed great reliance on an understanding of the literary and historical background to a work, on examination of the psychology and views of the author and the social background to a work. Above all the New Criticism demanded a 'close reading' of the text itself, seeing that text as an independent item that can be explained and understood purely in terms of itself, without reference to the author, literary history or sociological background. The New critics demanded objectivity, which in their terms meant close attention to the text itself. A poet who was very much a product of the 1930s, W. H. Auden, gave unintentional support to the school in his poem 'In Memory of W. B. Yeats' when he wrote of a poem being an object cast upon the waves, totally divorced and separate from its author once it has been written, forced to exist as a poem regardless of why or when it had been written.

New critics were very aware of ambiguity and the ironies that existed within a text, the potential of language to hold several, sometimes opposed meanings, within itself. The classic expression of this is to be found in William Empson's *Seven Types of Ambiguity*. This leads on to the New critics' emphasis on the importance of language, a specific form of literary language that cannot be paraphrased or shortened without severing the veins and arteries that define its existence.

Irony, ambiguity and paradox are central to the New critics' view of literature. Despite their own rejection of sociology or 'background' information, it is difficult not to see in the New criticism a reflection of the 1930s, when all values were challenged but very few new ones created. By insisting on a retreat to the text, and a single-minded concentration on that to the exclusion of almost all else, the New critics can act as an emblem for the lost and tortured 1930s. They can also act for much more, as their influence is still very strong in academic and university circles, despite all the later movements that have arisen. The New Criticism spawned one phrase which seems to have achieved critical immortality, the *intentional fallacy*. This was the supposed error of interpreting a literary work by referring to the intentions and hopes of its author. The success of the concept of the 'intentional fallacy' may have something to do with the fact that it reflects common sense. If every author who had wished to produce a classic work had done so, undergraduate courses in English Literature would need to last for a century. Quite clearly a work of literature has to stand and fall on what it is, not on what its author intended it to be. Intelligent and persuasive authors such as Henry James and George Bernard Shaw could write illuminatingly on their work, but the New critics did succeed in establishing that such views should not determine one's understanding of a particular work. For that reason alone, despite their being unfashionable, they are worth reading today. They are also worth reading because the majority of them can write effectively and well, something which sadly is not true of many more contemporary authorities.

## Phenomenology and the Geneva School

**Phenomenology** sprang from the work of a man who was a philosopher rather than a literary critic. The German Edmund Husserl (1859–1938) set out to describe and define human consciousness. One of his premises proposed very strong, inseparable links between the person who thinks a thought and the object that in Husserl's world is created by that act of thinking. Phenomenology was developed by Martin Heidegger (1889–1976) in Germany and by the Polish Roman Ingarden, but when phenomenological criticism is mentioned it is often shorthand for the **Geneva School** of critics, a group linked largely through their working at the University of Geneva.

The Geneva School is highly subjective, and thus very different from **Formalism** and **New Criticism**. For the Geneva School a work of literature is an expression in words and print of the unique personality of its author, and thereby of human consciousness. The reader must empty his mind of all preconceptions, and in so doing will by the act of reading become at one with the mind of the author. The work of literature is therefore an agency for achieving a unique form of empathy, of direct and vivid communication with the author. It is this communion with another mind that is at the heart of the experience proposed by the School. Phenomenology tends to disregard the historical background to a work, a link with the New critics, but differs from New Criticism in that it also disregards form, preferring instead to concentrate on the content of a work.

## Stylistics

Stylistics is part of the search for an objective, scientific method of analysing literary texts, and has been a strong influence since the 1950s. As might be expected, Stylistics concentrates on the *style* of a work, and how an author chooses to express himself, and is therefore less concerned with what is being said. Stylistics is much more concerned with form than it is with content. It leans quite heavily on *linguistics*, and throughout it can be seen as one of the numerous branches of critical theory which have what amounts to a distrust of the author, of feeling and subjectivity, and which seek to define and ratify literature in the manner in which science proper defines its subjects.

One aim of stylistics is to define a work of literature in terms of its patterns of speech, diction, metre and rhythm, its sentence structure and syntax, its grammar and grammatical structure and its use of rhetorical figures of speech, imagery and so on. All these, it will be noted, do not need any awareness of the author, what the author intended to say or indeed any theme to a work. However, the stylistic fingerprint of a work can, once deduced, be related to the individual personality of an author, or the cultural and historical norms of a given period. The stylistic interpretation of a work is therefore first established, and can thereafter be related to author or sociological, historical and biographical features.

Stylistics is a very diffuse area, influencing a number of schools and theorists, and also the victim of occasional ridicule. As with many of the theories studied here, the ridicule does not diminish the value of Stylistics but merely acts as a restraint on some of its excess. Structuralism in particular would benefit from some of the same treatment, a sense of humour and proportion not being the most noted feature of that pattern of thinking.

## Structuralism

Structuralism is arguably the most difficult of modern theories of criticism and the most divorced from normal, everyday thought. It was born and bred in France, and inaugurated in the 1950s by the cultural anthropologist Claude Lévi-Strauss, who in turn owed a debt to the real founding father of the movement, Ferdinand de Saussure and his book on linguistics published in 1915. Much of its difficulty comes from the fact that its founding fathers and its subsequent mummies and daddies have developed a fondness for inventing their own language and terms of definition. The problem is not a new one. Generations of Economics first-year undergraduates, and numerous A-level students, have been caught out and perplexed by the fact that a simple term such as 'marginal' means something totally different in Economics from what it means in ordinary life. It is a besetting sin of those who theorise on literary and critical theory that they insist on choosing words in normal usage to refer to something completely different.

At its heart, Structuralism proposes that there is no such thing as objective reality in literature. The basic element of all literature, the *phonemes* or elementary speech sounds of a language, do not have a permanent or obvious meaning. Instead, their meaning is created by the internal relationships, stresses and patterns which they set up amongst themselves. Key definitions in the theory are the *signifier* of meaning, which can be written or spoken language, and the *signifieds*, or meanings created by the signifier. Structuralism perceives a number of differing levels of meaning and interpretation: each level up organises the lower level into complex combinations and functions. Language is a 'signifying system', signals of meaning which reach their potential through bouncing off each other, and not from any relationship to the author or sociological, background factors. There is thus an implicit system of meaning to any 'signifying system' or language structure; some of this is understood by those who use it, but much is not. It needs the Structuralist critic to explain the otherwise inexplicable.

Structuralism is directly opposed to **mimetic criticism**, which sees literature as an imitation of reality, and to **expressive criticism**, which sees literature as being linked to the feelings and views of the author. It tries to isolate criticism within a theory of linguistics and language structure, and to divorce it from all other factors. It has been criticised for being too formalist, and for its insistence that the text is a closed system, cut off from any external input. Structuralism opposes the view that literature is a mode of communication between author and reader. Perhaps most of all Structuralism presents the view of one of its founders, Roland Barthes, that 'the author is dead'. The reader is similarly dismissed, though in 1975 there was a branch of the movement which shifted interest onto the reader as an element in literature and criticism. Structuralism looks at many of the concepts and words generated by criticism over the years and sees these merely as conventions acquired from earlier reading or the prevailing culture. Structuralism beats an old drum when it states that by frustrating or altering accepted standards of language it reveals the tacit conventions and codes that govern language and our interpretation of it, thus shocking, stirring and stimulating us into a new awareness of those codes. The real problem with Structuralism is that it seeks to destroy the theory that literature reflects, imitates or seeks to recreate external reality, yet to many ordinary readers this idea underpins their attitude not only to literature but also to art in general. In this area Structuralism reflects developments in modern art away from pictorial representations of reality and into more abstract forms, forms which can be guaranteed to outrage at least some elements in society. That outrage need not be taken too seriously, in that in an earlier age it greeted the news that the world was round. The 'common-sense' view of the function of literature and criticism is attractive by virtue of simplicity, but not always convincing. It is as well to remember that from a common-sense viewpoint it is quite clear that the Sun revolves round the Earth.

## Deconstruction and poststructuralism

Once Structuralism had become established, the French thinker Jacques Derrida took Saussurian linguistic concepts and some of the ideas of Structuralism to create **Deconstruction**, a term which is almost interchangeable with **Poststructuralism**. Derrida took the Structuralist fondness for coining new words several stages further. His work can be described as 'complex and elusive', but also as full of 'esoteric jargon', 'linguistic word play' and as being 'turgid'. Deconstruction believes that there is nothing outside the text of a work, no absolute certainties, and no key to the intentions of an author. Derrida was able to study a passage and produce from it a more or less conventional reading, and then apply the principles of deconstruction to show that the actual language or signifiers in the text 'deconstructed' that interpretation and made it meaningless. Thus all writing deconstructs itself. The relationship between a word or phrase and its intended meaning is variable and in a permanent state of flux, so it is impossible to ascribe a fixed meaning to it. Structuralism posed a theory based on a structure of language and the way it operates; poststructuralism denies the existence of that structure, and almost the existence of any structure. Derrida is gentleman enough to admit that his own writing deconstructs itself immediately it has been written. In fairness to him it should be noted that his theories were evolved to cope with all language, and not specifically as methods of literary criticism.

## Feminist criticism

Feminist criticism became established in the late 1960s, but as with so many of the theories discussed here it was a formalisation of concerns and ideas that had been in existence for many years. There is also no single voice of Feminist criticism. Feminist critics can write from a Structuralist, Marxist or any other stance, though under the general umbrella of Feminist criticism. Feminist criticism is more dynamic than any other literary or critical theory at the present time, and is expanding with the fervour of an evangelical revival. It has also produced a large number of very readable and very profound works of criticism, in contrast to many of the schools named above, which have produced large numbers of rather incestuous works on criticism itself.

At the heart of feminist theory is the belief that society is wholly *patriarchal*, organised, controlled and ruled by the male sex, in the interests of men and with the aim of subordinating women to men in all areas of life, work and culture. Marxism merely translates this in its own terms by seeing women as a subordinate social class. As a part of male domination, women are conditioned to accept and promulgate the view of women that allows them to be dominated, so that they become a major element in their own enslavement. Whilst the anatomical difference between the sexes is a fact, the association between one's gender and a host of other features – all the things that go to make up our concept of what is 'feminine' and what is 'masculine' – is a 'cultural construct', a fabrication of that same male-dominated society, with no objective existence in fact. Women are not born; they are made by society in an image of convenience. It is thus a fallacy that men are brave, strong, rational, creative, and women passive, emotional and supportive, but the expectation that this is true produces the reality, in the manner of a self-fulfilling prophecy. Feminist critics show how the odds have been stacked against women throughout literature, and in particular how literature has been dominated by men writing for men. In the great landmark of Renaissance culture, *Hamlet*, the hero is male and women either derided or subjugated, sexually treacherous or weak. In American culture with novels such as *Tom Sawyer* or *Huckleberry Finn*, women are at best peripheral figures (an advantage for a male writer in writing about children is the extent to which women can be relegated to having only a minor function), at worst interfering busybodies who cannot understand and wish to tame the essential male adventurousness and imagination of the boys. Language is also shown to be almost hopelessly biased towards male dominance, starting from the common term for our species being 'mankind'. **Gynocriticism** is criticism that deals exclusively with literature written by women, in all its aspects. Attempts have been made to define a specifically female subject matter, a specifically female tradition of writing and a specifically female style. Feminist critics have also sought to redefine the accepted list of great works, rescuing large numbers of female writers from obscurity, and establishing quite large numbers of female writers as worthy of the attention hitherto denied them. French feminists have tended to follow the pattern of most French exploration of literary and critical theory, and gone for critic-to-critic exploration of the 'theory' of gender in writing. The search of Structuralists of both genders for a 'theory' is often only equalled in strength by their inability to explain it once they have found it.

For the student dipping her or his toe into critical and literary theory for the first time Feminist criticism is arguably the best place to start. It has a huge variety of works to choose from, it is often very well written and provocative and it preaches a clear and logical message, in the process managing to add significantly to scholarly and academic understanding of many major and minor works.

## Reader response criticism

Reader Response criticism takes as its centre and starting point the response of the reader to a given work of literature. Reader Response critics by and large accept that the meaning of any work of literature depends to an extent on the individual reader. Thus with the distrust of authority that typifies so many modern critical theories, Reader Response criticism argues that there is no single 'correct' meaning for a work of literature. However, Reader Response critics find it hard to agree what it is that shapes a reader's response, how much control the author can exert over his reader's response and where one distinguishes between what is a determined and absolute fact in a work of literature, and what is movable and unfixed in the light of the response of the individual reader. In what is something of a relief from certain other schools, the theory does acknowledge the reader, and acknowledge sometimes the reader as a co-partner in the act of creation; the act of reading is a creative act which completes the work created by the author.

Structuralist critics accept part of Reader Response critical theory, inasmuch as their theory rests in part on the concept that the reader approaches a work of literature with preconceived structures of language in his or her head. On the other hand, Deconstructionists base their theory on the fact that the reader reads any writing as a collection of differences that spawn contradictory meanings, and so for both schools an awareness of the reader is an essential starting point. True, Reader Response critics start with the idea of exploring what happens when a reader's eyes meet a text for the first time. After that, they differ wildly, but if nothing else Reader Response criticism justifies its existence by recognising that the reader is an element in the act of literary creativity. **Reception Theory** is a historical application of Reader Response theory, first proposed by Hans Robert Jauss in 1971, and still seen as primarily a German movement. For Jauss and for many others literature only fully exists with the active participation of the reader. There will be moments of *indeterminacy* in any text, and to fill in these blank or grey areas the reader will apply the knowledge of his or her own culture and background to what is offered. This is the *horizon of expectation* by which any text will be measured. These horizons change in different historical periods, and so each age or generation will produce a different interpretation of text. Reception Theory is distinguished from Reader Response criticism in general by its awareness of history and changing perspectives.

## Semiotics

At the end of the nineteenth century the American philosopher Charles Sanders Peirce founded a study he called 'semiotic', and in 1915 Ferdinand de Saussure independently proposed a science to be known as 'semiology'. Both names can be used to describe the science of semiotics, or the many and varied methods by which humans communicate with each other through 'signs'. In theory, these signs can include the postures we adopt, the clothes we wear, even the music we like, all of which send a signal to fellow members of the species and are a form of communication. In practice, Semiotics, like so many recent critical theories, concentrates on language and linguistics. It has become associated with Structuralism because of the influence of de Saussure on it. Inevitably the study of the signs that humans exchange with each other descends into detailed technicality early on in its exposition, and there is no substitute for detailed reading for those interested in this area of theory.

## Speech act theory

Speech Act theory is a linguistics-based approach to criticism, outwardly slightly daunting because of its technicality, but very rewarding when pursued. It is particularly associated with the work of the philosopher J. L. Austin as expressed in 1962 in his posthumous book *How to Do Things With Words* and carried on thereafter by John Searle. Austin proposed three categories of language. The act of uttering is described as the *locutionary act*; the act performed in saying something (warning someone, praising them, reprimanding them, and so on) is known as the *illocutionary act*; and what is achieved as the result of something being said (such as having persuaded someone from a course of action or argued them into it) is known as the *perlocutionary act*. All these speech acts can be judged as being successful or not, but a major factor in the decision as to their success requires attention to what Austin defines as the *felicity conditions*, or certain facts surrounding the act of speech or writing. Before Austin's work there was a tendency to see the sentence as a fully enclosed, complete unit of speech. Austin expanded this simplistic view, showing some of the pressures and ancillary factors that influence the meaning and effect of the sentence and all language. In 1977 Derrida launched an attack on Searle and Speech Act theory, under the banner of Deconstruction. This was almost inevitable as Deconstruction attempts to refute any codified and systematic explanation of the way language works.

If the message of Speech Act theory seems to be rather clouded, it is worth stopping and thinking the next time one utters a sentence such as, 'It was cold yesterday.' This could be a simple statement of meteorological fact. In a novel about nuclear holocaust it could presage the end of intelligent life on earth, with a blanket of dust blotting out the sun's rays from the planet's surface. In a work about relationships 'cold' could act as a symbol for those relationships. Why and how these meanings are arrived at is one of the concerns of Speech Act theory. Applied to direct speech from a character in a literary work it can lay bare the unspoken presuppositions and implications that underpin that speech, acting in linguistic terms much in the way that psychoanalytic, Marxist or Feminist criticism act in showing the reality beneath the skin in psychological, political or gender terms. Speech

Act theory also has much to say about prose narratives, what is intended by the author in these, and what is understood by the reader. Some Speech Act theorists propose a new *mimetic* theory, arguing that many of the major forms of literature are attempts to imitate ordinary discourse.

## Postcolonialist theories

The term 'postcolonialist' is in some respects similar to Marxist and Feminist critical theory, in that the one, single term can be used to cover a multitude of essentially different approaches which have only one thing in common. In terms of postcolonialist theory that one thing is the experience of being colonised. Postcolonial in fact replaces the politically incorrect term 'Commonwealth literature', the Commonwealth being the very loose bonding on nations which at one time or another had been part of the British Empire. The experience of colonisation imposed a foreign language on native cultures, and very often imposed a large part of a foreign culture. Postcolonial theory, where it has any unity, starts from the assumption that colonised nations in using the language of the colonial power began to share and form that language partially in their own image and to their own usage. Some theorists distinguish between English (the language spoken in England) from english, the language as it evolved in the countries controlled by England.

Postcolonialists can argue that **variation** of the language is the first phase of development, followed by **abrogation** (denial of and rebellion against the imposed language), followed finally by **appropriation** (the use and modification of the language for the users own purposes).

Postcolonialism is not merely concerned with language. It deals also with the cultural impact of colonisation, often using the phrases **centre** and **margin** to describe the colonial power and its colonised nation. The relationship between the centre and the margin is frequently the study and the interest of postcolonialist theory.

Postcolonialism has been criticised for being such a wide description that it becomes so vague as to be useless, and criticised because of the danger it brings of seeing a work of literature only through the glass of the author or works colonial history, and allowing neither any other identity. The latter criticism is probably less valid than the former. There are critics who might try to persuade us that Charles Dickens's *Hard Times* can only be understood from an exclusively Marxist viewpoint, just as there are feminist critics who try to persuade us that the only possible vision of George Eliot's *Daniel Deronda* is the one wholly informed by the feminist viewpoint. In practice the most influential critics are those who persuade us that a major dimension of these books can lie in these perspectives, whilst still allowing for other perspectives to be exercised. Similarly, I do not believe that the only whole vision of Shakespeare's *The Tempest* is contained in the postcolonial view of that play: I do believe that I will never look at the play in the same way again having seen how postcolonial theories can inform one's vision of it.

One major use of postcolonial theory is the interesting comparison it allows between writing in 'english' from countries colonised by England (Africa, Australia, Canada, India, parts of the middle and far east including Sri Lanka and the West Indies) and writing in 'english' from countries who were either never colonised to the same extent or who left the Empire very early on. North America and Ireland are two examples.

Postcolonial theory can be associated with post-structuralism and deconstruction in particular, and has by now spawned the inevitable sub-groups, amongst which can be included 'orientalism'. Rather more healthily it has evolved alongside far greater interest in writing in English by non-native speakers, and may have contributed to that rise.

## Historicism, New Historicism and cultural materialism

Historicism is criticism that examines a work of literature within the context of its historical setting, and elevates the historical perspective of a work to a central position in its understanding. Historicism is to a certain extent a reaction against New Criticism and also against Structuralism and Deconstruction. On the other hand, Marxist criticism can be seen as a branch of Historicism. Cultural Materialism if the name often given to the British version of New Historicism.

New Historicism claims to react against many of the tenets of the older Historicism. They would deny that there is or can ever be one single view of History. Historians cannot claim that their work is detached or objective: we are all the prisoners of our own historical context. All history is, in effect, just as much a 'story' as the apparent story that the author tells. Detailed historical examination allows us to see the 'discourses' that underpin the writing of the time, and which the author is often unaware of as an influence on his or her work.

New Historicism has been particularly successful in studying Romantic literature and the literature of the Renaissance.

## Gay, lesbian and queer theories

The gay liberation movement of the 1970s sought to challenge repression of homosexuals and at the same time encourage 'gay pride', challenging a homophobic society by the presentation of same-sex love as admirable, rather than worthy of hate-filled denial. The inevitable result of increasing sexual liberalisation was an attempt on the part of the gay community to 'reclaim' literature and texts that had hitherto been hidden, just as feminism reclaimed texts by women or early feminist writers. In addition there has arisen criticism which seeks to interpret and evaluate a wide range of texts from the viewpoint of their sexuality. Freud and Michel Foucault have been major influences.

Gay, lesbian and queer theories are typical of much poststructuralist development in that they tend to place under the one umbrella criticism that is both immensely diverse within itself, and which owe part-allegiance to other critical theories. Feminism deals at least in part with a denial of equality that became institutionalised within a patriarchal society, which links it to gay studies in general and to lesbian studies if only through the common denominator of denial and institutionalised oppression. Sexuality is a part of all history, hence links with New Historicism, and so on. This has not stopped considerable antagonism between feminist and gay theoreticians. It is difficult to see much coherence in gay and lesbian theories at present. This is not testimony to their worth, more testimony to their relatively late arrival on the scene.

## Further reading

### General

All the major publishers have their own introduction to critical theory, often adding to general introductions 'readers', or collections of essays.

- Peter Barry, *Beginning Theory. An Introduction to Literary and Cultural Theory* (Manchester University Press, 1995): an excellent brief introduction.
- Culler, Jonathan, *Literary Theory. A Very Short Introduction* (Oxford University Press, 1997): useful, but not divided up into sections on the various critical theories, and therefore of limited use for the student who wishes insight into one or more specific theories.
- Terry Eagleton, *Literary Theory. An Introduction* (Blackwell, 1996)
- K. M. Newton, ed., *Twentieth Century Literary Theory* (Macmillan, 1997): an excellent, detailed 'reader' survey of all major theories.
- Raman Selden, Peter Widdowson and Peter Brooker, *A Reader's Guide to Contemporary Literary Theory* (Prentice Hall/Harvester Wheatsheaf, 1997): another effective survey, now in its fourth edition.

### Archetypal criticism

- Robert Graves, *The White Goddess* by (Faber, 1959)
- G. Wilson Knight, *The Wheel of Fire* (Methuen, 1949)

### Deconstruction and Structuralism

- Roland Barthes, *The Pleasure of the Text* (Blackwell, 1975)
- Julian Wolfreys, *Deconstruction. Derrida* (Macmillan, 1998)

## Feminist criticism

- Mary Eagleton, ed., *Feminist Literary Criticism* (Longman, 1991)
- Elaine Showalter *A Literature of Their Own: British Women Novelists from Bronte to Lessing* (Virago, 1982)
- Sandra Gilbert and Susan Gubar, *The Madwoman in the Attic* (Yale University Press, 1984)
- Helen Keyssar, *Feminist Theatre and Theory* (New Casebooks, Macmillan, 1995)
- K. K. Ruthven, *Feminist Literary Studies: An Introduction* (Cambridge University Press, 1984)

## Lesbian, Gay and Queer Theories

- Henry Abelove and Michelle Aina Barak and David M. Halperin, *The Lesbian and Gay Studies Reader* (Routledge, 1993)

## Linguistic criticism and Structuralism

- Jonathan Culler, *Structuralist Poetics* (Routledge & Kegan Paul, 1975)
- Leonard Jackson, *The Poverty of Structuralism* (Longman, 1991)

## Marxist criticism

- Terry Eagleton, *Marxism and Literary Criticism* (Methuen, 1976)
- Francis Mulhearn, ed., *Contemporary Marxist Literary Criticism* (Longman, 1992)

## New critics

- I. A. Richards, *Principles of Literary Criticism* (Routledge & Kegan Paul, 1961)
- Cleanth Brooks, *The Well-Wrought Urn* (various editions)
- F. R. Leavis, *The Common Pursuit* (Hogarth Press, 1984) and *The Great Tradition* (Penguin, 1983)

## New Historicism

- John Brannigan, *New Historicism and Cultural Materialism* (Macmillan, 1998)

## Phenomenology and the Geneva School

- J. Hillis Miller, *Charles Dickens: The World of His Novels* (Oxford University Press, 1958)

## Postcolonial Criticism

- Bart Moore-Gilbert, *Postcolonial Theory. Contexts, Practices, Politics* (Verso, 1997)
- Michael Parker, *Post-Colonial Literatures* (New Casebooks Series, Macmillan, 1995)

## Psychoanalytic criticism

- Maud Ellman, ed., *Psychoanalytic Literary Criticism* (Longman, 1994)
- Ernest Jones, *Hamlet and Oedipus* (1949)
- Lionel Trilling, *The Liberal Imagination* (Oxford University Press, 1981)

## Semiotic theory

- Jonathan Culler, *The Pursuit of Signs* (Routledge & Kegan Paul, 1981)

## Speech act theory

- John Austin, *How to Do Things with Words* (Oxford University Press, 1975)
- John R. Searle, *Speech Acts: An Essay in the Philosophy of Language* (Rendel, 1980)

# Index

**Bold** figures indicate main entries